Bennington

and the Green Mountain Boys

Bennington
and the Green Mountain Boys

*The Emergence of Liberal Democracy
in Vermont, 1760–1850*

ROBERT E. SHALHOPE

The Johns Hopkins University Press   Baltimore and London

© 1996 The Johns Hopkins University Press
All rights reserved. Published 1996
Printed in the United States of America on acid-free paper

05 04 03 02 01 00 99 98 97 96   5 4 3 2 1

The Johns Hopkins University Press
2715 North Charles Street
Baltimore, Maryland 21218–4319
The Johns Hopkins Press Ltd., London

Library of Congress Cataloging-in-Publication Data will be found
at the end of this book.

A catalog record for this book is available from the British Library.

ISBN 0–8018–5335–4

For Robert

Contents

Acknowledgments

Preparing these acknowledgments brought to mind fond memories of people and places I encountered while learning about Bennington and the Green Mountain Boys. Whether working in the cramped quarters of a town clerk's office or enjoying the wonderful facilities of the region's research libraries, I experienced gracious and helpful assistance. The staffs at the Boston Public Library, the Congregational Library, the New England Historical and Genealogical Society, Widener Library, the Andover-Harvard Theological Library, the American Antiquarian Society, the Beinecke Rare Book and Manuscripts Library, the Park-McCullough House in North Bennington, Vermont, and the Vermont State Library in Montpelier were particularly helpful. It gives me great pleasure to be able at last to acknowledge their assistance. Individuals at the Bennington Museum and the Vermont Historical Society merit special thanks. Gene Kosche and Ruth Levin made my stay in Bennington a pleasure; Mary Pat Brigham and Barney Bloom did the same for me in Montpelier. Because of their kind hospitality, these towns will always remain special to me.

Any scholar fortunate enough to enjoy the kind assistance of such people is twice-blessed to be able to devote an extended period of time to working in their collections. A grant from the College of Arts and Sciences at the University of Oklahoma and a fellowship from the Charles Warren Center for Studies in American History at Harvard University afforded me the privilege of fifteen months of uninterrupted study. I owe a particular debt of gratitude to Bernard Bailyn, who was not only a gracious host at the Warren Center but has long set an illustrious standard of scholarship for all historians to follow.

Upon completion of the manuscript, it was my good fortune to be able to draw upon the expertise of John Brooke, Ronald Formisano, Louis Masur, and Edward Rhodes. Each of these scholars read the manuscript in its entirety and offered insightful criticism. I greatly appreciate their help. My colleague David Levy merits a special note of thanks. He, too, read the entire manuscript and his painstaking efforts were of immeasurable assistance to me. Dave has always given generously of his time and talent and I am happy once more to be able to express my appreciation to him. I would also like to thank Robert J. Brugger and Joanne Allen of the Johns Hopkins University Press. I genuinely appreciate Bob's continued interest in my work and am particularly thankful for Joanne's meticulous copy editing. The careful attention of all these people has made this a much better book. I, of course, take full responsibility for its shortcomings.

Finally, I would like to thank my family for their abiding support. My parents have constantly encouraged my interest in history and for this I will always be grateful. My daughter, Adelaide, and son, Robert, have long been my greatest champions. Over the years I have drawn strength from their pride and their love, which I return fourfold. Most of all, I want to thank Emma for her enduring love and heartfelt enthusiasm for my work. Without her this book would not have been worth the effort.

Introduction

The United States today stands as one of the foremost liberal democracies in the world. Its champions praise the economic autonomy,
personal liberties, and political democracy enjoyed by the people and
extol the fluid, open, and prosperous nature of American society. And
yet such circumstances have not always prevailed. Indeed, for some
time historians and political theorists have been actively debating the
origins of liberal America.[1]

Generally united in a belief that America was not born a liberal
democracy, that it gradually became a materialistic, competitive, and
self-interested society, these scholars differ most often over the timing
and the significance of liberalism's emergence within American society.
Intimately related to such issues is the problem of assessing responsibility for the triumph of liberalism in America. Here there is no
consensus. Many depict members of the commercial classes as the principal agents of liberalism; others believe that vast numbers of common,
ordinary people were willing participants as well. The former portray
American society as riven by class tensions — capitalist entrepreneurs
versus communitarian advocates of a traditional moral economy —
whereas the latter emphasize the competitive individualism of most all
Americans.

We know that the early years of the republic were a transitional
period during which America changed from a traditional to a modern
society. How Americans viewed themselves during this transformation,
however, is less clear. Some scholars have argued that Americans clung
desperately to their belief in republicanism, a value system that empha-

sized communal values and social solidarity. Others insisted that liberalism, with its aggressive individualism, its open promotion of interests, and its strident materialism, replaced republicanism during this era. In recent years a synthesis of these views emerged. Most now agree that one cultural form did not displace the other; rather, like "templates overlying one another," they existed simultaneously.[2]

Interestingly, throughout the nineteenth century, a time when the nation became one of the most liberal societies in the world, no clear-cut, sustaining ideology of liberalism emerged in America. Even after British devotees of Adam Smith and Jeremy Bentham fashioned a powerful liberal ideology in England, most Americans continued to view themselves as republicans. They clung to a harmonious, communal view of themselves and their society even while behaving in a materialistic, competitive manner. Because of this stubborn affinity for republicanism, the liberal, democratic society that emerged in nineteenth-century America became a paradoxical blend of the traditional and the modern. Caught up in market forces over which they had little control and, perhaps, even less understanding, Americans obstinately tried to understand their changing world in familiar terms. More often than not, the socioeconomic transformations taking place throughout American society, which were increasingly complex and quite often confusing, gave rise to unintended consequences.

This was certainly true in Bennington, Vermont, where three strains of republicanism vied for dominance during the late eighteenth and early nineteenth centuries. Out of this clash between the egalitarian communalism of Strict Congregationalists, the democratic individualism of Green Mountain Boys, and the hierarchical elitism of Federalist gentlemen emerged an entirely new political culture: a liberal democracy. None of the participants in this process anticipated such a result. Indeed, none of them fully comprehended what they had created. But then few, if any, ever completely understood how they and their society had changed over the years.

What follows is the story of these changes and how the townspeople of Bennington responded to them. Actually, it is many stories, for the various individuals and groups involved embraced quite different perceptions of themselves and the world about them. Embedded in these stories is the ebb and flow of class tensions, religious differences, cultural conflicts, political partisanship, and economic competition. Contained within them too are valuable insights into the birth of liberal America, a process they reveal as far more subtle, complex, and ironic than commonly perceived. In addition they provide wonderful access to the dynamics of democratic liberalism and the manner in which that belief system became a powerful shaping force in modern American society.

Whatever the ultimate resolutions of these varied stories, they all had roots in the migration during the late eighteenth century of thousands of individuals into the area known as the New Hampshire Grants. To understand these stories and the larger mosaic of which they were a part, we must begin with that migration.

PART ONE: ORIGINS

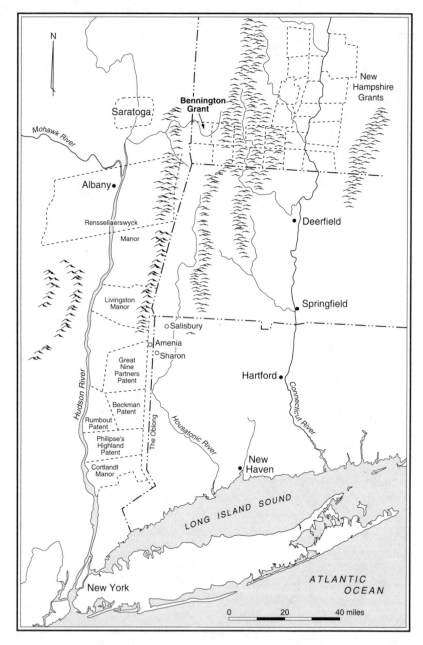

New York manors and New England towns, c. 1770. Adapted from Sung Bok Kim, *Landlord and Tenant in Colonial New York: Manorial Society, 1664–1775* (Chapel Hill: University of North Carolina Press, for the Institute of Early American History and Culture, 1978), and Earle Newton, *The Vermont Story: A History of the People of the Green Mountain State, 1749–1949* (Montpelier: Vermont Historical Society). Used with permission.

1. Separate Paths to the Grants

That God hath given to every Man an unalienable Right (in Matters of his Worship) to judge for himself as his Conscience receives the Role from God by his Word, and hath blessed them that have appeared to stand uprightly for the Liberty of Conscience in all Ages, and particularly our Fore-fathers, who left their pleasant native land for an howling Wilderness, full of savage Men and Beasts, that they might have Liberty of Conscience; and they found that their merciful and faithful GOD was not a wilderness to them, but drove out the Savages before them, and as it were dunged the Land with their Carcasses, and planted Churches and Colonies; He also gave them Favour in the Sight of their King and Queen, so that their Majesties granted to, and indulged their Subjects in this Province with a Charter, in which, among other great Favours, Liberty of Conscience (in the Worship of GOD) is given all Christians (except Papists). By this Liberty granted to us, we understand that no one religious Sect or Society, hath any Power, to constrain another, or any of another Sect, or Society, to pay to the Maintenance of their Worship: But nevertheless there are some Ecclesiastical Laws, so call'd that are so understood by them that have the Execution of them, that they oblige all Persons and their Estates in the Town where they live, to pay to the maintenance of the Town or Parish Minister or Ministers (except they be of the Denomination of Church-men or are of the Church of England, or Annabaptists or Quakers) tho: they can't in Conscience Worship with them; nor pay to their Worship, or the Maintenance of their Ministers; yet by Vertue of those Laws, some of His Majesty's most loving Subjects are Imprisoned, and others have their Goods and Chattels destrained from them, and great Waste is made of them, with which these should glorify GOD and Honour the King, (and need it to maintain their own Families, Worship and Ministers) and as these Oppressions are still carried on, your Excellency and Honour Petitioners, humbly pray, that your

Excellency and Honour may be the happy Instrument in the Hand of GOD, *of
unbinding of these heavy Burdens, and letting the Oppressed go free, by forbidding
any Person's being Imprisoned, or his Goods or Chattels being destrained, for to pay
any Ministers Rates on whose Ministry they don't attend. And we as in Duty bound
shall ever pray.*

> *Ebenezer Wadsworth of Grafton*
> *Samuel Robinson of Hardwick of Worcester*
> *Richard Seaver of Roxbury in Suffolk Ct.*
> *Oct. 17, 1754* [1]

When Samuel Robinson, a deacon in the Separate Society of Hardwick, entered the General Court of the Colony of Massachusetts to
deliver a petition drawn up by a convention of Separate Congregationalists, he did so with mixed feelings. He was a committed localist,
feeling that problems should be confined to the rough equality and
communal values of one's own township if at all possible. Consequently,
five months earlier he had approached the freemen of Hardwick. They
met "to see if the town will release a number of the inhabitants of the
town from paying towards the support of the settled minister in said
town, who assemble and meet together for religious worship by themselves, and are generally called Separates." The townspeople rejected
the Separates' appeal.[2] This decision prompted Robinson to gather in
convention with men who had experienced similar frustrations in other
townships. These men were neither social radicals nor political revolu-
tionaries. They were not agitating for the separation of church and
state, nor were they championing heterodoxy; they desired nothing
beyond tax-exempt status for Separates. And yet the issue of exemption,
or toleration, for Separate Congregationalism greatly disturbed the
established authorities within the New England colonies.

The furor over Separatism resulted from spiritual awakenings that
erupted in Massachusetts and Connecticut throughout the 1730s and
1740s. Initially these revivals were sporadic affairs affecting only local
parishes. With the appearance of evangelists such as George Whitefield, Gilbert Tennent, and James Davenport, however, the tone of
religious unrest changed dramatically. In progressively more extreme
language these men attacked those ministers and church members who
had not had a personal saving experience. Whitefield declared that
he was "verily persuaded the Generality of Preachers talk of an unknown, unfelt Christ. And the Reason why Congregations have been so
dead is, because dead Men preach to them."[3] At the conclusion of his

tour through New England in the fall of 1740, during which he spoke to great numbers of avid worshipers, Whitefield observed that "most that preach, I fear do not experimentally know Christ."[4] During the winter of 1740–41 Tennent kept up the attack in New England upon an unconverted ministry — "blind Guides" and "dead Dogs, that can't bark" — that produced churches filled with helpless sheep without a shepherd. He advised parishioners who found themselves under a "carnal" or "unconverted" minister to leave him and go to one who had accepted redemption.[5]

The assaults of Whitefield and Tennent created a highly charged emotional atmosphere and widespread soul-searching, not only by the thousands who had heard them but by a good number of established ministers as well. Many of the latter welcomed Whitefield and Tennent to their parishes and opened their pulpits to them in the hope that they could provide spiritual nourishment in a particularly anxious time. Such hospitality on the part of the orthodox ministry ceased, however, shortly after James Davenport began his barnstorming tour of New England in 1742. Davenport would appear in a town and immediately interview its minister. If he decided that the man was not spiritually awakened, he would publicly attack him forthwith and urge his parishioners to abandon him. Davenport advised that if they could not find a nearby church with a converted minister, they should separate themselves from the established parish churches and form their own congregations composed entirely of the spiritually pure. Soon, to the horror of the orthodox ministry, lay preachers — men without a college degree or the sanction of a legitimate ministerial association — appeared throughout the colonies exhorting others to join them in a spiritual awakening.[6] Above all, itinerant evangelists, whether ordained ministers or lay preachers, convinced great numbers of people that a sudden miraculous outpouring of God's grace was upon them. None who received the "new light" of God's love could doubt this. They could no longer believe that God worked only through such earthly intermediaries as an established clergy or a hierarchy of civil authorities. Instead, God communicated directly through his chosen few regardless of their rank or learning; he brought grace directly to the common people and called upon ordinary men and women to be his new ministers. "The common people," declared one evangelist, "claim as good a right to judge and act for themselves in matters of religion as civil rulers or the learned clergy."[7]

Like so many others, Samuel Robinson fell under the sway of evangelists of the new light. For him, though, George Whitefield always remained his favorite preacher.[8] Perhaps Whitefield's promise of peace, harmony, and love within a redeemed community of equals brought solace to a man caught up in the pursuit of the main chance in a society teeming with opportunities for enterprise, aggrandizement, and appropriation. Born to Samuel and Sarah Robinson on April 4, 1707, Samuel spent his youth in Cambridge, Massachusetts, where his father and mother kept a tavern in their home. In 1721 his father sold the house and moved the family to Westborough, in Worcester County, an area beginning to experience rapid growth and development. Three years later Samuel's father died. Within two years the local authorities had appointed Sarah's brother, Jedediah Brigham, the nineteen-year-old youth's guardian. Whether he was apprenticed to a carpenter while living in Cambridge or learned the trade from his uncle, by the time Samuel reached his majority he had become a skilled carpenter. This, along with the education he received in the common schools of Cambridge, helped him to thrive as a house builder, or joiner, when he began life on his own in Rochester, Massachusetts. By 1732 he had returned to Worcester County, where he married Mercy Leonard of Southborough. Although the couple took up residence in Grafton, Samuel did not sever all ties with Rochester. Several of the most prominent proprietors in the recently confirmed grant of Lambstown resided in that town, and young Robinson realized full well that in an agrarian society land ownership was vital for social advancement. Consequently, when these men sought out settlers in order to fulfill the terms of their charter, Robinson eagerly took part in a drawing of lots in December 1733. Not only did he draw one 103-acre lot, but he managed to purchase another of 100 acres from a participant in the drawing who did not wish to move to the rugged hill country of Worcester County.[9] Thus began a lifetime of aggressive land acquisition.

By early 1736 the Robinsons had moved to Lambstown, where Samuel intended to take up farming. This was a not an easy undertaking. The heavily forested, hilly, and rocky terrain of the area gave way grudgingly to the arable fields and roads necessary for agricultural prosperity. Success came only after the most tireless and arduous effort. At the same time, though, an individual's very presence, particularly if he was a freeholder, afforded him a position of relative prominence in this sparsely populated frontier region. Thus, when Lambstown's some sixty settlers held their first meeting in February 1737, they elected Samuel Robinson to the important posts of clerk and selectman.[10]

From that time on he played a large role in the affairs of the town. Indeed, during his first decade of residency Robinson served three terms as selectman, four as clerk, and two as town assessor; in addition, he filled lesser offices, such as those of highway surveyor and deer reeve. He even constructed the town pound.[11]

Often the tasks his fellow townsmen assigned Robinson took him outside the town. They repeatedly selected him to represent their interests to the proprietors at their annual meetings in Roxbury, and they occasionally asked him to present the town's grievances to the General Court in Boston. Robinson's trips to the Gray Hound Tavern in Roxbury were always to convince the proprietors either to pay their share of the town's costs for creating and maintaining roads and bridges, constructing a meetinghouse, supporting a minister, and providing common schools or to allow the town to levy the taxes necessary to finance these vital community needs. Trips to the State House in Boston more often than not entailed requests that the town be exempted from paying taxes levied either by the county or by the commonwealth. Sometimes one set of authorities was set against another. On March 5, 1739, for example, the General Court acceded to the demands of the townspeople over the strident opposition of the proprietors and passed an act incorporating the Lambstown settlement as the township of Hardwick.[12]

Incorporation gave town members what they had long desired: local autonomy. The people of Hardwick trusted their locally elected leaders, men closely identified with their own needs and desires, and whenever possible avoided association with outside authorities. Consequently it was fifteen years after incorporation before the voters of Hardwick elected a delegate to the Massachusetts General Court. Their choice, Timothy Ruggles, appeared to fit the role perfectly. The son of one of the wealthiest of the original Lambstown proprietors, Ruggles had moved to Hardwick in 1753 to develop his deceased father's extensive properties. A prominent attorney with a degree from Harvard, Ruggles had already served nine terms in the General Court. In addition, he had excellent political connections within the provincial government. Soon after emigrating to Hardwick, Ruggles had received commissions as justice of the peace, judge of the court of common pleas, chief justice of the same court, and brigadier general in the state militia. Beyond that, he had served as speaker of the house for two terms.[13]

Ruggles served as Hardwick's representative to the General Court for sixteen consecutive terms. With the exception of a single vote cast in his first term, on which he received specific instructions from the town, he voted consistently with the governor. Identifying with the larger interests of the commonwealth, Ruggles became a central figure in the provincial hierarchy. For this reason the voters of Hardwick refused to elect him to local town offices. By keeping Ruggles out of such offices they could erect a barrier between their local community and the intrusions of higher authorities.[14] Through this means they sought to perpetuate the local unity and autonomy that alone could ensure their values and traditions. They wanted no provincial hierarchy culminating in the distant figure of a governor or a king to intrude upon their world. Locally validated leaders naturally emerged within their township, but the impulse to level society by valuing membership within the local community above all else would impel such men to be responsive to the community's values. Most of all, the inhabitants of Hardwick wanted to be left alone in their relative equality, with the means to prosper and the right to shape their own moral and political worlds. For this reason they turned to men like Samuel Robinson rather than Timothy Ruggles when electing a selectman or an assessor.

Robinson was certainly a logical choice. He was one of a number of men who had persevered and prospered within Hardwick. He had accomplished this not only by wresting a subsistence from the difficult terrain but by constantly remaining alert to potential commercial opportunities. He had first settled in the isolated western part of the township; however, through careful buying and selling of property, he had managed to create a farm on the turnpike that passed through the town. Deeply committed to commercial success, Robinson strove assiduously to further the needs of a market economy even if this meant taking significant risks. For this reason he joined with like-minded individuals throughout the colony in supporting the Land Bank, or "Manufactory Scheme," in 1740. This called for him to mortgage his property in exchange for paper bills that would gradually be redeemed in payments of manufactured or agricultural products. The sole purpose behind the scheme was to provide an ample supply of commercial paper so that entrepreneurial opportunities would not be restricted to prosperous seaboard merchants, who alone could circulate their private bills of credit.[15] With fellow Land Bankers Christopher Paige and David Sabin, Robinson managed to garner the town's support. On May 18, 1741, the town meeting voted to accept Land Bank bills in payment for all town debts.[16] That same year Hardwick's rate list revealed these three men to be among the town's five most prosperous inhabitants.[17] Although the Land Bank failed, Robinson did not cease his commercial striving. His homestead eventually comprised over nine hundred acres. In addition, he owned over one thousand acres in other parts of Hardwick and in Greenwich, Connecticut.[18]

During the time when Robinson was working to achieve a measure of secular prominence within Hardwick, he also assumed an increasingly prominent role within the town's religious life. His association with the church began on November 17, 1736, when he and eleven other men joined together to form the Church of Christ in Lambstown. On that same day a council of ministers representing the presbyter ordained Rev. David White, a recent graduate of Yale, as the new church's minister. Several weeks later church members elected Christopher Paige and Joseph Allen to serve as deacons.[19]

Over the years the congregation faced problems common to most churches in the area: the minister's salary must be paid and an adequate meetinghouse maintained. While such issues presented difficulties for the congregation, they could be overcome by communal cooperation and hard work. Such was not the case, however, when church members gathered in the meetinghouse on September 9, 1747, "to hear and consider Deacon Christopher Paige's reasons for absenting himself from the public worship and ordinances of God." After prayerful consideration, the church laid Paige "under censure" and suspended him "from the sacrament of the Lord's Supper."[20] Thus began a long and agonizing confrontation between the church and its most prominent deacon. In June 1748 a church council convened in Hardwick to take up the matter. Paige refused to yield his point and suffered a second admonition.[21] Still he would not relent. For the deacon the issue was spiritual: to compromise was to sin, to barter with the devil. The disruptive power of the new light had emerged within Hardwick.

Actually, the momentous wave of religious enthusiasm that swept over New England engulfed Hardwick as early as October 1740, when George Whitefield spoke to hundreds of avid listeners in an open field in nearby Brookfield. Although he "preached, with little freedom at first," Whitefield recalled that "at last, many were melted down."[22] A number of those "melted down" by his words returned to Hardwick filled with the spirit and eager to hear more of God's redeeming grace from the pulpit of their own church. They experienced only disappointment and frustration, however, for the Reverend White continued to read bloodless sermons composed from dense theological tracts.[23] Like so many other orthodox pastors in the region, he closed his pulpit to itinerant evangelists, forbade members of the congregation to speak freely of their personal conversion experiences during church services, and opened church membership to all—the unconverted as well as the converted.[24]

As a result of White's behavior, many church members began to suspect that he epitomized the ministers being denounced by so many evangelists. To many folks, including Samuel Robinson, White did indeed resemble a "blind guide" or a "dead dog that could not bark." Troubled by these anxieties, Robinson had to search his soul when he was called upon to become a deacon on April 30, 1746. He delayed giving an answer, and although he eventually accepted the post, Robinson remained deeply distressed by White's behavior and the official actions of the church. Finally, at a church meeting on March 2, 1749, he "desired the church that he might lay down his office of deacon."[25] The church complied. The following month Paige also resigned his deaconship.[26] Then, on July 25, 1749, church members voted to call a council of ministers to advise them whether to dismiss or to censure the "dissatisfied brethren" within their midst, namely, Samuel Robinson, James Fay, Benjamin Harwood, Silas Pratt, and George Abbott Jr.[27]

Separation ultimately came to Hardwick early in 1750, when the church voted to seat its members within the newly finished meetinghouse—"the highest payers in the highest seats."[28] No longer willing to accept this traditional means of reinforcing the social hierarchy of the secular world within the church, a number of New Lights broke away, formed a separate church, and erected a meetinghouse on Samuel Robinson's farm. There they shared in the blessed spirit with John Roberts, a lay exhorter, and elected Robinson, Fay, and John Fassett as their deacons. Based on the Cambridge Platform, the new church's covenant created a community of true believers. Since only those individuals who had personally experienced the saving grace of God would be admitted, this was genuinely to be a church of equals. All members were free to sit where they chose and to share their glorious revelations freely with their brothers and sisters. Here at last the saved could find spiritual calm.

While the pietism of Hardwick's New Lights may have brought them an inner peace, it also brought them into conflict with civil authorities, who stubbornly denied them status as a new denomination and forced them to pay taxes in support of the orthodox Congregational Church. In many areas where New Lights' consciences would not allow them to pay such taxes civil authorities forcibly confiscated the property of Separates and often dragged men and women off to jail.

These actions, as well as the fact that Hardwick refused to exempt him and his fellow church members from parish taxes to support David White, led Robinson to join fellow Separates in the convention at Sutton, Massachusetts, on May 22, 1754, that resulted in the petition to the General Court requesting tax-exempt status for Separate congregations. The General Assembly peremptorily refused.[29]

The Separatist movement distressed members of the established order not only in Massachusetts but throughout New England. Lay exhorting elicited particular fear and hatred because it threatened the dominance of the educated clergy over religious discourse. Worse, it accorded equality in religious affairs to all people; granted legitimacy to the oral culture of simple folk, whose spontaneous outbursts contrasted shockingly with the gentry's literary culture; gave ordinary people the idea that they, rather than the established clergy, were responsible for their own souls; and disrupted the hierarchy by granting members of the lower orders privileges generally reserved only to an educated elite. In addition, the open forums of Separate churches allowed common folk to gain a sense of moral equality with those toward whom the traditional order had always taught them to defer. To tolerate the Separates as bona fide dissenters and either grant them exemption from taxes or the right to tax themselves to support their own churches would have been unthinkable. To allow them the freedom to proselytize would be to give free rein to attacks upon the established system. What was permitted the few Baptists, Quakers, and Anglicans within New England would have proved disastrous if it were granted to the thousands of Separate Congregationalists. Therefore, in many areas Old Lights, representatives of the standing order, harassed Separates unmercifully. Local authorities declared Separate meetings illegal and arrested, fined, and jailed their ministers and lay exhorters for disturbing the peace. When Separates refused to attend the regular Sabbath worship of established churches, they suffered fines and public disgrace in the stocks.[30]

Members of the Separate Society of Hardwick were required to pay the parish tax to support David White, but beyond that they endured no harassment. Indeed, the majority of voters in Hardwick, the same individuals who refused to grant tax exemption to the Separates, elected Samuel Robinson to the position of selectman in five consecutive years, beginning in 1752.[31] In addition, when war broke out with France in 1754, many of these same individuals, together with young men not yet eligible to vote in town meetings, elected Robinson captain of Hardwick's militia company.

During the Seven Years' War Robinson served in four separate campaigns. He was at the bloody English "victory" at Lake George on September 8, 1755, where he served under provincial authorities. Then, throughout the campaign of 1756 Robinson and his fellow Massachusetts volunteers, now commanded by British officers under Lord Loudoun, blundered about in the vicinity of Lake George while the French built Fort Carillon (Ticonderoga) at the south end of Lake Champlain. In 1757 Robinson returned to Hardwick to raise troops for the relief of Fort William Henry, near the southern tip of Lake George. He had little success; Hardwick men had become thoroughly disgusted with British officers. Consequently Robinson saw no action during this season. Then, during the campaign of 1758 he raised a company that participated in the disastrous frontal assaults on Fort Ticonderoga ordered by Major General James Abercromby. For the remainder of the summer Anglo-American troops, their morale shattered, constructed a new post, Fort George, near the ruins of Fort William Henry. During the year 1759 Robinson took part in the capture of Fort Ticonderoga by troops under the command of Jeffrey Amherst. He did not serve in 1760; instead he remained in Hardwick, where the townspeople elected him moderator of the September town meeting.[32]

Robinson's military service had been a grueling experience. At the same time, though, it had been tremendously instructive. Serving under British officers reinforced his commitment to localism. Like many other provincial soldiers, he perceived these men to be arrogant, class-conscious elitists. He rebelled against the thought of a hierarchy of such individuals — men of no fellow feeling for his community and its values — exercising authority over him and his neighbors.[33] Robinson's travels to and from the campaigns in which he participated proved valuable to him in another way. He found the land he traversed particularly attractive. The land lay within an area commonly known as the New Hampshire Grants, a vast tract of unoccupied land located north of Massachusetts, between the Hudson and Connecticut Rivers. With the French and Indian threat removed, this land held out seemingly boundless possibilities to those willing to risk their lives and their livelihoods in a veritable wilderness.

The lure must have become increasingly attractive to Robinson following his return to Hardwick. Like other communities, Hardwick experienced a period of upheaval during and after the war. Taxes had been driven to the highest level in the history of the province, a tremendous public debt had been created, and at one point the provincial government had been brought to the brink of bankruptcy. At the same time, there had been great infusions of British money to support the war effort. Robinson had been handsomely paid for his services, but while he had more hard money in hand than at any previous time, he also faced the likelihood that taxes and other provincial levies would be higher than ever before. More troubling were signs of change within Hardwick itself. For example, Timothy Ruggles had developed a handsome estate that included an enclosed park where he and his gentlemen guests could ride and hunt deer. In addition, Ruggles traveled about in a stylish carriage, the only such vehicle in a town where few could afford more than an oxcart. With his close ties with provincial authorities and his genteel deer-hunting associates, Ruggles appeared more and more like the British officers Robinson had encountered. What was worse, the authority of provincial officials like Ruggles seemed to be encroaching constantly upon the prerogatives of the townspeople. And there were still taxes to be paid to support a church that Robinson and his fellow Separates refused to attend.

In November 1760 Robinson made a critical decision. In that month he began to buy land rights from the proprietors of Bennington, a six-square-mile tract of land granted by Governor Benning Wentworth of New Hampshire in 1749.[34] This grant lay six miles north of the Massachusetts border and approximately twenty miles east of the Hudson River. By the summer of 1761 Robinson had clearly determined his course: he sold his six-hundred-acre homestead in Hardwick.[35] He meant to stake his future on the development of yet another frontier region. This time, however, he would be the new township's leading proprietor. Many Hardwick Separates decided to join him, and in late May the first contingent left for Bennington. Several months later Samuel Robinson, carrying the church covenant with him, led nearly thirty more families to their new home on the Grants.

By His Excellency
Sir HENRY MOORE, *Baronet,*
Captain General and Governor in Chief in and over the
Province of New York, and the Territories depending thereon
in America
. A PROCLAMATION

Whereas it appears by Proof on Oath, That William Pendergast, of Beekman's Precinct, in the County of Dutches, Yeoman; Jacobus Gonsales of the same

Precinct, Yeoman; Silas Washburn, of the South Precinct, in the same County, Blacksmith; James Secord, of the same Precinct, Yeoman; Elisha Cole, of the same Precinct, Yeoman; Isaac Perry, of the same Precinct, Yeoman; and Micah Vail, of Beekman's Precinct aforesaid, Yeoman; have commited HIGH TREASON. *In Order therefore that the said Persons may be brought to condign Punishment; I have thought fit, by and with the Advice of His Majesty's Council of this Province, to issue this Proclamation; hereby strictly enjoining and commanding all Magistrates, Justices of the Peace, Sheriffs, and all other Civil Officers, and all other Person and Persons whomever, within the said Province, to apprehend, or Cause to be apprehended, all and every the Persons above-named, and charged with having committed* HIGH TREASON *as aforesaid, and them, and every of them, to secure and bring before any of the Justices of the Supreme Court of judicature, to be examined concerning the Premises, and dealt with according to Law: And I do hereby promise the Reward of* ONE HUNDRED POUNDS, *as offered by my Proclamation of the Thirtieth Day of April last, for apprehending the said William Pendergast; and also the Reward of* FIFTY POUNDS *for apprehending each of the other Persons so charged as aforesaid, to be paid to the Persons apprehending them respectively, so that they be secured to be proceeded against as the Law directs. And all His Majesty's loving Subjects are exhorted and enjoined not to harbour, conceal, or otherwise either directly or indirectly, give any Aid or Assistance whatever to any the Persons so charged as Traitors as aforesaid; as they will thereby become Principals in the Treason and render themselves liable to Punishment accordingly.*

GIVEN *under my Hand, and Seal at Arms at Fort-George, in the City of New-York, the Twentieth Day of June,* 1766, *in the Sixth Year of the Reign of our Sovereign Lord* GEORGE *the Third, by the Grace of* GOD, *of Great-Britain, France, and Ireland, King, Defender of the Faith, and so forth.*

H. Moore.

By his Excellency's Command,
Gw. BANYAR, *D. Secry.*[36]

At the time when Governor Moore proclaimed Micah Vail and others guilty of high treason these men were taking part in a revolt against the landlords of vast estates within Dutchess County, New York. These "traitors" demanded longer leases, lower rents, and the opportunity to hold land in fee simple. Beyond that, they wanted families that had been forcibly evicted from their farms to be able to return to the land. In order to accomplish this, they gathered a great many local farmers into armed companies. Directed by a Committee of Twelve under the nominal leadership of William Prendergast, these bands roamed

Dutchess County intimidating local officials and tenants who remained loyal to the landlords. They burned barns, tore down fences, removed roofs from the homes of their opponents, and threatened bodily harm to all who did not support them. On June 6, 1766, they thoroughly terrorized the sheriff at Poughkeepsie, forced him to open his jail, and freed one of their men who had been imprisoned for refusing to pay rent to his landlord.[37]

This last action led to the governor's June 20 proclamation of treason. More important, on the previous day General Thomas Gage, commander in chief of British forces in North America, had, at Governor Moore's request, dispatched a regiment of regulars to aid civil officials in their attempt to restore order within the county. A week later, while marching through the Oblong, these troops encountered a company of insurgents commanded by Micah Vail, a member of the Committee of Twelve.[38] Shots rang out and two British soldiers fell, critically wounded. Enraged by this encounter with people whom they considered "peasants," the regulars swept forward. Scattering in the face of this attack, Vail and most of his men escaped into the countryside. Prendergast and many of his supporters were not so fortunate: later that same day they fell captive to the British.[39]

The tensions that led Micah Vail and so many of his neighbors to take up arms resulted from deep-seated antagonisms against the owners of immense estates within Dutchess County. The fundamental conflict, indeed the flash point of the rebellion, involved land. Who would control it? On what terms? Underlying this struggle was another of equal volatility, namely, the clash of cultures that emerged within the region between the Hudson and Housatonic Rivers, where New England and New York frontiers overlapped. There Yankee settlers and Yorker landowners found themselves at odds over more than simply the land.

During the late seventeenth and early eighteenth centuries an aristocratic provincial gentry had emerged in New York's Hudson River valley. A few families had gained exclusive control over vast areas of land. A single manor, Rensselaerswyck, contained over a million acres; the Philipse Highland Patent encompassed 205,000 acres. As early as 1710, when the population of Dutchess County numbered just under five hundred, the county's entire 800 square miles had been patented to several dozen individuals. Most of these men were absentee landlords; some never set foot on their property, while others appeared once a year only to collect their rents.[40] Those who did reside on their estates adopted a quasi-feudal way of life. When, for example, a wedding took place on one of the manors, just "as on rent day, the tenants gathered before the manor hall to feast and wish happiness to the bride while within a lavish banquet was spread for the Van Cortlands, Livingstons and other river families."[41]

Leaders of these river families were men of immense social prominence, economic power, and political influence. And yet they were not invincible. In fact, by the middle decades of the eighteenth century the great patentees' domination of the land appeared increasingly tenuous. The vastness of their estates and the indefinite boundaries that naturally resulted from such enormous holdings contributed mightily to their problems, as did their own cupidity. By purposely misrepresenting various landmarks many of these manor lords defrauded Indian tribes of thousands of acres of land.[42] As a result, the land titles of a great many New York grandees remained clouded.

To make matters worse, the great landowners faced an increasingly unsympathetic imperial officialdom. Since the beginning of the eighteenth century the royal government had tried to restrict the size of grants, to encourage actual settlement upon the land, and even to subject patents to forfeiture if they were not fully settled and developed. The Board of Trade instructed New York's governors to restrict patents to two thousand acres, to insist upon an orderly improvement of such lands, and to enforce the collection of quit rents. Such instructions resulted not only from vast land grants having been made in the late seventeenth century but from the additional circumstance that most of this land still remained vacant and unproductive by the middle of the eighteenth. Settlement on these patents initially took place along the Hudson River and then gradually spread eastward. So massive were these grants, however, that by mid-century immense areas still lay unused. Despite the efforts of men such as Cadwallader Colden, surveyor general of the colony and later lieutenant governor, little reform took place. The landlords were simply too powerful. Either through gaining patents for dummy partners or by manipulating the colonial legislature, they managed to circumvent the efforts of royal officials to restrict the size of patents as well as Colden's attempt to resurvey the colony in order to open up uncultivated areas to settlement. As a consequence, enormous tracts of fertile land lay vacant in those areas closest to the New England frontier.

Such an expanse of virgin land was tempting indeed to New Englanders, many of whom firmly believed that "every private man" was entitled to "a share in the general property."[43] In addition, most still subscribed to the traditional belief that the earth belonged to its cultivators. Customarily applied to the lands of nomadic Indian tribes, this doctrine seemed just as relevant when the uninhabited soil of absentee landlords was at stake.

The lure of vacant lands, in the context of unextinguished Indian titles, colonial boundary disputes, the seeming support of royal officials for the actual settlement of unoccupied lands, and the increasing shortage of good land within the New England colonies, proved overwhelming. New Englanders swarmed into eastern New York and took up land legally wherever they could and simply squatted where they could not. It was during this time that Micah Vail emigrated from Connecticut to the Beekman Patent, in eastern Dutchess County. In 1753 he purchased fourteen acres with rights to common land, the cutting of firewood, and the ranging of cattle and horses. For this he paid fourteen pounds "current money." His deed also required that he pay one-half a "Schepel" of "Good merchantable winter wheat for quit rent" each year.[44]

Vail and his fellow New Englanders, accustomed to governing themselves in their own townships and unalterably committed to a freehold system of landownership, set out to secure these traditions in their new surroundings. The aggressiveness of their efforts and the egalitarian zeal that characterized their personal behavior offended the patricians of the Hudson River valley. Accustomed to the deferential habits of their Dutch and German tenants, the landowners viewed these newcomers as "conceited," "litigious," "vulgar," "insolent," and "cunning." Totally exasperated with New Englanders, one genteel New York lady finally exclaimed: "They flocked indeed so fast, to every unoccupied spot, that their malignant and envious spirit, their hatred of subordination . . . began to spread like a taint of infection." Worse yet, "elegance or refinement were despised as leading to aristocracy."[45]

So strong were New Englanders' sense of self-righteousness and their "hatred of subordination" that even British troops did not escape their irascibility. Small detachments of soldiers entering areas close to the Connecticut border often encountered a decidedly unfriendly reception. Such befell Sergeant Cassedy and ten troopers when, in search of deserters, they approached Crum Elbow Precinct (Amenia) in the Great Nine Partners Patent during the fall of 1761. When the British sergeant questioned Jonathan Mead, a local blacksmith, the latter declared that he knew nothing about the deserters and made it clear that even if he knew of their whereabouts, he would conceal it from any and every "lobsterback." The troopers then proceeded to the nearby house of a family whose daughter had reputedly married one of the deserters and settled in for the evening. In the middle of the night Mead and some thirty accomplices broke into the house, dragged the soldiers out into the road, beat them severely, and then kept them captive for the remainder of the night. The next morning a precinct constable and officer in the neighborhood militia came with a warrant for the troops to appear before the local justice of the peace. Justice Roswell Hopkins, refusing to hear their defense, showered the troopers with "many abusive expressions" and sent them on their way. Their captain, upon reporting the incident to his superiors, could only conclude that the inhabitants of the Nine Partners "are a riotous people and Levellers by principle."[46]

While "levellers" such as Roswell Hopkins and Jonathan Mead were harassing British regulars, these same men and many of their neighbors were taking steps to remove themselves from the Yorker authority these soldiers represented. Three months after their encounter with British soldiers, Roswell Hopkins, Gideon and Jonathan Ormsby, and other neighbors met in the same room in which Hopkins had upbraided Cassedy and his men; this time, however, they gathered as proprietors of the township of Danby in the New Hampshire Grants.[47] Other like-minded individuals had received charters for the townships of Manchester, Pawlet, Rutland, and Hardwick (Mt. Tabor) from Governor Wentworth of New Hampshire, to which they intended to emigrate as soon as possible. They assumed that once on the Grants, they, rather than a group of elite landlords, would control the land; with such control would come the chance to shape their own lives.

Other settlers dealt with their landlords in quite a different manner. Early in 1755 violence broke out on the Livingston and Van Rensselaer estates. In fact, by the middle of that year a small-scale border war had erupted. Over the next several years many fields, houses, and barns went up in flames, and there were bloody skirmishes between bands of armed men. This turbulence resulted from the overlapping border claims of New York and Massachusetts, unextinguished Indian claims, the aggressive expansion of settlers from Massachusetts supported by that colony's General Court, and the stubborn determination of the manor lords to extend their patents as far eastward as possible. The violence subsided somewhat with the outbreak of the French and Indian War in 1757. During that same year the Board of Trade fixed the boundary between New York and Massachusetts along a line twenty miles due east of the Hudson River.

Tensions simmered uneasily in the Hudson River valley until the heirs to the Philipse Highland Patent began to press their claims to the easternmost reaches of that grant. The area was inhabited primarily by settlers from New England who had resided there for several decades. Most had squatted on the land with the proprietors' full knowledge but with no formalized lease arrangements; others had purchased title or accepted long-term leases from the Wappinger Indians. In late December 1764 the proprietors brought ejectment suits against fifteen individuals holding Indian leases. Convinced that crown officials were sympathetic to actual settlers and to those holding Indian titles, these men banded together and raised a fund to finance a single test case. Unfortunately, they discovered that every attorney in the province had been retained by the other side.[48] The trial, which resulted in the tenants' being evicted without compensation for their improvements, convinced most settlers that the justice system in New York was hopelessly under the control of the large landholders. A popular perception soon arose that "those who had been turned out of possession had an equitable Title but could not be defended in a Course of Law because they were poor." And since "poor Men were always oppressed by the rich," the outraged settlers were determined "to do them justice."[49] Beyond that, many believed it was "high Time great men such as the Att Gen [John Tabor Kempe] and the Lawyers should be pulled down."[50]

Organized under the Committee of Twelve and the armed bands of Prendergast, Vail, and others, settlers throughout Dutchess County set out to reinstate those evicted by the proprietors and to ensure more favorable conditions for all. Prendergast himself had been evicted, and Vail, perhaps fearing for the validity of his own title, joined those who resented the landlords' control over all avenues of economic advancement. Consequently, these exasperated Yankees destroyed their opponents' property and terrorized provincial officials by holding their own mock judicial tribunals, conducted before "bars" constructed of log rails. Recalcitrant prisoners were often "tied to a White Oak tree and whipped as long as the mob thought proper and then carried out of the County and there kicked as long as they tho't proper."[51]

The intervention of British regulars brought these tribunals to an end. From July 29 to August 14, 1766, the Supreme Court of New York met and tried some sixty men who had participated in the rebellion against the landlords. Composed of representatives of the great patentees as well as some of the colony's largest land speculators, the court sentenced some of the convicted rebels to the pillories and levied fines upon others. Then, on August 6 William Prendergast came before the bar. Several days later the court pronounced a sentence that unmistakably revealed its members' true feelings: the prisoner was to "be led back to the Place whence he came and from thence shall be drawn on a Hurdle to the Place for Execution," where he "shall be hanged by the Neck, and then shall be cut down alive, and his Entrails and Privy members shall be cut from his Body, and shall be burned in his Sight, and his Head shall be cut off, and his Body shall be divided into four Parts, and shall be disposed of at the King's Pleasure."[52]

While Prendergast and other rioters were standing trial in New York, Vail made his way toward the New Hampshire Grants. Soon to be followed by Roswell Hopkins, the Mead family, and a host of others from eastern Dutchess, he meant never again to submit to the authority of Yorker landlords or their minions.

November 12, 1745 — reasons given by Joseph Safford for separating from church

1) Because that the Church walk disorderly in refusing to be organized with Officers according to Gospel Rule

2) Because that the Chh. admit Members to Communion with them who are not able to say that they believe that Christ is formed in them or that they have acted Faith in him

3) Because that the Church hold Persons in Covenant & not Members in full Communion, the things which I believe to be contrary to any Precept or Example in the Word of God[53]

When Joseph Safford spoke out before the members of the Congregational Society of Newent (Lisbon) Connecticut he joined hundreds of fellow Congregationalists in the Norwich area in expressing dissatisfaction with their churches and their ministers. Clearly, George Whitefield's visit in June had ignited a religious firestorm in Norwich. Those who accepted the new light he offered abandoned the established churches in droves. As a result of Safford's decision, the Newent church met on January 17, 1746, and voted his reasons for separating himself from communion to be "insufficient." Church members then declared "separation to be disorderly walking and unanimously agreed to warn all separates of their confusion."[54] Four years later, upon reviewing the case of Joseph Safford and others, the church concluded that these individuals "have continued in their disorderly walking."[55]

Members of the Newent church took such time and exercised such care with a man like Safford because of his long and faithful service to both the church and the community. The Saffords had been among the pioneer families in the Newent area. Joseph's grandfather, John, had purchased land in the crotch formed by the confluence of the Shetucket and Quinebaug Rivers as early as 1695.[56] Shortly thereafter he had moved his family from Ipswich, Massachusetts, where he, his sons, Joseph, John, and Solomon, and his grandson, Joseph, had been born. The Saffords prospered in Newent. On March 5, 1729, young Joseph married Anna Bottoms of Norwich, and the couple set up housekeeping on their own. Their first child, Anna, born the next year, was followed by ten more children over the next several decades.[57] By 1734 Joseph had gained sufficient wealth to take the freeman's oath.[58] Later that same year his fellow townsmen elected him to the position of tithingman.[59] In years to come he would serve as collector of the town rate, a town lister, and a grand juryman.[60] He also became proprietor of the town's only gristmill.

If Joseph Safford was a solid member of the Newent community when the religious excitement occurred in the early 1740s, he and his extended family were also respected members of the church. His uncle John had been among the twelve signers of the original church covenant in 1728. At that time John Safford, Jeremiah Tracy, and ten others had renounced the Saybrook Platform of 1708, which restricted the ordination, approval, and dismissal of ministers to clerical associations and tied the churches more closely to the power of civil authorities, and pledged themselves to support the Cambridge Platform under the ministry of Daniel Kirtland.[61] Additional members of the Safford family also owned the covenant and played active roles in the life of the church. They, with other devout members of the congregation, would gather between church services to listen to one of their number read aloud from a large folio volume of the works of Richard Baxter.[62] In addition, Joseph's father participated on committees to order the affairs of the society and to determine the minister's salary; he also served as collector of the society's rate.[63]

In spite of his family's long association with the church and the efforts of the church to keep him in the fold, Safford could not resign himself to the decision made in 1745 by the Newent Congregational

church and other Congregational churches in the Norwich area to
accept the Saybrook Platform as their rule of discipline. Worse yet, the
Norwich churches decided that even though "it is esteemed a desirable
thing that persons who come into full communion offer some publick
relation of their experience, yet we do not judge or hold it a term of
Communion."[64] On December 6, 1750, Joseph finally declared himself
"released from all obligation to the church he first joined, as if he had
never joined, because the church has in his opinion broken covenant
with God & with him in practice but not in principles."[65]

For its part, the church considered the actions of Joseph and other
Separates to be "disorderly & irregular." In particular, Joseph and Anna
Safford had "cast most uncharitable reflection on the church." Tracy
had even "taken upon himself to preach—not called by God to do
so according to the church." The church then ruled these members
"blameworthy"; they had "cut themselves off from Church communion." As a result of this "unscriptural separation," the "Church [with-
drew] from them."[66]

The split in the Newent church was irrevocable. Joseph and Anna
Safford, Tracy, and four others formed a Separate church, pledged
themselves to support the Cambridge Platform, and built a meetinghouse near Safford's mill.[67] At first Tracy administered the ordinances
and preached; then in November 1751 the congregation, whose numbers eventually grew to nearly sixty, voted to call Bliss Willoughby, a
"teaching Brother" in the church, to be their minister.[68] After Willoughby's ordination the congregation had to consider the problem of
"being destitute of deacons." Finally, on May 14, 1755, church members installed Joseph Safford and Andrew Tracy as their deacons.[69] The
pure church Joseph Safford had so desired and demanded—gathered
under the "old Platform," ministered to by an enlightened brother, and
organized "according to the Gospel Rule"—was at last a reality.

Having created a more perfect church, Safford and his fellow Separates quickly discovered that they, as well as their church, must live in a
decidedly imperfect world. The idealism inherent in the Cambridge
Platform collided with the harsh political realities symbolized by the
Saybrook Platform. The Old Light established order in Connecticut
meant to crush the Separate movement. As early as May 1742 the
Connecticut Assembly had passed an "Act for Regulating Abuses and
Correcting Disorders in Ecclesiastical Affairs," intended to smother
the New Light excitement. This act decreed that any licensed minister
who preached or exhorted in any parish other than his own without the

permission of the settled minister and a majority of the congregation in that parish would forfeit his right to a legal maintenance under the laws of the colony; that all members of a ministerial association would lose their legal right to maintenance if their association licensed a minister or otherwise interfered with matters properly within the jurisdiction of another constitution; that no minister could receive his legal maintenance until he could certify that he had not violated either of the above laws; that any person who preached or exhorted within a parish without the permission of the established minister and a majority of the congregation of the church of that parish must post a bond of one hundred pounds until the county court could determine what course should be taken; and that if a stranger from outside the colony, whether a licensed minister or not, preached or exhorted within a parish without the permission of the settled pastor and a majority of his congregation, that person should be treated like a vagrant and be sent beyond the boundaries of the colony.[70]

Five months later the assembly legislated out of existence the "Shepherd's Tent," a seminary established by Separates in New London to train their own ministers. It also passed a law prohibiting any church or parish from choosing a minister who did not have a college degree. Then in May 1743 the assembly repealed the Toleration Act of 1708. Henceforth all those who dissented from the ecclesiastical laws of the colony must apply to the assembly for exemption. Such would be granted only to those who could be clearly distinguished from Presbyterian or Congregational beliefs: Separate Congregationalists could expect no relief.[71]

The established clergy also attempted to stem the tide of religious enthusiasm building in the colony. Realizing in the summer of 1745 that George Whitefield intended to visit Connecticut, the General Association of the Churches of Connecticut met and resolved that since there were "many errors in doctrine and disorders in practice, prevailing in the Churches in this land, which seem to have a threatening aspect upon the Churches," and since "Mr. George Whitefield has been the promoter, or at least the faulty occasion of many of these errors and disorders," it "would by no means be advisable for any of our ministers to admit him into their pulpits, or for any of our people to attend his administration."[72]

While neither the legislation of the colonial assembly nor the pronouncements of Old Light clergymen could keep people from flocking to hear Whitefield, the power of the state could be brought to bear on those who separated themselves from the established churches as well as on the men who preached without official sanction. Local constables and collectors of the parish rates, operating under the old laws against nonpayment of rates and nonattendance upon the worship of the Sabbath, assessed fines, seized goods, and incarcerated hundreds of Separates and many itinerant evangelists.[73] Often such repression reached Draconian levels. The experience of a Norwich woman became commonplace. A collector appeared at her home late on a rainy night and found her seated at the fire reading the family Bible. Quite sick, she had wrapped herself in thick clothing and blankets. Assuming that under these conditions the woman would relent, the collector insisted that she pay her rate. She refused to abandon her principles, and the officer took her off to prison, where she languished for nearly two weeks until an anonymous person paid her tax.[74]

Such intense self-righteousness characterized Separates in the Norwich area. Essential in strengthening their fortitude against the persecution of the established authorities, this absolute certainty in the rectitude of their moral beliefs played a central role in their own churches as well. Indeed, it became the key to church discipline. In a community of ardent believers all members became their brother's keepers; each person who owned the covenant must not only subject his or her own soul to constant self-scrutiny but search out potential weaknesses in others in order to labor with them and bring them to an awareness of their own faults. However, the final decision regarding an individual's spiritual purity lay with the full congregation. Only that body could admonish or forgive. Once forgiven and received back into full communion, the penitent resumed the status of a visible saint and enjoyed the unmitigated love and affection of all members of the church family.

The ability of Separates to discern the spiritual state of others, to separate saints from sinners, came not from a set of legal or formal principles but rather from the new light within. Separates believed this "key of knowledge" to be so infallible that a true Christian could be known from an unbeliever "as clearly as a sheep may be known from a dog."[75] Certain that God illuminated the perception of the regenerate, a Separate minister unequivocally declared that a believer, "having Divine Light shining into the Understanding, and the Love of God (or pure Charity, which is the same), ruling in the Soul, is also to know certainly that such and such Persons are true Converts, or the Saints of God."[76]

The idea of God's illumination became central to the life of the

Newent Separates, and discipline within their congregation sprang from a devout belief in the key of knowledge. The power to admonish or to forgive unreservedly emanated entirely from this principle. This became manifest when Bliss Willoughby was "overcome with a strange mistery or Iniquity" in the fall of 1749. Although he had been legally married to Hannah for a number of years, Bliss publicly announced that God intended Mary Smith, a sister in the church, to be his wife. Mary declared the same. Bliss brought Mary into his home, "kept company with her many times," and told Hannah that she might remain within the house but he would have nothing to do with her. Church members labored with both Bliss and Mary, but to no avail. Finally, on November 28, 1749, a church council composed of Separate ministers from nearby towns met in Newent to deal with the case. Upon being brought before the council, Bliss stated that Hannah was not his wife; instead "God had shown him Mary Smith was to be his wife." Thus he not only lived with Mary but also broke the Sabbath, sang carnal songs, kept company with carnal people, and blasphemed against the word of God. Solomon Paine, a Separate pastor from Canterbury, then prayed and invited Bliss to repent. When Bliss refused, Paine declared him given up to Satan for destruction and forbade all fellowship with him.[77] Within a year, however, Bliss renounced his relationship with Mary and repented before the church, whose members forgave him and received him back into communion. A month later Bliss and Hannah renewed their marriage covenant, and a year after that the church called Bliss to be its minister.[78]

Discipline within Deacon Safford's church remained unrelenting. He intended to see that all members adhered to their promise "to oppose all sin and error in ourselves" when they signed the church covenant.[79] Thus, the church declared Keziah Bishop unworthy of communion for holding it lawful to dance and to sing carnal songs; excommunicated John Ashbro for excessive drinking, withdrawing from communion, and defrauding fellow members; cut off Isaac Lamphare for holding a household baptism; and admonished Hannah Hunter for singing carnal songs, foolish talking, and scoffing.[80] Finally, on May 21, 1756, the church admonished Deacon Safford's own daughter, Elizabeth, for "sinfully withdrawing from [the] sacrament of [the] Lord's supper and [for] living in friendship with this world." Three months later the congregation declared that Elizabeth Safford and Hannah Hunter "were gone out from them and members were to look upon them as heathens and 'publickans.'"[81]

By the fall of 1761 Joseph Safford and a good many members of his congregation had decided to emigrate to the New Hampshire Grants, where they intended to join Samuel Robinson's band of Separates in Bennington. While they may have learned of Robinson's plans through the web of Separate contacts that spread throughout Connecticut and Massachusetts,[82] it was more likely that Deacon Safford's cousin Joseph alerted them to Robinson's emigration. The cousins had both been born in Ipswich in 1705. One had moved to Connecticut, the other to Hardwick, Massachusetts, where he had become Samuel Robinson's neighbor and fellow church member.[83] His son Challis had served on Colonel Timothy Ruggles's staff with Samuel Robinson Jr. during the French and Indian War; another son, Phillip, had enlisted in Captain Robinson's company during that same conflict.[84]

However Safford and the others learned of Robinson's plans to settle in Bennington, they intended to join him. There they could escape the constant persecution of Old Light civil and ecclesiastical authorities. There, too, they might be able to live free of the worldly ways that tempted their sons and daughters, ways that drove their children to become "publickans." With this hope, Deacon Safford led a small group of Newent Separates northward in the fall of 1761. Shortly thereafter, Nathaniel Clark joined them, bringing with him the covenant and fragmentary records of the church. Sternly devout New Lights, Clark and Safford meant to create a perfect community on the Grants, one that would be peaceful, pious, and harmonious.

Ethan Allen did, in a tumultuous and offensive manner, with threatening words and angry looks, strip himself even to his naked body, and with force and arms, without law or right, did assail and actually strike the person of George Caldwell of Salisbury, aforesaid, in the presence and to the disturbance of His Majesty's good subjects.[85]

For this action Thomas Hutchinson, Salisbury, Connecticut's justice of the peace, fined Ethan Allen ten shillings on September 3, 1765.[86] A little more than a month later Allen met Caldwell and Robert Branthwaite on the road. Allen struck Branthwaite, and when Caldwell attempted to intervene, Allen "in a violent and angry manner stripped off his cloaths to his naked body" and hit Caldwell on the head with a club. When Branthwaite grabbed at the club, Allen hit him again. Just at that point the local constable appeared and took all three men into custody. Shortly thereafter, Allen again "stripped off his cloaths to his naked

body and in a threatening manner with his fist lifted up repeated these
malicious words three times: 'You (meaning George Caldwell) lie you
dog' and also did with a loud voice say that he would spill the blood of
any that opposed him."[87]

Even prior to his encounter with George Caldwell, Ethan Allen was
no stranger to Justice Hutchinson's court. In August 1764 he and his
brother Heman had become involved in a legal dispute with Samuel
Tousley, one of the town's original settlers and a solid member of the
church, over several of Tousley's pigs that had invaded the Allens' garden. Even though Tousley had retrieved his pigs, the Allen brothers
went to his house, took the pigs, and "impounded" them in the pen of a
friend. Tousley went immediately to Justice Hutchinson, who ordered
the pigs released on a writ of replevin. Tousley did not, however, let the
matter rest there; he charged the Allens with trespass and theft and
demanded damages. Arguing his own case before Hutchinson, Ethan
"averred" that the pigs had not been stolen. Instead, he had them
legally impounded, as was every citizen's right when animals roamed
freely and damaged another man's property. Hutchinson did not see it
that way. He ruled that the Allens had acted outside the law and that the
pigs had not been placed in a legally constituted pound. He then fined
them ten shillings and awarded Tousley five shillings in damages.[88]

Hutchinson's ruling settled the matter of the pigs but did not bring
an end to problems between the Allen and Tousley families. Ethan
meant to get his legal pound of flesh. Earlier that same year Samuel
Tousley's brother, John, had borrowed a small sum of money from
Ethan that was payable, with interest, on demand. In light of recent
developments, Ethan made that demand. When Tousley refused to
pay, Ethan swore out a complaint against him with Justice Hutchinson,
who quickly ordered Tousley to make good the note.[89] Bad feelings did
not cease with that order, however. Soon thereafter Heman struck
Samuel Tousley in the face, for which Hutchinson fined Heman sixteen
shillings and issued a stern warning regarding such behavior in the
future.[90]

Hutchinson's admonition apparently took effect with Heman, for he
did not appear in Salisbury Justice Court again. The same was not true
of Ethan, who refused to restrain either his tongue or his contempt for
legal restrictions that he considered ignorant or unnecessary. Connecticut's prohibition against the use of smallpox serum without proper cer-
tification from local selectmen struck Ethan as one such entirely senseless restriction. Not only did he have himself inoculated but he publicly

excoriated the law in the strongest language. While Salisbury's selectmen did not take offense, its minister, Jonathan Lee, did. When Ethan
learned of this, he let fly a string of epithets to the effect that he meant
always to have the satisfaction of being prosecuted for disobeying outrageous laws. Such did in fact take place. Reverend Lee brought Ethan
before Justice Hutchinson, not for breaking the colony's law regarding
inoculation, but for flaunting its prohibition against blasphemy.[91]

Before emigrating to Salisbury in 1762 at the age of twenty-four,
Ethan displayed few, if any, aggressive traits. He was certainly a self-
sufficient and energetic young man. He had to be: his father, Joseph,
died when Ethan was just seventeen, and Ethan, as the eldest child,
assumed responsibility for the homestead and for helping his mother,
Mary, with his seven sisters and brothers. At the same time, Ethan
intended to better himself; like his father, he meant to advance as best
he could within the relatively fluid social and economic environment of
western Connecticut.

Joseph Allen had grown to maturity in Litchfield, Connecticut.
Raised by his widowed mother, Mercy, he had inherited a small plot of
uncultivated land upon her death in 1728. By 1740 he had managed to
increase his landholdings sufficiently to rank within the middle range
of Litchfield property owners.[92] By that time, too, he had wed Mary
Baker of nearby Woodbury, and the couple's first child, Ethan, had
been born on January 10, 1738. Still, Joseph was not content. Even
though he had improved his stature as a property holder, the freeholders of Litchfield had never called him to serve in any of the offices
within their purview. In fact, he had been entirely overlooked by the
emergent social and political order within the community. The religious life of Litchfield too distressed Joseph. As the wave of religious
enthusiasm sweeping throughout New England engulfed his church,
Joseph Allen became increasingly uncomfortable. Concerned far more
with the head than with the heart, Allen's rational, or Arminian, religious perspective placed him at odds with the New Light majority
of the Litchfield church. His religious liberalism as well as his desire
for social and economic advancement prompted Joseph to relocate his
family.[93] In 1740 the Allens moved to the frontier town of Cornwall,
where Joseph had become a proprietor.

In Cornwall Joseph Allen immediately gained the stature denied
him in Litchfield, although certainly Cornwall was a far more primitive
environment. From the outset he regularly served as moderator of the
town's meetings and as a selectman.[94] The freeholders also chose him as

their agent to the General Assembly to deal with delinquent proprietors. In addition, Joseph served on the committee that hired a liberal, Solomon Palmer, as Cornwall's settled pastor.[95] Beyond that, he participated in the regular divisions of land made by the proprietors. This enabled him to become one of the more successful men in Cornwall, where he consistently ranked just within the top quartile of the town's rate list. In more established towns, such as Woodbury or Litchfield, Allen's wealth would have placed him only at the top of the lowest quartile.[96]

Life in Cornwall was good for the Allens. Over time both their farm and their family grew and prospered. Joseph regularly sent Ethan, who by now had seven younger sisters and brothers, with grain from the farm to Cornelius Brownson's gristmill in Woodbury, twenty miles to the south. There he could visit with his cousin Remember Baker and members of the Brownson family. At the same time, Joseph worked to instill his own liberal religious beliefs in his eldest son's mind. Ethan, a curious youth, was an apt pupil. Recognizing the boy's intellectual proclivities and anxious that his son enjoy opportunities that had been denied him, Joseph determined that Ethan should have a college education so that he might become a professional person, perhaps even a minister. In any event, graduation from college was the necessary prerequisite for achieving a position of substance and social position, for becoming a gentleman, in eighteenth-century Connecticut. Therefore, to ready his son for admission to Yale, Joseph arranged for him to study with Rev. Jonathan Lee of Salisbury. Early in 1755 Ethan went to live in Salisbury. In April, however, Joseph died, and Ethan immediately returned to Cornwall to take charge of the family farm. He would be denied a formal education, with all its advantages, just as his father had been before him.[97]

If Joseph Allen never gained the kind of education he sought for his son, he had certainly achieved respectability in the town of Cornwall. The farm Ethan began to oversee contained over five hundred acres and an abundance of livestock, including two sets of oxen.[98] Ethan remained in charge of the farm for over six years. During that time he successfully sued one of his father's debtors in the name of the estate, served fourteen days in the militia under Captain Moses Lyman in a fruitless attempt to come to the defense of Fort William Henry in the summer of 1757, and helped his cousin Elihu Allen buy a farm in Cornwall by loaning him fifty pounds.[99] All the while, though, Ethan realized that his father's property must eventually be divided among all the family. Since he was the eldest son, his share would amount to two-ninths of the estate. With such a small piece of property, he could look forward to years of hard labor with little prospect of attaining even the position and prosperity of his father. To rise in the world and prosper, he must constantly be alert to whatever economic prospects might arise. In January 1762 Ethan grasped what he perceived to be just such an entrepreneurial opportunity. With the half-interest he maintained in Elihu's farm as financial backing, Ethan joined with John Hazeltine of Uxbridge, Massachusetts, in obtaining the rights to dig iron ore from a hill owned by Samuel and Elisha Forbes near Salisbury.[100] Intent upon establishing an iron forge, these men, joined by Heman Allen, then purchased timber and coal rights on a nearby mountain.[101]

Ethan left the farm in Cornwall and moved to Salisbury, where he intended to establish his own family. On June 23, 1762, he married Cornelius Brownson's daughter Mary and brought her back with him to Salisbury, where they shared a home with Heman and his wife. Early the next year Allen and his partners purchased the land and forge of Leonard Owens.[102] In that same year, on December 29, 1763, the probate court in Litchfield distributed the estate of Joseph Allen, freeing Ethan to expand his investments in Salisbury.[103] The forge flourished, and so did Ethan. He gained a position comfortably within the middle range of the Salisbury Grand List.[104] Ethan was not satisfied, however. Always eager to find greater economic opportunities, he and Heman sold their share in the forge to George Caldwell of Hartford, Connecticut, in October 1765.[105] Heman invested his portion of the payment in a general store in Salisbury. For his part, Ethan meant to buy into a partnership in a lead mine in Northampton, which would bring him greater returns than had his one-sixteenth share in the Salisbury forge. In any event, Ethan's departure from Salisbury was not a smooth one. He left following the encounter with George Caldwell that ended up in Justice Hutchinson's court. Ethan set out for Northampton with his wife and their newborn son, Joseph, early in 1766, leaving behind a checkered social and economic experience. In many ways his life in Salisbury had been unsettling. In one quite important way, though, his years there would have a profound effect upon him: he had formed a lasting friendship with Thomas Young, a physician residing in neighboring Amenia, New York.

Born in 1731 in Ulster County, New York, the son of recent immigrants, Thomas Young grew up in the shadow of the great manors of the Hudson valley. He was an extremely inquisitive and precocious youth who received the best schooling available in West Windsor. By and large, however, Thomas was self-taught. He was a voracious reader, and his father supplied him with volumes ranging from the classics to John Locke. Eclectic in his reading, Thomas always showed the most interest in botany and physical science. At the age of seventeen he became the apprentice of a local physician. Two years later he began practice on his own and migrated into the region along the boundary between Connecticut and New York. There he married into a family of Palatinate Germans and settled in the area of Crum Elbow Precinct (Amenia), New York.[106]

By the time Young reached maturity he had become a firm believer in maxims gleaned from Alexander Pope's *Essay on Man*. Central to his way of thought was that all of nature's truths could be reduced to a few fundamental ideas or principles. Young held fast to certain basic precepts of social, religious, and political thought. In religion his rationalism led him to become a confirmed deist. The strength of his own convictions, as well as his impatience with conventional wisdom, frequently brought him into conflict with established authority. Such was the case in 1757, when local officials in Dutchess County indicted him for blasphemy for referring to Jesus Christ as "a knave and a fool."[107]

Young also grew to resent entrenched privilege and the skewed distribution of wealth and power that resulted from a hierarchical order. In his mind, the entitlement granted to the wealthy few unfairly inhibited the advance of many men of talent and ability who lacked social position. He came by these sentiments honestly; his parents, Scotch-Irish Presbyterians, had "grown more and more dissatisfied with the government" in Ireland before they migrated to America.[108] Once settled in Ulster County, the Youngs prided themselves on their link to the unpretentious Clinton family, "which they prize[d] much more than to have been related to the assuming family of Livingston."[109] It may very well have been one of the "assuming" Livingstons who so disdainfully told young Thomas at school one day that he would "have a great estate to manage, which will require all the knowledge I can gain to manage it, and support my rank. But if you can gain a knowledge of pounds, shillings and pence, it is all you will ever have occasion for."[110] That remark, and the special privilege it signified, galled Thomas Young from that day forward.

By the time he settled in Amenia Thomas Young had formed a deep antipathy toward men of wealth; he was bitterly indignant of their inordinate power and privilege. His politics sprang as much from these beliefs and his personal experiences as from his reading in political theory. The vaunted balance of the British constitution meant little to him. Checking and balancing the king, lords, and commons was not nearly as important, in Young's opinion, as protecting ordinary people from the power of wealth. For him the complexities of political science could be reduced to a simple maxim: governments existed to restrict the dominion of the rich and the powerful. Young believed that whenever "the upper part of a nation . . . have the authority of government solely in their hands," they would "always be for keeping the low people under." Consequently, threats to society came from an "encrease of property" that caused its owners to become not only "haughty and imperious" but "cruel and oppressive" as well. Such people inevitably viewed themselves as "above the law."[111] Young himself admired the ancient Saxons, who he felt "considered every man alike as he came out of the hands of his maker — riches with them gave no power or authority over the poorest person in the state." It had been the Normans who introduced "that infernal system of ruling by a *few dependent favourites*, who would readily agree to divide the spoils of the lower class between the supreme robber and his banditti of feudal lords."[112] Quite clearly, Young enthusiastically supported those residents of Crum Elbow characterized as "Levellers by principle."

Thomas Young's ideas struck a responsive chord with Ethan Allen. Allen's rationalism, his as yet inchoate religious beliefs, gained form and structure from Young's articulate deism. And his basic egalitarianism, his commonsense approach to law and social custom, took on sharper focus during his long conversations with Young. Denied a college education, forced to make his way on the strength of his own abilities, Allen listened closely to Young's critique of the gentlemen of privilege who gained special opportunities, not as a result of their own merit, but because of their social and political connections. Young, the radical democrat, helped hone Ethan's perception of the relationship between landed wealth and power. As a result of his association with Young, Ethan's latent sense of the injustice suffered by common people at the hands of established authorities also assumed greater clarity. Like Young, however, Ethan formed his beliefs as much from his own experience as from the teachings of others. Young did not shape a mindless youngster in his own image; instead, he helped bring Ethan's youthful, rather incoherent beliefs to maturity. After exchanging ideas with his friend, Ethan would spend hours alone attempting to capture his thoughts on paper; his relationship with Young had re-kindled the philosophical curiosity of Ethan's youth.[113]

During this time of intellectual ferment between the two men, Young composed a pamphlet that integrated many of his principal beliefs. In it he focused his social and political critique upon a problem that bore directly upon the lives of many New Englanders: the control of land by wealthy men with political influence. The pamphlet, *Some Reflections on the Disputes between New York, New Hampshire, and Col. John Henry Lydius of Albany*, dealt with the claim of Colonel Lydius, a Dutch Indian trader from Albany, to a large tract of land on the eastern shore of Lake Champlain. Lydius, who affirmed his title by right of purchase from the Mohawk Indians and a subsequent reconfirmation by the governor of Massachusetts, had attempted to sell plots of this land to settlers from New England on extremely favorable terms. New York authorities had intervened to prevent this on the grounds that Lydius had no legitimate claim to the land.[114] Young supported Lydius with a vengeance. In his eyes, the dispute was one between an individual whose policies would open up a vast area of land to small investors and arrogant colonial authorities whose actions represented the monopolizing interests of wealth and power. If the Lydius claim prevailed, land speculation, the premier path to economic advancement, would no longer remain the sole prerogative of the wealthy; ordinary individuals might have a chance to further themselves in a manner long dominated by their superiors.

Young equated the "monopolizing enemies" of Lydius with those who oppressed the common man, and his *Reflections* resounded with stinging attacks upon them. When, for example, opponents of Lydius scoffed at his generous terms of sale, Young asked, "How many gentlemen, in the province of *New York*, keep thousands of acres of excellent soil in wilderness, waiting till the industry of others round them, raise their lands to three, four, or more pounds per acre?" He demanded to know "who, that has the most superficial acquaintence with the country, can esteem the buyer of such lands any other than a slave during life?" Noting that "Liberty and Property (*the Household Gods* of Englishmen) have called loudly for our *blood* and *treasure*," Young exclaimed: "We the common people, have freely lavish'd both."[115] All that such people now asked was equity, a fair chance to advance themselves through the possession of land. "On presumption the bone was common, and each had equal right to strive for it," Young declared that none were "riotous despisers of lawful authority"; instead, all had "waited much to [their] detriment" until they could "plainly see [their] enemies": men took the land of honest, hardworking farmers "by law craft and illegal fraud, of the worst kind, being carried [out] *under cover of [the] law.*"[116]

In October 1764, shortly after completing his *Reflections*, Young moved to Albany. The ideas so stridently expressed in that pamphlet, a distillation of the long hours spent in conversation with Ethan Allen, remained, however, very much alive within the younger man. Even before Young left Salisbury, Allen had begun to challenge established authority. He displayed little deference toward his social superiors when he personally "impounded" Samuel Tousley's pigs. And when Young inoculated him against smallpox, Allen vociferously defied the town's elected officials to do anything about it. After Young's departure for Albany, Allen continued to flaunt social conventions in his blunt, straightforward manner. He backed down from no man, regardless of rank or status. As George Caldwell discovered, Allen would "spill the blood of any that opposed him." Allen displayed this same aggressively independent frame of mind when he emigrated with his family to Northampton. Less than a year later, on July 15, 1767, the selectmen of Northampton warned him, his wife, and his children out of town.[117]

Ethan Allen had offended more than just the town authorities in Northampton. His partnership in a lead mine with his brothers-in-law, Abraham and Israel Brownson, not only had failed but had degenerated into a series of lawsuits and hard feelings between him and his wife's relatives.[118] Fortunately, relations with his own kin had remained more cordial. When they returned to Salisbury, Ethan and his family moved in with Heman, whose general store was flourishing. In addition, two other brothers, Levi and Heber, had begun to invest in property in Salisbury.[119]

With his family secure, Ethan began to take long excursions into the New Hampshire Grants, where he hunted and trapped. It was the land itself, however, that attracted him. That, and the possibilities for economic advancement through the kind of land speculation so forcefully advocated by his old friend Thomas Young. Consequently, in May 1770 Ethan purchased an entire proprietor's right in Poultney and an additional five hundred acres in New Haven for a total cost of twelve pounds.[120] Both these townships lay in the Grants. There Ethan Allen, the democratic entrepreneur, intended to stake his future; there he meant to achieve the social and economic success that had eluded him in Salisbury and Northampton.

On the 17th of April 1753, Jonathan Fowler of Westfield, husbandman, for good will and respect to Jedediah Dewey, John Noble, George Granger, Ebenezer Bush, Abel Morley, Israel Dewey, Moses Kellogg, Pompey Negro, and Nathaniel Collins, who being incorporated into a body whom I look upon to be a church of Christ, for which reason I grant unto them land near Little River on the south side of a certain brook upon Bridge Hill or Dewey's Hill, or near the place where Josiah Dewey's house formerly stood on the east side of the highway, near the dwelling house of Asa Noble: bounded west on said highway, east on land of said Fowler, north on the brow of the hill or his own land, south on said Fowler's land, containing fifty foot square to build a house for the worship of God, so long as they, their successors, and followers shall use and improve the same for that use and no longer.[121]

The day after Jonathan Fowler executed this deed members of the Separate Congregational church of Westfield, Massachusetts, erected a meetinghouse on the property.[122] Less than a year later two Separate Congregational ministers ordained Jedediah Dewey pastor of this church.[123] Within several more years the congregation grew to nearly forty adult members.[124]

The man installed as pastor of the Separates in Westfield came from a family with deep roots in the community and its established Congregational church. Indeed, Jedediah Dewey's grandfather and namesake, along with his two brothers, Thomas and Josiah, had been among Westfield's original settlers.[125] Born in Windsor, Connecticut, the three brothers moved in 1660 to Northampton, Massachusetts, where they operated a corn mill. By 1667 they had migrated southward to Westfield, which was then part of Springfield and thus under the powerful sway of John Pynchon. There, with Pynchon's son-in-law, Joseph Whiting, the Dewey brothers established saw and corn mills.[126]

The Deweys became prominent citizens in the larger community as well. Following the creation of the township of Westfield in 1669, all three repeatedly served as selectmen and in other positions of trust.[127] With Joseph Whiting's departure in 1677 the Deweys assumed full control of Westfield's only saw and corn mills. In addition, Thomas owned a tavern and Jedediah served as an ensign in the local militia.[128] All of the brothers farmed large parcels of land, and Jedediah was also a skilled wheelwright.[129]

The Deweys prospered with the growth and success of Westfield. They were also prominent members of the church. Thomas and Josiah became foundation men in the town's Congregational church when it formed shortly after their arrival in the area. In 1671 Thomas served as the church's messenger to procure a minister in Boston and had to struggle through a terrible winter storm in order to accompany Rev. Edward Taylor back to the community. Josiah became the church's first deacon.[130] Their brother Jedediah joined the church on September 28, 1680.[131] None of them took church membership lightly; for them church members truly were visible saints. Not only must each individual have undergone a saving experience but each must offer a public relation of that conversion. Such "relations" were vital to the well-being of the individual member and the corporate body of the church. They stood as the only palpable manifestations of the crucial covenant between God and man; without them the church could have no meaning.

Josiah Dewey's own public relation, carefully recorded by the Reverend Taylor, exemplified this religious intensity. In his personal statement Dewey painstakingly described the state of his soul from the age of thirteen, when "God was pleased to give me some discovery of my miserable state," until he joined the church more than ten years later. At one point, with "swarms of iniquities that came in upon me beseeging me on every Side," he recalled that he was so "a shamed of mine own righteousness" and developed "such an indignation against mine own heart, that many times laying hold on my breast, me thot that could I come at it I could even tare it out of my Body, & cast it a way." With the support of his parents, Christian friends, and various ministers, Josiah managed to overcome the deep spiritual despair and persevered in his soul-searching. Finally, one day, "going away into the field musing thereon, I felt a strong perswasion arise in me, of the Love of God in Christ through the riches of Grace, as made me cry out my Lord, & my God, my Saviour & my Redeemer." Then, "passing on as it were in an heavenly Rapture, & inflamed with these Considerations, on a sudden the whole face of things seeming to be changed, & I hurd me thoughts as it were these words, a Pardon, a Pardon, Christ hath purchased a Pardon." Astonished that "the wonderful Free Grace of God . . . Should ever be bestowed on such an unworthy Sinner, as I was," Josiah's "heart was as it were Swallowed up with admiring & praising God, that for sometime, especially in private Duties, I could scarece thinke of any thing Else."

For a time he was so "strongly perswaded of [his] own Salvation . . .

that [he] feared not to challeng a dispute with Satan about it." However, "God withdrawing himselfe again, let me se my own weakness . . . the Lord Shewed me the continuall need I was in of a momentary Supply of his Grace." Josiah went to his minister, who told him that "God had carryed [him] through dangerous ways, & Set [him] on the top of the Hill: & that [his] worke was to watch against Temptations." As a result of this conversation, Josiah felt ready to join the church. Doubts and fears did not vanish, however, and he "forbore about halfe a year." At that time "it pleased God to afflict me th[at] I kept my bed mostly a day or two, which brought me to consider what God might aim at by it, & fearing lest it might be a neglect of Communion with God & his People I earnest sought Go[d] in the matter desiring that he would be pleased to discover it to me by raising me up again; & it pleased God so to answer me, as that within an hour, or two, I was able to go about my business." Josiah immediately sought out the elders of the church and expressed his desire to join in communion with them. "Being joyned I may truly say I have seen God here, & there, in his Ordinances & in h[is] Providences, in his Mercies, & in Afflictions."[132]

This same spiritual fervor carried through the next generation. Jedediah Dewey's eldest son, of the same name, placed himself "under the watch of the church" on August 24, 1705. It was not until March 30, 1712, however, that he felt able to own the covenant. In the interim his wife had been brought into the church as a full member.[133] The faith of the young Jedediah, was, however, to be sorely tested.

Born in Westfield on April 11, 1714, the third-generation Jedediah grew to maturity in the tradition of the Deweys. The Reverend Taylor baptized him at birth, and his parents raised him within the Congregational church.[134] Like the Dewey men before him, he became a skilled carpenter as well as a farmer. His farm was decidedly smaller than theirs, however, and his prospects for enlarging it much less favorable. The landholdings of his grandfather had been divided through partible inheritance into a number of small farms. The eldest son, Jedediah the second, had inherited a house and about twenty-two acres, and three other sons had each received twenty to thirty acres.[135] Over the years Jedediah managed to add only a little more than twenty acres to his holdings. Upon his death in 1728 this estate was divided among his wife, two sons, and six daughters.[136] Upon reaching his maturity, the third Jedediah found himself forced to buy the various shares held by his siblings simply to reconstitute the original farm. He began to do this following his marriage to Mindwell Hopkins of Windsor, Connecticut, on April 4, 1736. But in order to increase his holdings beyond those of his father, Jedediah had to search for land farther and farther away from his own homestead. His chances for prospering within Westfield proper were becoming increasingly circumscribed.[137]

If Jedediah's life as a carpenter and a farmer became somewhat troublesome, so too did his spiritual life. In 1735 a religious revival spawned by Jonathan Edwards in nearby Northampton spread to Westfield; young Jedediah joined the church two years later.[138] Caught up in the excitement of the revival, he had disregarded important changes that had taken place within the church in Westfield. In 1728 church members had voted that individuals wishing to join the church would "be left at their liberty as to the giving the chh. an account of the work of saving conversion." Henceforth "Relations" would be "looked upon as a matter of indifferency." The church also accepted the Halfway Covenant by approving a motion suggesting that "all Baptized Persons who were come to years of understanding and were capable of discipline belonging to this congregation should be lookt upon subjects of discipline."[139]

These changes, which struck at the very heart of what the Deweys and so many others had always believed, troubled Jedediah. His anxieties increased following George Whitefield's visit to the area in the fall of 1740. Whitefield preached several sermons to Edwards's church in Northampton, where the "congregation was extraordinarily melted by every sermon; almost the whole assembly being in tears during a great part of the sermon." He then proceeded to Westfield, where he spoke "to a pretty large Congregation, and with considerable Power at the latter End."[140] Apparently Jedediah felt the power of Whitefield's attack upon unconverted ministers and members of the congregation who had not experienced the saving grace; on January 3, 1749, a meeting of the church noted that Jedediah had withdrawn himself from the Lord's table for some time. At that same meeting they heard his reason for separating from them: "That the Church admitted Members without care to know whether they had saving Faith." Considering this justification insufficient, the church appointed a committee to confer with their erring brother.[141] A year later committee members reported that they had little reason to believe that further labor with Brother Dewey would be of any use. He had "joined himself to a Separate Society" and had "taken upon him[self] to preach." The church then discussed whether to excommunicate Dewey but could reach no consensus. The following month the congregation accepted the Reverend Ballantine's advice regarding all those who had withdrawn from the church for reasons of conscience. Rather than excommunicating these people, it would be "sufficient to vote them no longer Members of the Church."[142]

After dealing with Jedediah, church authorities began to summon others who had separated from them to appear before the congregation to give their reasons for separation. Those who did so declared that "the Church deneyed the power of Godliness," "the Church admitting Members who had no Grace," "because private Brethren had not liberty to exercise their Gifts & to speak when they were filled," "that they [the church] allowed natural men as Such to come to the Sacrament of the Lords Supper," and "that they hold that natural men as Such may be called into the work of the Gospel ministry."[143]

These Separates ardently believed in the old ways; they cherished the covenant of grace and a church composed exclusively of visible saints. Intent upon keeping alive the fervent spirit manifested so plainly in the public relations of Josiah Dewey and so many others, they meant to purge the corrupt influence of "natural" men from the church. Such beliefs brought them into conflict with Old Light authorities as well as with New Light ministers offering the refined Edwardsianism of "Consistent Calvinism" or the "New Divinity."[144] The sophisticated principles espoused by these two groups competing for control of New England Congregationalism were anathema to simple folk like the Westfield Separates.

John Ballantine personified all that Old Light Congregationalism represented in the minds of Jedediah Dewey and his fellow Separates. He came from a wealthy Boston family. His father, a solid member of the church in Brattle Square, had been register of deeds for Suffolk County, and his mother was a Winthrop. During John's senior year at Harvard his father died. Even with a large inheritance, though, John remained committed to the ministry and received both a bachelor's and a master's degree from Harvard.[145] Within two years after being settled as Westfield's established minister in 1741, Ballantine married a Dedham woman and brought her back to Westfield in a carriage he purchased for the occasion. Since Ballantine's "chair" was the single such vehicle in a town accustomed only to oxcarts and lumbering farm wagons, it created quite a stir.[146] Such a luxury drew attention to the amenities enjoyed by a settled minister. Ballantine's salary, which was princely when compared with those of most Westfield residents, together with the home provided by the town, rankled men like Jedediah Dewey and may have elicited their envy as well.

If Ballantine's ostentatious display of wealth offended many of his parishioners, so too did his acceptance of any and all individuals into the church. Like his liberal colleagues at Harvard, Ballantine believed God's grace to be conditional. As a result he recognized an expanded role for human effort in achieving redemption. Through constant and diligent application of the means of grace — prayer, Bible reading, and close attendance upon the learned clergy — individuals could be brought to salvation. Thus, as many people as possible should be welcomed into the church, where they would fall under the tutelage of an educated ministry. Ballantine's acceptance of "natural" men within the congregation deeply troubled Jedediah and others within the Westfield church. Perhaps it was for this reason that the pastor paid Dewey a personal visit in the fall of 1743.[147]

In any event, Ballantine's behavior during this same time was as troubling as his theological principles. He openly subscribed to Charles Chauncey's *Seasonable Thoughts on the State of Religion in New England*, published in Boston in 1743, a vitriolic blast against George Whitefield and the New Light revivals sweeping the region.[148] Two years later Ballantine joined a group of Connecticut ministers who accused Whitefield of espousing false principles, being "deeply ting'd with Enthusiasm," displaying "a very censorious Spirit by slandering the Ministers and Colleges in this Country," and "having caus'd Divisions and Offences contrary to the Doctrine which we have learn'd of Christ."[149] For Dewey and others "deeply ting'd with Enthusiasm," it was Ballantine and his liberal colleagues, not George Whitefield, who committed gross offenses against "the Doctrine which we have learn'd of Christ."

The Westfield Separates were disturbed not only by Ballantine's liberalism but by many of the ideas being propounded by New Light advocates of the New Divinity as well. Intent upon countering the Arminianism of the liberals while at the same time embracing the spiritual fervor of the revivals, these men strove to rationalize the idea of man as a moral agent by means of the traditional Calvinistic belief in the divine sovereignty of God. They worked toward this goal by claiming that God's dominion was absolute, regeneration was completely unconditional, and man must be entirely self-denying and totally submissive to God.[150]

Yale became the bastion of New Divinity thought, and its graduates began to fill back-country pulpits in western Massachusetts and Connecticut, where they expounded the principles of their mentors. Israel Dewey, Jedediah's cousin and a foundation man in the Separate church in Westfield, encountered one such pastor shortly after he moved his wife and ten children to Sheffield, Massachusetts, in 1757. There Israel heard Samuel Hopkins just as Hopkins was beginning to formulate the ideas that would make him one of the leading New Divinity theologians in New England. It was not a pleasant experience for Israel. Hopkins maintained God's sovereignty to be so absolute that God did not simply permit sin to exist but actually willed it. In addition, to emphasize the entirely unconditional nature of regeneration, he declared that God considered the awakened sinner who employed the means of grace such as prayer or Bible reading to be even more vile and degraded than the unawakened sinner who disregarded prayer and the Bible.[151]

Such pronouncements from the pulpit stunned Israel. How could God will sin to exist on earth when he was its most powerful opponent? How could any person be damned for praying or reading the Bible? Should not these practices in fact make up the heart of every true Christian's daily life? Baffled by these issues, Israel entered into private discussions with Hopkins and exchanged letters with the pastor in which he expressed the belief that Hopkins was preaching ideas "pregnant with a train of the most deformed Monsters, that ever were born in the Kingdom of Irreligion." In his mind, "the plain and manifest Design of the Scriptures is to declare against Sin" and "if there is any God, he is a holy God, if he is a holy God, his Will is holy; if his Will is holy, Sin and Wickedness which is Unholiness, can't be agreable to his Will and Pleasure, and exactly as he would have it."[152]

Israel Dewey's discomfort did not end with this exchange of letters. By word or by action he must have made it clear during one of Hopkins's sermons that he disagreed with the pastor, for on March 23, 1758, a church meeting voted that Dewey ought to be dealt with for his "disorderly behaviour in the time of preaching in the meeting-house lately." On April 20 Dewey appeared before the church and admitted that he was "out of the way in his conduct." Since he promised to reform, the church voted to allow his disturbance to pass without a public censure. However, when Dewey remained adamant regarding the nature of sin, the church voted to defer its decision for additional consideration. Finally the church decided to "admonish" Israel before the entire congregation "to be more modest and earnestly seek further light, as we look upon him ignorant and much out of the way."[153] For his part, Dewey, whose belief in the evil of sin and the promise of salvation to the awakened sinner never wavered, considered it his duty to oppose Hopkins and all other ministers as long as they opposed the truth as he knew it.

Jedediah Dewey did his best to uphold these same simple truths as a Separate minister. Thus, he attended a convention of Separate ministers at Stonington, Connecticut, on May 29, 1754, in order to discuss the practice of infant baptism. The convention itself was being held in response to the opposition to this practice on the part of a great many Separate Baptists. Indeed, their opposition was becoming a divisive issue among Separates and threatened to tear apart a number of congregations.[154] Dewey and his church stood by the traditional position and continued to baptize babies at birth. He also took seriously his responsibilities to his fellow townsmen. During the summer of 1757 he served as chaplain to Captain Ezra Clapp's militia company on its march northward to relieve Fort William Henry.[155]

Upon his return from service with the militia Dewey began to assess his life in Westfield. He remained committed to his ministry, and yet the opportunity to prosper, to expand his farm, appeared to be lessening each year. His cousin and lifelong friend Israel had already left with his family. In late fall 1757 Jedediah decided to do the same. He traveled to Crum Elbow Precinct (Amenia), where he worked as a joiner while searching for good farmland. In May 1758 he sold his Westfield homestead to his brother Martin; four months later he paid more than four hundred pounds for nearly two hundred acres of land in Crum Elbow Precinct.[156] He settled there with Mindwell and their six children.

The move from Massachusetts to New York did not necessitate any compromise of Dewey's religious principles. In fact, the area around Crum Elbow Precinct was a hotbed of Separatism. A Separate church, "Carmel in the Nine Partners," had been formed there in 1748. Two years later Solomon Paine, who had organized the first true Separate or Strict Congregational church in Connecticut in 1744, had helped ordain his nephew, Abraham Paine, as pastor of this church. The church adhered closely to traditional Congregational beliefs and maintained a strict discipline over all its members. On one occasion the congregation met to labor with several members "for the indulgence of an Antinomian and party spirit." According to the church's own records, this "solemn assembly continued from Wednesday morning in solemn fasting, lamentation, prayer and confession, from the rising of the morning till the stars appeared on Saturday night."[157] Dewey became an enthusiastic member of this congregation, which included Stephen, Roswell, and Weight Hopkins, as well as the Paines and the Mead family, when he came to Amenia.

In February 1762 Dewey applied to the Separate church in Westfield for dismissal as its minister in order that he might become pastor in Amenia. The Westfield church denied his request.[158] Consequently, Dewey worked to unite the Westfield and Amenia churches. The fact that many people from Westfield, including his brother Martin and his family, had settled in Amenia strengthened his resolve. In any event, he did not intend to return to Westfield. Mindwell had died on May 29, 1760, shortly after the birth of their eighth child, and six months later Jedediah had married Betty Buck of Amenia.[159] His ties to Amenia had become far stronger than any link to Westfield.

With the passage of time, though, life in Amenia became increasingly unstable. Disputes over land titles between New England settlers and New York patent holders became more and more troublesome, and occasional violence erupted. In addition, many of Dewey's neighbors and fellow church members, including Roswell and Weight Hopkins, had emigrated to the New Hampshire Grants. Dewey must have begun to wonder whether he had made the right decision when he settled in Amenia. Then in May 1763 the Separate church in Bennington asked him to become its pastor.[160] Two months later he met with Samuel Robinson, Jonathan Fassett, and several other members of that church, who offered him the right of land set aside for the church within the township as well as a regular salary if he would become their pastor.[161] A full right of land in a developing town promised far greater rewards than a farm in an increasingly unstable environment. In addition, like John Ballantine, he would enjoy the status of a settled minister. In Bennington he could have all this and still maintain his religious beliefs inviolate.

On August 14, 1763, a council of Separate ministers met in Westfield, where they voided a contract to merge the Westfield and Amenia congregations into one church. At the same time they united the churches of Westfield and Bennington.[162] Shortly thereafter Jedediah Dewey, his wife, and family left for the Grants.

My next object was to make a map of the township of Mansfield, with the allotments & Survey-bills thereof, agreeable to the bond etc., I had given the proprietors of Said town the preceedig Summer. I soon completed the map; but turning my

attention to the field books, that Captain Remember Baker and I had kept, a diffi-
culty arose in my mind, for my object was to sell out of Mansfield at all events, and if
possible to get the ninety pounds for the survey, etc. A great proportion of the corners
of said lots were made on Spruce or fir timber, and if I described them as such, it
would show the poorness of the town, and raise many questions that I wished to avoid.
I made use of a stratigem that answered my purpose. In my survey bills, I called
Spruce and fir gum-wood, a name not known by the people of Sharon (the place
where the proprietors lived). They asked what kind of timber gumwood was. I told
them tall Straight trees that had a gum, much like the gum on cherry trees etc.
While the proprietors were busy in inspecting the map, Survey Bills, etc., I took aside
the brother of one of the principal proprietors, who was an ignorant fellow and owned
two rights of land in the town. I tryed to buy his rights, but he dared not sell them
without first consulting his brother. By this the proprietors all got the alarm that I
wished to purchase, and land in Mansfield was considered of consequence. I was urged
to sell back to the proprietors the twenty rights I had bought, which I did, and
obtained the ninety pounds for the survey, etc., which I considered of more conse-
quence than the whole town. Having closed this business satisfactorily to myself, I
returned to my brother's and had a hearty laugh with my brothers Heman and
Zimri, on informing them respecting the gum-wood etc.[163]

The land that Ira Allen so gleefully disposed of in the fall of 1772 lay
in the township of Mansfield on the New Hampshire Grants. Following this transaction Allen still held thirty proprietor's rights on the
Grants, in the townships of Bolton, Duxbury, Moretown, and Middlesex, for which he owed Samuel Averill £150 to be paid in "neat cattle"
over the next eighteen months. In addition, he had taken out a bond for
six more rights of land payable at the same time as his other debts.[164]
Following his trip to the area of the Onion (Winooski) River to survey
Mansfield, however, Allen decided to rid himself of all these holdings
except for those in Middlesex. This would enable him to acquire land
closer to Lake Champlain, which he believed would become far more
marketable in the near future because of its easy access to water trans-
portation. To do this he intended not only to convince Averill to take
back his land but to make a profit on the exchange.

Allen approached his objective indirectly. Instead of proceeding
straight to Averill's home, he visited with two of his own uncles who
lived nearby. These relatives held a party, to which they invited Averill's
sons. Upon learning from his boys that Ira Allen was in the neighborhood, Averill immediately sent word that he would like to meet with
him about the Onion River lands. Not wishing to reveal that he too was

eager to discuss these lands, Allen responded that he would drop by Averill's on his way back to Salisbury, where he was living with his brothers Heman, Zimri, and Levi. But first he meant to spend several more days with his relatives. When Ira finally called on him, the older man asked him to stay the night and then accompanied him to Heman's home in Salisbury the following day. Once there, Averill proposed to surrender Allen's notes in return for the deeds and the bond. Allen refused on the grounds that the land had increased in value and that he planned to settle there. Averill said that he would renew the conversation when he returned from a trip to the Grants. Following Averill's departure, Heman, certain that the man would not return, upbraided Ira for not accepting the offer. Ira responded that he meant to hold out in the hope of gaining a large profit. When Averill did return through Salisbury without stopping, Ira suffered even more verbal abuse from his brothers, yet he stubbornly maintained that he would still turn a profit in his dealings with Averill.[165]

A short time later Ira again called upon his uncles who lived near Averill. Again he arranged it so that Averill would conclude that his purpose was to visit relatives. This time, however, he also let it be known that he had hired his cousin Jesse Baker to help him survey townships and to make settlements on the Onion River. Finally, one evening Ira went to Averill's home. Mrs. Averill informed him that her husband would be back later and invited him to stay the night. He accepted and within a short time told Mrs. Averill that he intended to settle on the Onion River and that he meant to survey all the townships and cut a road through to the area. Since Mr. Averill owned so much of the land involved, he would naturally be expected to stand a large proportion of the expense. After convincing Mrs. Averill of the tremendous costs her husband might soon face, Allen affected drowsiness and finally acceded to her suggestion that he go immediately to bed. This too was part of his scheme, for having previously spent a night with the Averills, he knew that only a flimsy partition separated his room from theirs. Consequently, when Mr. Averill returned, Allen could overhear everything he and his wife had to say about the Onion River lands. His plan worked to perfection. As he recalled later, "I learned all the secrets, and went quietly to sleep, and did not hurry myself in the morning." Knowing full well what Averill would surrender and what he would not, Ira gained more than even he had thought possible. In exchange for the rights of land in Bolton, Duxbury, and Moretown, Averill canceled all of Allen's debt to him; in addition, Ira returned to Salisbury owning the ten rights to land in Middlesex free and clear. And all this had not cost him a shilling.[166] Just as in his relations with the Mansfield proprietors, Allen's ingenuity, as well as his disingenuousness, served him well. Barely twenty-one years of age, Ira Allen had thoroughly absorbed the aggressive, entrepreneurial practices of an increasingly market-oriented society.

The belief that the individual must protect his own interests in any business transaction came quite naturally to Allen. Like his brothers and sisters, he had been forced to rely upon his own resources from an early age. Just three years old when his father died in April 1755, Ira, the youngest of eight children, lived on the Allen homestead with his family and attended common schools in Cornwall until his elder brothers began to sell off their shares of the estate. Ethan and Heman left for Salisbury in 1762. Four years after that Heber sold his twenty-five-acre portion of the estate; Levi followed suit two years later.[167] By this time Ira's mother, Mary, had moved to Goshen, Massachusetts, to live with her eldest daughter, Lydia, and her husband, John Finch.

Following the breakup of the homestead in Cornwall, Ira and his brother Zimri migrated to Salisbury, where they joined Heman and Levi in whatever business ventures offered a profit. There in September 1769 Ira invested with Heman and Levi in 350 hogs. Assisted by several other men, Ira and Heman drove these animals nearly seventy miles in order to fatten them on beechnuts along the Connecticut River near Hatfield, Massachusetts. To accomplish this, they had to struggle through a bitter winter storm that made it nearly impossible to follow the blazed trees that marked their path. In January 1770 Ira drove 150 of the best hogs to Albany, over eighty miles away, and sold them for a good profit. Upon his return he moved the other animals to Sunderland, where he had to find corn and shelter for them. In April the Allen brothers bought 200 additional hogs, which they fattened on beechnuts until Ira drove them to Albany during the summer, and again the brothers turned a nice profit.[168]

During the time that he was involved in fattening and marketing pigs, Ira repeatedly encountered individuals who occupied a higher social station than he. During two such experiences he gave full vent to feelings he harbored toward his social superiors. The first incident occurred in Sunderland, where Ira was bargaining with local farmers to buy corn for his hogs. He came upon a tavern whose owners had a reputation for being overbearing in their treatment of poor folk. Whether out of envy of their relative wealth, resentment toward their social station, or simply for sport, Allen meant to embarrass the tavern keepers. Although he had gold in his pocket, he feigned poverty and acted in the most obsequious manner toward the landlady, who, as anticipated, treated him with contempt. Finally, after enduring repeated slights from the woman and having leftovers placed before him for his dinner, Ira took two gold coins out of his pocket, laid them on the table, and, without attempting to eat a mouthful, asked for his bill. At the same time he exclaimed for all to hear that he expected it would be high, since he was certain that the cooks had been at least a week preparing the meal. He then experienced great glee when the landlady, at the sight of his money, bustled about to serve him a good dinner. His satisfaction grew as bystanders who had witnessed the entire charade joined him in humbling the woman.[169]

After Allen returned from driving the last of the hogs to Albany, his horse strayed away. He took a bridle and set out on foot to find it. One Sunday evening he tacked up an advertisement for his stray horse at a public house kept by Mr. Todd, a preacher. When Ira turned to leave, Todd, who was also the local justice of the peace, ordered him not to travel on the Sabbath. It was late in the evening, and since he was tired Allen decided to submit to the law and remain for the night. The following morning, when he gave Todd a gold piece to change, the man turned it over several times in his hands, "appearantly considering how to get the most of it," and promptly ordered Ira to pay a fine of ten shillings for breach of the Sabbath laws. Allen argued that he had peaceably complied with Todd's request to cease his travels and that searching for a lost horse was both customary and consistent with the Scriptures. However, the "briliancy of the gold exceled my arguments, and the fine was insisted on." Ira refused and stormed out. Todd sent several men after him, and they quickly succeeded in bringing him back. Still, Ira remained adamant in his refusal. Finally, however, submitting to the inevitable, he relented and paid his fine.[170]

Payment of the fine did not end Allen's skirmish with Justice Todd. When Ira put on his hat to leave, Todd lectured him regarding disorderly behavior and ordered him to remove his hat and pay close attention to what was being said to him. Responding that any traveler had the privilege of wearing his hat in the barroom of a public house, Ira maintained that since he had paid his fine, he was at liberty to do as he pleased. The justice, considering Allen still to be in his courtroom and thereby responsible for behaving in a respectful manner, continued his harangue. Ira insolently replied that he paid Rev. Jonathan Lee of Salisbury for any preaching he had to endure. Todd immediately placed him "under keepers for contempt of authority." A terrible altercation ensued during which Todd threatened to send Ira to prison, to which he expressed great pleasure since this would take him near home, where his brothers could pay his bail.[171] The confrontation finally ended when Todd agreed to release Ira on the condition that he publicly confess to his misdeeds. Ira expressed his willingness to comply if only Todd would tell him what to say. Todd supplied him with a long "story," and Ira started in; soon, however, he forgot his lines. Todd repeated the confession; Ira again botched it. Finally, upon reciting his admission in its entirety, he impudently added that he was also guilty of original sin.[172]

Allen left Mr. Todd's tavern seething with anger and filled with a venomous indignation toward gentlemen and the established authority they represented. He meant to take his revenge upon this class of individuals in any way he could. Quick as he was to harass his superiors, however, Ira would expend any amount of time and energy to help friends and family. Shortly after returning to Salisbury following his bout with Justice Todd, he went to Goshen to help tend his eldest sister Lydia, who was desperately ill. To obtain the medicines prescribed by her doctors, Ira rode more than 120 miles without rest. Despite his heroic efforts, his sister died a few days after his return. At about this same time his mother suffered a stroke. Ira attended to her for nearly a month, until she could be moved to Salisbury, where Heman insisted she be brought to live in his home.[173]

After helping transport his mother to Heman's, Ira traveled north into the Grants, where he perused the area around Castleton and Hubbardton. He bought several proprietor's rights of land in Poultney and intended to seek out Captain Isaac Searles of Wiliamstown, Massachusetts, one of the largest proprietors of Hubbardton, in order to buy more land in that town. Upon discovering that Searles was in Boston, Ira returned to Salisbury, where he helped Heman and Levi with a business they had initiated early in 1771. Levi, involved for some time in the Indian trade around Detroit, had returned with deerskins that he, in partnership with Heman, meant to make into leather pants. They obtained the use of a fulling mill on the Housatonic River and employed some Irish leather dressers and tailors. Ira spent several months working with these men in the mill.[174]

During the time that he labored in the mill Ira managed to contact Captain Searles, to whom he and Zimri paid sixty-four pounds for nearly ten thousand acres of land in the township of Hubbardton. In the fall of 1771, accompanied by Remember Baker, a skilled surveyor, Ira set out to establish the boundaries of his property. To accomplish this, the two men found it necessary to run the north and west lines of Castleton, which had not yet been completely surveyed, in order to locate the township of Hubbardton. While doing this, Ira came across an excellent tract of intervale land in Castleton. When he and Baker discovered that no lines had been run near this piece of property, they surveyed it along with some other land near their own property. So rugged was the terrain and so haphazardly had it been previously laid out that a man with a compass and a chain had nearly free rein in creating boundary lines. As a consequence, when Allen and Baker ran their lines to locate the Hubbardton boundaries, they included over fifteen hundred acres of land previously considered to be within the township of Castleton. By the time they had laid out some individual lots in Hubbardton, however, the two men had run out of supplies and had to live off the land.[175]

When Ira returned to Salisbury for the winter, he again dressed leather for Heman and Levi. In March 1772 he decided to learn the surveyor's art and worked with a master for seven days.[176] During that same month he and Zimri sold one and one-half shares in their father's estate. The half-share was Ira's; as a minor he merged a portion of his inheritance with that of his older brother in order to be able to sell it.[177] This money enabled the bothers to invest in lands in Poultney. In May Ira and Baker set out once more to run lines in Hubbardton. Again they ran out of supplies and had to live off fish they managed to catch until they finally struggled into a settlement in Castleton. After recuperating from the terrible fatigue that he had suffered, Baker returned home. Allen, however, "commenced Surveyor for myself, and never after went to a master to learn a rule."[178]

While surveying lots for Zimri and himself in Poultney, Ira encountered his eldest brother, Ethan, who was hunting deer. Ethan invited his brother to accompany him on the hunt. Ira, always more intent upon business than upon pleasure, hesitated. However, when he realized that Ethan, who had traveled the region many times while hunting, could locate prize areas of vacant lands for him, he took his rifle as well as his compass and accompanied his brother. During the long and grueling trip Ira noted that Ethan often "took a quicker step" in the belief that his younger brother would falter. Instead, Ira took great pleasure in recalling that "the real facts were that for a few days [Ethan] could out travel me, in the wilderness." After that, however, "on a long seige and corse fair, raw pork, etc., I could out do him."[179]

Ira enjoyed comparing himself with Ethan. He often told a story about challenging his strapping brother to a race in Salisbury. Standing on the edge of a bog filled with a tangle of underbrush, Ira bet Ethan that he could beat him to a lone hickory tree standing on the far side of the swamp. Tearing through the muddy water and snarled branches, Ethan made straight for the tree. In the meantime, Ira, who knew of a hidden path around the swamp, took off swiftly in that direction. Both brothers reached the hickory at the same time. Ira, being so much smaller, considered this quite an accomplishment.[180] In relating the tale that compared him favorably with Ethan, though, Ira was oblivious to the real import of the story: it illustrated a clear contrast in the brothers' essential character. Ethan, a man of great candor, approached life in a blustering, open, straightforward manner. Ira, far more introspective, exercised guile and cunning in his relationships with others.

During the time that he had spent hunting with Ethan, Ira pondered the economic future of the New Hampshire Grants. Calculating the advantages that might arise from owning land contiguous to Lake Champlain, he decided to investigate that area. When he did travel along the Onion River near Lake Champlain, Ira decided that this was where he wanted to invest his greatest time, effort, and money. Ira believed that the region would become a booming economic success because of its proximity to markets in Montreal and Quebec. Unconvinced by his younger brother's reasoning, Ethan tried to discourage him; for his part, Heman told Ira that he would never have sufficient capital to buy the land or to make settlements upon it. Ira responded that he would purchase the land on credit and take surveying jobs to pay the expense of exploring the country. Heman reconsidered and gave his brother a letter of credit for two hundred pounds. With this Ira purchased fifty-two rights of land in the township of Mansfield, as well as bonds for six additional rights. Beyond that, he contracted with the proprietors of Mansfield to survey the township, lay out fifty-acre divisions to each right, and build six "possession Houses" on the land in return for ninety pounds. Impressed with his brother's enterprise, Heman loaned Ira thirty dollars in cash to support the expedition. Ira then made Remember Baker a partner in the surveying expedition. Baker, who was to supply all the necessary men and material, agreed to take payment when the proprietors compensated Ira upon the completion of the job.[181]

In the fall of 1772 Baker and Ira proceeded to the Onion River, where they found fertile areas of open land along the river near Lake Champlain. Even though he did not own this land, Allen declared to the group that he intended to make a farm for himself there one day, laid out several lots, and made some small improvements on them. When the men reached Mansfield and began to survey the township, they discovered, much to Ira's chagrin, nothing but steep, rocky mountainsides covered with "gum" trees. Upon climbing to the top of one of the tallest of these trees, Ira could see the entire countryside that made up the township of Mansfield. It was at this time that he, "the owner of very near one third of the town," realized that he was unable to find enough open land for even "one good farm" in the entire township. Baker did not miss the opportunity to chide Ira unmercifully for his abilities as a land speculator.[182] Such taunts only served to intensify Ira's determination to rid himself of his Mansfield land and to invest in the area where he wished one day to have his own farm. In any event, the men proceeded to survey the boundaries of Mansfield in order to fulfill their contract with the proprietors.

Upon completion of the survey, Ira returned to Salisbury with three main objectives: to divest himself of his property in Mansfield; to bargain Samuel Averill out of his choicest property on the Onion River at no cost to himself; and to convince his brothers to join him in investing in land along the Onion River as close to Lake Champlain as possible. By January 1773 Ira had accomplished all three. In that month he formed a partnership with Remember Baker and his brothers Ethan, Heman, and Zimri. Together they created the Onion River Land Company.[183] With the establishment of this business venture, Ira Allen, determined to achieve wealth and distinction by whatever means possible, linked his fortunes inextricably to those of the New Hampshire Grants.

2. The Grants in Jeopardy

On June 18, 1761, twenty-two men, women, and children made their way along a narrow trail blazed through the dense forest north of Williamstown, Massachusetts. The women and small children rode on horseback, while the men led strings of horses loaded with the families' belongings. As the group sensed they were approaching Bennington Township, excitement spread. When they came within sight of the slashed trees marking the southern boundary of the town, several of the women raced their horses in an effort to be the first to enter the township that was to be their new home. Thus did families from Hardwick and Amherst, Massachusetts, led by Samuel Robinson Jr. become Bennington's first permanent settlers.[1]

Although he had yet to move to Bennington as a resident, Samuel Robinson Sr. had visited the township on several occasions. In fact, he had been there as recently as April, when he had led a party of men who marked out land rights for settlement and left a cache of supplies that would be of great use to those who followed. Then in the late summer of 1761 he led a group of Separates from Hardwick and the neighboring hill towns of Ware, Amherst, and Sunderland to his settlement in Bennington. Others came after: that fall Joseph Safford arrived with a contingent from Norwich, Connecticut, and the following year Stephen Fay led another group of families from Hardwick, as did Nathan Clark and Ebenezer Walbridge from Norwich.[2] Separates all, these individuals intended to establish the special kind of community based on equality, trust, and Christian discipline that had been denied them in their native states.

Upon their arrival, the new settlers confronted the immediate necessity of obtaining food and shelter if they were to survive in a virtual wilderness environment. In order to conserve the small supply of staples they had on hand, they hunted wild game and harvested the native berries that abounded in the forest around them. They could also draw upon the nearby Walloomsac River and its numerous tributaries for a plentiful supply of fish.

The families cooked over open fires and slept under lean-tos made from freshly cut tree limbs covered with pine branches until log houses could be constructed. Upon completion, these homes had massive stone fireplaces with chimneys made of split sticks plastered on the inside with clay. The roofs and gable ends were made of poles covered with loosely woven split wood, bark, and brush. Some houses had floors made of hewn logs, but most rested on hard-packed dirt. Many had doors made out of slabs split from basswood and windows covered with oiled paper. Others simply had blankets hanging over the openings cut for doors and windows. The occupants of these homes often had cause to regret taking such temporary measures; it was not at all unusual for a bear to brush aside a blanket, enter a home, drive its occupants up into the loft, and make a meal out of whatever food was simmering over the fire. Even those families living in more fully completed homes did not escape occasional frights from wild animals. One evening Marcy Robinson was at home with three small children when a pack of wolves approached the house and tried to find a way in. Marcy's desperate pounding on the door did not frighten the animals away; they left only after she opened the door and ran among them screaming fiercely and waving burning branches she had removed from the fireplace.[3]

While some men constructed log homes, others sowed fall grain, the seed for which the senior Samuel Robinson had brought to the town site the previous April. The townsmen planted most of this seed in fertile pond beds they drained by destroying beaver dams. They also found some plots of open intervale land along the Walloomsac and its larger branches. After planting in these areas, however, the inhabitants of Bennington faced the arduous task of clearing the dense forest to create more arable land. By late fall and early winter many settlers had begun this process in order to be ready to plant in the spring.

Once the pressing needs of survival had been met, the residents of Bennington began to create the institutions necessary to govern their town and shape its character. On February 11, 1762, the proprietors, individuals who had purchased full rights of land from the original grantees under the New Hampshire charter awarded by Governor Benning Wentworth in 1749, held a meeting at the home of John Fassett. After electing Samuel Robinson moderator and John Fassett clerk, they proceeded to their primary order of business: locating a site for the township's meetinghouse. They turned the matter over to a committee composed of Robinson, John Safford, and Fassett. Then, after the rights and quarter rights of land that had already been laid out had been confirmed (each right contained 360 acres), the meeting adjourned.[4]

At ensuing meetings the proprietors assumed their primary responsibilities: allocating and determining the use of town land, establishing the location and the dimensions of all roads and bridges throughout the township, assessing landowners to pay for these improvements as well as to construct a meetinghouse and a school house, and fostering enterprises deemed essential to the town's well-being. To further the latter, at their March 31, 1762, meeting the proprietors gave Robinson and Joseph Safford five acres of land and the privilege of building a corn mill there. They also promised the two men forty dollars if the mill were in operation by August 1 and offered forty-dollar bounties to have sawmills built in the eastern and western sections of the town.[5] In order to fulfill their obligations more efficiently, the proprietors organized themselves into committees and elected certain of their number to fill standing offices. Robinson served as moderator and treasurer of the proprietary, while Fassett filled the positions of clerk and collector. These two men, along with James Breakenridge, made up the original committee charged with taking care of the "prudentials of the propriety."[6] Additional committees arbitrated boundary disputes between neighbors and laid out town lots in the village proper.[7]

By the winter of 1769–70 the proprietors had ceased meeting as a separate body. The bulk of their responsibilities had long since been assumed by officers or committees elected by the annual town meeting. Actually, the proprietors and the town meeting had coexisted for some time. The first town meeting had assembled only a little more than a month after the initial proprietors' meeting, and more often than not, individuals selected to prominent positions by the proprietors simultaneously held the most influential offices within the town government. Thus, Fassett repeatedly presided as moderator of the town meeting, Joseph Safford held the position of treasurer, Moses Robinson filled the office of clerk, and men such as Breakenridge, Samuel Robinson, Fassett, Henry Walbridge, Samuel Safford, and Stephen Fay repeatedly served as selectmen.[8]

Although the same men filled the principal positions of the town and the proprietary, the constituencies that elected them were quite different. Only holders of proprietary rights — large landholders — could be members of the proprietary; however, all adult males qualified as voters in the town meeting. Indeed, participants at Bennington's first town meeting, held March 31, 1762, instituted an important precedent: "Every inhabitant and Freeholder have Free Liberty To Vote in Said Town Meeting."[9] Although fully committed to the principle of egalitarianism in their community, the townspeople of Bennington had no intention of creating an environment of unrestrained individualism. Consequently, when the town voted to support the forty-dollar subsidy to promote the construction of sawmills, its citizens also mandated that the owners of these mills could not charge more than two dollars per thousand board feet of lumber.[10] Participants in these early town meetings desired that citizens in their community live within an atmosphere of corporate harmony; each individual should contribute toward the well-being of the larger whole. To foster such an environment, the Bennington town meeting created offices such as sealer of leather, sealer of weights and measures, haywards, constables, tithingmen, fence viewers, and deer reeves. The primary responsibility of the men filling these positions was to enforce communal standards, to shape the social and economic behavior of Bennington's citizens in such a manner as to subordinate individual desires to the good of the greater community. Above all else, town officials wanted to foster the ideal of egalitarian communalism.

This same egalitarianism permeated the church in Bennington from the time of its formation, December 3, 1762. On that date the Churches of Christ from Hardwick and Sunderland joined together to create one church. Participants at this meeting elected John Fassett clerk and adopted a covenant pledging themselves to walk in brotherly love and to abide together in Christian harmony. In addition, they committed their church to the principles of the Cambridge Platform. This commitment, however, rested on important exceptions stemming from the difficulties many Separates had experienced in Massachusetts and Connecticut. Members of the Bennington church specifically rejected provisions within the Cambridge Platform recognizing the power of civil authorities to intervene in church affairs. Local control, not a state-supported ecclesiastical hierarchy, would be the rule in Bennington.[11]

The church met two weeks after its formation to provide for preaching and to establish the manner in which new members would be accepted in the future. After choosing Samuel Robinson as their moderator, those present agreed that all individuals offering themselves for membership in the church must be rigorously examined. If they failed to give full satisfaction, particularly regarding their conversion experience, they must "stand propounded" for an indefinite period of time. The church members then chose Joseph Safford, Elisha Field, and John Fassett to examine the religious principles of prospective members and to provide preaching for the church.[12] By choosing men who had served as deacons in the towns from which most settlers in Bennington had emigrated — Norwich, Sunderland, and Hardwick — members displayed their concern that all segments within their church receive fair and equitable representation within its councils.

The following year, church members, anxious to have a settled minister among them, initiated proceedings that required the full and harmonious cooperation of the church, the proprietors, and the town. The church began this process by issuing a call to Jedediah Dewey on May 24, 1763. Upon receiving a positive response from him, church members sent a three-man committee to Westfield, Massachusetts, to discuss settling Dewey in Bennington. The church also requested that Separate churches in Plainfield, Scotland, and Suffield send their pastors and elected delegates to act as a church council "in Settling M. Dewey amongst us."[13] That same day the proprietors voted to give Dewey the minister's right of land if he came to Bennington.[14] On August 14 the council of Separates requested by the Bennington church met in Westfield, where they voided a contract between the Westfield and Nine Partners churches and joined those of Westfield and Bennington.[15] In October the town voted its consent to the church's actions.[16] Then on November 1 the proprietors granted Dewey title to the minister's lot; the town also created a committee to set up a home for Dewey.[17] Finally, through the concerted efforts of the church, the proprietors, and the town government, Bennington had a settled minister.

Jedediah Dewey's arrival in Bennington was the source of great satisfaction for the town's church. It was also the cause of some concern. One question constantly plagued church members: how was their minister to be paid? There was no standing order on the Grants, no system to support settled ministers with tax money imposed on all residents by a sympathetic colonial assembly. There could be no compulsory tax in Bennington; those who attended the church must bear full responsibility for paying its minister. In May 1764 the church took an important first step when it voted that "the Society have a right to act with the

Church in proposing any method to support the Gospel provided they in no ways infringe on the privileges and liberties of the Church."[18] In this vote the Bennington church, like all Congregational churches, drew a clear distinction between the "church" and the "society." The church consisted solely of individuals who had experienced saving grace, whereas the society included those who had not yet been saved. Only church members could participate in the sacrament of communion and take part in the governance of the church. Thus, the decision to allow the society to act with the church in deciding the manner in which Dewey's salary would be raised represented a departure from orthodox Congregational practice that reflected the essentially egalitarian nature of the Bennington church.

At a meeting held nearly four years later, on February 8, 1768, church members reiterated their commitment to the democratic principle that all who were asked to support the church should have the right to participate in making decisions that determined how that support was to be raised. A majority of the church "voted that Church & Society should stand all in an equal right about proposing any method or voting in any meeting about the support of the gospel for the present year." At this same meeting members of the church and the society adopted a voluntary subscription method of support, elected Stephen Fay to be treasurer, and chose Fay, Samuel Safford, and Moses Robinson to serve as assessors.[19] Four months later church members elected Joseph Safford and Eleazar Harwood as their deacons.[20] The Bennington church at last stood fully organized.

During the time in which members of the church wrestled with the dilemma of how to support their minister, the men of Bennington took steps to meet whatever problems might arise regarding their community's defense. On October 24, 1764, all able-bodied men of the town between the ages of eighteen and sixty met and organized themselves into a militia company. They elected John Fassett captain and James Breakenridge lieutenant of their company.[21]

At first there appeared to be little need for such an organization. The town flourished within an environment seemingly free of external threats. Population increased at a rapid rate as great numbers of individuals and families from Massachusetts and Connecticut migrated onto the Grants. Large tracts of forest land had been cleared and put under cultivation. A traveler passing through Bennington as early as the summer of 1765 testified to the extent of the labor expended by the settlers when he observed the area's "very fine Land or Plowland or Meadow."

In fact, he considered Bennington's Timothy Meadows "quite the best I ever saw."[22] As a consequence of their arduous efforts, Bennington's farmers and mill owners were beginning to thrive. Not only did they produce ample supplies of grain and flour for the inhabitants of Bennington but they were able to sell or trade their surplus to the immigrants passing through the town en route to settlements further north on the Grants. Roads passable by oxcart had been cut through to Albany on the Hudson River, opening additional trade possibilities.

Bennington began to assume a more prosperous appearance. At the center of the village stood the meetinghouse, a plain wooden building with no steeple. The more successful citizens of the town replaced their log cabins with wood frame houses. John Fassett's tavern thrived. Stephen Fay became the innkeeper of a large, two-story frame building located near the meetinghouse. Taking its name from a stuffed cougar mounted atop a tall post in front of the building, Fay's Catamount Inn drew travelers from a wide area. Like the Catamount, Bennington itself was rapidly becoming the center of activity for that portion of the Grants lying west of the Green Mountains.

From the perspective of a traveler lodging at the Catamount, Bennington must have seemed a pleasant village composed of industrious families gathered in peace and harmony. Such an impression was not entirely accurate, however. In fact, since the settlement of Jedediah Dewey uneasiness had spread among many of the townspeople. This tension did not stem from the fact of Dewey's settlement, but from the decision allowing the society to share equally with the church in any determination about how the pastor was to be supported.

Discontent first surfaced within the church when some members refused to pay their share of Dewey's support. By June 1766 the church felt compelled to appoint a committee to call on the delinquent brethren in the hope that they might give security for the required sums.[23] None did. Instead the breach within the church widened. On June 13, 1768, several discontented members brought charges before the church against those individuals who constituted the majority in the vote taken on February 8 allowing members of the society an equal voice with members of the church in deciding how to raise money to support the pastor. That same majority had elected two members of the society, Stephen Fay and Samuel Safford, to serve as assessors for the subscription list that had been created. In addition, Fay had been elected treasurer. The "agrieved Brethren," former members of the Sunderland church, believed that these actions contradicted the covenant of the

Bennington church, violated the Cambridge Platform, and created "contentions and Divisions" within the church.[24] In their minds, only full church members could participate in votes to raise money to support the pastor; equally important, only full members were eligible to serve as treasurer or assessor for the church. Until the church addressed these issues in a manner satisfactory to them, these doctrinaire members refused either to contribute to Dewey's salary or to attend church services. In addition, they insisted that as long as divisions remained within the church, Parson Dewey should not administer the sacrament of communion.

The controversy over the proper relationship between the church and the society initiated a four-year period during which members of the church worked assiduously to bring their dissident brethren back into the fold.[25] They were unsuccessful. To make matters worse, additional members refused to pay their subscriptions and withdrew from the church. Still the church stood firm: Dewey administered communion regularly, and church members strictly followed the "Gospel Rule" by first "labouring" with those who had withdrawn from communion and then "admonishing" them. Most important, church members would not relent. Behind the resolute leadership of John Fassett and Samuel and Moses Robinson the Bennington church remained resolutely committed to its egalitarian principles.

By the winter of 1771–72 the dissident faction had begun to meet in the home of Ithamar Hibbard, an itinerant evangelist who served as their pastor.[26] The Bennington church acquiesced. No excommunications resulted from this separation, nor did it cause any ruptures in the town. Dissidents who held town offices previous to their separation continued to be elected to these offices. Moreover, whatever religious tensions had existed over the last half-dozen years quickly faded in the face of far more serious issues facing every member of the Bennington community.

The first sign of this impending turmoil appeared as early as the winter of 1763–64. On December 28, 1763, Lt. Gov. Cadwallader Colden of New York issued a public proclamation declaring the Connecticut River to be the eastern boundary of his colony. Basing this claim on a seventeenth-century grant made by Charles II to the duke of York, Colden warned all those who had settled west of the Connecticut River under grants made by the governor of New Hampshire that "they could not derive a legal Title under such Grants." He then enjoined the sheriff of Albany County to list the names of all individuals living on the New Hampshire Grants so that "they may be proceeded against according to Law."[27]

Colden's proclamation threw settlers on the Grants into a state of alarm; title to their land, granted by the authority of a royal governor, had now been declared faulty by another of the king's representatives. Their concern abated somewhat when Governor Wentworth published a rejoinder to Colden's statement. Declaring that the 1739 settlement between New York and Massachusetts established the eastern boundary of New York twenty miles east of the Hudson River, Wentworth unequivocally maintained that "New Hampshire may legally extend her western Boundary as far as the Massachusets [sic] claim reaches." Therefore, settlers on the Grants "may be assured that the patent to the Duke of York is Obsolete, and cannot convey any certain Boundary to New York that can be claimed as a Boundary." Wentworth then ordered all "Civil Officers" of his colony to "continue & be diligent in exercising Jurisdiction in their respective Offices, as far Westward as Grants of land have been made by this Government."[28]

Samuel Robinson, who had been appointed a justice of the peace by the New Hampshire Assembly in February 1762, took seriously Governor Wentworth's injunction to remain active in exercising the authority of his office on the Grants. During the first week of August 1764 he accompanied Deputy Sheriff Samuel Ashley of neighboring Pownal Township and John Horsford and Isaac Charles of Williamstown to the farm of Hans Jurry Creiger in Pownal. The previous year Horsford and Charles had purchased several New Hampshire rights of land in Pownal. They discovered, however, that three Dutch families had been living on this land for several decades under a seventeenth-century New York patent.[29] The Massachusetts men took their complaint to court in Portsmouth, New Hampshire, where they won ejectment suits against the Dutch settlers; Robinson and Ashley then rode with Horsford and Charles to serve those suits and to dispossess the settlers. On Friday, August 3, the four men arrived at Creiger's, where they turned the unfortunate man and his family out of possession of their farm. In addition, they confiscated a parcel of Indian corn and impounded Creiger's cattle, which they held until he paid forty-five dollars to redeem them. On the following Monday, Robinson and the others dispossessed Peter Voss and Bastien Deal from their land. They had not traveled far, however, before the sheriff of Albany County rode up with two New York justices of the peace and some thirty armed men, placed Robinson and his colleagues under arrest for violating New York jurisdiction, escorted them to Albany, and lodged them in jail.[30]

Upon learning of this affair, Governor Wentworth immediately requested that Governor Colden order the release of Robinson and the others. Wentworth considered it "an act of cruelty to Punish Individuals for disputes between two Governments." In his mind, "Jurisdiction is the Main Thing," and that should be left to the king to decide. When Colden laid Wentworth's letter before the members of his council, they responded that Robinson's actions had taken place "within the undoubted Jurisdiction" of New York and that Robinson and the others must therefore "answer in a legal course of Justice."[31]

Released on bail, Samuel Robinson returned to Bennington during the second week of September badly shaken by his encounter with the New York authorities. It was not his incarceration in Albany that upset him; rather, it was the realization of the serious nature of the jurisdictional dispute rapidly developing between New Hampshire and New York. Robinson's anxiety, shared by others holding New Hampshire grants, heightened with the passage of time. Finally, proclamations published by Colden and Wentworth in April 1765 confirmed their worst fears: the king in council had declared in favor of New York.[32] The Board of Trade, responding positively to Cadwallader Colden's continual stream of letters outlining New York's position,[33] had recommended to the king on July 20, 1764, that the Connecticut River be fixed as the boundary between New York and New Hampshire. On that same date the king in council issued a decree to that effect.[34] The king and the board may have been reacting as much to the tension developing between Great Britain and New Englanders over Parliament's power to legislate for the colonies as they were to the actual circumstances of the dispute. Colden himself stressed the ideological differences between New York and the New England colonies in his efforts to sway the board. He doggedly maintained that governments in New England rested on "Republican Principles & those Principles are zealously inculcated on the Minds of their Youth in opposition to the principles of the Constitution of Great Britain." On the other hand, New York's colonial government was "established as nearly as may be after the modell of the English Constitution." Given these circumstances, Colden asked, "Can it then be good Policy to diminish the extent of the Jurisdiction in his Majesty's Province of New York, to extend the power and influence of the other?"[35] In the end, for whatever reason, the king in council granted New York full jurisdiction over the New Hampshire Grants.

The king's order in council naturally created great uneasiness among settlers on the Grants. This anxiety resulted as much from what the order did not say as from what it actually did say. The decree clearly established the boundary between New York and New Hampshire, but it failed to answer other vitally important questions. Did the order, for example, involve simply a change of political jurisdiction from New Hampshire to New York? Or did it mean the transfer of land titles to that colony as well? If so, would holders of New Hampshire grants be required to receive confirmation of their deeds from New York authorities? At what cost? And finally, would the king follow well-established precedent and insist that the government of New York respect the rights of actual settlers whenever there was any dispute over land titles? Since Governor Wentworth had granted 128 townships totaling nearly three million acres prior to the king's order in council, such questions took on considerable importance for a vast number of individuals holding title to their land under his auspices.

In an attempt to address the issue of individuals or families "actually settled" on the Grants, the governor and council of New York issued an order "in Favor of the Occupants under New Hampshire, who were settled before the 22nd Day of May, 1765." Declaring that "the dispossessing of such Persons might be ruinous to themselves and their Families," this decree instructed the surveyor general of the colony not to "make Return on any Warrant of Survey, already, or which may hereafter come to his Hands, of any Lands so actually possessed under such Grants, unless for the Persons in actual Possession thereof, as aforesaid."[36]

On the surface this order appeared to be simple and straightforward; however, such was not the actual case on the Grants. Land titles there became increasingly confused and contradictory. Colden, acting in his capacity as interim governor, bore the largest share of the responsibility for this. By November 1765 he had issued patents for nearly 170,000 acres in the disputed area. The great bulk of this acreage included land previously granted by Wentworth. In fact, Colden described one patent of 10,000 acres as "lying partly within the townships of Shaftsbury, Glastenbury, Sunderland and Arlington, formerly granted under the Province of New Hampshire." Colden also laid out the Princetown Patent, comprising 26,000 acres, to his friends John Tabor Kempe, James Duane, and Walter Rutherford in an irregular shape roughly twelve miles long and three miles wide in order to incorporate only the rich bottom lands along the Battenkill River. As a result, the patent, which cut across the New Hampshire townships of Arlington, Sunderland, and Manchester, incorporated farms already under cultivation in these towns as well as saw- and gristmills being constructed in Arlington by Remember Baker. Colden also issued 154 military patents, totaling 131,800 acres, to British officers and men who had served in the French and Indian War. These too conflicted with New Hampshire grants made in and around Bennington.[37]

Samuel Robinson worked desperately to protect his property and that of others on the Grants. He inquired whether Colden would issue patents confirming actual settlers in possession of their land, only to discover that nothing could be done; the Liberty Boys' violent opposition to the Stamp Act in New York prevented the distribution of the stamps necessary to validate such legal actions.[38] Robinson, hoping to protect the claims of established settlers within the bounds of the Princetown Patent, also cooperated fully with Duane and Rutherford when they toured the area in the summer of 1765.[39] During that same summer Robinson visited Thomas Hutchinson, lieutenant governor of Massachusetts, in the hope that the latter might intervene with the British government on behalf of settlers on the Grants. By this time Robinson clearly recognized what was at stake: if the British government did not uphold New Hampshire titles, he and many others faced economic ruin. He would be forced either to abandon his lands or to become a tenant on such unfavorable terms that an investment of more than one thousand pounds would be destroyed.[40]

Early in November Sir Henry Moore arrived from London to assume the governorship of New York. Cadwallader Colden remained as his lieutenant governor. A lady familiar with Moore considered him "a mere shew governor." She had lived in Albany long enough to realize that Colden would continue "to do the business, and enjoy the power in its most essential branches, such as giving patents for land." For his part, "Sir Harry," who "had never thought of business in his life," would remain "gay, good-natured, and well bred, affable and courteous in a very high degree." Indeed, "if the business of a governor was merely to keep the governed in good humour, no one was fitter for that office than he."[41]

For their part, settlers on the Grants took heart when they learned of Moore's arrival; perhaps he would be more sympathetic to their plight. Determined to present their case before Moore and perhaps to gain concessions they had not been able to wrest from Colden, settlers in the Bennington area sent Robinson and Jeremiah French of Manchester to New York. Surely the new governor, bringing an entirely fresh perspective to the office, would enter into serious negotiations with them regarding land titles on the Grants. With this in mind the two men set out for New York early in December.

Robinson and French could not have met with Governor Moore at a more unpropitious moment. Since his arrival in New York early in November Moore had faced urban riots in opposition to the Stamp Act as well as rural uprisings along the Hudson River led by William Prendergast and his lieutenants. Even before he set foot in the colony, Moore had been warned by the British secretary of state to be alert for troublesome elements within the colony. In fact, he carried instructions from the secretary to employ "the utmost Exertion . . . and Vigour necessary to suppress [the] Outrage and Violence" of "the Lower and more ignorant of the people."[42] Moreover, by the time he met with Robinson and French the governor had been in the colony long enough to absorb local animosities toward New Englanders, which far exceeded Colden's suspicion of the "Republican Principles" of these people. In the minds of those deeply resentful of "Obadiah or Zephaniah, from Hampshire or Connecticut," Yankees always "came in without knocking; sat down without invitation; and lighted their pipe without ceremony; then talked of buying land." Immediately after that these impudent people invariably "began a discourse on politics, which would have done honour to Praise God Barebones, or any of the members of his parliament." Worse, "these very vulgar, insolent, and truly disagreeable people . . . flocked . . . to every unoccupied spot" they could find. As a result, "their malignant and envious spirit, their hatred of subordination, and their indifference to the mother-country, began to spread like a taint of infection."[43]

Moore nonetheless greeted the men from the Grants cordially and allowed them to present their case to the council. In order to buttress the claims of bona fide settlers, he asked them to prepare a list of all individuals who actually resided on the Grants. This they did.[44] Then the governor as well as members of the council expressed their willingness to confirm, when possible, the land titles of true settlers. This would be done at no cost to the landholders. Beyond that the New York officials would make no promises; while they were willing to protect the twenty- and thirty-acre plots that individual settlers had under actual cultivation, they had little intention of confirming titles to entire townships held by proprietors for speculative purposes. It was clear from their conversation that if they confirmed title to larger tracts of land, the fees demanded by the colony of New York for such transactions would be quite high.[45]

Robinson and French left the council meeting extremely agitated. It seemed clear to them that New York authorities, responding to British pressure, meant to confirm only small holdings, to protect individual yeomen. Apparently, large grants of land, the traditional path to prosperity within the colonies, were to be reserved entirely for New York gentlemen like John Tabor Kempe and James Duane.

Concern among proprietors holding New Hampshire grants mounted throughout the spring of 1766. Finally, on June 22, the governor and council of New York issued an order that prompted these men to take action. That order, published in newspapers throughout New England, required all individuals holding New Hampshire grants to appear before the council within three months to confirm their titles. The land of those who did not appear and failed to send an attorney in their stead would be granted to others.[46] In response to this order, nonresident proprietors throughout New England held meetings and appointed agents to represent them before the council. As these agents returned to their communities subsequent to their negotiations with New York officials, word spread that confirmatory grants would be prohibitively expensive. The various proprietors consequently sent their agents to general meetings held at Deerfield, Massachusetts, New York City, and Quaker Hill on the Oblong. Out of these meetings came a plan to petition the king to confirm New Hampshire grants. If their petition succeeded, the concerned proprietors could avoid the New York fees and thus secure their investments on the Grants.

Samuel Robinson was the logical choice to deliver these petitions to the king; he was a settler himself and had as much at stake as any other single individual. His passionate commitment to the cause meant that he would willingly undertake such a long and difficult trip. Robinson sailed for London in December 1766 carrying twenty petitions bearing the signatures of more than six hundred proprietors or purchasers of rights on the New Hampshire Grants.[47] Shortly after reaching London Robinson contacted William Samuel Johnson, an attorney from Stratford, Connecticut, who had recently arrived to serve as Connecticut's colonial agent. The two promptly initiated a cooperative effort in the interests of the settlers and proprietors holding New Hampshire land titles on the Grants.[48] First, they met with a secretary of the Board of

Trade in order to gain some insight into the government's perception of their mission. This meeting convinced them that British officials, under the impression that Wentworth's grants were either speculative or fraudulent, would protect only the rights of authentic settlers. The two men then decided to substitute a single new petition bearing only Robinson's signature "on behalf of himself and more than one thousand other Grantees" for the numerous petitions Robinson brought to London. In this way they hoped to obscure the fact that most property on the Grants was in fact held by nonresident proprietors.[49]

The petition itself recited the basic grievances of those holding New Hampshire titles: a great many people had purchased land grants in good faith from a royal governor; at the time of purchase no grantee had any reason to doubt that the territory now in question lay within the colony of New Hampshire; following the orders in council of July 20, 1764, the petitioners had attempted to gain confirmation of their lands from New York authorities in a legal and peaceable manner; they had been unsuccessful because New York officials had either granted much of this land to others or demanded prohibitively high fees to issue legal titles. The petition went on to claim that "upwards of one thousand families" were now settled on the Grants. Many of these had been "in actual Service of your Majesty in the late War carried on for the defence of your Majesty's Dominions in North America and particularly of the Lands in Question." Most had "expended their whole and others the greatest part of what they were worth in purchasing the said Grants and Surveying and settling the said lands." To turn them out would risk "the hazard of their utter ruin and Destruction." The petition asked the king to confirm Wentworth's grants; in addition, it asked that the Grants either be made into a new and distinct colony or be returned to the jurisdiction of New Hampshire.[50]

Robinson and Johnson submitted their petition to Lord Shelburne on March 20. From there it went to the privy council and then to the committee on plantation affairs. Once the petition became thoroughly enmeshed within the governmental bureaucracy, it became abundantly clear to Robinson and Johnson that they were facing an extremely long and troublesome process. The various British officials would demand statements from the New York authorities, which, in turn, would necessitate a hearing requiring Robinson's presence as a witness. The two men would therefore have to remain in London for an extended period of time. This worked no special hardship on Johnson, a man of means who received a salary from the Connecticut government. Such was not the case with Robinson; he quickly spent his meager supply of cash and had to rely upon sporadic contributions sent by various of the petitioners he represented in order to subsist. As a result, he lived in penury. Robinson's only solace during the months he waited for the British government to act was his relationship with George Whitefield. He attended Whitefield's Sunday services regularly and listened intently to the sermons of the spiritual leader he had admired for many years.

If Whitefield provided a balm for Robinson's spiritual life, Sir Henry Moore became the bane of his secular existence. In a letter dated April 11, 1767, Lord Shelburne severely chastised Moore for his handling of the affairs mentioned in Robinson's petition. He made it plain that under no circumstances was Moore to disturb any resident on the Grants who held a valid New Hampshire title. In addition, he informed Moore that the king vested the power of granting lands in his governors "for the purpose of accommodating not distressing setlers." This was especially true for "the poor and industrious." Moore should realize that "any perversion of that Power" could only be considered "highly derogatory both from the dignity of their Stations and from that disinterested Character which a Governor ought to support, and which His majesty expects from every person honored by him With his Commission." Beyond that, Shelburne expressed outrage at the "unreasonableness of obliging a very large Tract of Country to pay a *Second Time* the immense sum of thirty three thousand pounds in Fees according to the allegations of this Petition."[51]

Moore blamed Robinson for these attacks upon his integrity and character; he meant to have his revenge. While responding as best he could regarding conflicting land grants and the payment of fees for confirmation of titles, the governor remained thoroughly deferential toward Shelburne. Moore could not, however, contain either his outrage or his class bias when discussing Robinson. He attacked Robinson as a speculator who had requested confirmation of forty-five townships of land. Naturally, as governor, he had viewed this petition "so very absurd that it was treated as it deserved and rejected." He also challenged the contention that many of the petitioners had served honorably in the late war. Moore declared that Robinson had done little more than drive an oxcart for the settlers; beyond that he exclaimed that it "must be obvious to every one that very few Levies could be made at that time in a Frontier Country exposed to all incursions, and which had scarce any inhabitants at all in it." Finally he closed by observing that a petition containing so many falsehoods must "have been the

Offspring of a very bad Heart." In fact, "the head must likewise have been impaired," for "how else should a man of one of the lowest & meanest occupations at once set up for a statesman and from a notion that the wheels of Government are as easily managed and conducted as those of a Waggon, take upon him to direct the kings Ministers in their Departments." Moore, claiming to "have been taught to treat with so much respect, those whom His Majesty is pleased to honor with his confidence," closed with a clear implication that the word of a gentleman must surely take precedence over that of an oxcart driver.[52]

On July 24, 1767, the king in council ordered Governor Moore "to desist from making any Grants whatsoever of any Part of those Lands [the Grants], until your Majesty's further Pleasure shall be known."[53] Although no final decision had been made regarding the substantive issues of Robinson's petition, the king and the privy council did not want the issue clouded further by additional grants in the disputed area. Moore nonetheless took this as an implied criticism of his official behavior. Indignant that he should be castigated by the king and certain that Robinson's petition lay behind the embarrassment he was suffering, Moore continued to slander Robinson's character. He even accused Robinson of being a counterfeiter and a notorious troublemaker of low character.[54]

While Moore maintained a constant diatribe against him, Robinson worked with Johnson during the summer and fall to spark official interest in moving his petition through the various channels of government. For his part, Johnson eventually concluded that the poverty of the petitioners "rendered them unable to give the cause that effectual support, which was necessary to give it proper weight, and render the application to the crown as regular and respectable as its importance and the usual course of proceedings in cases of this kind justly required." As a consequence, the cause wore the aspect of "*forma pauperis*, which is an appearance seldom made or much regarded in this country."[55]

In addition to lobbying as best he could in favor of the petition, Robinson sought out opinions on the proper course for the settlers on the Grants to pursue while waiting for a final decision by the king in council. An essentially conservative man who believed firmly in law, order, and social discipline, Robinson finally advised the landholders in Bennington "to fulfill the duty required in your grants made by Wentworth that are not yet meddled with by New York, for if Wentworth's charters should not be held good, then the land would be the king's, and he never dispossessed any settlers." On the other hand, "where New

York has made grants, give up no possession till they come in course of law, and then apply for a special jury for the trial of each case."[56]

Robinson's constant and exhausting efforts on behalf of his settlement ended in late October, when he fell seriously ill with smallpox. He died on October 27, 1767. Johnson took up a collection to pay the funeral expenses, and George Whitefield performed the service. Robinson was buried in the churchyard directly opposite Whitefield's house.[57] To those who knew him well, it must have seemed entirely appropriate that Robinson should come to rest at the very doorstep of the man who had ignited a spiritual fire within him nearly twenty-five years earlier. Ironically, that fire had helped impel Robinson on the long journey that had just ended.

If Samuel Robinson's odyssey was over, that of his family and others on the Grants continued. They faced the threat of losing not only their property but the very means of maintaining an independent livelihood as well. The future for which so many had risked so much was now clearly in jeopardy.

3. The Emergence of the Green Mountain Boys

.

In the years following Samuel Robinson's death Bennington's leaders attempted to follow the course of action he had recommended: they
strove to remain strictly within the limits of the law in the defense of
their property. In an effort to keep abreast of those limits, Samuel Robinson Jr., who, like his father, had great respect for the law, conferred
regularly with Peter Silvester, an Albany attorney. He then shared his
information with the Bennington Committee, to which he had been
elected to replace his father. This committee, composed of town selectmen and officers of the proprietary, had been formed to assume responsibility for the town's interests in the jurisdictional dispute with New
York authorities.[1] Its other members, like the Robinsons, were cautious
men who favored legal means to uphold their land claims.

As long as Henry Moore was governor, Robinson and the Bennington Committee had few concerns.[2] Stung by the criticism he had received from royal authorities, Moore refused either to make new grants
in the area or to confirm those that had already been made. The possibility for conflict was thereby held to a minimum. These circumstances
changed, however, with Moore's death in September 1769. Cadwallader Colden became acting governor once more and pursued a much
more aggressive land policy. He issued land patents on the Grants in
areas where he claimed no previous New Hampshire titles existed.
Then, in an effort to encourage settlement of Yorkers in the region,
Colden pressed forward the survey of these lands as well as of tracts
held by residents of his colony under previous patents. As a result, a
great many New York surveyors began to move onto the Grants.[3]

Such an influx of New York surveyors would have proved troublesome under any circumstances, but conditions on the Grants had
changed drastically since 1764, when the king established the Connecticut River as the boundary between New York and New Hampshire.
Even before that time, Colden had complained of the presence of New
Englanders "in appearance no better than . . . Pedlar[s] . . . Hawking &
selling [their] pretended Rights to . . . Townships on trifling considerations."[4] These "pedlars" became even more common following the
king's decision; after that time a great many proprietors of New Hampshire grants, no longer certain of the validity of their land titles, subdivided their rights and sold off small plots even more cheaply than
before. Hundreds of New Englanders, anxious for an opportunity to
own land, eagerly purchased these tracts, settled their families, and
began to farm their new property.[5] Confident that the king would
protect the rights of actual settlers, these people had little regard for
New York law or its representatives; they meant to defend their holdings by whatever means necessary. Many looked to individuals such as
Micah Vail, James Mead, or Benjamin Cooley for leadership in their
defiance of New York authorities. These men, embittered by their
experience on the Oblong and determined not to lose their farms again,
had taken up land in Danby, Rutland, and Pittsford. Another veteran of
strife on the Oblong, Roswell Hopkins, settled his family in Bennington. He, and increasing numbers of small landholders like him, displayed little patience with either New York surveyors or New York
sheriffs. Such men would not hesitate to employ force to defend their
land titles. As a consequence, conditions on the Grants were extremely
volatile by the fall of 1769.

Colden chose this moment, however, to send out commissioners and
a surveyor to partition the Walloomsac Patent, which had been granted
some thirty years earlier.[6] By the middle of October word reached
Bennington that this survey party was drawing near. On October 19
James Breakenridge led several hired men into his fields to pick corn. A
group of armed neighbors accompanied them. Shortly thereafter John
Munro, a resident of Shaftsbury who held a New York commission as
justice of the peace for Albany County, entered the field and informed
Breakenridge that the contingent from Albany would soon be there.
Munro advised Breakenridge not to attempt to prevent these men from
completing their survey. If he did, Munro warned, he would be liable
to prosecution under the law. To emphasize this point, Munro read
Breakenridge the riot act. As he listened to Munro, Breakenridge ob-

served the survey party at the western edge of his field. To prevent trouble, he asked his neighbors to go home or at least to leave his field. At this same moment Samuel Robinson, who had just returned from a conference with Peter Silvester, joined Breakenridge in urging the bystanders to leave. The men did withdraw a short distance, but only after Breakenridge and Robinson threatened to abandon the confrontation with the New York authorities altogether if they remained.

As members of the Bennington Committee, Breakenridge and Robinson entered into a conference with the New York commissioners. When asked by the Yorkers why so many armed men stood nearby, they responded that they "could not tell [since they] had no connection with their Being together and had Desired them to withDraw out of the field." At the same time, Breakenridge and Robinson expressed the hope that the men from Albany "would not take any advantage: for our People Did Not understand Law." Following this exchange, the representatives of the two sides stated their respective positions on the matter at hand. The Bennington men claimed that the Walloomsac Patent lay entirely within Albany County and that since the survey party was east of the twenty-mile line, it was infringing upon land granted by New Hampshire. Further, "his Majesty had forbide them [New York authorities] Making any Grants on ours or hindering our Settlement." In answer the Yorkers claimed that all New Hampshire grants were invalid. Breakenridge and Robinson responded that if the commissioners proceeded with the survey, "they must Run it as Disputed Land." With this statement the two men took their leave. The Yorkers quickly called them back to ask if their neighbors intended to intervene. The two responded that they were not part of that group, "for we Did Not intend to Break any Law or Expose our selves." When the Yorkers declared that Breakenridge and Robinson should stop the survey if that was their true intent, the two men again answered that they would not "unless they would Tell us what way we could without Breaking any Law for we had not braken any Law Nor Did Not Intend to." The Yorkers then asked them to talk to their neighbors to ascertain whether they meant any harm to the survey party.

Robinson and Breakenridge now found themselves negotiating with the assembled crowd. They reported the conversation with the Yorkers to their neighbors and advised them not to attempt to stop the survey by force. The settlers agreed only after Robinson and Breakenridge consented to take several of their number along "as Evidences" when they returned to tell the Yorkers to run the survey only as "Disputed

Lands." The Yorkers would not consent to this. Robinson and Break-enridge then bid them farewell and returned to their homes.[7] The survey party, intimidated by the presence of so many armed men, returned to Albany.

The encounter at Breakenridge's farm, combined with news Robinson brought from Albany that a number of ejectment suits were being filed there by New York claimants to land held by settlers with New Hampshire titles, greatly upset residents in and around Bennington. Agents for the towns of Arlington, Bennington, Manchester, Pownal, Shaftsbury, and Sunderland met together and responded to the crisis by sending two petitions to John Wentworth, who had replaced his uncle as governor of New Hampshire in June 1767. One contained the names of 470 settlers, and the other bore only the signatures of the six town representatives; both were in the hand of Samuel Safford, a member of the Bennington Committee. These petitions complained of the injustice of being placed under New York jurisdiction, expressed concern over the pending ejectment suits, and asked Wentworth to use his influence with the king on behalf of settlers on the Grants.[8]

In December New York Governor Colden unnerved Bennington's leaders even further. On December 19 he issued a proclamation declaring that "a Number of armed Men, tumultuously and riotously assembled," had forcibly prevented New York officials from completing the partition of the Walloomsac Patent. He named James Breakenridge, Jedediah Dewey, Samuel Robinson, Nathaniel Horner, Henry Walbridge, and Moses Robinson as the "principal Authors of and Actors in the said Riot and Breach of the Peace" and called for their arrest.[9] Breakenridge and Robinson responded by addressing a petition directly to the king. Claiming to represent more than eight hundred "Owners & Possessors" of land granted by Governor Benning Wentworth, the two men reiterated the principal arguments put forward in the petition of Samuel Robinson Sr. ten years earlier. They did, however, go beyond that petition to portray hundreds of settlers that had "expended the whole, and others the greatest part of what they are Worth in . . . Purchasing, Clearing, and Cultivating these Wilderness Lands," facing ejectment suits at the hands of "sundry Persons of Wealth and influence within the Province of New York." If the king did not intervene to confirm New Hampshire titles, these hardworking farmers and "their numerous Families" would be "utterly Ruined and Perish thro' want of Bread" in order "to gratify those Men of Wealth & Power who have covetted [their] Possessions and sought [their] Ruin."[10]

No matter how much Bennington's leaders hoped for direct intervention by the king, they could not avoid facing their adversaries in
court. The Supreme Court of New York had scheduled nine ejectment
cases for the June term of the Albany circuit. Since the issues at stake
in these cases transcended the specific individuals named in the suits,
interest spread far beyond Bennington. The influential New York attorney James Duane and the colony's attorney general, John Tabor
Kempe, were to represent the plaintiffs. Both of these men had grown
wealthy through large-scale land speculation. Indeed, Duane and
Kempe had a great deal at stake in the upcoming trials: both had vast
holdings in the same area as the plaintiffs they represented.[11]

The defendants too had numerous supporters. Proprietors of New
Hampshire grants living throughout Connecticut, Massachusetts, and
the Oblong stood to lose far more than the nine settlers if Duane and
Kempe won their cases. Many of these proprietors met first at Sharon
and then at Canaan, Connecticut, in order to formulate a course of action.[12] The men decided to pool their resources and engage Jared Ingersol of New Haven, one of the leading attorneys in the colony, to defend New Hampshire titles before the Albany court. At their meeting
in Canaan the proprietors also delegated Ethan Allen to ride to Portsmouth to procure the necessary documents to support New Hampshire
land titles, after which he was to proceed to New Haven and accompany Ingersol to Albany.[13]

On June 28, 1770, the bell in the cupola of the massive three-story
city hall in Albany rang out to announce that court would soon be in
session. The ringing of the bell was a prelude to an elaborate courtroom ritual intended to instill proper respect for the authority of the
supreme court justices.[14] The judges soon appeared in long, full-curled
wigs and sumptuous clothing. Each man knew full well how to dress in
the manner "expected from one in his station."[15] In order to "advance the Dignity Authority Solemnity and Decorum of the Court" the
judges wore "Robes and Bands," and the king's counsels, Duane and
Kempe, appeared in "Bar Gowns and Bands" similar to those worn at
Westminster.[16] Such splendor must have been not only awe-inspiring
but positively intimidating to ordinary provincials called to appear before this august body.[17]

The justices tried four cases on June 28. In the first, they decided
against James Breakenridge on the grounds that his farm lay within the
twenty-mile limit and was therefore clearly within the Walloomsac
Patent, which predated Breakenridge's New Hampshire grant. In the

three subsequent cases the judges found in favor of the plaintiffs after refusing even to admit the defendants' New Hampshire titles into evidence. They based this refusal on the grounds that the disputed region had always been within the boundaries of New York. Consequently, all New Hampshire grants made within this area were null and void. Once this decision had been made, the five other settlers against whom ejectment suits had been served saw no reason to suffer the expense of a court trial; therefore, these cases never came before the justices.

The defendants and their supporters were disappointed, frustrated, and angry; some appeared restive. Noting this, and realizing that they needed the cooperation of settlers on the Grants if they were to make good their own investments in the area, Duane and Kempe asked Ethan Allen whether he would help calm the people on the Grants and assist in bringing about an accommodation between the settlers and the New York owners. When Allen hesitated, Kempe reminded him that ofttimes "might makes right." To this Allen replied that "the gods of the valleys were not the gods of the hills." When Kempe asked for an explanation of this remark, Allen responded that if Kempe "would come to Bennington the meaning should be made clear to him."[18]

Had either Duane or Kempe visited Bennington following the ejectment trials, Allen's message would indeed have become clear. Strident opposition against the "gods of the valleys" swept over the Grants. The resistance began with an informal meeting in Bennington led by Rev. Jedediah Dewey. Having no faith in the New York courts, the townspeople gathered at the Catamount Tavern did not consider an appeal of the June decisions. What was the use? Not only the prosecuting attorneys but Robert R. Livingston, one of the supreme court justices who had ruled against them, held large grants in the area. To make matters worse, John Dunmore, the new governor of New York, was actively patenting vast tracts of land on the Grants to New Yorkers. Worse still, much of this land was in his own name.[19] Thus, in response to Dewey's earnest advocacy, the assembled crowd resolved that until the king made a final decision regarding Samuel Robinson's petition of 1767, the defendants would not surrender their farms. If necessary, writs of possession would be resisted by force. Those in attendance also decided that the town should take the land of Breakenridge and Josiah Fuller under its special protection. They intended to defend these farms, which had been the object of special attention during the ejectment trials, with particular vigor.[20]

Following this meeting, opposition to Yorkers became more forceful. On September 26 a band of armed men gathered at Breakenridge's farm and forcibly prevented another attempt by New York commissioners to survey this land as a part of the Walloomsac Patent. While pleased that his farm had not been surveyed, Breakenridge grew increasingly apprehensive regarding the use of extralegal force. Ever hopeful that the king would act on their previous petitions and intervene to protect the Grants, he and Samuel Robinson prepared yet another petition to the king. In this document they expressed their dismay at the manner in which the New York court refused even to consider "the Least Evidence we were able to Produce in Favour of our Said Grants From New Hampshire." Finally, they stressed that if the king did not act soon, a great many honest settlers would be dispossessed "with [their] Families Into ye Open Wilderness."[21]

The desire of Breakenridge, Robinson, and others to employ lawful means to protect themselves and their land claims became ever more difficult. This was particularly true after November 1, when Governor Dunmore declared that the Walloomsac survey had been prevented by "a riotous and tumultuous Body of Men" and ordered the arrest of Silas Robinson and three other individuals as the principal leaders of this breach of the peace.[22] New York authorities also indicted twelve additional settlers for participating in the "riot."[23]

During the last week of November Henry Ten Eyck, sheriff of Albany County, set out to apprehend these people. By keeping to the woods and approaching the town from the north instead of by the main road from Albany, Ten Eyck, a deputy, and John Munro managed to avoid detection and apprehend Silas Robinson at his home. They hurried their prisoner back along the route by which they had come. When they reached the house of a friendly farmer in New York, they took lodgings for the evening. During the night around forty men from Bennington arrived and demanded the prisoner's release. Munro sent for help, and before daybreak the would-be rescuers discharged their weapons into the air and left. Ten Eyck proceeded to Albany, where he placed Robinson in jail.[24]

In December a New York constable and several deputies managed to arrest Moses Robinson, another of the men indicted by Dunmore for preventing the Walloomsac survey. These Yorkers were not, however, able to escort their prisoner back to Albany. Instead, a large party of settlers, their faces blackened to disguise their identity, rescued Robinson by force. When the constable informed them that they were breaking the law, "they damned the Laws of New York, and said they had better Laws of their own." Following these exclamations, they sent the Yorkers flying for their lives.[25]

The tension between Yankees and Yorkers grew even stronger with the coming of the new year. On January 5, 1771, Sheriff Ten Eyck attempted to serve writs of possession on Breakenridge and Fuller. When he arrived at Breakenridge's farm, the sheriff found a determined group of men who threatened "to blow his brains out" if he proceeded. The same scenario took place at Fuller's home. Ten Eyck had no choice but to withdraw without serving the warrants. About this same time Munro managed to serve two writs of possession on farms in Shaftsbury, where he did not encounter the organized resistance becoming characteristic in Bennington.[26] This lack of opposition in the Shaftsbury area was short-lived, however. By the end of May groups of armed men there had begun to threaten the lives and destroy the property of settlers holding New York titles. They also forcibly prevented Albany County constables from performing their duties within Shaftsbury.[27]

This behavior convinced New York officials in Albany that special measures would be required to gain possession of the Breakenridge farm. Ten Eyck called the Albany County militia to his aid. Early on the morning of July 18 the Sheriff left Albany at the head of a band of nearly three hundred men that included Abraham Cuyler, mayor of Albany, as well as such prominent attorneys in that city as Christopher and Robert Yates.[28] The settlers in Bennington were ready to meet them. Breakenridge's family had been moved to a neighbor's farm and Captain John Fassett had arranged his militia company — augmented by the presence of a good many fiery young men, such as Ethan Allen, Robert Cochran, Remember Baker, and Weight Hopkins — in such a manner as to place anyone approaching Breakenridge's house in a cross fire. Well-armed men barricaded themselves inside the house and had a red flag that could be run up the chimney if they required the assistance of the men stationed outside.

On the morning of June 19 a small advance party of Yorkers led by Mayor Cuyler approached Breakenridge and asked him why so many men had gathered with the apparent purpose of preventing the sheriff from doing his duty. Breakenridge replied that the town had taken over his farm and that he had no say in the matter. After more discussion the two men agreed that Cuyler would withdraw and wait thirty minutes to give Breakenridge the opportunity to reconsider and convince his neighbors to abandon the farm. At the end of this time Breakenridge sent a message that his property would be held at all costs. Ten Eyck ordered the Albany militia forward. The vast majority of these men, small farmers who were far more sympathetic with the settlers in Bennington than with the gentlemen of Albany, refused to obey. As a result, Ten Eyck led only a small group of notables to the Breakenridge farm. When these individuals arrived at the house, Robert Yates informed those gathered around Breakenridge that disputes between loyal subjects of the king must be settled in court. The settlers readily acknowledged themselves to be loyal subjects but maintained that they had no faith in New York courts. More importantly, they declared that their agent in England had recently given them assurances that the king would soon decide the issue in their favor and had advised them in the strongest terms to hold onto their possessions in the meantime. This they intended to do, come what may.

When Ten Eyck realized that the settlers were not going to give peaceable possession of the farm, he grabbed an axe and stepped toward the door. At that instant the Bennington militiamen took aim at him with their muskets. Seeing that he was in an untenable position, Ten Eyck withdrew. When he reached the main body of his own militia, he ordered them to Josiah Fuller's farm. Again, none would comply. Instead, leaving the Bennington settlers in possession of their land, the militiamen dispersed and returned to their homes.

The confrontation at Breakenridge's farm had a profound effect on the residents of Bennington and the nearby townships of Sunderland, Manchester, Dorset, Rupert, Pawlet, Wells, Poultney, Castleton, Pittsford, and Rutland. Assuming that New York authorities would persevere in their attempts to exercise complete jurisdiction over the Grants, each township elected a committee of safety to direct opposition to Yorker activities in their locale. In addition, the committees stood ready to coordinate their efforts to form a common defense.[29] Like the committees in the other townships, Bennington's committee was composed of the town's most prominent citizens. Chaired by Nathan Clark, the group included John Fassett, Moses Robinson, Samuel Safford, Samuel Robinson, Simeon Hathaway, Henry Walbridge, Ebenezer Walbridge, and Jonas Fay.[30]

Shortly after the committees of safety were created, ad hoc military companies also formed in these same townships. The rank and file of these groups, composed primarily of young men determined to defy New York authority by whatever means necessary, elected individuals such as Remember Baker, Micah Vail, Robert Cochran, James Mead, Benjamin Cooley, Weight Hopkins, and Peleg Sunderland to be their captains. Many of these men had been actively involved in the tenant rebellions of Dutchess County; all now served under Ethan Allen, who appointed himself colonel. Allen and his captains thus took it upon themselves to become the defenders of all those holding New Hampshire titles. In addition, they did not hesitate to harass any Yorker, from those serving in some official capacity to those merely unfortunate enough to hold their land under a New York grant. Since the officers of Bennington's established militia company — Fassett and Breakenridge — shied away from the increasingly aggressive and extralegal tactics being employed by Allen and the others, these men would not recognize Allen's authority. As a result, Seth Warner, a respected member of the community,[31] recruited an irregular armed band in Bennington and served as its captain.[32]

By late summer 1771 members of these various companies, who generally identified themselves as "New Hampshire Men,"[33] had become quite active. They pulled down or burned the fences and haystacks of farmers settled under New York titles, and they appeared in the dead of night to terrify these poor souls. On one such occasion eleven men threatened a settler with his life and then granted him a week to turn his land over to a New Hampshire claimant. At the end of that time a hundred men, "some of whom disfigured with Black; others with wigs and Horse Tails, and Women's caps and other Disguises; and armed with Guns, Swords, Pistols, and clubs," returned to ransack the house in search of the hapless man, who had fled for his life.[34]

More often than not, the New Hampshire Men spurned disguises. Thus, in the middle of an early August night Seth Warner led some men to the home of a Yorker living near Bennington. They called the farmer and his family outside and pulled the terror-stricken man's house to the ground. In September a group under the leadership of Ethan Allen drove a New York surveyor off the Grants when he attempted to run lines near Clarendon.[35] The following month Allen and Remember Baker took a band of their followers to the farm of another Yorker who had settled in Rupert. They burned the man's house and warned him to "Go your way now & complain to that Damned Scoundrel your Governor." After that, both Allen and Baker exclaimed: "God Damn your Governour, Laws, King, Council & Assembly." When their victim protested, Allen cried out: "G——d Damn your Soul, are you going to preach to us." He then proceeded to inform the man that no constable would survive an attempt to arrest any of the group involved in this incident. If, by chance, one of them were ensconced in the Albany jail, the others would tear the building down and rescue him.[36]

This lawlessness elicited disgust and contempt from William Tryon, who had become governor of New York the preceding July. As governor, Tryon was convinced that it was "good policy to lodge large Tracts of Land in the hands of Gentlemen of weight and consideration" rather than with ordinary individuals like Allen and his followers. These gentlemen would "naturally farm out their lands to Tenants," which in turn would create the "subordination" necessary to maintain good order.[37] In his view, the "Subordination which arises from Distinction in Rank and fortune" was "friendly to Government and conducive to strengthening the hands of the Crown." Moreover, such a hierarchy might well prove to be "the only counterpoise against a levelling and Republican spirit, which the popular constitutions of some Colonies, and the Temper of their Inhabitants, who are spreading themselves throughout this Continent, so naturally excite."[38] Tryon felt that drastic measures must be taken to assert royal authority on the Grants. He called for the arrest of Allen, Baker, Cochran, and six others. Knowing the difficulty sheriffs would have in apprehending them, he placed a bounty of twenty pounds on the head of each rioter. The governor also ordered all officials to report the names of every individual involved in any manner in the rioting on the Grants so that they could be dealt with to the full extent of the law.[39]

Tryon's clumsy attempt at intimidation had very little effect on the Grants. Indeed, Seth Warner celebrated New Year's Day with a public review of his company. The men spent the day shooting at marks posted near Warner's house, toasting their officers, drinking to the success of Wentworth's grants, and damning all Yorkers. Warner and his officers recruited a good many men during the course of the day; neither he nor his subordinates made any effort to hide the fact that every man who joined them took an oath to uphold New Hampshire grants in open defiance of Tryon's proclamation.[40]

That same week an unlucky Yorker wandered into the Catamount Tavern while Samuel Robinson was reading Tryon's proclamation to an assembled crowd. When asked his opinion of the governor's contention that New York held jurisdiction over the Grants, the man answered that he thought this was true. Upon hearing this, Ethan Allen approached him from the rear, struck him several times, and declared that "you are a Damn Bastard of old Munro's" and that good New Hampshire men would soon "make a hell of His House and in turn burn him in it, and every son of a bitch that will take his part." The stunned man responded that even if those individuals who considered their New Hampshire titles to be legitimate were correct, might would overcome them. Allen wondered aloud how the Yorker could be "such a Damn fool" and asked him if New Hampshire men had not always prevailed in their confrontations with New York officials. He bragged that his men controlled the area one hundred miles to the north and that if his opponents ever attempted to come onto the Grants again, "we shall Drive them two hundred miles and send them to hell." Then, playing upon the governor's name, Allen exclaimed: "So [his] name is Tryon, tri on and be Damn[ed] he shall have his match if he comes here."[41]

During the next several months New York authority suffered additional indignities. In February a proclamation signed by Ethan Allen, Remember Baker, and Robert Cochran appeared throughout the Grants. Claiming that James Duane and John Kempe had "by their menaces and threats greatly disturbed the public peace and repose of the honest peasants of Bennington, and the settlements to the northward," posters offered rewards totaling twenty-five pounds to any person or persons who would deliver these Yorkers to Landlord Fay's in Bennington.[42] Then late in March John Munro, accompanied by a dozen men, surprised Remember Baker at his home, took him captive, bound him, placed him in a sleigh, and raced toward Albany. They had proceeded barely twenty miles, however, before a group of Bennington men intercepted them. At first sight of the "Bennington mob," Munro's men fled, leaving the justice and his deputy to be captured by Baker's friends. Once Baker's escape had been assured, the men from Bennington released Munro and his constable, who immediately beat an ignominious retreat.[43] Munro's embarrassment was not yet complete, however. Shortly after the Baker affair, Seth Warner, accompanied by a single companion, rode close to Munro's house in Shaftsbury. The justice and some of his supporters hastily blocked the path of the two men. An angry exchange ensued. Calling for his men to help him arrest the captain of the Bennington rioters, Munro grabbed the bridle of Warner's horse. Warner immediately leveled him with the flat side of his cutlass and left him groveling in the road.[44]

Soon after Munro's abortive attempt to take Warner, Robert Cochran and some of his men captured a team of New York surveyors who were attempting to run lines in Rupert. The New Hampshire men "tried" the Yorkers and then beat them with clubs. Following this, Cochran and his followers publicly humiliated the Yorkers by exposing them to "every species of derision" while escorting them off the Grants. They finally dismissed their victims with the solemn pronouncement that death would be their fate if they ever presumed to return.[45]

At the same time that he and his captains were displaying their disdain for Tryon's proclamation through their actions, Allen also responded to the governor in print. In March and April he published two essays, "Lover of Truth and Reason" and "Friend of Liberty and Property," in the *Connecticut Courant*. Refuting New York's claim to the Grants in great detail, Allen maintained that once the duke of York's grant had become extinct, all the disputed area had reverted to the crown. As a consequence, New Hampshire authorities, as representatives of a crown colony, had every right to grant land in this region. This was particularly the case since the king had asked the governor of New Hampshire to take over the only fort (Fort Dummer) in the territory. Allen reasoned that if the crown compelled the governor of New Hampshire to defend these lands, it should also allow him the privilege of making grants within them. He then recounted all the usual arguments in support of New Hampshire claims: The settlement of New York's eastern boundary with Connecticut and Massachusetts also established its border with New Hampshire; the best proof of this was the fact that "all the antient maps" showed it that way. It was, Allen insisted, "the common understanding of the nation of both learned and unlearned" that New York's eastern boundary lay twenty miles east of the Hudson River. Further, since "common people are not capable of judging upon a higher principle," they should not be punished for innocently trusting the power and authority of the royal governor of New Hampshire. In any event, honestly acquired property rights should never be affected by changes in political jurisdiction.[46]

For all his careful refutation of New York's claim to the Grants, Allen's recitation of familiar arguments supporting New Hampshire land titles actually assumed a perfunctory role in his essays. The central thrust of his message lay elsewhere. Like Thomas Young's *Reflections*, Allen's essays exhibited a deep-seated resentment of gentlemen of wealth and power who used their social and political influence to exploit common folk.[47] Thus, he presented innocent, hardworking yeomen on the Grants as in danger of being exploited by avaricious aristocrats who controlled the legal mechanisms of their society. In his view, the controversy on the Grants pitted "numerous families settled upon the land" against "certain mercenary, intriguing, monopolizing men of the city of New York and elsewhere." No "person of good sense [could possibly] believe that a great number of hard laboring peasants, going through the fatigues of settlement and cultivation of a howling wilderness, [were] a community of rioters, disorderly, licentious, [and] treasonable persons." Quite the contrary, the "brave inhabitants" of the Grants were "leige subjects to George the third." The guilty party was Governor Tryon; he was attempting "to enslave a free people."[48] For this reason, and this reason alone, "bold spirited Men" banded together to defend themselves from the "execrable Cunning of New York." If they did not, "the Yorkers would so punish and bring to Poverty every patriotic generous and valient Man."[49] Thus, far from being the lawless rioters pictured by Tryon, residents on the Grants were simply industrious farmers attempting to wrest an honest living from the soil while beset by the machinations of greedy aristocrats.

While Ethan was composing his second essay, rumors began to circulate that Governor Tryon was on his way up the Hudson with a regiment of British troops to put down the riotous activities on the Grants. Settlers in and around Bennington readily believed these reports; many remembered all too clearly how British regulars had crushed the uprising led by William Prendergast six years earlier. In response to this crisis, members of the committees of safety in and around Bennington met with Allen and his captains in order to discuss this challenge. All in attendance agreed that they must oppose the governor. However, when they began to consider how this might be accomplished, tension developed between the town elders on the committees of safety and the more aggressive leaders of the armed bands, who now referred to themselves as Green Mountain Boys.[50] The town leaders, always cautious and circumspect, favored sending a flag of truce to the governor, hoping that some accommodation might be reached without violence. Allen and his captains accused the committeemen of being timid and argued vehemently that Tryon would only respect a strong show of force. Finally, the older men pledged Allen their full support in whatever he decided; they did not, however, wish to help plan any aggressive actions the military leaders might deem necessary. Saying that they would leave this entirely to Allen and his captains, they left the meeting.[51]

News of this decision greatly bothered some of the more cautious Bennington settlers. Upset over the possibility of an armed confrontation, James Breakenridge proceeded to Portsmouth, where he petitioned Governor John Wentworth to use his official station to intervene with the king on behalf of the settlers. Breakenridge wanted the king to confirm New Hampshire titles and to return the Grants to that

colony's political jurisdiction.[52] Above all, he wanted the controversy to
be solved by lawful means.

Following their meeting with the committees of safety, Allen and his
men prepared to meet Tryon's expected attack. They brought two cannon, a mortar, and a supply of ammunition from the old fort of East
Hoosick (Williamstown) and coordinated plans among the various
companies of Green Mountain Boys for the defense of Bennington.[53]
As it turned out, these efforts were unnecessary; although troops actually did sail up the Hudson, they were en route to various forts in the
west. More important, no governmental officials accompanied them.

Within a month of their desperate preparations for battle, the inhabitants of Bennington did in fact hear from Governor Tryon. To
their surprise, a letter arrived addressed to the Reverend Dewey in
which the governor offered an olive branch rather than a sword. In
a spirit of compromise, he invited them to send representatives to
New York City to discuss their complaints. Under the impression that
Breakenridge, Dewey, and Stephen Fay were Bennington's principal
leaders, Tryon suggested that these men represent the town.[54] He specifically disallowed Ethan Allen and four of his captains as possible
delegates because they had been declared outlaws.[55]

During the third week of June the various committees of safety met
in Bennington to discuss the governor's overture. Anxious for a peaceful settlement of their dispute, these men selected Stephen and Jonas
Fay to carry a letter to Tryon outlining their grievances in a simple,
straightforward manner. Claiming to be "his Majesty's liege and loyal
subjects of the Province of New York," they declared that their original
land grants lay within the boundaries of New Hampshire. After 1764,
when the king altered those boundaries, the government of New York
had made grants in the area as if land ownership had been transferred
along with political jurisdiction. New York authorities had then pursued "illegal and unconstitutional" means to dispossess settlers holding
New Hampshire land titles. Worse still, these same authorities had
proceeded to indict and attempted to capture "sundry persons, who are
bound by the Law of self and family preservation to maintain their
liberty and properties." In sum, the settlers on the Grants freely recognized New York's political authority over them; even under these circumstances, though, they "must closely adhere to the maintaining our
property."[56]

When the Fays left for New York City, they carried not only the
response prepared by the principal leaders of Bennington and nearby

townships but also one written by Ethan Allen. This letter, signed by Allen, Seth Warner, Remember Baker, and Robert Cochran, went far beyond reiterating the conventional arguments regarding the legitimacy of New Hampshire land titles. In fleshing out the principal ideas he had offered as a "Lover of Truth and Reason" and a "Friend of Liberty and Property," Allen began to sharpen his perception of the larger issues involved in the controversy over land titles on the Grants. In his view, a violent struggle was developing on the Grants that pitted a small cadre of wealthy gentlemen against an entire community of settled and industrious yeomen and their families.[57] Thus, a "certain number of designing men," as a result of their social and political prominence, had received patents from the governor of New York for land on the Grants already being farmed by settlers holding New Hampshire titles. Then, in order to turn a large profit without any labor on their part, these same individuals, through their control of the courts, had dispossessed settlers who had "expended their several fortunes, in bringing their farms out of a wilderness state, into that of fruitful fields, gardens and orchards." As a result of these ejectments, "universal slavery, poverty and horror, emblematically appeared in every countenance."

Allen also claimed that New York authorities were heedlessly shattering the protection-allegiance compact between the people and their rulers that was the very essence of civilized society. Like many other colonists, Allen accepted as a given this popularized version of John Locke's social contract.[58] Thus, he exclaimed that no individual or community could be "supposed to be under any particular compact or Law, except it pre-supposeth, that Law will protect such person or community of persons in his or their properties." If this were not the case, "the subject would, by Law, be bound to be accessary to his own ruin and destruction, which is inconsistent with the Law of self preservation; but this Law being natural as well as eternal, can never be abrogated by the Laws of men." In Ethan's opinion, this was exactly what was happening on the Grants, where "Law has been rather used as a tool (than a rule of equity) to cheat us out of the country, we have made vastly valuable by labour and expence of our fortunes." In this case "a set of artful, wicked men . . . seek[ing] our ruin, thereby, to enrich themselves . . . under colour of punishing rioters, and a zeal of loyalty and veneration for good government, rob the inhabitants of their country." Finally, in exasperation Allen asked: "Can any man, in the exercise of reason, make himself believe that a number of Attorneys and other gentlemen, with all their tackle of ornaments, and compliments, and French finesses, together with their boasted legality of law . . . have just right to the lands, labours and fortunes of the *New-Hampshire* settlers?"[59]

Shortly after Stephen Fay and his son left for New York City, another letter of Allen's appeared in the *Connecticut Courant*. Hoping to draw an even sharper contrast between honest, hardworking settlers and "wicked, inhuman, most barbarous, infamous, cruel, villainous and thievish" representatives of New York authority, he wrote a lurid narrative of Munro's capture of Remember Baker on March 22. He described how the Yorkers had broken down Baker's door with axes and forced their way inside. Following that, Munro had slashed off Baker's thumb with a cutlass, while the other "Ruffians" were "Mawling, Beating, and Bruising his Children." When the Yorkers had finally escaped with Baker strapped to a sleigh, three "loyal and faithful Subjects to the Crown of Great Britain, whose Banner they mean ever more to live and die under" had pursued them until more brave men could assist in rescuing their comrade.[60]

After Landlord Fay and his son returned to Bennington from their meeting with Governor Tryon, it appeared that Ethan's letters might no longer be necessary. The Fays brought quite a favorable report from the Council of New York. After a lengthy and detailed exposition of the legitimacy of the New York claim to the Grants, this report expressed "great tenderness to a deluded people who are in danger of forfeiting the Favour of the Crown by resisting the authority of the Laws." It recommended that the governor suspend all prosecutions of people on the Grants until the king made a final decision regarding the entire matter. The settlers would thereby be able to hold their land in quiet possession until that time. All that was asked of the people of Bennington and the surrounding area was their peaceful conformance with the civil laws of New York.[61]

On July 15 a large group of settlers gathered at the meetinghouse in Bennington to discuss the Fays' trip to New York City. Upon learning of the council's report and Governor Tryon's letter in support of its findings, the assembled crowd voted unanimously to accept the terms of peace offered them. To celebrate the occasion, Warner's company fired salutes with their muskets as well as the cannon that stood in front of the meetinghouse. The crowd drank to the king, Governor Tryon, and the Council of New York. Their final toast celebrated "Universal peace & Pelenty liberty & Property."[62] It appeared that peace had come to the Grants at last.

The harmony and good feelings of July 15 lasted less than a month. This was because of an incident that occurred while the Fays were in New York. During that time Remember Baker and Seth Warner received word that William Cockburn, a New York surveyor whom Ethan Allen had run off the Grants previously, was running lines in the area of the Onion River. Baker and Warner immediately set out at the head of a group of Green Mountain Boys to punish him. En route they encountered a settlement of Yorkers established on lands along Otter Creek claimed under New York patent by Colonel John Reid. Baker and Warner drove these people off and proceeded to the Onion River, where they captured Cockburn. As they were making ready to try him before one of their informal courts, word of the truce with Tryon reached them. In light of this development, the Green Mountain Boys released Cockburn without punishment.[63]

Governor Tryon did not take a sanguine view of these incidents. On August 11 he wrote a letter to the inhabitants of Bennington and the surrounding area accusing them of behaving in a "disingenuous and dishonorable" manner. He insisted that Colonel Reid's tenants be put back in possession of their lands immediately or the settlers must suffer the "fatal consequence that must follow so manifest a breach of public confidence."[64]

In response to Tryon's letter, committees of safety from Bennington and ten neighboring towns convened at Manchester on August 27. The meeting, chaired by Nathan Clark, approved a letter written two days earlier by the Bennington committee. This letter argued that the dispossession of Reid's tenants on Otter Creek, as well as the action taken against Cockburn, had occurred before the public meeting held at Bennington on July 15, from which time the people on the Grants "reasonably Compute the Date of public Faith, and sacred Bond of Friendship." In any event, Tryon had to realize that the presence of Reid's tenants on land taken from New Hampshire settlers and Cockburn's attempt to survey land already granted by New Hampshire constituted "a manifest Infringement on our Property, which has all along been the Bone of Contention." Committee members then pledged themselves to two articles of faith: to protect and maintain their property and to "use the greatest Care and Prudence, not to break the Articles of Publick Faith, or insult Governmental Authority."[65] Their great hope was that the truce they had ratified with Tryon would remain intact.

That truce came to a definitive close barely a month after the Manchester meeting when Ira Allen, Remember Baker, and five others encountered Benjamin Stevens, a New York deputy surveyor of lands, running lines near the mouth of the Onion River, where both Allen and Stevens were in charge of survey expeditions. The New Hampshire men captured Stevens and his party, beat them, threatened them with death if they ever returned to the Grants, and turned them loose. The New York authorities immediately issued a warrant for the arrest of Baker and Allen and placed a bounty of one hundred pounds on the head of each man.[66] This prompted the committees of safety on the Grants to meet at Manchester on October 21. Alarmed at the prospect of more violent confrontations, the assembled committee members elected James Breakenridge and Captain Jehiel Hawley of Arlington to carry yet another petition to the king. Hawley, preferring to seek New York confirmation for his land, refused to go,[67] and Breakenridge proceeded alone to London. In the meantime, settlers on the Grants could only hope that they would remain in peaceful possession of the lands.

Tranquility did not, however, prevail. Instead, the Green Mountain Boys became ever more aggressive in their opposition to any and all Yorkers. Early in August more than one hundred Green Mountain Boys, led by Ethan Allen, Remember Baker, and Seth Warner, descended upon a group of Scottish families settled by Colonel John Reid on Otter Creek. Having dispossessed a group of Reid's tenants from this exact location the previous year, the Green Mountain Boys meant this time to convince even the stubborn colonel that no Yorker could hold land on the Grants. They turned men, women, and children out of their homes, burned the structures to the ground, ruined crops in the fields, and totally destroyed a gristmill that Reid had constructed on the creek. When one of the tenants asked Baker by what authority or law he and his men committed such acts, Baker responded that "they lived out of the Bounds of the law." Brandishing his weapon, he exclaimed that "this was his law." To another frightened Yorker Baker explained that he had a commission to perform this duty. Holding up his hand to display the stub where Munro had cut off his thumb, "he call'd [this] his Commission." Before Allen and his men left, he informed Reid's stunned tenants that if any of them attempted to stay and hold possession of the land for Reid, he would have them tied to a tree and skinned alive.[68]

By the time they led this foray to Otter Creek, in August 1772, Allen and Baker, like Breakenridge, the Robinsons, and other leading families in Bennington, had a considerable economic investment to protect. In January 1773 they joined with Ira, Heman, and Zimri Allen to form the Onion River Land Company. Throughout the winter and spring the partners traveled about buying as much land as they could in the Champlain valley. Since most speculators now considered New Hampshire titles in this region to be tenuous at best, they were willing to sell at bargain prices. Paying solely with promissory notes, the partners amassed a large portfolio of land titles along Lake Champlain.[69] Indeed, on June 1 an advertisement appeared in the *Connecticut Courant* in which "Ethan Allen and Company" offered for sale on easy terms forty-five thousand acres of prime land at the mouth of the Onion River.[70] Clearly, whatever chance Ethan and the others had for economic success depended entirely upon making good their New Hampshire titles. Under no circumstances, then, could New York's claim to the land on the Grants be allowed to stand. All Yorker settlers and all Yorker authority must be kept out of the Grants.

During the fall of 1773 the Green Mountain Boys increased the intensity of their attacks on Yorkers. This occurred largely because during the previous year the government of New York had split the area between the Hudson River and the Green Mountains off from Albany County and established the new county of Charlotte, in the process creating a whole range of new county offices to be filled. The Green Mountain Boys directed their ferocity against anyone who accepted these commissions. Their first target was Benjamin Spencer, a resident of Durham (Clarendon) and a newly appointed justice of the peace for Charlotte County. In the middle of the night of Saturday, November 20, Ethan Allen and Remember Baker, at the head of a large contingent of Green Mountain Boys, broke down the door to Spencer's house and dragged the horrified man out of bed. Following considerable cursing, Allen declared Spencer to be "a damned old offender" and announced that everyone in Durham must hold their lands under New Hampshire title and submit to the rules of the Green Mountain Boys or have their property destroyed and their lives endangered. Allen's followers then took Spencer away under heavy guard.[71]

Early on Monday morning the Green Mountain Boys put Benjamin Spencer on trial. They erected a "Judgement Seat," and Allen, Baker, Seth Warner, and Robert Cochran took their places as judges. Spencer, forced to stand with his hat in his hand, heard the charges brought against him: he had applied to the government of New York for a title to his land and induced others to do likewise; contrary to the standing orders of the Green Mountain Boys, he had accepted a commission to serve as a justice of the peace under New York authority; as justice of the peace he had issued a warrant against a settler holding New Hampshire title to his land; and, finally, he was using his influence to induce settlers in the area to declare loyalty to the laws of New York. After the charges had been read, Baker insisted that Spencer be whipped. The other judges disagreed; instead, they decided to burn Spencer's house. When that had been accomplished, Allen and Baker told the unfortunate man that if he did not like their methods, he could apply to the government of New York for redress. For their part, however, "they damned the Government, said they valued not the Government nor even the kingdom; That force was force in whatever Hands, & that they had force and power sufficient to protect themselves against either." Before leaving Durham, Allen and his band of men set fire to several other houses and thoroughly terrorized the inhabitants of the township.

Five days later Jacob Marsh, another justice of the peace in Charlotte County, suffered a similar fate. Captured by Warner and Baker while passing through Arlington, Marsh faced a judgment seat occupied by Samuel Tubbs, Nathaniel Spencer, and Phillip Perry. Warner charged him with purchasing land under a New York title, discouraging settlers from holding New Hampshire titles, and accepting a commission from the governor of New York. Baker also charged that Marsh had publicly reproved him for damning the governor of New York and had threatened to bring charges against him for swearing and blasphemy. Baker demanded that Marsh be whipped severely, but the court merely ordered him not to encourage settlement under New York titles nor to discourage those holding New Hampshire titles; in addition, he must give up his New York commission as a justice of the peace. If he did not obey these conditions, his house would be burned. Before being released, Marsh received a slip of paper signed by the three judges. It certified that Marsh "haith ben Exseamined, and had on fare Trial. So that our mob shall not medeal farther with him as long as he behaves Sartified by us his Judges to yet." When Marsh returned to his home he discovered that an entirely different company of Green Mountain Boys, under the leadership of John Smith, Peleg Sunderland, Benjamin Cooley, and Sylvanus Brown, had already been there. They had removed the roof from his house and done a great deal of damage about his farm. From that time on, Marsh refused to act in his capacity as justice of the peace of Charlotte County.[72]

The violence perpetrated upon Spencer and Marsh not only cowed these two men but intimidated other Yorkers who witnessed their persecutions into following the dictates of the Green Mountain Boys. The trials instituted by the Green Mountain Boys during the fall of 1773 also served an important symbolic function. They subjected the august power and authority of the New York courts to popular ridicule. Ethan Allen had been in the Albany courthouse in June 1770 when the Supreme Court of New York decided the ejectment cases. He had seen how members of the gentry intimidated simple folk with their power, authority, and aristocratic bearing. To have New York officials stand hat in hand before a judgment seat occupied by ordinary citizens not only publicly humiliated these individuals but subjected them to a leveling experience as well. The courts of the Green Mountain Boys were spontaneous, open affairs in which the opinions of common, everyday individuals counted as much as those of the finest gentlemen. Their judgment seats stood as powerful symbols that justice on the Grants sprang from the people themselves, not from an aristocratic hierarchy.

As a consequence of the actions of Allen and his followers, most inhabitants of Durham purchased New Hampshire titles to their lands and submitted to the rule of the Green Mountain Boys. One man, however, did not: Benjamin Hough continued to petition New York authorities for aid and protection. In addition, Hough notified Tryon that Ethan Allen, Seth Warner, Remember Baker, Robert Cochran, Sylvanus Smith, John Smith, and Peleg Sunderland were the "principal actor's in these Violences." He also informed the governor that these men were "encouraged and excited to the Perpetration of these daring offences, by men who do not openly appear, but are chosen by the rest as Councilors and Advisors of all their Measures." His investigations led him to conclude that James Breakenridge, Jedediah Dewey, Samuel Safford, and Stephen Fay were the true leaders of the Bennington Mob. If Tryon intended to send troops in to put down the riots, they must apprehend these men as well as Allen and his followers.[73]

In his letter to Governor Tryon, Hough clearly recognized the alliance that existed between the leading men of Bennington and the Green Mountain Boys. There was, of course, no way for him to realize what an uneasy alliance it was, that it had been brought into being through the force of circumstances rather than the shared characteristics of the two groups. Bennington's leading men were intensely religious social conservatives, men with a deep respect for established authority and tradition as well as an abiding reverence for communal values. Ethan Allen and his followers could not have been more different. They were aggressively individualistic, profane, and had little patience with authority or tradition; they existed for the most part outside the influence of any organized church or community. Still, the two groups did have certain things in common. They both harbored an egalitarian distrust of genteel elites and the undue influence wielded by gentlemen within their society. Most important, though, they had all staked their fortunes, large or small, on New Hampshire land titles.

In response to the actions of the Green Mountain Boys, the New York Assembly passed an act on March 9, 1774, proclaiming that a riotous condition existed on the Grants. That same day Governor Tryon issued a proclamation calling for the arrest of Ethan Allen, Warner, Baker, Cochran, Sunderland, Brown, Breakenridge, and John Smith as the principal leaders of those "distinguished and known by the Name of the Bennington Mob." In addition, he placed a bounty of one hundred pounds on the heads of Allen and Baker and fifty pounds for the capture of each of the others named in the proclamation.[74]

These measures by the New York Assembly and governor brought a quick reply from the committees of safety on the Grants. Convening in Arlington on March 16, in a meeting chaired by Nathan Clark they declared unequivocally that settlers on the Grants had faced "an unequal and biassed Administration of Law, ever since our unhappy Misfortune of being annexed to a Government in which the Interest of the greater Part of the leading Gentlemen thereof are in direct Opposition to our's." In contravention of all law and equity, these gentlemen had undertaken "to be judges in their own case." If settlers on the Grants submitted "to their executions of law, and become obedient and submissive subjects of their designing government, we must soon yield to be their tenants and slaves." Then, having thoroughly absorbed Ethan Allen's perspective as well as his language, the committee exclaimed that it could only "be shocking to common sense" to observe New York authorities bringing such outrageous charges against "thousands of hard labouring, industrious, honest peasants, who are, in truth, loyal subjects of the crown of Great Britain, for their violations of law and government." This was all the more shocking since the New York authorities themselves were guilty of breaking the king's order of July 24, 1767, prohibiting them from making any grants in the area. These authorities, not the honest settlers, were the true violators of the law.

Following this expression of their sentiments, the assembled committeemen voted four resolutions. The first declared their absolute allegiance to the king, their "political father." Next, because they had purchased their land in good faith from one of the king's governors, they remained determined to maintain their property against all opponents until "his Majesty's Royal Pleasure shall be known on the Premises." Third, since the settlers had never made any resistance to government beyond that "which the Law of God and Nature enjoyns on every intelligent, wise and understanding Being," and since the actions of New York officials were "contrary to the Spirit and Design of the good and righteous Laws of Great-Britain, which, under a just Administration, never fail to secure the Liberty and Property of the Subject," the settlers bound themselves, "at the Expence of our Lives and Fortunes," to defend any of their neighbors indicted by the New York government. Last, while every measure necessary would be taken to defend their land, inhabitants of the Grants would act only in a defensive manner. Further, they would "always encourage due Execution of Law, in civil Cases, and also in criminal Prosecutions, that are so indeed; and that we will assist, to the utmost of our Power, the officers appointed for that Purpose." Before adjourning, the committeemen voted to have their statement published in the newspapers so that any New York official who might "presume to take the rioters aforesaid" would know that they did so "on their peril."[75] With this public letter the committees of safety solidified their ideological affinity with the Green Mountain Boys.

During the second week in April the Green Mountain Boys themselves published a response to the New York Assembly's act declaring them to be outlaws. Written by Ethan Allen, this rejoinder to Tryon and his government stated definitively that the "Spring and moving Cause" of the opposition to New York officials was "Self-Preservation." If New York authorities would only withdraw their patents and quiet the settlers in possession of their land, all inhabitants on the Grants would become peaceful, orderly, and submissive citizens of that colony. Until such time as the government of New York, ruled by "a Number of designing Schemers, and Land-Jockeys," obeyed the law, though, settlers on the Grants would band together to defend themselves. Indeed, even if the recently enacted New York law afforded "indemnification" for killing or capturing individuals on the Grants, there was "no indemnification for so doing, from the *green mountain boys*; for our lives, liberties and properties are as verily precious to us, as to any of the King's Subjects." The authors then challenged any and all who wished to take possession of the settlers' land or execute any of the so-called outlaws to come forward, since they stood "ready for a Game of Scalping with them." So that there could be no mistaking their intent, the Green Mountain Boys declared themselves to be "under Necessity of resisting, even unto Blood, every Person who may attempt to take us as Felons or Rioters as aforesaid: for in this Case it is not resisting Law, but only opposing Force by Force." All those whom Tryon had designated outlaws except James Breakenridge signed the response. Then, as a postscript, those who did affix their signatures to the document added that Breakenridge had "never been concerned with us in any Mob whatever; but that he hath always relied on a good Providence, and the regal Authority of Great-Britain for the Confirmation of the New-Hampshire Charter; exclusive of all forcible Measures whatever."[76]

Five months after writing this letter, Allen published a pamphlet of over two hundred pages in which he presented the case for the New Hampshire settlers in fulsome detail. Printed in Hartford and circulated throughout New York and New England, his *Brief Narrative of the Proceedings of the Government of New York* reprinted all the material relative to the controversy between New York and the settlers on the Grants that had appeared in the newspapers. In addition, he offered a lengthy, closely reasoned analysis of the history of boundary disputes that New York had carried on with Massachusetts, Connecticut, and New Hampshire. His argument fully substantiated the legitimacy of the settlers' claims; he left no doubt that the early settlers had every reason to assume the authenticity of their land titles. Finally, he countered at some length and with great cogency a widely circulated pamphlet detailing New York's claim that the Connecticut River formed its eastern boundary with New Hampshire.[77]

Allen's *Narrative* provided the settlers on the Grants a complete explication of the arguments that had been employed against New York authorities for nearly a decade. More than that, it offered them a graphically detailed exposition of the struggle taking place between rich and powerful men of prominence and poor, simple working people. In the first ten pages Allen drew as sharp an image as his prolix style would allow of a contest between a small faction of aristocratic gentlemen and an entire community of hardworking farmers. In many ways, then, the *Narrative* represented an attempt on Allen's part to clarify ideas that had nettled him since the days he spent in Salisbury deeply engaged in conversation with Thomas Young. The same animosity against entrenched privilege and the unfair advantages gained by the rich and powerful in a hierarchical society that had animated those conversations now permeated Allen's thought. Throughout his writings, he struggled to develop an ideological perspective based upon an egalitarian society of independent landholders. In such a society, land speculation — the key to social and economic advancement in an agrarian society — would not be the exclusive prerogative of gentlemen. All men, regardless of their rank in society, would be free to buy, sell, and trade land for profit.[78] Every man should have equal access to all avenues of economic opportunity within his society.

Allen slowly began to articulate a position — a yeoman persuasion — that validated the efforts of ordinary citizens. He felt compelled not only to laud the characteristics of the common man but to reveal the fraudulent practices and pretensions of all gentlemen. Thus, he described how the "crafty, designing, & monopolizing" government of New York patented "to certain celebrated Attornies and principal Gentleman in the Province, the very Lands on which the New-Hampshire Settlers dwelt."[79] These same "Favourites and Gentlemen of Influence" brought suit in New York courts to take possession of the settlers' land. There, "the Plaintiffs appearing in great Fashion and State, which together with their Fraternity of Land-monopolizers, made a briliant Appearance." For their part, "the Defendants appearing in but ordinary Fashion, having been greatly fatigued by hard Labour, wrought on the disputed Premises, made a very disproportionable Figure at Court." The result was foreordained: "Interest, Connection, and Grandeur, easily turned the Case against the forlorn Defendants."[80] Outside the courtroom, the same "extreme Fatigue, Hunger, and infinite Hardships the inhabitants had undergone in the Settlement and Cultivation of a Wilderness Country" contrasted sharply with the "Attornies and wealthy Gentlemen . . . of New-York which fared sumptuously every Day" while "perusing . . . old obsolete and abdicated" charters to gain some advantage without labor.[81]

The same contrast between manly yeomen and effete gentlemen characterized the confrontation following the ejectment trials. Driven to "the Extremity of either quiting their Country and Possessions, or mak[ing] forceable Opposition" to New York officials, the settlers "put on Fortitude, and chose the latter Expedient." For their part, the gentlemen attorneys, "a cringing, fawning, deceitful Fraternity; not enured to the Horrors of War, or any thing Heroic, durst not Fight for their own Claims." Instead, they followed their "accustomed Way," which was to "deceive, cheat and over reach the Commonality of their Species, under a pretence of Law, Justice, good Government and a great pretended Zeal of Loyalty, etc." Hiding behind the facade of law and government to pursue their own selfish ends, these gentlemen "extended their Influence into the General Assembly of the Government, and sway[ed] that whole Legislative Body" to their ends by causing the hardy yeomen who were simply defending their own liberty and property to be declared rioters. The full force of the government could then be employed to serve the selfish ends of a small faction of gentlemen.[82] All "Law, Order, and *good* Government" became in the hands of such men *"Horns of Iron, and with them do they push the Poor and Needy, when they get them into their Net."*[83]

In many ways the Green Mountain Boys, particularly in the manner they treated captured Yorkers during the fall and winter of 1774–75, acted out the beliefs that Ethan attempted to articulate in his *Narrative*. This often meant subjecting gentlemen, with all their pretensions, to the scorn and ridicule of the common people. Such was the fate of Dr. Samuel Adams of Arlington. A man of affluence and substantial property, Adams held his land under a New Hampshire title. However, following the riot act passed by the New York legislature on March 9, he advised all who would listen to settle under New York titles. In addition, he became extremely critical of the actions of the Green Mountain Boys. When neighbors repeatedly warned him to keep still, Adams armed himself with a brace of pistols. Assuming that this action, in combination with his stature as a gentleman, would shield him from any mob action, Adams persisted in his obstreperous ways. One day, though, a group of Green Mountain Boys caught him off guard, took him captive, and escorted him to the Catamount Tavern, where he endured a trial for his "crimes." His punishment consisted of being tied to a chair and hoisted up to dangle just beneath the grinning catamount that graced the tavern's signpost. The good doctor, dressed in his finest, remained in this ludicrous posture for several hours, all the while enduring the merciless jibes and taunts of a crowd on onlookers. Finally, the Green Mountain Boys released him with the simple advice to go and sin no more.[84]

Benjamin Hough suffered quite a different experience at the hands of the Green Mountain Boys. A marked man since the New York Assembly had mentioned his name as a complainant in the riot act of March 9, Hough fell captive to Peleg Sunderland, James Mead, Benjamin Cooley, and other Green Mountain Boys on January 26, 1775. These men transported him to the township of Sunderland, where they incarcerated him until January 30. On that day he came before a judgment seat occupied by Ethan Allen, Seth Warner, and five others. The charges against him included complaining to the New York authorities about the treatment Benjamin Spencer received at the hands of the mob; discouraging people from joining the mob in its activities; and accepting a commission as justice of the peace of Charlotte County. Hough declared that he had every right to do all these things. After some deliberation, the judges sentenced him to two hundred lashes. In addition, they banished him from the Grants. If he returned he would receive five hundred lashes. Following this, several men stripped off Hough's shirt and tied him to a tree; four others took turns delivering his punishment. Allen and Warner then signed a slip of paper declaring that Hough had received punishment for his crimes and was thereby granted safe passage off the Grants.[85]

Two months after his trial, Hough signed a deposition in New York City regarding the power of the Green Mountain Boys. He declared it to be his belief "that neither the said Sheriff or his officers dare to venture within the District, where the Rioters live, without express leave from the Leaders of the Mob."[86] In early April, Lt. Gov. Cadwallader Colden corroborated Hough's statement in a report to the earl of Dartmouth. Noting the "farther outrageous and most illegal proceedings of the Bennington Rioters," Colden claimed that in his opinion "the authority of Government is entirely lost among them, and I am afraid can not be restored but by Force."[87] Thus, by mid-1775 the Green Mountain Boys held clear sway over the Grants; they and the yeoman democracy they advocated had triumphed over the genteel aristocracy of New York. How long this triumph would last in the face of changing circumstances and an influx of new migrants to the Grants only time could determine.

The humiliation of Dr. Samuel Adams, the whipping of Benjamin Hough, and the application of the "beach seal" by various Green Mountain Boys, as the dramatic scene appeared in Zadock Thompson's *History of the State of Vermont* (1842). (Courtesy of the American Antiquarian Society)

The Reverend Lemuel Haynes of Rutland, a black minister, delivering a sermon at Bennington's old First Church on March 31, 1816. Many guest preachers occupied the church's pulpit during the early years of the nineteenth century. Oil painting by William Tefft Schwarz, c. 1938. (Courtesy of the Bennington Museum)

Prisoners Taken at the Battle of Bennington. A fanciful view of the events immediately following the great American victory of August 16, 1777, the anniversary of which occasioned celebration in Bennington for many years afterward. Oil painting by LeRoy Williams, c. 1938. (Courtesy of the Bennington Museum)

The View of Bennington, by Ralph Earl (1798), captures the village before construction of the new meetinghouse. The State Arms Tavern and the courthouse, focal points of the uphill community, appear in the background, behind Isaac Tichenor's mansion; downhill folk clustered around the Dewey Tavern and the old meetinghouse in the right foreground. (Courtesy of the Bennington Museum)

Elijah Dewey, by Ralph Earl (1798). Earl depicted his subject as a man of considerable means, seated proudly in front of his tavern, which for many years was the traditional gathering place of Bennington Federalists. (Courtesy of the Bennington Museum)

Thomas Jefferson and James Madison pause in front of the old Cantamount Tavern during their 1791 tour of New England. The town's illustrious hosts included Elijah Dewey, Isaac Tichenor, and Moses Robinson. Oil painting by LeRoy Williams, c. 1938. (Courtesy of the Bennington Museum)

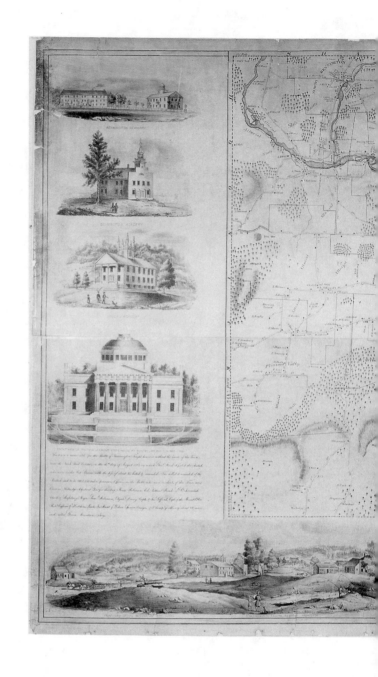

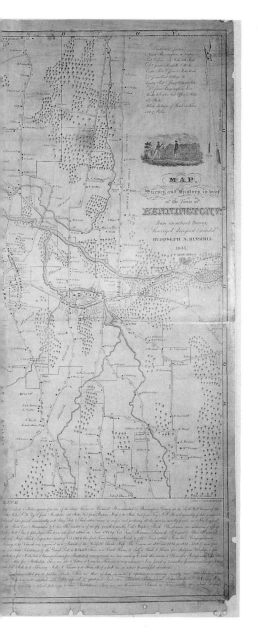

Joseph Hinsdill's map of Bennington (1835), in which he not only located each homestead and place of business within the township but also included portraits of the Bennington Seminary, the Bennington Academy, the Union Academy, and the Bennington Furnace, the principal edifices in the town. For some idiosyncratic reason, Hinsdill also pictured the capitol building in Montpelier. (Courtesy of Special Collections, University of Vermont)

PART TWO: CHANGE AND CONFLICT

4. Newcomers to the Grants

And inasmuch as I have heretofore been duly ordained an officer in Christ's kingdom, by "the laying on of the hands of the presbytery," whereby I am invested with full power and authority to administer, sealing ordinances, and to do all the duties of a minister in God's house; and inasmuch as I can receive no new, nor even any accession of power by a re-ordination; I do now, without some of the usual ceremonies of an installment, thus publicly acknowledge and declare myself to be under the most sacred vows to exercise my office, and to do all the duties of the pastor of this church, according to the tenor of the charge given to Timothy or Titus, or to any other pastor of new testament description, so long as God in his providence shall continue me with you. And, in reliance on divine grace, I do engage to exercise this my office for your edification and not destruction, that I may hope to present you as a chosen virgin to Christ, to whom I am to give account, that you and I may rejoice together at his appearing.[1]

With this statement Rev. David Avery made it plain to the members of the Separate Congregational church in Bennington that he had no intention of submitting to the Strict Congregational tradition that called for the membership of each church to ordain its own minister. There would be no laying on of hands by the Christian brotherhood in Bennington; no investiture of their new minister by the saints of this church would take place. In Avery's mind, ordination by the presbytery was not only sufficient, it was definitive. Indeed, the presbytery was the only institutional authority he would recognize. No matter how arbitrary he might appear or how overbearing his position might seem, Avery would not alter his stance on this issue. The church capitulated.

Installation ceremonies proceeded on May 3, 1780, without Bennington's new pastor ever being ordained by the church membership.

Avery's attitude regarding ordination was by no means atypical. By his own admission, he held to certain church principles with "inflexible adherence." The precepts to which he clung so doggedly related primarily to church discipline and the power of the pastor in each congregation. For Avery, the Apostle Matthew's exegesis of "Fraternal Correction" (Matthew 18.15–18) constituted "the only Rule of chh. discipline." For him the church, through its members, was solely responsible for disciplining those who behaved in disorderly or ungodly ways. Within each church, though, the authority of the pastor superseded even the majority opinion of the members themselves. In addition, the power of the church not only supplemented but actually surpassed that of the state.[2] Thus, from David Avery's perspective, he, as pastor of the church, assumed ultimate responsibility for guiding and shaping the lives of the citizens of Bennington.

Avery's exalted perception of himself and his position in society belied his own humble beginnings. Born April 5, 1746, in a remote northwestern section of Norwich, Connecticut, known as Bozrah, he was the eighth child in a family of ten, the youngest of six boys born to Lydia and John Avery. David was extremely bright, but his parents could not afford to provide him with any education beyond that available in the local district schools. As soon as he was old enough, they apprenticed him to a house carpenter.[3]

An opportunity to improve himself by means of a better education did exist in nearby Lebanon, Connecticut. There, Rev. Eleazar Wheelock, pastor of the local Congregational church, had started a school to convert Indians to Christianity and to introduce them to the ways of white civilization. Anxious to extend the influence of his school into Indian country itself, Wheelock wanted to train missionaries to go among the various tribes in western New York. To accomplish this, he accepted a small number of English youths into his school each year. Wheelock selected young men from humble circumstances who displayed excellent intellectual potential. In return for their promise to serve as missionaries, he provided a free education. In addition, he had worked out an arrangement whereby his best students could attend Yale College at no expense to them. To protect his investment, however, Wheelock required all charity scholars to sign a bond requiring them to repay all the costs of their education if they did not take up missionary work among the Indians following their graduation.[4]

In the fall of 1764, having been chosen as a charity student, David Avery moved to Lebanon and began his course of instruction under Eleazar Wheelock. He lived on the upper floor of the school building with his fellow scholars, both white and Indian. On the floor below, Wheelock and his tutor taught English to the Indian students and Latin and Greek to those charity scholars preparing to attend college. Wheelock also stressed religious and manual training. All students attended morning and evening prayers daily and two church services each Sunday. They also worked on Wheelock's farm at specified periods of each day. Here too Wheelock did not distinguish between white and Indian students; all had to perform manual labor.

Wheelock attempted to instill a competitive work ethic in his Indian students and a sense of humility in his white scholars. He adamantly insisted that his English students must never demean either their Indian colleagues or agricultural labor. Toward this end he required that "all the English students in the college and school treat the Indian children with care, tenderness and kindness." He insisted that "no English scholar, whether supported by charity or otherwise, shall, at any time, speak diminutively of the practice of labor, or by any means cast contempt upon it, or by word or action endeavor to discredit or discourage the same."[5] There was simply no place for cultural pretension at Wheelock's school.

The same could not be said of social conditions at Yale, where Avery and four other students from Wheelock's school enrolled in the fall of 1765. President Thomas Clapp, following Yale's tradition of ranking students in each class according to the social status of their families, placed the five charity students at the bottom of the entering class. Each time they sat down to a meal in the commons or took their appointed places in the classroom or the chapel they suffered social humiliation. Their assigned seats broadcast their inferior breeding, their lack of refinement.[6] Little wonder, then, that David felt greatly relieved when the college abandoned this practice during his junior year. He exulted that it was no longer "he that has got the finest coat or largest ruffles that is esteemed here at present." Instead, "the class henceforward are to be placed alphabetically, the students may expect marks of distinction put upon the best scholars and speakers."[7] Not everyone welcomed this change; in fact, one outraged traditionalist declared that "the new Method" might well "save the Governours of the College Some Trouble, and prevent some Reflections from some few particular Gentlemen, who think their Sons have not their due Place." However, such a radical change would surely "disgust Gentlemen, whose Sons must perhaps Stand the lowest, and have one brot up by Charity or of the meanest Parentage often at their head."[8] David Avery did indeed now stand at the head of his class.

That class rank now depended upon the alphabet rather than social prominence did little, however, to diminish the emphasis upon social hierarchy that pervaded Yale's rules and regulations and dominated the behavior of its tutors and its students. Even an individual such as David Avery, born to a modest family and schooled in humility and manual labor by Eleazar Wheelock, would find it difficult not to absorb the pervasive sense that Yale produced gentlemen and that gentlemen should be accorded special privileges in any properly structured society. They alone possessed sufficient education, reason, integrity, and selflessness to guide and shape their community's affairs.

In the fall of 1768 Wheelock interrupted Avery's education at Yale with the request that he accompany Jacob W. Johnson as a missionary to the Oneida tribe in western New York. Shortly after joining Johnson, Avery and his colleague attempted to persuade English colonial officials to prohibit the sale of Indian land to whites. The two men contended that such sales inhibited their missionary work: the constant alienation of land disrupted the process of civilizing and Christianizing the Indians.[9] The efforts of the missionaries came to nothing, and because of poor health Avery returned to Yale in December 1768, where he graduated the following summer.

Following his graduation, Avery remained in Lebanon for nearly a year to study theology with Wheelock. Then he agreed to assist Samuel Kirkland, one of Wheelock's most prized pupils, on a missionary tour among the Oneida. Before leaving to join Kirkland, however, Avery suffered a bout of ill health and claimed that he was too weak to undertake such a formidable task. Instead, he went to assist Rev. Samuel Buell, a longtime supporter of Wheelock's charity school, at his parish in East Hampton, New York. Serving as an itinerant, Avery preached in Sag Harbor, Southampton, Westhampton, and other towns near the eastern tip of Long Island.[10]

When preaching, Avery spoke extemporaneously in a loud, clear voice and often became quite animated while exhorting his listeners to repent of their sins and come to Christ. Very often he felt the spirit moving within him; on numerous occasions he recalled in his diary that he spoke with "great freedom," that "Jehovah appeared to be present," or that the "Good Lord was pleased to enable me to speak with boldness, without Fear of Man."[11] He must have had some success, for alongside notations of his own emotions Avery mentioned a number of women being "almost [in] agony" following a prayer session that went well past midnight. On another occasion he observed that "the good Lord was pleased to add his Signal Blessing — A No. were sensibly pricked in! — Sighs — Tears — Sobbs — [*illegible*] — seemed to Mount toward Heaven." It was not at all unusual for him to record that "one or two I saw in tears" or a "Number of youth in Tears & Sighs — Children of God refreshed."[12] At times like these he would exclaim, "Oh! how glorious does G. appear when He begins to work," "Oh! how sweet is Communion of Saints."[13]

While he expressed a willingness to be sent wherever the Lord might please, Avery became increasingly reluctant to go where Eleazar Wheelock requested. With the passage of time, he grew more convinced that he wanted to be a classical scholar, to occupy a settled ministry rather than pursue the humble life of a missionary to Indians. Tension mounted between Avery and his mentor. Wheelock continually requested that Avery take up an Indian mission; Avery repeatedly assured him that he would but then found reasons to forestall an actual commitment. There was also the matter of money. If Avery did not pursue missionary work, he was bound to repay Wheelock the costs of his education. Finally, on August 29, 1771, he was ordained as a missionary from Wheelock's school, which was now located in Hanover, New Hampshire, and had been incorporated as Dartmouth College. The next month Avery took up his duties as Kirkland's assistant among the Oneida.[14]

Avery's tenure as a missionary did not last long. In the spring of 1773 he returned to Hanover with the news that the Oneida did not intend to allow an additional minister among them and that Kirkland himself would likely be driven from their midst. In addition, Avery claimed to be in poor health. Wheelock could only conclude that his protégé "appear[ed] entirely disinclined to return to them [the Oneida] again."[15] In fact Avery was not inclined to return to any Indian tribe. Instead, he took up itinerant preaching through the breadth of southern Massachusetts and northern Connecticut in search of a permanent ministerial position. He must have been well received, for three towns — Somers, Connecticut, and Uxbridge and Gageborough, Massachusetts — extended invitations for him to settle among them. He accepted the call of Gageborough, in Berkshire County, and his installation ceremony took place in that newly settled town in March 1773. Later that same year

Dartmouth College conferred a master of arts degree upon him. This may have indicated Wheelock's acceptance of Avery's decision or simply that the elder man had tired of battling his stubborn pupil. The issue of money still remained, though. In this too Avery outlasted his creditor; after several years of fruitless requests for payment, Wheelock simply gave up and canceled the debt entirely.[16]

Church members in Gageborough looked forward eagerly to having Avery as their pastor. He had made a powerful impression upon them when he preached in their town during his itinerant period. Those brief exhortations, however, had been their only encounters with him. When they extended him a call, they knew him only in the pulpit, where he exuded the common touch of an evangelist filled with the new light. Only after Avery arrived in Gageborough did the townspeople realize that they had hired a man who considered himself a gentleman. Not only that, their genteel new preacher adhered dogmatically to the sophisticated tenets of New Divinity theology.

Once in Gageborough, Avery intended to replicate the life of refinement he had known at college in New Haven. In fact, even before moving to Gageborough Avery had taken steps to have a house designed for him by the same Albany draftsman who had drawn the plans for President Wheelock's home at Dartmouth. He wanted the design "adopted to be convenient for a parson or scholar, as well as a private gentleman."[17] A gentleman's life proved difficult to attain, however, in a recently established township inhabited by farm families struggling to wrest a living from the Berkshire wilderness. In fact the church to which Avery had been called did not even have a building for its services. Furthermore, the townspeople had never ratified the church's call to Avery. As a result, payment of his salary, which should have come from a tax imposed by the town, was irregular at best.

Immediately Avery began an unrelenting assault upon town officials to create what he considered to be a proper religious environment in Gageborough. He demanded that a church structure be built and made it abundantly clear that the town must pay its minister an ample and regular salary. Given Avery's heightened sense of his own importance as well as his belief in the superiority of religious over secular authority, his battles with the town government were constant and tempestuous. The young minister believed that he knew what was best for Gageborough and had no tolerance for those who disagreed with him.[18]

Avery assumed an equally sanctimonious attitude in theological matters. Most Congregational churches accepted individuals as full members upon receiving a letter of recommendation from an established minister of the church they had previously attended. Not so Avery. A local minister took offense when he learned that people bearing letters of recommendation from him were not being accepted as full members in the Gageborough church as a matter of course. When he questioned Avery about this and several other religious principles, he received a forty-eight-page reply lecturing him on church doctrine and dogma.[19]

Avery's letter, written in a most patronizing tone, touched first upon the matter of church membership. He proclaimed that saving grace was the sole qualification for full membership. On such a vital matter as this Avery simply could not take the word of another minister; instead, he required all those seeking communion within his church "to give account of their gracious experiences." Knowing himself to be possessed of the inner light, he personally examined all prospective members in an attempt to "know the heart of [each] candidate." Only those he judged to be pure of heart — having had the saving experience — could become full members of his church.[20]

Avery was certain that "not all churches are of Christ." Not all ministers followed his exacting standards; indeed not all ministers had experienced saving grace themselves. As a result, there were far "too many Stoddardean churches" — churches practicing open membership — in New England. To accept members simply on the basis of letters of recommendation was to open the church "to the threat of Arminians, Socians, & Arians."[21] Such would clearly not be the case in Gageborough.

Avery then addressed the issue of a common charge against him, namely, that he taught that unregenerate men ought not to pray. The complex doctrines that Avery, like Samuel Hopkins, Edward Bellamy, and other proponents of the New Divinity, preached offended a great many of his less sophisticated listeners.[22] This was certainly the case respecting his views on unrepentant men and prayer. In his effort to reinforce the total sovereignty of God and the complete degradation of man, Avery taught that the love of God constituted the essence of prayer and that any prayer that did not emanate from such love was blasphemy. Consequently, the prayer of an unrepentant individual was vile in the eyes of God. Only after such individuals had accepted Christ could they pray with the love of God in their hearts. Then, and only then, would their prayers be worthy.[23]

Such reasoning confused most of Avery's congregation, whom he described as "not the most accurate reasoners."[24] For these people, raised on simple religious fundamentals, Avery's pronouncements smacked of heresy. They believed that all men should seek redemption and that the best way to prepare themselves for salvation was through prayer. If sinners were told not to pray, how were they to be saved? What was to ensure moral authority within society if impenitent men were not brought to the Lord through prayer? Although Avery was aware of such misgivings, he did little to assuage them. Instead, intolerant of what he perceived to be ignorance and absolutely certain of his own rectitude, he adhered even more rigidly to the intricate Calvinism propounded by New Divinity theologians.

Ironically, in view of his elitist attitudes, Avery developed a considerable following among the common folk of Gageborough. This resulted primarily from his growing opposition to the policies of Great Britain that began to appear in Berkshire County shortly after he settled there. Caught up in the spirit of the Liberty Boys, Avery preached sermons that became increasingly political in response to the British Parliament's enactment of the Coercive Acts in the spring of 1774.

Upon learning of the clash between British regulars and colonial minutemen at Lexington, Massachusetts, Avery gave clear voice to the fear that the forces of power threatened to undermine American liberties. He preached a farewell sermon to his parishioners in which he told them that he was leaving to join in the fight against the British. Then, following the church service, he entreated the men of Gageborough, "by every motive of patriotism, and as they valued liberty and abhorred slavery, not to turn a deaf ear to her cry," to join him.[25] Twenty parishioners answered his call, elected Avery their captain, and marched to Cambridge to join the American army gathering under George Washington. When Avery arrived in Cambridge in April 1775, he received a captain's commission and began service with the Continental Army that would last nearly five years. Throughout this time he served as chaplain in William A. Patterson's Massachusetts regiment, which became the Fifteenth Continental Infantry, and Col. Henry Sherburne's Sixteenth Additional Continental Regiment.[26] Because of his extended absence from Gageborough, Avery requested and received a dismissal from that church in April 1777.[27]

For Avery the Revolution became a great regenerative crusade, an opportunity for Americans to cleanse themselves and their society of the moral imperfections and iniquities that plagued them. Just as the conversion experience brought peace and love to the heart of the repentant sinner, the Revolution could create a fresh, new world of lib-

erty in America. During one exhortation to the troops Avery proclaimed that if Americans could "*break* EVERY YOKE: and *let the* OP-
PRESSED go FREE," if they could "break off [their] sins by *righteousness*,
and [their] iniquities by showing *mercy* to the *poor*;" if they would "by
faith and repentance flee to the *blood* of JESUS to cleanse [their] *polluted*
land from its manifold transgressions," then, and only then, could
America "become IMMANUEL's *land*, a *Mountain* of *Holiness*, a *Habita-
tion* of *Righteousness!*" When all this came to pass, the "LORD's *spiritual*
Empire of Love, Joy, and *Peace* [would] flourish gloriously in this *Western*
World."[28]

Committed to helping bring "Immanuel's land" into existence,
Avery threw himself into the task of redeeming the common soldiers
under his care. He urged them to awaken: "Open your Eyes & see what
is before you—! Act like rational Beings—don't rush blindfolded into
the Flames—! Every step you take brings you nearer to your home!!!!!"
He never let them forget that "the Devils stand rady—waitg. to hail
you welcome to your *own home!* Hell is moved from beneath to meet
you at your coming.—oh! then flee from the Wrath to come! lest you
soon follow judas to your own home!"[29] Before the troops went into
battle, Avery would remind them that "unconverted sinners are required, by God, to cast away all their transgressions—& make them a
new heart & a new Spirit, *immediately*, on Pain of death."[30]

As Avery went from camp to camp urging ordinary soldiers to repent,
he became increasingly convinced of the need for men like himself to
serve as America's moral guardians. He noted again and again that the
troops were "very sinful, & awfully secure." Indeed, there were "but
few, very few, who dare to speak for God."[31] His heart trembled "on
account of the sin, vanity, and almost every vice, which are rampant
thro' the camp." He bemoaned the fact that "even the poor sick soldiers,
whom I often visit in the hospitals, in general, appear very hardened and
secure—many of them die as stupid as brutes."[32] All this caused him to
lament "the alarming state of our land." Americans were "a people of
unclean lips . . . our Army—all ranks—our towns—cities—shall not
G's Soul be avenged on such a Nation as this."[33] For Avery, the American cause was just, the reformation necessary, but the material with
which he and other leaders had to work was weak. The common people
of America very much needed the shaping hand of their genteel leaders.

Even as he labored with the troops of the Continental Army, Avery
remained mindful that he would need a ministerial position when the
war ended. He was, therefore, receptive to an invitation that came in

the late fall of 1778 to preach as a candidate for the pastorate of the Presbyterian church in Newburyport, Massachusetts. Because of his strong views on the authority of the pastor within the structure of any church government, however, he did not receive a call to become New-buryport's pastor.[34] Clearly, his tenure as an officer in the Continental Army had done nothing to lessen Avery's self-righteous belief in his own moral and intellectual rectitude. In fact, his military experience led him to demand of his followers even greater obedience and discipline. He emerged from military service with an air of tremendous authority, a commanding presence. As one observer noted, "Apart from his band and black coat, he might have been taken for a general instead of a chaplain in the army, as he actually had been."[35]

In August 1779 Avery received another request to preach as a candi-date for a settled pastorate. This invitation came from the Separate Congregational church in Bennington, Vermont, whose original pastor had died in December the previous year. Avery's sermons must have made a favorable impression on the church, because in January its members chose a committee to investigate his religious principles more closely. In spite of the reservations repeatedly expressed by one mem-ber of that committee, John Fassett, the church voted in late February 1780 to extend a call to Avery. He accepted, submitted his resignation to the Continental Army on March 4, and proceeded to Bennington, where his installation ceremony took place on May 3.[36]

On the day of his installation Avery addressed both the church and the society. He expressed confidence that the zeal and faithfulness of the "visible believers" would cause them to "concur with him in every prudent measure for the reviving and supporting of church-discipline; to the end that the erroneous may be corrected, the vicious & the impenitent may be excluded, & that the just may be vindicated & encouraged." This was of the utmost importance, because only in this manner could the church in Bennington "become conspicuous as a city on a hill; and in this way will your *King* greatly desire your beauty."[37] When he turned to the society Avery distinguished between an evange-list and a pastor. A pastor had a clear relation to the church, it being his duty to lead in the church's discipline; an evangelist had no such charge. Avery considered himself a pastor. He saw it as his function "to notice your morals, to seek your best interests, & to watch for your souls & the souls of your children."[38]

David Avery left no doubt that he took it to be his personal respon-sibility as pastor to mold the lives of his followers within the church.

Anyone listening to Avery that day could easily perceive that Bennington's new minister assumed not only that it was the prerogative of the church to discipline its own members but also that it was well within the authority of that institution to shape the secular society of the town as well.

Worcester, August *14*, *1777*
To the PUBLIC

THE PRINTING BUSINESS *in Worcester having by compact devolved on the subscriber, he flatters himself that a constant attention to business will enable him to give universal satisfaction.*

As his entrance on the business is attended with considerable expense, he hopes those ladies and gentlemen who continue their papers for the present year, but have not complied with that useful custom of one half advance, will, as soon as they conveniently can, comply with the same, for which they shall receive due credit, and the hearty thanks of the Public's most obedient & humble servant

ANTHONY HASWELL [39]

With this announcement Anthony Haswell embarked upon his first experience as a newspaper editor and printer. He did so in difficult times. The Revolution had created social and economic distress throughout Massachusetts, and Haswell faced a chronic shortage of paper, type, and ink. Above all, he struggled against financial instability. Runaway inflation and a shortage of specie created terrible hardships for his subscribers and advertisers. Haswell had to dun his customers constantly in order to meet his operating expenses. More often than not his efforts failed; as a consequence he operated perpetually on the verge of bankruptcy.

Such straitened economic circumstances were not unusual for Haswell. He had lived modestly since his birth in Portsmouth, England, on April 6, 1756. His parents, William and Elizabeth, raised him, along with his brother William and sister Betsey, in a house on Penny Street that was plain even compared with others in that working-class district of the city.[40] Anthony's father struggled to support his family on wages he earned as a carpenter in the nearby dockyard.

By the time Anthony turned fourteen his mother had died and his father intended to remarry. William Haswell Sr. may have been anxious to establish his two boys away from Portsmouth prior to settling into his new marriage. In any event, he signed aboard a merchant vessel as a ship's carpenter and took William and Anthony with him. After sailing throughout the Mediterranean the Haswells arrived in Boston during the winter of 1769–70. The father immediately set out to find positions for his sons. He quickly apprenticed William to a shipbuilder, and after a bit longer he managed to arrange an apprenticeship for Anthony with a potter. Having accomplished this, he planned to sail for Portsmouth as soon as he could find a berth. Unbeknownst to the boys' father, his departure would be the occasion for Anthony's initial encounter with what the youth could only consider an unreasonable and high-handed person of authority.[41]

Anxious to see his father off, Anthony arose, dressed, and crept out of his master's house before dawn on the day the ship was to sail. As he rushed toward the docks Anthony had the misfortune to encounter a local tithingman. Even more unfortunate, the day was Sunday. No one was to be on the streets unless he or she was on the way to or from church services. Implacable, the man stood firm in the face of Anthony's earnest entreaties to allow him to pass by so that he could embrace his father one last time. Seething with anger at what he perceived to be an arbitrarily imposed injustice, Anthony returned to his master's house without a glimpse of his father. Several days later, noticing the tithingman walking ahead of him on the street, Anthony picked up a brick, threw it, and struck his antagonist in the back of the head. The blow felled the man instantly. Terrified that he might have killed the man, Anthony ran off, only to suffer days of painful remorse. His pangs of conscience finally ended when he later recognized the man walking about the streets in good health.[42]

Whatever relief Anthony experienced at seeing the tithingman alive turned to sadness when he learned that his brother must return to England. Shortly after his arrival in Portsmouth the boys' father wrote to ask that one of them return home because relatives of their mother suspected that he had abandoned the boys, perhaps even sold them to the navy. A former brother-in-law threatened violence toward him unless he could prove himself innocent of such aspersions. Only the personal appearance of one of the brothers could save their father from a terrible beating. Since William could more easily secure passage, he became the chosen son. Therefore, shortly after receiving his father's letter William sailed for Portsmouth, leaving Anthony entirely alone in a strange city.[43]

With the departure first of his father and then of his brother, Anthony lost his most intimate sources of personal support and companionship. Then a dramatic event occurred on the evening of March 5, 1770, that greatly affected his life and helped him form meaningful new relationships. While standing among a crowd near the Custom House on King Street, Anthony saw eight British troopers open fire upon the civilians crowding about them. In that moment, "when the blood of the Sons of Liberty stained the pavements of Kingstreet, in Boston, shed by the hands of British murderers," Haswell vowed to support "the heroism of Samuel Adams, William Mollineaux [sic] and numerous others, who took command of the incensed and armed Bostonians, evaded the chicanery of the insidious Governor Hutchinson, and drove the murderers from the town."[44] The Boston Massacre wedded Haswell to the American opposition to British authority, an authority that he and so many others considered both arbitrary and tyrannical. If his outrage drew Anthony toward the Sons of Liberty, his remarkable knack for composing patriotic verse and songs brought him to the attention of these men, who welcomed the talented youth into their midst.[45] Within this fellowship Haswell regained the bonds of mutual support and comradeship lost when his father and brother had left him. At a critical time in his life he found a cause that gave his life meaning and compatriots whose sympathetic friendship provided him with a sense of brotherhood.

The same wonderful ability to write songs and verse that pleased his companions in the Sons of Liberty enabled Haswell to get a position where he could make fuller use of his talents. This came about as a result of divisions among the employees at the pottery works where Anthony served as an apprentice. Most of his fellow workers, recent immigrants from England, remained steadfastly loyal to their homeland. Some, like Haswell, had become ardent patriots of the American cause. Each group enjoyed baiting the other by singing ditties articulating their sympathies and ridiculing their opponents. One day, while the British loyalists were in full voice Anthony composed a song on the back of a large platter that had been spoiled previous to being fired. After his rivals had finished, Haswell began to sing his new composition. Just at that moment the proprietor of the shop appeared; Anthony quickly fell silent and threw the dish into a bin of spoilt pottery. A bit later the owner summoned Haswell into his office and asked the youth where he had learned the song he had been singing; Anthony responded that he had written it himself.[46]

Soon thereafter Anthony received a summons to appear at his master's home. He proceeded "with fear and trembling to the house, and was shown into the parlor where the gentleman was with a number of other gentlemen."[47] The assembled group asked him to sing some pieces that he had composed. Patriots all, they expressed the greatest pleasure with the songs and asked Anthony if he would not rather be apprenticed to a printer than to a potter so that he might make better use of his abilities. When he responded in the affirmative, several individuals in the room declared their intention to support him in whatever manner they could. One gave him a suit of clothes, and another presented him with ten dollars. More important, Haswell's master released him so that he could be apprenticed to Isaiah Thomas, owner and editor of the *Massachusetts Spy, or Thomas's Boston Journal.*[48]

When Haswell joined Thomas he became intimately involved with one of the leading whig editors in Massachusetts. He accompanied Thomas after the editor fled to Worcester in April 1775 following the battle of Lexington. When Thomas established the *Massachusetts Spy* in Worcester he placed the defiant message "Americans! — Liberty or Death! — Join or Die!" on his paper's masthead. From the moment Thomas set up shop near the courthouse on May 3, 1775, the *Spy* became virtually the voice of the Worcester County Convention, the Revolutionary institution responsible for directing the political, military, and judicial affairs of the county.[49]

Haswell remained with the *Spy* until the winter of 1776, when he joined a local militia unit that formed in response to General Washington's desperate call for additional soldiers.[50] Haswell's company joined Washington's army in the vicinity of White Plains, New York, and suffered through a grueling retreat through New Jersey to the Delaware River. The weather turned cold, rain pelted the troops, and the roads turned into rivers of mud. Washington's army lost hundreds of tents when it evacuated New York, and none of the militia units joining him brought any with them. Men had to sleep on the icy ground, unprotected from driving sleet storms. The relentless march exhausted the men and wore out what little clothing and blankets they had. "There are few coats among them but what are out at elbows," noted a British officer, "and in a whole Regiment there is scarce a pair of breeches."[51] An American observer exclaimed that "without blankets, medicines and the proper care of physicians, they are reduced to the lowest ebb of human wretchedness."[52] Haswell recalled marching "with a musket on my shoulder, unsheltered at times and barefooted for days, living on a single ration per day, precariously served, and scarcely sufficient for sustenance."[53]

Although neither the weather nor the equipment of the men had improved by late December, their morale certainly took a turn for the better when Washington halted their retreat and led them in bold attacks upon the enemy. His movements shielded by a blinding sleet storm on December 26, 1776, Washington managed to surprise the Hessian troops encamped at Trenton and score a smashing victory. He then moved toward Princeton. The troops again had to make exhausting marches along roads that had turned into endless tracts of mud. On January 3, 1777, Washington's men attacked a British force at Princeton. After hard fighting during which they had to dislodge the enemy from Nassau Hall, they gained another complete victory. Following his success at Princeton, Washington took his army northward to Morristown, where he put it into winter quarters.

On March 1 Haswell's term of enlistment expired. He immediately returned to Worcester, where he rejoined the *Spy*, now under lease to William Stearns and Daniel Bigelow, two Worcester attorneys. Since he had completed his apprenticeship prior to his enlistment, Haswell returned to much larger responsibilities. In fact, since Bigelow and Stearns devoted the majority of their time and attention to their legal duties, he may well have had complete charge of the operation. Then on August 14, 1777, the paper appeared under a new title: *Haswell's Massachusetts Spy Or American Oracle of Liberty*. Barely twenty-one years of age, Haswell, having taken over the lease from Bigelow and Stearns, became the editor of one of the leading newspapers in Massachusetts.

In the first issue to appear under Haswell's name Stearns and Bigelow recommended the new editor to the public as "a MASTER of his BUSINESS, and a staunch friend to the Cause of America."[54] Beyond placing his name in the title of the paper, Haswell changed very little. He retained the same format and devoted as much energy as Thomas had to furthering the Revolutionary effort. On October 9, 1777, Haswell did replace the motto on the masthead, "Undaunted by Tyrants we'll DIE or be FREE," with a Latin phrase, "Lectorum delectando, pariturque monendo — Nos populo damus."[55] Since he had absolutely no understanding of Latin, Haswell must have enlisted the aid of someone only slightly less ignorant of the language than himself. In any event, no matter how clumsy the grammar, he clearly intended that his paper serve as a watchdog to warn the people of impending dangers to their freedoms. Above all else, he wanted to keep his readers vigilant so that they might better protect their liberties. Only in this way could America remain a virtuous republic.

By this time Haswell had become thoroughly imbued with the belief that America represented a land of virtue and liberty that must free itself from the tyranny of Great Britain. At one point he exclaimed: "Rejoice Americans, in the common course of human events your triumph over your cruel enemy is certain, virtue has ever been the charge of omnipotence, and altho' we may for a while be punished for our sins, we shall, if we make that [virtue] the favoriable rule of our conduct, prove in the end compleatly victorious."[56] Another time he referred to America as "our Zion."[57] Always, though, Haswell envisioned America — this virtuous Zion — from an egalitarian frame of reference. His simple origins, strengthened by his experience as a common soldier, shaped his ideological perspective: he always extolled the simple and the ordinary. Analyzing Sir William Howe's activities around Philadelphia in January 1778, for example, Haswell speculated that the commander of the British forces in America was not likely to risk a battle. Howe must surely remember his last excursion, when, "notwithstanding his formidable appearance, and all the clamour of his emissaries, thereabouts, the *half starved*, *barefooted* Americans, were not to be intimidated."[58]

While Haswell's patriotic fervor never languished, it must have been difficult to maintain in the face of serious problems he encountered as an editor. He constantly had difficulty obtaining paper of good quality. Ofttimes he was unable to acquire even poor paper in sufficient quantity to print his newspaper in the normal manner. At such times he could only "beg leave to inform our customers that we are again put to the disagreeable necessity of printing on paper a size smaller than we usually do."[59] On these occasions not only was the paper smaller in size but it contained only half as many pages as usual. Haswell also confronted a chronic deficiency of type and ink of good quality.

Through his own ingenuity, as well as the patience of his customers, Haswell managed to surmount these problems. One difficulty he simply could not overcome, however, was the lack of money. Haswell and his customers, suffering from the terrible inflation and scarcity of specie caused by the war, faced real economic hardship. In February 1778 he asked every customer behind in his payments to "pay up his arreages," and he requested his other customers to advance payment for six months or a year. If the price of newspapers fell during the next year, he would extend their subscription; if prices advanced, he would not raise his rate beyond the present one of twenty shillings per year.[60] If a note of particular urgency crept into Haswell's appeal for money, it was because of his wish to purchase much of the printing material in the office from Isaiah Thomas. Claiming that he had agreed to this purchase in order to keep the printing office in Worcester and that his own wish was "to settle in this town," Haswell hoped that his customers would come to the support of this "young beginner."[61] Unfortunately, his plea went unrewarded.

In March he again addressed his customers. Their lack of response had now "put it out of his power to make the intended purchase" of the printing materials. Claiming that every newspaper in Massachusetts except his own had raised its price from twenty to forty shillings per year, Haswell now called for his customers to pay at the weekly rate of seven pence per paper. If this expedient failed, he could not guarantee the continuance of the paper.[62]

Actually, the maintenance of the paper assumed an importance for Haswell beyond keeping a press alive in Worcester. He planned to marry in April and needed to be sure of earning a livelihood. Although his customers did not respond, he and Lydia Baldwin proceeded to be married on April 23, 1778. Haswell was not, however, able to retain the lease on the paper. His name appeared on the *Spy* for the last time on June 18, 1778, after which Isaiah Thomas took over proprietorship. Perhaps to reassure those readers who had become loyal to Haswell, Thomas announced that he was resuming control of the paper and that "Mr. HASWELL, who has published this paper for ten months past, will be connected with the business."[63]

The Haswells remained in Worcester for nearly two more years. Then in 1781 they moved to Hartford, Connecticut, where Anthony joined the printing firm of Hudson and Goodwin. The young couple stayed in Hartford only a year; by May they had taken up residence in Springfield, Massachusetts, where Anthony had formed a partnership with Elisha Babcock, a paper maker. Together they published the *Massachusetts Gazette or the Springfield and Northampton Weekly Advertiser.* The first issue appeared May 14, 1782. Four months later the partners changed the name of their paper to the *Massachusetts Gazette or the General Advertiser.* The two men also carried on a general printing business under the name Babcock and Haswell.[64]

Haswell faced the same problems with the *Gazette* that he had endured as editor of the *Spy*. He and his partner found themselves forced to make constant appeals to their customers to pay their subscription fees. Anthony and Lydia did enjoy a bit of assistance from her father, Nathan, who on one occasion promised to send some money, "but if it does not come in better than it has this week I shall send you but little."[65]

On May 13, 1783, the *Gazette* announced the dissolution of the partnership between Haswell and Babcock. Henceforth Elisha Babcock would exercise sole proprietorship over the newspaper. Haswell had ended the partnership after meeting with a committee charged with procuring a state printer for the Vermont legislature. This committee had offered the bounty of state patronage if Haswell would locate a press in Bennington.[66] The promise of state support must have seemed like a godsend to the Haswells, who now had two children to support. Young Anthony had been born in Worcester on November 17, 1780, and Elizabeth in Springfield on February 20, 1783. Haswell quickly accepted the committee's proposal.

With the financial assistance of his father-in-law and credit extended by Daniel Bigelow, Haswell bought a simple hand press and a supply of type. He loaded this equipment and all his family's worldly possessions into an oxcart and set out with his wife and children for Vermont.[67] The family reached Bennington in this humble manner in time for Anthony Haswell, the egalitarian young democrat, to publish the first issue of the *Vermont Gazette* on June 5, 1783.

Camp, at Fredericksburg
October 3, 1778

Dear Friend, — I lately saw a letter to our friend B——, in which you make very kind mention of my name, but was not a little surprised that you have so long neglected to write me. I immediately examined the letters which have passed between us, and found you were one in my debt; and depend on it, I shall demand payment without conscience.

Before this reaches you, I shall, in all probability, have resigned. My wages, which are my sole dependence, are by no means equal to my expenses. I am already in debt, and a continuance in the service, to me affords no other prospect than that of utter ruin. If I resign, unqualified as I am for business, and without friends, at least powerful friends, I shall find myself extremely embarrassed — and often apply to myself certain lines of Thomson with a little alteration:

A quick returning pang
Shoots through the conscious heart where honor still,
And great designs against the oppressive load
Of poverty, by fits impatient heave.

Although it is a great mortification to me to resign, it is a greater to hold the rank, and not be able to support the character of a gentleman. I forbear any reflections on the country, yet cannot but pity the condition of the officers, many of whom I know to be in a worse condition than myself, as they are more reduced, and have more to provide for. It is very shocking to think that many brave fellows who have been accustomed to command others, and to be treated with respect, who have a thousand times exposed their lives, have spent their estates and ruined their constitutions in defence of their country, must soon with their families be reduced to want. And perhaps derided and insulted by those whom they have defended. Forbid it, humanity! forbid it Heaven. You will, as a friend, pardon these apprehensions, gloomy indeed, but, as I think, founded in reason.

I shall spend the winter in Salisbury, Connecticut, in the study of law; though I cannot but regret that it is not in my power to spend considerable time in general studies, before applying myself to a particular one. Opportunities of writing will doubtless be less frequent after I leave the service, but I shall embrace every one that occurs, and shall from your friendship expect the same. And I will also promise to write a better hand, or procure some one to copy. Winter quarters are now in agitation. Litchfield is talked of for this division. Where they will be, is uncertain as yet. I think, from all appearances, we may reasonably conclude that the glorious contest draws near a glorious conclusion, when, with the blessing of heaven, we may enjoy the sweets of liberty in peace.[68]

One week after writing this Nathaniel Chipman tendered his resignation as a lieutenant in the Continental Army. In his letter to his commanding officer Chipman declared that a lieutenant's "wages are in no degree equal to his expenses." Consequently, "he must necessarily have some other resources, or make a contemptible appearance; he must, in fact, become a beggar." Since Chipman had only his salary to depend upon, he felt that he had no choice but to resign. His sensitivities as a gentleman were at stake; for him it was "a great mortification to be obliged to resign, but a greater to hold the rank, while unable to support the character, of an officer."[69]

Chipman left the Continental Army in October 1778, extremely conscious of his stature as a gentleman. Such concern for gentility did not, however, characterize the family into which he had been born.

Chipman was descended from solid yeoman stock; his father, Samuel, had brought up all six of his boys "in habits of unremitted and patient industry."[70] An equally strong commitment to the "staid habits of the puritans" characterized all the Chipmans of Salisbury, Connecticut.[71]

The Chipman family had lived in Salisbury since Nathaniel's grandfather, Thomas, first arrived there with his wife and five sons — Thomas, John, Amos, Samuel, and Jonathan — shortly after the formal organization of the town in October 1741. In March 1743 Thomas Chipman, "Yeoman," purchased 50 acres that included a dwelling house, a gristmill, a sawmill, a one-fourth part of an ironworks, and a one-fourth part of the dam that powered the mills.[72] The following year he acquired an additional 180 acres.[73]

The elder Thomas must have been a man of more than modest means when he immigrated to Salisbury, for the property he purchased shortly after his arrival cost him more than sixteen hundred pounds. In any event, he ranked second out of the fifty-nine inhabitants who appeared on Salisbury's rate list for 1744.[74] Two years later he ranked first.[75] Chipman's comparative affluence in this newly formed township on Connecticut's westernmost frontier, combined with his industrious character and religious piety, soon brought him into positions of authority in the town government and the church. Chipman's fellow townsmen repeatedly turned to him to fill the most important positions in their purview. They first elected him a selectman in December 1744.[76] From that time on they frequently called him to that position, and they elected him moderator of the town meeting on numerous occasions. He served as town treasurer and as Salisbury's first representative to the Connecticut General Assembly. In addition, he was the first justice of the peace named for Salisbury by the colonial legislature.[77]

Chipman assumed an equally prominent role in Salisbury's Congregational church. Indeed, he played an instrumental part in acquiring and settling its first minister, Jonathan Lee, a recent graduate of Yale. In 1744 the town elected Chipman to a committee to negotiate with Lee regarding the terms of his settlement.[78] Chipman soon became the central figure in this process. The town voted that "Mr. Jonathan Lee and Mr. Thos. Chipman appoint ye time Mr. Lee be ordained & ye men to Do ye Work."[79] When Lee's ordination took place in Salisbury on the morning of November 23, 1744, the first order of business was to gather the church. Under the watchful eyes of visiting ministers, Jonathan Lee, followed in order by Thomas Chipman and nine other men, signed the church covenant. This task completed, "The Counsel owned them as a *Chh* of Christ and a Sister *Chh*."[80] The "Saints" of the church then elected the Reverend Lee to be their minister, and the ordination ritual took place.

Not long after Lee's ordination the inhabitants of the town and members of the church acknowledged Chipman's efforts in securing their first settled pastor. On January 4, 1745, the saints of the church elected Thomas their first deacon.[81] Over time both the town and the church continued to recognize Chipman's prominence in their affairs. In April 1746, when the town decided to replace its log meeting house with a larger frame building, its citizens chose Chipman to carry on the necessary negotiations with the General Assembly regarding a site.[82] After costs for the new structure became burdensome, townspeople again turned to Chipman, this time sending him to the General Assembly to gain permission for the town to levy a special tax on nonresident landholders.[83] In both instances he succeeded in accomplishing the town's goals.

By 1752 the new structure had been completed; its pulpit, pews, seats, and galleries had been installed. It was almost ready for church services. First, however, town officials had to "dignify," or seat, the meeting house. Taking into account status, age, and property valuation on the town's Grand List, they assigned pews and seats according to the "dignity" of each individual or family in the town.[84] At times such as this the prominence of men like Thomas Chipman, long recognized by his fellow townspeople, received official public affirmation. Hierarchy, the cement holding together any respectable society, had been duly reinforced in Salisbury.

When Thomas Chipman died on August 5, 1752, he was one of Salisbury's most respected and affluent citizens, a town patriarch. His sons, while valuable and respected members of the community, never achieved such wealth or stature. Thomas Jr., who purchased the original homestead and ironworks from his father in 1746, devoted himself to iron production.[85] Through hard work he managed to gain sufficient wealth to rank in the upper third of the Salisbury Grand List, but he never approached the prominent position his father had occupied, nor did he enjoy the same status in the community.[86] Although twice elected a selectman, far more often he occupied such positions as tithingman, poundkeeper, or lister of the tax rate.[87] John, Amos, and Jonathan could not match the limited success of their eldest brother; they consistently ranked closer to the middle range of the Grand List and held far fewer and less prestigious offices in the town.[88]

Like his brothers, Samuel strove to make a place for himself in Salisbury. He began buying land as early as 1745. Eventually, however, he sold all the property he had acquired except for twenty acres and a town lot.[89] He opened a blacksmith's shop on the lot, married Hannah Austin of Suffield, Connecticut, and moved to the twenty acres, where the couple intended to raise a family. Hannah gave birth to Nathaniel on November 15, 1752. He was the first of six boys born to the Chipmans.

Committed to hard work and rigorous discipline, Samuel and Hannah Chipman raised their sons in a strictly ordered household. They respected the Sabbath, observed all its laws, and attended church services with punctual regularity. For the Chipmans, though, regular attendance at church "was scarcely more of a religious exercise than the government of their famil[y], the education of their children, industry in their several callings, honesty in their dealings, submission to the civil and ecclesiastical authorities, and the performance of all their moral duties."[90] The Chipmans raised their boys "as well by fear as by affection." They knew full well the value of education, but at the same time they firmly believed that unless a child "be governed in part by fear of his parent, and act in obedience to his authority, there will seldom be that hardy vigor of intellect, which is so useful in every department of life." Such a home environment "created in the child an habitual submission to the will of his earthly parent — an important if not an indispensable preparation for an habitual obedience to the will of our heavenly Parent."[91]

Samuel Chipman was a diligent, hardworking man who expected his sons, when they reached the proper age, to work as long and arduously as he. As soon as they were able, he kept his boys constantly employed either on the farm or in his blacksmith shop. Samuel subjected all members of the family, himself included, "to an orderly system, no departure from which was ever permitted." Every member of the family arose early, worked tirelessly throughout the day, and retired punctually at an early hour. Samuel and Hannah did, however, read more than most ordinary laboring people. On winter evenings they instilled this love of learning in their boys by having each member of the family take turns reading aloud from books selected at the town library. Any issues raised by the book being read became the subject for a lively conversation to which every member of the family was expected to contribute.[92]

Samuel and Hannah clearly desired their boys to acquire "that hardy vigor of intellect" so essential to leading a full and useful life. This was especially true of Nathaniel, who, like other children in Salisbury, attended common schools during the winter months and labored on his father's farm during the rest of the year. Seeing that their eldest son thrived on intellectual challenges, Samuel and Hannah decided that he should have a college education. In order to prepare him for the entrance examinations at Yale, they released him from his farm duties for nine months. During that time he studied classical languages and literature with Rev. Jonathan Lee. The son of an artisan himself, Lee had gradually risen to a position of affluence and prominence subsequent to his graduation from Yale. Indeed, by the time Nathaniel Chipman studied under him Lee had become one of the most prosperous Congregational ministers in western Connecticut. Salisbury's pastor realized full well what a college education could mean for an intelligent and ambitious lad in Nathaniel's modest circumstances. Consequently, he gave freely of his time and knowledge in order to prepare his pupil for the entrance examinations.[93]

In the fall of 1773 Nathaniel traveled to New Haven to be examined for admission to Yale. He underwent the scrutiny of President Naphtali Daggett and his tutors, John Trumbull and Timothy Dwight, who tested his competence in Latin, Greek, arithmetic, and English grammar. Satisfied regarding Nathaniel's academic preparation, they finally asked him for "suitable Testimony of a blameless Life and Conversation."[94] He doubtless provided them with a letter from the Reverend Lee, whose word as a minister and a Yale graduate surely sufficed. Nathaniel then paid his tuition and gave the steward a bond for his first quarter's room and board in Old College Hall, where he had been assigned a room by President Daggett. Daggett also entered the names of all the members of Chipman's class in alphabetical order. Fortunately for Nathaniel, the college had abandoned the practice of ranking students according to the status of their parents. As the son of a country blacksmith, Nathaniel would have been assigned a position among the lowliest of his class.[95]

The elimination of the status system for ranking students at Yale by no means indicated that the administration did not believe in hierarchical relationships. Indeed, a belief that social hierarchy—a cohesive order in which all individuals knew their proper sphere, moved contentedly within it, observed and respected social distinctions, performed the social functions allotted to their station, and deferred to their natural superiors—constituted the essential foundation of the larger world outside the college permeated the thought of Yale's ad-

ministrators and formed the very essence of what they meant to inculcate in their students. The subtle gradations of subordination necessary
to sustain such a hierarchical society pervaded the rules and regulations
of the college. Its "Laws," which the president required each student to
purchase and to keep in his possession at all times, clearly outlined the
kind of moral, social, religious, and academic behavior expected of Yale
men if they were to become gentlemen. Students must pattern their
lives according to the Scriptures, respect the Sabbath, avoid immoral
behavior, dress in good taste, and always act like gentlemen. Above all,
every scholar was "required to shew all due Honour and Reverence
both in Words and Behaviour to all his Superiors, viz. Parents, Magistrates, Ministers, and especially to the President, Fellows, and Tutors
of this College."[96]

To instill such respect for "Decency and good Order" the college
"Regulations" laid down a number of hard and fast rules. All students,
for example, were "forbidden to wear their Hats (unless in stormy
weather) in the front door-yard of the President's or Professor's House,
or within Ten Rods of the Person of the President, Eight Rods of the
Professor and Five Rods of a Tutor." In addition, they must "rise and
stand, when the President or Professor is entering or going out of the
Chapel; nor shall they take up their Hats, after Public Exercise, until all
their superiors have gone out." Further, all undergraduates were "to be
called by their *Sur-names*; Bachelors of Arts have the titles of *Sir* pre-
fixed to their names, and the title of Mr. is given to Masters of Arts."[97]

While Chipman's Salisbury background may not have prepared him
to become a gentleman, his family's penchant for system and order fit
nicely with the college curriculum, especially the capstone of a Yale
education, an intensive concentration on moral philosophy under the
exclusive tutelage of the president during the senior year. In this course
President Daggett depended almost entirely upon John Locke's *Essay
Concerning Human Understanding* and William Wollaston's *Religion of
Nature Delineated*. In Daggett's hands, as in those of so many other
Congregational ministers, Locke's *Essay* became a means for providing
religious certainty, for elucidating biblical truth, and, above all, for
linking that certainty and truth to the established order.[98] *The Religions
of Nature Delineated* provided even more support for traditional authority. Wollaston stressed the value of education by declaring that individuals could act upon their own judgments "in respect of such things as
are private, and concern themselves *only*," but even then they should
preserve "a due deference to them, who differ from them, and . . . have

more knowledge and literature than themselves." Private judgments were one thing, but when "a society is concerned" individuals must give way to "them to whom the power of judging is intrusted." For Wollaston, those endowed with "the power of judging" were the educated gentry. In his mind, "the reason why the *many* are so commonly in the wrong and so wretchedly misjudge things" was that "the generality of people are not sufficiently prepared, by a proper education, to find truth by reasoning."[99] Wollaston's ideas made perfect sense to Yale men, who upon graduation meant to take their place in society as educated gentlemen to whom the masses should defer and whom they should entrust with the power of judging. Wollaston's stern advice to each individual in society to "behave himself according to his *subordination* or place in the community" could only strengthen such attitudes.[100]

Chipman and his classmates reinforced the bonds between gentlemen and expanded their literary efforts informally outside the regular curriculum. Each undergraduate at Yale joined one of two literary societies, Linonia or Brothers in Unity. Chipman affiliated with the latter. Members of these organizations gathered to discuss, orate, or debate whatever topics they chose. Both societies posed questions to their members and then formed an answer by consensus. The Linonians, for example, put the question, "What thing is the most delightful to Man in the World?" The answer: "Virtuous Men will take greatest Delight in virtuous Actions, but what is most delightful to most Men is getting Money." For their part, the Brothers in Unity reached such conclusions as "an unconverted person should not preach" and "women ought not to have a share in civil government."[101]

Such inquiries gave way to more somber issues as political tension between the American colonies and Great Britain intensified. As early as 1774 two candidates for the master of arts presented a dialogue at commencement exercises entitled "The Rights of America and the Unconstitutional Measures of the British Parliament."[102] In February 1775 students formed their own military company. One of its members observed that the "College Yard constantly sounds with, *poise your firelock, cock your firelock etc.*"[103] On April 21, 1775, the campus erupted: news of the battle of Lexington filled the country with alarm and "rendered it impossible for [students] to pursue [their] studies to any profit."[104] Chipman responded to the crisis by composing an impassioned poem replete with the powerful images — tyranny, virtue, corruption, liberty — reverberating throughout the colonies. In his most fervent lines Chipman implored his readers to honor those who fell at Lexington:

"Think on those heroes who resigned their breath, / No tool of tyrants, ministers of death. / Who firm, the rage of tyranny withstood, / And Seal'd the cause of liberty with blood."[105] Shortly after writing this, Chipman left Yale to accept an ensign's commission in Colonel Charles Webb's Second Regiment in the Connecticut Continental line.[106]

Because of the turmoil created by the Revolution, Yale did not hold its annual commencement celebration in September 1777. Instead, the president granted diplomas to the graduating seniors in July. He awarded Chipman a diploma *in absentia* even though he had not been able to take his final examinations.[107] In fact, while the president was giving his classmates their diplomas, Chipman and his regiment were supporting General Washington's desperate attempt to keep Sir William Howe away from Philadelphia. After suffering sharp defeats at Brandywine Creek on September 11 and at Germantown on October 4, however, Washington had no alternative but to allow the British forces to occupy Philadelphia. Then, in order to maintain the presence of an American army close to the city, Washington put his troops into winter quarters at Valley Forge, some twenty miles to the north.

By the time the American forces arrived at Valley Forge they were in deplorable condition. The first task facing the troops was to build log huts to shelter them from the winter cold. General Anthony Wayne reported that his men would be "covered in a few days, I mean as to huts, but naked as to clothing—they are in that respect in a worse condition than Falstaff's recruits for they have not one whole shirt to a Brigade."[108] A colonel in the Fourth Massachusetts line observed that "the State has not supported the troops with one single article for more than three months past" and there were "at least 400 men in the Brigade which I belong to that have not a shoe nor a stocking to put on and more than that number have not half a shirt apiece."[109] Rations were another serious problem. Men often had only cold water for breakfast and a mouthful of meal for dinner. In March 1778 the troops received only three ounces of meat and three pounds of flour for an entire week's rations.[110] Soldiers began to drift away from camp and return to their homes. In April Chipman observed that "the officers of the army are at present in a great dilemma, whether in contempt of poverty and the unmerited reproaches of their ungrateful constituents, they shall still continue in the service of their country, or quit, and join with the rest of the world in the pursuit of riches." He felt certain that "if something is not done, most of them will resign, and that soon."[111]

Shortly after Chipman expressed these fears Washington took the army out of winter quarters. Nathaniel's spirits, as well as those of the other officers who had persevered, began to rise. The army, having been drilled throughout the winter by Baron von Steuben, emerged from Valley Forge a much better disciplined fighting force than it had been. Chances were good that it would soon be tested in battle, since Sir William Clinton, who had replaced Howe, had evacuated Philadelphia and was making his way across New Jersey. Finally, on June 28, 1778, the two armies clashed in a fierce battle near Monmouth courthouse. The following day Clinton withdrew his forces from the field. He eventually rendezvoused with the British fleet, which carried his army to New York. Washington followed, and by early fall the American army had settled in near White Plains, where it had been encamped nearly two years before.

On October 10, 1778, Chipman tendered his resignation. In his letter to General Washington he declared: "With reluctance would I quite the service of my country, could I subsist myself in it with honor." In fact, he claimed that he stood "ready, in behalf of my country, to sacrifice every consideration of interests as far as may be consistent with honor." Unfortunately, his wages no longer "afforded an honorable subsistence." Since he was "unable to answer the demands of my creditors, it will be in their power to ruin me when they please."[112] As a gentleman he could not endure the humiliation any longer.

The heightened sense of honor that pervaded Chipman's letter of resignation resulted in large measure from his experience as an officer in Washington's Continental Army.[113] Convinced that "proper discipline and Subordination" were essential to the creation of an effective army, Washington fostered the belief that social hierarchy supported military hierarchy.[114] Consequently, in order to gain the necessary authority over common soldiers, an army's officers must be gentlemen. Just as a true gentleman kept a proper distance between individuals of high and low station, an officer must rigidly enforce the strict subordination of rank so essential to the creation of a disciplined professional army. Thus, even though most junior officers in the Continental Army were "the Sons of Farmers or Mechanicks, who had quit the Plow or the Workshop," under the pervasive influence of General Washington they tried desperately to become gentlemen.[115] Quickly, then, a group consciousness developed among Continental officers, a consciousness that set them off from the common soldier or citizen. Military rank bestowed upon many of them a status that they could never have achieved outside the army. And with this change in status came a change in their attitudes and values as well. Not only must an officer do all in his power to preserve his own stature but all others, civilians as well as enlisted men, must publicly acknowledge his position.

Chipman returned to Salisbury in the fall of 1778 a very different man than when he had left five years earlier. His years at Yale had ingrained within him the belief that a social hierarchy was not only a natural development within a society but an essential one. It provided the stability and order so vital to the existence of a civilized culture. His experience as a Continental officer reinforced this belief and strengthened his commitment to the subordination that should exist among the various ranks within that hierarchy. He believed that in all societies there were men whose talent, education, and cosmopolitan outlook set them apart. These individuals — gentlemen in civilian life and officers in the military — furnished the natural leadership to which ordinary citizens should defer; they alone should assume responsibility for shaping their society.

Because his parents and brothers had migrated to the Grants in 1774, Nathaniel was on his own when he arrived home in the fall of 1778. Since there were no lawyers in Salisbury at this time, Chipman may have moved to nearby Sharon, where John Canfield took in students who read law with him.[116] Regardless of where he lived while in Litchfield County, Nathaniel maintained a close friendship with Uriah Tracey, a classmate at Yale who was studying law in the town of Litchfield.[117] This relationship reinforced the social attitudes Chipman had acquired during his years at Yale and in the army. In fact, his good friend believed that the Revolution created "too much liberty and equality." Not only that but, he argued, "this state of liberty and equality must be broken up, and we must have a king here, but he must not be called king, as it would startle the old whigs — but he must have the essential requisites of a king." In addition, "we must have a body of nobility, but they must not be called noblemen for the same reason, yet must have all the essentials of a body of noblemen." And finally, "we must have an established religion and an established clergy. The people must be reduced to a condition of hard labor and ignorance, and then they will be safely governed."[118]

Chipman made rapid progress as a student of the law. On January 1, 1779, he wrote an old college classmate that he planned to take the attorney's oath in March. He thought that after that he would settle in Bennington, "where I shall indeed be *rara avis in terris*, for there is not an attorney in the state."[119] On March 2 he reported that he had passed the bar in Connecticut and was "in full march to the capital of the empire," meaning that he intended to take up residence in Vermont. Realizing full well what opportunities there were for trained lawyers in a frontier environment, he jovially noted to a friend and fellow attorney that he could not "but laugh to think what a flash we shall make, when we come to be members of congress." Still, he expressed mock vexation when he pondered "how many steps there are by which we must mount to that pinnacle of happiness." These included "first, an attorney; then, a selectman; a huffing justice; a deputy; an assistant [state representative]; a member of congress."[120]

By April 1779 Nathaniel had joined his family in Tinmouth, Vermont. Two months later, on the second Tuesday of June 1779, the superior court, meeting at Rutland, appointed Nathaniel Chipman, Esquire, attorney at law, swore him in, and licensed him to plead at the bar in the state of Vermont.[121] Chipman assumed that the common citizens of Vermont would naturally look to him and individuals like him to provide direction and leadership in their society. He fully expected the inhabitants of this new republic to surrender "the power of judging" to gentlemen such as himself.

Thursday 20 of May [1789] set out for Williston where governor Chittenden lives. — baptised five children, rode through ye woods, 14 miles, ye riding as bad as it could be, almost half of ye trees in ye woods blown down by ye violence of ye wind last year. Came to one Deacon Talcotts and he accompanied me to his Excellency's Governor Chittenden's. A low poor house. — a plain family — low, vulgar man, clownish, excessively parsimonious, — made me welcome, — hard fare, a very great farm, — 1000 acres — hundred acres of wheat on ye onion river — 200 acres of extraordinary interval land. A shrewd cunning man — skilled in human nature & in agriculture — understands extremely well ye mysteries of Vermont, apparently and professedly serious.[122]

The observations made by Rev. Nathan Perkins, a prominent Presbyterian minister from Hartford, typified the reactions of refined individuals to the character and habits of Thomas Chittenden. Despite their own affluence or his political prominence, Chittenden and his wife, Elizabeth, simply refused to make distinctions for wealth or station. Instead, they treated anyone well disposed toward them with an egalitarian bonhomie. An unsuspecting group of gentlemen and their ladies learned this when they paid a formal call on the Chittendens at noontime and accepted an invitation to dinner. These cultivated people experienced quite a surprise when they heard a tin horn call workers in from the field at the same moment that they themselves had been asked to come to the table. Surprise turned to shocked amazement when they discovered that they were to share that table with the farm laborers. One of the ladies ventured to ask if "servants" always came to table with the family. Elizabeth, immediately sensing the hauteur lurking behind the inquiry, responded: "They do; but I have been telling the Governor, as *they* did the work, *we* ought to give them the first table and take the second ourselves."[123]

For Thomas Chittenden such modest behavior came quite naturally. Born on his father's farm in East Guilford (Madison), Connecticut, on January 6, 1730, he grew up in a family of simple habits, frugality, and industry. The boy worked on the family farm in an isolated region near the Hammonasset River from the time he had strength enough to help out. He attended the local common schools only when his father did not need his assistance on the farm. He had no exposure to genteel people or habits; his industrious, plain, and pious neighbors were the only society he knew.[124]

Early in 1748, shortly after his eighteenth birthday, Chittenden decided to strike out into the world beyond East Guilford. He traveled to New London, where he shipped out on a merchant vessel bound for the West Indies even though King George's War still raged between England and France and American ships ran the risk of capture by an enemy naval vessel. Perhaps the danger strengthened the resolve of an eighteen-year-old farm boy to try his hand at sea. In any event, Tom's ship sailed down the Atlantic coast past the Carolinas, Georgia, and Florida. Shortly after clearing the Bahama Channel, it encountered a French man-of-war, whose crew quickly boarded the American ship and took its sailors captive. The French captain then took what he wanted of the cargo, burned the vessel itself, and put its crew off on a nearby West Indian island. Left to fend for themselves, the American sailors finally managed to reach a friendly port. Chittenden, determined "never again to leave his plough, to go ploughing on the deep," worked his way back to Connecticut.[125]

Having purged his wanderlust, Chittenden returned to his father's farm. He did not, however, remain there long. By the winter of 1748 he was in Salisbury, Connecticut, where he apparently planned to remain; on January 3, 1749, he registered his mark with the town authorities. From that time on, "a sloping crop off of under side of left ear" would distinguish his animals from those of his Salisbury neighbors.[126] In the fall of 1750 Tom returned to East Guilford and married Elizabeth Meigs, the daughter of one of the Chittendens' longtime neighbors. The couple took up residence in Salisbury.[127] Tom's honesty and industriousness must have favorably impressed the townspeople, because in December 1749 they elected the nineteen-year-old newcomer to the position of lister.[128] Tom's father too was impressed with the way his son had begun to make his own way. In April 1750 he traveled to Salisbury, where he bought a portion of a lot containing a small frame house and a barn. He let Tom and Elizabeth move into the house, and when Tom turned twenty-one, his father, "in consideration of Love, Goodwill and Affection to my loving Son Thomas Chittenden for and towards his advancement in the world, accounting it to the value of 550 pounds Old Tenor toward his part of my estate," deeded the property to the young man.[129]

The house was comfortable. Elizabeth tended the garden and orchard that came with their house lot, and Tom began to work for neighboring farmers in order to earn enough money to purchase his own farmland. Since both husband and wife had been raised in simple, hardworking families, the frugality required to save enough money to buy land came naturally to them. Their efforts soon brought results. In February 1754 Tom purchased ten acres of excellent land, and in December of that year he acquired 210 additional acres.[130] The following year he bought a town lot adjacent to his own and two more portions of land totaling nearly one hundred acres.[131] This land, together with the income from Tom's diligent labor in his fields, qualified him to be sworn in as a freeman of the town in April 1756.[132]

Over the next several years Chittenden managed to acquire additional pieces of property.[133] Whenever he bought or sold land during this period, he did so with the intent of creating a single farm large enough to generate an ample income. He succeeded. In 1756 he ranked near the middle of the Salisbury Grand List.[134] Five years later he ranked second out of more than two hundred individuals who appeared on the rate list.[135] Unlike the original proprietors of the town, who had made a great deal of money simply through the sale of property that had been granted to them, or others who had garnered large profits through the shrewd purchase and sale of land, Chittenden earned his income exclusively from farming.[136] Arduous physical labor, rather than shrewd speculation, propelled his success.

Chittenden's neighbors recognized and respected him for such diligence and hard work. In 1750, even before he had turned twenty-one or been made a freeman of the town, the residents of Salisbury elected him to be a surveyor of highways.[137] Six years later they elected him a constable and collector of the tax rate for the north end of the town. Over the ensuing six years they called him to this position annually and made him collector for any special rates they enacted.[138] Clearly, the residents of Salisbury held young Tom Chittenden in high regard.

The respect the men of Salisbury had developed for Chittenden became most apparent in the fall of 1763, when, on October 6, they elected a captain for their militia company.[139] Their experience in the French and Indian War had taught these men lessons about themselves and their society that they would not soon forget. Most of all, their service under British officers — men drawn overwhelmingly from the ruling class and accustomed to life in a stratified society — had filled American volunteers with a bitter hatred for such haughty and authoritarian leaders.[140] They wanted to be led by men of their own choosing, men like themselves whom they knew personally and trusted implicitly. The common citizens who served in the town's militia company wanted to be led by a man they respected; yet this man must be as plain and ordinary as they, a man totally without social pretensions. They chose Tom Chittenden.

The trust and respect manifested by members of the local militia company toward Chittenden were shared by the voters of Salisbury, who elected him one of the town's selectmen in December 1763.[141] Then, in October 1764 they chose him to be one of their representatives to the Connecticut General Assembly.[142] With this election, Chittenden, who had never presumed to be anything beyond a simple, hardworking farmer, simultaneously held the three highest offices the citizens of Salisbury could bestow upon him.

Chittenden's election to the colonial assembly involved him in issues far larger than those with which he dealt as a local selectman. Indeed, he became caught up in tensions affecting all the American colonies at his first session of the Connecticut General Assembly, which met at New Haven on October 11, 1764. Connecticut's colonial agent in London had warned Governor Thomas Fitch as early as March that the British Parliament intended to impose a stamp tax upon the American colonies, and discussion among the delegates at the October meeting centered upon the impending Stamp Act. They immediately took under consideration a report prepared by a committee formed during the previous legislative session to help Governor Fitch articulate the col-

ony's opposition to the proposed tax. These resolutions, which gained
the overwhelming support of the General Assembly, appeared late
in the year in a pamphlet entitled *Reasons Why The British Colonies
in America Should Not Be Charged with Internal Taxes, By Authority of
Parliament Humbly Offered In Consideration In Behalf of the Colony of
Connecticut.*[143]

The resolutions passed by the General Assembly stressed that no
laws could be made or abrogated without the express consent of the
people voiced through their own elected representatives.[144] Connecticut's legislators believed that this constituted the very essence of English freedom. In their minds, English common law supported the same
premise; subjugation to law was voluntary, not forced. Thus, the people
were bound only by those laws to which they had given their consent.
This was not the case with the Stamp Act. And if the people of Connecticut were to be taxed without their consent, "they cannot, indeed, be
said to enjoy even so much as the Shadow of *English* Liberties."[145]

*Reasons Why The British Colonies in America Should Not Be Charged
with Internal Taxes* rested on a belief firmly held not only by members of
the Connecticut General Assembly but also by their counterparts in
other colonial legislatures. The belief that the people pledged their
allegiance to their king in return for his protection of their personal
safety and his preservation of their essential rights undergirded most
colonists' perception of government and society. By the 1760s, however, many colonists had begun to stress the ruler's obligation to protect
his people, rather than their duty to grant him their fealty. If he did not
honor his responsibility to them, if he broke his portion of the covenant, the people were free to question their allegiance to him. If rulers
failed to protect them, the ruled had every right to defend themselves in
whatever way they considered necessary.[146]

Thomas Chittenden was perfectly familiar with the main premises
of the protection-allegiance covenant. His perception of this compact
differed in no essential way from the voluntary, contractual manner in
which members of the the Connecticut militia viewed their service in
the army during the French and Indian War. For Chittenden as for any
colonist involved in raising crops for the market, contracts were, in
addition, a central part of everyday life and thought. Thus, while he had
no familiarity with the writings of John Locke, or any other author
espousing a compact theory of government, Chittenden did have an
excellent intuitive sense of the contractual relations between rulers and

their subjects. In addition, his own essentially democratic inclinations prompted him to support those in Connecticut who were leading the opposition to Parliament's attempts to tax the colonies.

During the fall of 1765 the opponents of the impending stamp tax formed themselves into Sons of Liberty in town after town throughout the colony. These organizations whipped up hostility against the Stamp Act and forced Governor Fitch to call a special session of the legislature to meet on September 19 in order to formulate the colony's response to Parliament's action. The delegates appointed commissioners to attend a special Stamp Act Congress in New York. When the regular session of the assembly met in October the representatives considered the report of their delegation to the Stamp Act Congress and instructed the colony's agent in London to fully support the resolutions of that Congress.[147] The legislature went beyond the resolves of the Stamp Act Congress, which merely emphasized that American citizens had not consented to the passage of the tax, to condemn the Stamp Act as "unprecedented and unconstitutional."[148]

On November 1, 1765, the Stamp Act went into effect despite colonial opposition, and Governor Fitch faced a difficult choice: to take the oath to uphold the law or to side with the opposition in his colony. Fitch's conservative instincts, as well as his respect for authority, caused him to take the oath to support the Stamp Act. He defended his actions in a pamphlet published in Hartford in 1766, *Some reasons which influenced the Governor to take and the Councillors to administer the Oath required by the Act of Parliament, commonly called the Stamp Act; Humbly submitted to the consideration of the public.*[149]

Fitch's submission to the oath and the publication of his pamphlet drove a wedge between conservative and radical elements throughout Connecticut. A contest emerged between the Sons of Liberty, intent upon voting the governor out of office, and conservatives who viewed this effort as an attack upon authority and good order in the colony. Rev. Jonathan Lee assumed the leadership of conservatives in Salisbury. Governor Fitch was, after all, one of the town's original proprietors, and his son Hezekiah lived in Salisbury and worshipped in Lee's church. Beyond that, Lee had, over the years since he came to Salisbury, forged excellent ties with the leaders of the standing order in the colony, and he had become one of the wealthiest and most orthodox Congregational ministers in western Connecticut.[150] This may have been the cause of his being invited to preach the election-day sermon before the colonial assembly on May 8, 1766.

Regardless of the reason he was chosen to preach to the legislature, the Reverend Lee took advantage of the opportunity to exhort his listeners to uphold legally constituted authority. He began by noting that "he who shares in the benefits of civil society and government, is confederate, and bound to obey authority." He claimed that "the authority of God takes place, and good conscience requires us to keep the peace, and submit to proper authority, so long as the design of government is inviolate." Rulers were "ministers of God, for good," and "he that resisteth the power, resists the ordinance of God." Finally, Lee observed that "the singular circumstances of the present day will justify me in observing to you, that the honour and authority of the king, Lords, and Commons, must be upheld by all lawful means."[151]

Lee's efforts failed; the citizens of Connecticut turned Fitch, along with four councilors who supported him, out of office. This resulted largely from the efforts of the Sons of Liberty in towns all over the colony. For their part, Salisbury's most radical whigs participated in a general convention of the Sons of Liberty from the towns of Litchfield County on March 31, 1766. At this meeting they heartily endorsed the resolutions opposing the Stamp Act that had been passed by the General Assembly in October of the previous year. In addition, they supported the exertions of the "Spirit of heaven-born Liberty which has displayed itself among our neighbouring American Colonies." In order to keep up a correspondence with their counterparts in the surrounding colonies, the convention elected a county correspondence committee composed of the most dedicated leaders of the Sons of Liberty.[152]

Tom Chittenden, Salisbury's member of the county committee of correspondence, assumed an increasingly prominent stature within the town as a result of this upsurge in popular participation in politics.[153] His fellow townspeople elected him both a selectman and a representative to the General Assembly for 1766, and over the next eight years they elected him to five additional terms in the colonial legislature and twice more to the town's board of selectmen.[154] When the General Assembly restructured the colony's militia in 1767, its members appointed "Thomas Chittenden, Esqr." to the rank of major of the Fourteenth Regiment.[155] Three years later the legislature made him a lieutenant colonel.[156] In 1772 and again in 1773 the General Assembly selected Chittenden to be a justice of the peace in Litchfield County.[157] With this appointment, he achieved all the influence and prestige generally associated with members of the gentry. Still, even though the colonial legislature accorded him the title "Esquire," Chittenden remained very much a man of the people, a leader with an extraordinary bond with the common, ordinary citizen. He never forgot his simple origins.

In addition to the prominent offices that he filled, Chittenden had achieved both economic success and personal happiness in Salisbury. His farm brought in a solid income, his family now included four sons and six daughters, and he had been able to build one of the largest two-story brick homes in Salisbury. Still, he was not sanguine about prospects for him and his family if they remained in Salisbury. Gloomy economic conditions descended upon Connecticut, conditions that may well have heightened the reactions within the colony to British taxation. As early as 1762 and 1763 there were widespread reports of farmers losing their lands because of an inability to pay their debts and merchants experiencing difficulty meeting the demands of their creditors. The colony's leading newspaper, the *Connecticut Courant*, reported in December 1764 that "Merchants and farmers are breaking: and all things going into confusion."[158] Land values also fell into a steady decline.[159]

By 1765 the economic outlook appeared even worse. In March the *Courant* reported that "the present state of this colony affords a melancholy aspect: foreign trade embarrassed, our private debts many, and the cries of the needy continually increasing."[160] Two months later the same newspaper reflected even deeper gloom: "Take it for granted, there is not one of your readers, but has heard that most melancholly sentence, repeated times without number, THERE IS NO MONEY; nor scarce he, who has not himself frequently joined in this epidemic complaint."[161] Shortly after the passage of the Stamp Act, even Governor Fitch described Connecticut as being "at a very low Ebb through the Poverty of the People the great Scarcity of Money etc."[162]

Conditions appeared to worsen as the decade wore on. Connecticut courts were overwhelmed with debt litigation. Moreover, Chittenden and his colleagues in the General Assembly found themselves forced to devote increasing time to petitions from private citizens asking for relief. Chittenden and the other Salisbury representatives even had to petition the assembly to avoid being held responsible for debts incurred when Jonathan Chipman defaulted as collector of the colony's tax in Salisbury.[163]

Hard times, the shortage of good farmland for his sons when they reached maturity, and the availability of seemingly boundless tracts of land and opportunity on the Grants all began to weigh heavily on

Chittenden's mind. His long acquaintance with Heman Allen, as both a
neighbor and a storekeeper in Salisbury, may have been the deciding
factor in influencing him to investigate land along the Onion River.
Accompanied by Ira Allen, he picked out a beautiful tract in the spring
of 1773. Upon his return from the Grants, Chittenden and his neighbor Jonathan Spafford accepted a bond in the amount of two thousand
pounds from Heman and Ethan Allen pledging these partners in the
Onion River Land Company to deliver each man a deed for six hundred
acres in Williston Township. The Allens assured Chittenden and Spafford "the same right to the said different pieces of land as the grantees
under New Hampshire originally had." On that same day, Chittenden,
Spafford, and another Salisbury neighbor, Abijah Pratt, gave their own
bond in the amount of five hundred pounds, which pledged them to
clear and improve the land they had just purchased.[164] After this, Chittenden and his family made preparations to move to their wilderness
property.

In May 1774 they all set out for the Onion River. Since no provision
had been made in advance for constructing a shelter on the land, the
Chittendens began their new life on the Grants cooking over an open
fire and sleeping under a lean-to constructed of freshly cut logs covered
with bark and hemlock boughs.[165]

AN ACT TO SUSPEND PROSECUTIONS AGAINST ISAAC TICHENOR ESQR;
COMMISSARY OF PURCHASES, FOR PUBLIC PURPOSES, UNTIL
THE RISING OF THE ASSEMBLY IN OCTOBER NEXT

June 27, 1781

*Whereas, it is made to appear, by sufficient Evidence, that there is due to Isaac
Tichenor Esqr:, late Commissary of Purchases, for the States of New Hampshire and
Vermont, and his Agents, for Public Purchases, the Sum of sixty five thousand one
hundred and eighty four Pounds nine Shillings and five Pence, Continental Money,
and one thousand three hundred and twenty four Pounds fourteen Shillings and two
Pence, in specie value; and that he hath taken due pains to procure the said Monies
from the public, but hath hitherto been unable to obtain the same. And Whereas,
the said Tichenor, and his Agents under him, have given their private notes of hand
to the several persons of whom they respectively have purchased, for the public; And
that said Tichenor and his Agents are in danger of being entirely ruined, if Actions
should be brought and supported on the notes before mentioned. Which to prevent,*

*Be it enacted, and it is hereby enacted, by the Representatives of the freemen of
the State of Vermont, in General Assembly met, and by the Authority of the same,
that all and every Action already commenced against said Tichenor and his Agents*

for public Purchases, by him or them made, shall be stayed until the rising of the next General Assembly in October next.

And that no Actions shall be supported, that may be commenced against said Tichenor, or his agents, for Purchases made in behalf of the Public, until the rising of the next Sessions of the General Assembly, in October next.

Provided nevertheless, *that if the said Tichenor shall receive the public Monies due him as aforesaid, before the rising of the General Assembly in October next; then it shall and may be lawful for every person, to bring his or their Action against said Tichenor, on the Notes aforesaid; Anything in this Act to the contrary notwithstanding.*[166]

More than a year after the Vermont General Assembly intervened to protect Isaac Tichenor from prosecutions for indebtedness he still had not been reimbursed by the Continental government. Fortunately for him, the courts in Vermont continued to shield him from his creditors. The same was not true, however, in New Hampshire, where if Tichenor did not personally reimburse the public creditors who relentlessly dunned him, he faced the prospect of "being committed to Goal as a common debtor."[167] To escape this unhappy predicament, Tichenor requested help from the central government. In response to his plea, the Continental Congress interceded on his behalf with the New Hampshire state legislature; as a result he managed to avoid imprisonment for debt as well as personal impoverishment.[168] Either of these would have been unbearable to Tichenor, who by the age of twenty-seven had managed to attain a measure of wealth and gentility far beyond what would have been possible for him in his native New Jersey. The state legislature there would certainly never have accorded him the honor of being addressed as "esquire."

Tichenor's roots in New Jersey consisted of solid yeoman stock. His great-grandfather Martin had migrated from France to Connecticut, where he took the freeman's oath in New Haven in August 1644. Seven years later he wed Mary Charles, who bore him five children.[169] In the summer of 1666 the Tichenors migrated with other families from Connecticut to the new settlement of Newark in the colony of New Jersey. At the time of his death in 1681 Martin Tichenor possessed an estate valued at £230.[170] Having taken part in every division of land since 1667, he had amassed enough property to place him in the middle rank of Newark farmers.[171] His status in the town never exceeded that position; Tichenor's fellow townsmen never called him to any office greater than hayward, a position he held only once, in 1673.[172]

Despite his lack of participation in town government, Tichenor maintained a comfortable position within the middling range of Newark yeomen and was a respected member of the church. This was not true of his descendants. His son Daniel refused to pledge support for the pastor in 1687, when the town substituted voluntary contributions for the mandatory rate that had previously fallen upon all residents.[173] Daniel's refusal may have resulted from a lack of religious fervor or from difficult economic circumstances. In any event, due to the practice of partible inheritance and the shrinking supply of arable land, each succeeding generation of Tichenors found it more difficult to acquire sufficient property to support their families comfortably. Consequently, Martin's son Daniel and his grandson of the same name experienced a loss of status in the township. The elder Daniel appeared in the town record only once, when residents asked him to look after boys and girls who misbehaved during church service.[174] The town also called on the younger Daniel but a single time, when it asked him to serve on a committee to establish the boundaries of a meadow lying within the town.[175] By the time the second Daniel created his will in 1759, he could only bequeath land to his two eldest sons. His daughters and younger sons, including Isaac, received only cash.[176]

Even though the Tichenor family had experienced a relative social decline, its members were fortunate compared with many residents in New Jersey. During the eighteenth century there was a pattern of declining landholding and increasing tenancy throughout the colony.[177] By mid-century a third of all adult white males held property of marginal or insufficient size to support their families; another third held no land at all. This created serious tensions between large proprietors and those desirous of acquiring land. Riots broke out during the 1740s as landless "clubmen" attempted to gain title to disputed tracts of land. Nowhere were there as many disturbances of this nature, nor as many participants in them, as in Newark. A tremendous antipathy arose against both the landed proprietors who monopolized the available land and lawyers and judges who represented their interests. In January 1770 more than a hundred armed Liberty Boys marched into Newark to block the opening of the county court and thereby prevent cases of individuals who had forcibly attempted to acquire land in the western portion of Newark Township from coming to trial. Local authorities managed to disburse the mob and establish order within the town. Arsonists, however, burned the barn and other outbuildings on the rural property of one of the county judges. This incident, as well as the riotous behavior that took place in Newark, greatly intensified the animosity toward both the legal profession and large landowners throughout the township.[178]

Neither Daniel Tichenor nor his eldest sons, Aaron and Daniel, appeared in records relating to these land riots. Holding their land free and clear, they were not likely to support the actions of the Liberty Boys. Daniel's third son, Isaac, exhibited no sympathies for those opposed to established authority. Anxious to join the ranks of the gentlemen who represented that authority, Isaac meant to attend the College of New Jersey in nearby Princeton. In September 1771 he gained admission by passing an entrance examination requiring him to "render Virgil and Tully's orations into English and to turn English into true and grammatical Latin, and to be so well acquainted with the Greek, as to render any part of the Four Evangelists in that language into Latin or English." In addition, he had to prove himself "acquainted with vulgar arithmetic as well as spelling the English language, and writing it without grammatical errors."[179] He paid his tuition and living costs for the first quarter and moved into Nassau Hall with the rest of the student body. It is likely that in order to afford tuition and room and board, which amounted to more than £25 per year, Isaac drew in advance upon an inheritance of £250 established in the will his father had registered in 1759.[180] Four years of college would strain this amount to the limit.

By the time Isaac entered Princeton, John Witherspoon, embarking upon his fourth year as president of the college, had worked great changes in the school's curriculum.[181] An advocate of the Scottish Enlightenment, he committed the college to a system of instruction grounded in the Common Sense philosophy of Francis Hutcheson. By advancing this new moral philosophy, Witherspoon broke away from the theological orientation associated with Jonathan Edwards, a former president of the college. Virtue became a subject for scientific inquiry rather than the result of divine grace. No longer did Witherspoon presuppose revelation to be the foundation for all knowledge; instead, he demonstrated the validity of revelation through the tenets of reason and science.

Graduates of Princeton left the college imbued not only with Witherspoon's intellectual concepts but with a distinctive set of social values as well. The trustees of the college expected graduates to become habituated "to subjection, and yet maintain their respective ranks without insolence or servility." In addition, they desired them "to cherish a sense of honour, without self-sufficiency and arrogance." Beyond that, the college should "inspire [its students] with such principles, and form them to such a conduct, as will prepare for sustaining more extensive connections, with the grand community of mankind."[182] In short, Princeton should shape its students to become gentlemen, men who understood that hierarchy constituted the cement that held a society together and that each place in the social hierarchy carried with it certain unquestioned obligations and responsibilities to ranks above and below.

Life for students at Princeton was not restricted to the confines of Nassau Hall. The extracurricular activities for most students centered around the Cliosophic Society and the American Whig Society. These two literary clubs, emphasizing forensic skills, became the focus for informal student discussions and camaraderie. Upon entering Princeton, Isaac Tichenor joined the Cliosophic Society, through which he became closely acquainted with the sons of prominent New York families such as the Livingstons, the Van Cortlands, and the Morrisses.[183] Of all the people with whom Tichenor came into contact within the Cliosophic Society, though, the man who exerted the most influence upon him was William Paterson. This aggressively ambitious lawyer had been a founding member of the Well-Meaning Club, which became the Cliosophic Society in 1770. Paterson frequently attended meetings of the Clios throughout the 1770s and served much like an adviser to its members. He brought to that society a wealth of business acumen as well as cosmopolitan professional contacts. Early in 1775 he made a presentation entitled "Address on the Rise and Decline of Nations" to a meeting of the Clios. In this address he alerted his listeners to the terrible threats posed to civil society by political corruption, tyrannical government, and moral decay.[184]

Paterson's audience had little difficulty identifying the opposing forces of liberty and tyranny in his address: the American colonies represented a liberty-loving people, while George III and the British Parliament stood for political corruption and decay. By this time students at Princeton had become thoroughly politicized. In fact, a year earlier, to demonstrate their sympathy for the perpetrators of the Boston Tea Party, a band of students had burned the college steward's entire store of winter tea while others tolled the college bell. Then they had proceeded to burn an effigy of Governor Thomas Hutchinson of Massachusetts, complete with a canister of tea tied about its neck.[185]

Following the battles of Lexington and Concord in April 1775, martial fervor spread through Princeton. During the graduation ceremo-

nies of September 27, 1775, Isaac Tichenor and his colleagues dressed
in homespun clothing to show their support for the position of resistance taken by the Continental Congress. Even before these commencement ceremonies took place, New Jersey officials prepared the
colony in accord with the plans for an American army promulgated by
the Continental Congress on June 17. The colonial legislature passed
an ordinance requiring every able-bodied male between the ages of
sixteen and fifty to join the state militia or pay a personal exemption fee
of four shillings a month.[186] Vast numbers of New Jersey men responded to this call. Isaac Tichenor's older brother Daniel became a
lieutenant in the militia, while his younger brother David acquired the
same rank in the Second Essex Regiment. Nearly a dozen of his cousins
enlisted in the militia as well.[187] As for Isaac, immediately after the
graduation ceremonies he left the colony and proceeded to Schenec-
tady, New York. There, either through the intervention of William
Paterson or the auspices of families such as the Van Cortlands or the
Livingstons, arrangements had been made for him to study law.

     Following his arrival in Schenectady, Tichenor earned a living by
teaching in the grammar school of Rev. Alexander Miller, a Princeton graduate and pastor of the town's First Presbyterian Church.[188] He
also became involved with an influential group of lawyers, land speculators, and merchants in the Albany-Schenectady area that included
Philip Schuyler, Christopher Yates, Jacob Cuyler, Robert Van Rensselaer, Peter R. Livingston, and Pierre Van Cortland. Several of these
men arranged for Isaac to serve as clerk and to keep the poll at an
important election of militia officers involving one of their key associates.[189] At the same time Isaac studied law under the auspices of these
same individuals.

     With the outbreak of the Revolution, this powerful coterie hoped to
be able to take advantage of the lucrative opportunities arising from the
vast demand for food and other materials made by the army operating in
their region.[190] After Philip Schuyler became commanding general of
the Northern Department, the entrepreneurial possibilities appeared
boundless. At first Schuyler served as his own quartermaster. He sold the
army great amounts of lumber and flour from his mills as well as other
material from his general store. In addition, he spread this governmental
largess among the Van Rensselaers, the Livingstons, and the Cuylers.
When Congress appointed Walter Livingston, Schuyler's nephew-in-
law, deputy commissary for the Northern Army, little changed. Lucrative contracts for army supplies continued to pass through the hands of

friends and relatives of Schuyler and Livingston. Indeed, Livingston himself received a contract to supply pork rations to the Northern Army that netted him a 700 percent profit.[191]

It was not long before complaints about such behavior began to appear throughout the states. Newspapers in all parts of the nation condemned commissary and quartermaster departments as "a herd of monopolizing, extortionate and peculating traders," as "those greasy, money-making fellows," and as "harpies which have preyed upon our vitals." Indeed, one Pennsylvania official referred to them as the "Common Enemy."[192] Problems within the procurement system that gave rise to such condemnation resulted more often than not from the manner in which the government paid its commissary agents. Each agent received a commission on every purchase that he made. Consequently, the higher the price he paid for the goods, the higher his commission. In light of these circumstances, Roger Sherman, a Connecticut congressman, could only observe that the commission system represented "such a temptation as an honest man would not wish to be led into."[193]

In the summer of 1777 the Continental Congress reorganized the procurement system. Joseph Trumbull became the commissary of purchases for all the Continental armies. He promptly removed William Livingston from his position as deputy commissary for the Northern Army, but after a bitter struggle within Congress James Duane, Livingston's brother-in-law and a close business associate of the Schuyler-Livingston group, managed to have Jacob Cuyler named deputy commissary of purchases in the Northern Department. Commissary Trumbull knew exactly what was at stake in the battle between New York and New England for control of this position. A year earlier he had accurately observed that "General Schuyler is willing to let anybody fight the battles that will under him, but let him command the chest, the commissary and quartermaster departments and he is pleased."[194] Schuyler and his associates realized full well the economic power wielded by the purchasing commissary and remained adamant that a member of their group should always fill this position.

Among Jacob Cuyler's first acts as deputy commissary of purchasing for the Northern Department was the appointment of Isaac Tichenor to one of the lucrative assistant deputy positions under him. The geographical area for which Tichenor was responsible included northwestern Massachusetts, the New Hampshire Grants, and western portions of New Hampshire. He was free to name his own assistants.[195] Officials within the commissary department naturally assumed that

Tichenor's position offered him the opportunity to reap large personal profits.[196]

Upon first taking up his duties as Cuyler's assistant, Tichenor operated primarily out of Williamstown, Massachusetts. He depended in large part upon Stephen Hopkins of Bennington to supply him with cattle, although Tichenor himself often supervised the movement of these cattle to Albany, where they could be apportioned to troops in the area.[197] He appointed Major Jonathan Childs to supervise purchasing in the eastern portion of the Grants and western New Hampshire, but here too Tichenor made personal trips whenever necessary. Hundreds of thousands of dollars passed through his hands, and he made a great many purchases on the strength of his own credit. At one point he owed upwards of one hundred thousand dollars in personal debt to citizens of New Hampshire.[198]

In the course of his activities as a purchasing agent Tichenor made numerous enemies, among them individuals desiring government contracts with whom Tichenor refused to deal; contractors unhappy with the prices they received; citizens who suspected Tichenor of profiteering at the expense of the war effort; and military officers convinced that he shirked his duties at the expense of their troops. As a result of one officer's accusations, Tichenor stood trial before a court-martial in Springfield, Massachusetts, in April 1780. Col. Moses Hazen accused him of dereliction of duty and "a Misapplication of the Public Money."[199] Tichenor considered the trial, which lasted over six weeks, beneath his dignity as a gentleman; from his perspective, "the greatest part of the time was spent in personal altercations and Reflections before the Court, which reflected little honor upon their Dignity, and established Hazen's indefatigable Baseness as a Prosecutor."[200] The court cleared Tichenor of all charges but recommended that he receive a reprimand from General Washington for failing to make every effort to supply the troops in his area with rum. Convinced that Tichenor had done everything in his power in this regard, Washington refused to comply with the recommendation.[201]

With the passage of time, Tichenor involved himself less with his duties as assistant deputy commissary and more with personal business affairs of quite a different nature. He also moved his base of operations to Bennington, where he joined several prominent local citizens in petitioning the Vermont General Assembly for large grants of land.[202] Soon after that he began to practice law in Bennington, and in March 1781 the freeholders of the town elected him clerk of their annual town meeting.[203] In August of that same year members of a local militia company elected him their captain.[204] The following month Bennington's freeholders chose Tichenor and Samuel Safford to represent them in the Vermont General Assembly, which soon thereafter appointed Tichenor a justice of the peace in Bennington.[205]

Within a short space of time after his arrival in their town the citizens of Bennington had bestowed tremendous status and prestige upon Tichenor. As a trained attorney and a man of affluence, gentility, education, and cosmopolitan connections throughout the new nation, Tichenor appeared to be an invaluable addition to the town. For his part, Isaac Tichenor, Esquire, fully intended to link his future with that of Bennington, a town that was rapidly becoming the political center of an expansive and potentially prosperous new region of the nation.

. . . yet this is a fine country for those who can plough and dig; but even they must take care to avoid the harpies who await their landing, and must immediately dash into the country. The members of the society for the abolition of slavery have not the least objection to buying an Irishman or Dutchman, and will chaffer with himself or the captain to get him indented at about the eighth part of the wages they would have to pay a country born. *But to tell the truth, they who are purchased generally do themselves justice, and run away before half their time is up.*[206]

With this observation, Archibald Hamilton Rowan, an Irish gentleman visiting America, quite unwittingly described nearly the exact circumstances under which Matthew Lyon, a fellow Irishman, arrived in New York in 1765. The only difference between Rowan's categorical statements and Lyon's personal experience was that Lyon suffered exploitation at the hands of a "harpy" even before he came ashore. In this case the captain of a ship bound for New York lured Lyon aboard by promising the fifteen-year-old boy that he could pay for his passage after earning sufficient money in America. Rather than keeping his word, however, the captain sold the lad as a redemptioner once the ship docked in New York.[207] The captain's actions gave credence to another of Rowan's observations: "Swarms of Irish are expected here by the spring vessels, and the brisk trade for *Irish Slaves* here is to make up for the low prices of flax-seed!"[208]

Being treated as an "Irish slave" infuriated Lyon; still, to be an indentured servant in America held out more promise for the ambitious youth than did life in Ireland. Born on July 14, 1750, in County Wicklow, Lyon had had a relatively pleasant early life.[209] His father, a Protestant tenant, held enough land on favorable terms to be able to place the boy in a school in Dublin, where he learned the rudiments of Greek and Latin.[210] His life changed abruptly, however, when the White Boy uprisings swept over southern and central Ireland in the early 1760s.[211]

Conditions for tenants, whether Protestant or Catholic, had always been difficult in Ireland. Rents paid to absentee landlords were burdensome, as were the tithes on the land paid to support the Catholic Church. The fact that many landlords permitted their tenants the free use of vacant and often swampy property — long considered common land by most peasants — was the only solace for many hard-pressed families. This allowed them to maintain at least a marginal existence; it also meant that they could remain on the land. The few tenants that held good land under equitables lease led reasonably comfortable lives; they might even hope to prosper. Whatever chance any tenants had for prosperity had grown increasingly dim, however, by the late 1750s. In 1758 and 1759 the British Parliament suspended the Cattle Acts, thus opening the English market for Irish beef, cheese, and butter. This, combined with a severe epidemic that decimated whole herds of cattle in England, created a tremendous demand for Irish beef and dairy products. Landlords throughout Ireland began to convert as much of their land as possible into pasturage in order to support more cattle. It was not long before they evicted those families and individuals holding tenuous leases, raised the rents of others in an attempt to force them off the land, and enclosed and drained common lands in a desperate attempt to gain more pasture land. To make matters worse for the tenants, Irish law exempted pasture land from church tithes. Consequently, the burden of supporting the church fell even more heavily on tenants, who had no choice but to keep their land under tillage, and thus subject to the tithe, in order to feed their families.

Of all the actions taken by the landlords, it was their enclosure of lands traditionally considered to be commons that caused the most anguish among their tenants. Free use of these areas had been a godsend to the poor. It had allowed them to supplement their meager subsistence in a number of important ways: they could dig peat for fuel, graze milk cows, or till small garden plots. Without access to such property, those families already living barely a minimal existence could not remain on their farms, while others, facing higher rents each year and desperate to find additional sources of support, were rapidly sinking toward a precarious condition themselves. Beginning in 1761 tenants in southern Ireland struck back using the only means they knew: violent protest.

Those who had been dispossessed of their land banded together with others who faced a similar fate, took secret oaths pledging themselves to mutual support and protection, and began to make night raids on the vast tracts of grazing land held by wealthy proprietors, dubbed "land pirates" by the insurgents.[212] Wearing white shirts over their clothing in order to be readily identified by their compatriots, these men destroyed the ditches and leveled the mounds of earth created by the landlords in their attempts to enclose the common lands. At first termed "levellers" by the authorities, these bands of men soon became more commonly known as "White Boys."

The White Boys were neither religiously nor politically inspired; they simply wanted to protect their livelihood and to avoid being forced off land their families had occupied for generations. An English lord familiar with circumstances in Ireland claimed that the outbreaks of violence resulted from "exorbitant rents, low wages, want of employment, farms of enormous extent let by their rapacious and indolent proprietors to monopolising land-jobbers, by whom small portions of them were again let and re-let to intermediate oppressors and by them subdivided for five times their value among the wretched starvers upon potatoes and water." In his mind, "misery, oppression, and famine" succinctly explained the White Boy insurgency.[213]

An anonymous pamphleteer who described the tensions between landlord and tenant resulting in violence in Munster claimed that "the law indeed, is open to redress [the White Boys]; but they do not know the laws or how to proceed; or if they did know them they are not equal to the expense of a suit against a rich tyrant." The same writer noted one other important fact: "the greatest part of these tenures are by verbal agreement, not written compact."[214] This author's final observation described the circumstances of men like Matthew Lyon's father, men who might be relatively prosperous tenants but did not hold a written lease that protected their tenure on the land. Thus, in a desperate attempt to retain a claim to his farm, Lyon's father joined the White Boy movement in his native Wicklow. Unlike most insurgents, though, he paid the ultimate price for his actions; he was captured and executed by the authorities.[215]

In 1763 Matthew's mother moved to Dublin, where she faced difficult times. Unable to keep her son in school, she was forced to apprentice him to a newspaper printer's shop to learn publishing and book-binding.[216] At nearly this same time a new biweekly newspaper began publication in Dublin. This paper, the *Freeman's Journal*, exerted a tremendous influence on Matthew and other young Irish boys in similar circumstances.[217] In the first years of its existence the *Freeman's Journal* was the vehicle by which Charles Lucas — ardent Irish nationalist, outspoken egalitarian reformer, and passionate supporter of Protestant causes in Ireland — broadcast his opinions.[218] Lucas, who at one time had been disfranchised and banished from Ireland for criticizing corruption within the Irish Parliament and agitating for that body's independence from English control, used the *Journal* to attack the oligarchic nature of Irish government and society and the restrictions imposed upon Irish self-government by the English Parliament. His clarion call, as well as that of others writing in the *Journal*, was to "openly declare ourselves the enemies of all tyranny, and of all sorts of tyrants, whether single or Hydras — the one or many-headed monster."[219] Lucas and others writing in the *Journal* singled out Ireland's prominent attorneys as the country's foremost "tyrants" and viciously attacked them for their corruption and venality. In the minds of these radical journalists, highly placed attorneys neither championed liberty nor protected the people. Instead, they formed the central bulwark in an Irish legal system that allowed the upper classes to exploit the peasants. These attorneys treated any White Boys brought to trial as dangerous threats to society and good order rather than as representatives of an oppressed underclass. In the eyes of Lucas and his followers, these representatives of the English judicial system exacerbated rather than ameliorated the injustices afflicting Ireland.

The rhetoric of Lucas and the *Journal* inflamed youths like Matthew Lyon against the corruption of the English and Irish Parliaments, the decadence of aggrandizing landlords, and the tyrannical and unfeeling upper classes in both England and Ireland. Matthew had personally experienced tyranny and corruption; he had seen his father lose his land and then his life to powerful landlords and the British legal and political authorities that supported them.[220] And he could see that someone of his lowly rank in society, no matter how talented or hardworking, faced tremendous social and political obstacles if he tried to rise above the class into which he had been born. It was no wonder, then, that Matthew, at the age of fifteen, fled his apprenticeship and turned his back on Ireland.

The trip to America strengthened the egalitarian instincts that he had acquired as a youth. It also fueled his burning hatred of what he considered to be corrupt authority. Shortly after his ship sailed, Matthew became violently ill and lay in a feverish state for many days. Upon regaining his senses he discovered that, except for a group of "fallen women" who had nursed him through his illness, he had been deserted by his fellow passengers. These women shared what little clothing they had with him when he discovered that he had been robbed of all of his belongings while delirious with fever. This simple act of kindness by women who had so few possession of their own touched Matthew deeply.[221] It helped instill in him a heightened, ofttimes frenzied sensitivity to anyone claiming pretensions to "high blood." He bridled at any suggestion of superiority on the part of other individuals; his immediate response to such people was that "he thought he had as *good blood* as any of them, as he was born of a fine, hale, healthy woman." Then, more belligerently, he might add that he made this claim even though he "could not say, it was true, that he was descended from the bastards of Oliver Cromwell, or his courtiers, or from the Puritans, who punished their horses for breaking the Sabbath, or from those who persecuted the Quakers or hanged the witches."[222]

Because of his experiences in Ireland and aboard ship, Matthew arrived in New York seething with indignation against the affectations of gentlemen; he harbored an intense desire to show up the sort of people who shunned him during and after his illness, to prove himself as good as or better than they. In addition, he particularly resented the captain, for it was just after the ship docked that this man betrayed him. When it came time to disembark, the captain — the gentleman, the authority figure whom Matthew had trusted — grouped Matthew with those individuals who had been unable to pay their own passage and sold them all as redemptioners. This action, following closely upon the acts of oppression the young boy had recently witnessed in Ireland, embedded in his mind an enduring hatred for the duplicitous and self-serving behavior that could be practiced by those in positions of trust and responsibility. It helped ingrain within him a zealous advocacy of fair treatment for common, ordinary individuals that he had difficulty keeping within reasonable bounds. A close friend, keenly aware of Lyon's personal strengths and weaknesses, claimed that his "leading trait of character was his zeal and enthusiasm, almost to madness itself, in any cause he espoused." He "never seemed to act coolly and deliberately, but always in a tumult and bustle — as if he were in a house on fire and was hurrying to get out." His friend fondly affirmed that, despite all this, Lyon's "Irish impulses were honest, and always on the side of human freedom."[223]

Jabez Bacon, a prosperous merchant from the town of Woodbury in Litchfield County, Connecticut, was the first American to experience Matthew Lyon's "Irish impulses." In New York City on business when Matthew's ship arrived, Bacon purchased the young Irishman's indenture. Several days later he brought his newly acquired servant back to Woodbury and put him to work in a thriving trade in pork that he carried on with merchants in New York City. Housed in a shack behind the "Red Store in the Hollow" that served as the hub for Bacon's business, Matthew helped tend the pigs that Bacon accepted from farmers who traded at his store. He also helped his master slaughter these animals and pack and transport the meat to New York City.[224]

Tempestuous as any master-servant relationship involving a youth with such an explosive temperament, Lyon's service under Bacon was also a genuine learning experience for him. Having left Ireland determined to achieve social and economic success in America, he could not have had a better teacher than Jabez Bacon, who was one of the wealthiest and most astute merchants in Litchfield County. Even in New York City Bacon enjoyed a reputation for being an extremely shrewd businessman because of his willingness to take calculated risks in order to turn huge profits. Such entrepreneurial tactics were not lost on young Lyon; he absorbed as much of Bacon's business acumen as he could. Nonetheless, even though it might have been to his advantage to remain with Bacon, Matthew became intractable, and the Woodbury merchant began to search for someone who would buy his servant's indenture.[225]

The tensions that developed between Bacon and Lyon mirrored those that were emerging throughout Connecticut. At the time that Bacon purchased Matthew's indenture, Litchfield County, like most of Connecticut, was embroiled in the Stamp Act controversy. Fiery opponents of this act formed themselves into Sons of Liberty in towns all over the county. Woodbury was no exception. With his insatiable hatred of tyranny and zeal for liberty, Matthew naturally espoused the cause of the local patriots. Bacon, who had business dealings with conservative merchants in New York, remained much more cautious. It was not long before Lyon's zealous temperament became too much for Bacon. He sold Matthew's indenture to Hugh Hannah of Litchfield for a pair of stags. From that moment on, Matthew's constant exclamation was "By the Bulls that redeemed me!"[226]

Lyon may have been redeemed from Bacon, but he still owed several years' service to Hannah. And even though Hannah was an ardent supporter of the Sons of Liberty, his relationship with his servant soon became anything but cordial. The strict, aggressive discipline of the master and the mercurial temperament of the servant was a volatile mixture. In many ways the young Irish boy should have made an excellent servant. He was strong and extremely quick-witted. When Hannah allowed him to attend the district school in Litchfield during the winter months, Matthew excelled in his studies. However, even at school he could not control his explosive temper. Nor would he curb his energetic sense of independence — considered impertinence by most of his superiors — whether at school or at work. Determined to break this rebellious spirit, Hannah beat Matthew with a stout rod at the least provocation. Finally, in a fit of temper, Matthew turned on his master, threw a wooden mallet at his head, and ran away.[227]

After escaping from the bondage of his master in Litchfield, Matthew went to work in the iron forges in Salisbury.[228] He received steady wages and by June 1772 had saved enough money to purchase one hundred acres of land in Cornwall, Connecticut.[229] Always seeking the main chance and willing to take risks if necessary, Lyon then participated in a drawing held by the proprietors of Wallingford Township in February 1773. These men, intent upon meeting the stipulations of the grant they had received from the governor of New Hampshire — to establish actual settlers on their grant — divided their town into one-hundred-acre lots, allowed potential settlers to draw for those lots, and then sold them to these individuals at quite modest prices. Lyon returned to Cornwall the owner of another one hundred acres of land.[230] A short time later, perhaps desirous of acquiring additional money to invest on the Grants, he sold his property in Cornwall.[231]

In June 1773 Lyon took another important step in his life; he married Mary Horsford of Cornwall, a distant relative of Ethan Allen and the daughter of a woman every bit as impatient with authority as he. In the case of Mary's mother the object of suspicion was the local Congregational church. In March 1764 the town authorities of Cornwall discharged the widowed mothers of both Ethan Allen and Mary Horsford from the Congregational church to the "dissenting collector" of the Episcopalian church.[232] With his deep-seated suspicion of established authority, Matthew Lyon certainly made a sympathetic son-in-law for the Widow Horsford.

While in Cornwall Matthew also came into regular contact with the

Allen brothers and Remember Baker, a native of nearby Woodbury. These men continually traveled about Litchfield County during the time Lyon and his new bride lived there. In fact, as partners in the Onion River Land Company, they persistently tried to persuade individuals and families in Connecticut and Massachusetts to purchase land on the Grants and to immigrate to the region. Any one of them could have influenced the young couple to move to the grants. Or the Lyons might have made this decision entirely on their own. Given Matthew's determined resolve to better himself, to achieve economic success however possible, a move to the Grants made perfect sense. This newly settled area held out far greater promise for social and economic advancement than did the more settled region of western Connecticut. In addition, the Grants had neither a religious establishment nor an entrenched landed gentry with which to contend. A man with aggressive social and economic ambitions could do well in such an environment. Even better, Matthew's democratic egalitarianism might prove to be an asset rather than a liability in such a fluid frontier region.

Having made their decision, Matthew and Mary moved to Wallingford in the summer of 1773. In January 1774 Matthew purchased an additional ninety acres of land in that town.[233] The young democrat had clearly decided to stake his future on the Grants. Here he could anticipate achieving the success denied him in a class-structured society such as Ireland. Resolutely committed to an open, egalitarian society, he was determined never again to be subjected to the kind of hierarchical society that he had left behind in Europe. He meant to prove himself the equal of any man and did not intend to allow any individual or group of individuals, no matter what their social position, to stand in his way.

5. Independence

Shortly after his arrival on the Grants, Matthew Lyon set about organizing a company of Green Mountain Boys. He and other "young-erly men" in his neighborhood armed and clothed themselves "uni-formly." They "hired an old veteran to teach us discipline, and we each of us took command in turn, so that every one should know the duty of every station."[1] Lyon soon had the opportunity to employ whatever military techniques he had managed to learn. Indeed, the clash between British regulars and colonial militia at Lexington and Concord, Massachusetts, on April 19, 1775, prompted all the American colonies to ready themselves for battle.

At the time of this alarm civil authority on the Grants rested in the hands of a grand committee created by a convention that met in Manchester on January 31, 1775.[2] Made up of the committees of safety from twenty-five towns, this convention created a temporary compact in order to maintain good order in the region until the king settled the dispute between the Grants and the royal government of New York. This compact empowered the delegates to "make such just and equal Rules, Injunctions, Constitution and officers as are judged necessary and expedient, for the best Good of the Inhabitants of this District." It prohibited all those holding New York commissions from filling any office on the Grants but allowed New York sheriffs to enter the Grants under certain specified conditions. They could enforce only those civil laws that did not touch upon disputed land claims and could not apprehend those declared outlaws by the New York legislature. If James Duane or John Tabor Kempe ventured onto the Grants, they were to be captured and escorted to Bennington, where they would be interrogated by "the Elders of the People" and the "principal Officers of the GREEN MOUNTAIN BOYS." Finally, the convention ordered the officers of all companies of the Green Mountain Boys to enforce the various provisions of the compact.[3]

The grand committee, under the leadership of Nathan Clark, assumed responsibility for administering the provisions of the compact once the convention adjourned. As chairman of the committee, Clark desired above all else to protect the land claims of those living on the Grants. At the same time, he wanted to maintain the best possible relations with the provisional government of New York. This became evident subsequent to the affair at Lexington and Concord when he, as a member of the Bennington committee of safety, signed the Albany Association protesting the "avowed design" of the British ministry to raise a revenue in America and expressing alarm at the "bloody scene now acting in the Massachusetts bay." Vowing "never to bee Slaves," Clark and thirty-eight other residents of Bennington pledged to support whatever measures might be recommended by the Continental Congress and the Provincial Congress of New York.[4] Clark also worked strenuously to coordinate the efforts of his own committee with those of the Albany Committee of Correspondence: he attended meetings of the larger group in Albany, kept in constant written contact with its leaders, and served as chairman of the committee of correspondence for the district that included Bennington and the New York towns of Cambridge and Hoosick.[5]

Cooperation with the colonial opposition to British authority was not, however, entirely without problems; in fact, it raised serious questions for the leadership on the Grants. These men had always believed that the king would render a favorable judgment in their controversy with New York. Now they had to consider what course to follow if colonial resistance to the crown became a full-scale rebellion. It was impossible to know what the king's attitude would be toward their land claims if they participated in an unsuccessful revolution against his authority. If, on the other hand, they joined a successful revolt, whatever government emerged in America might look with favor upon their cause.

These issues weighed heavily on their minds when Clark and members of the grand committee met at Bennington shortly after news of Lexington and Concord reached the Grants. In consultation with Ethan Allen and the principal officers of the Green Mountain Boys, they agreed to submerge their grievances against New York in the colonial struggle for liberty.[6] As a result of this decision they welcomed representatives of committees of safety from Connecticut and Massachusetts, who urgently pointed out the need to capture the British forts at Ticonderoga and Crown Point on Lake Champlain if the colonies were to secure their northernmost border. Allen sent out word to his captains to prepare their companies for action. On May 3 Clark's grand committee and a "committee of war" composed of officers of the Connecticut and Massachusetts militia met at Bennington and agreed that Allen should command the force sent to take the British fortresses. Col. James Easton of Pittsfield, Massachusetts, would be second in command, and Seth Warner would assume the third position.[7]

Early the morning of May 10, Allen and eighty-three men completely surprised the garrison at Ticonderoga, captured fifty prisoners, and took control of 120 cannon and a large supply of small arms and additional stores. Two days later Seth Warner's detachment captured the fortress at Crown Point and with it another sixty-one excellent cannon. Early in June a regiment of volunteers from Connecticut arrived at Ticonderoga, and Allen relinquished command of the fort to its colonel. Before leaving Ticonderoga, however, Allen met with a council of Connecticut officers, who recommended that he travel to Philadelphia in order to confer with the Continental Congress about the official status of him and his men. Allen and Warner proceeded to Philadelphia bearing a letter of recommendation from the chairman of the council of officers.[8]

The two men gained all they could have desired at Philadelphia. The Continental Congress agreed to pay the Green Mountain Boys for their service in capturing and garrisoning Ticonderoga and Crown Point; in addition, the Congress recommended that the New York convention, in consultation with Gen. Philip Schuyler, allow the Green Mountain Boys to serve as a New York regiment under officers of their own choice.[9] Two weeks later the New York convention grudgingly acceded to the congressional suggestion and passed a resolution allowing the Green Mountain Boys to form a regiment and to elect all their own officers except those of field grade. They could recommend individuals to serve as field officers, but the ultimate choice would be made by the convention.[10]

On July 26, 1775, members of the various committees of safety on the Grants convened at Dorset to select the officers for the regiment that had been approved by the Provincial Congress of New York.

These men, who elected Nathan Clark to chair the meeting and John Fassett to act as clerk, intended to keep control of the revolutionary movement on the Grants firmly in their own hands. For this reason they ignored a list of officers submitted by Ethan Allen to the Provincial Congress of New York earlier in the month that called for Allen to serve as lieutenant colonel and named his most aggressive captains as company commanders.[11] Instead, Clark and the other delegates elected Seth Warner lieutenant colonel by a vote of forty-one to five; following that they chose Samuel Safford to be the regiment's major by a margin of twenty-eight to seventeen and then selected captains, not naming Remember Baker, Robert Cochran, or Peleg Sunderland. Ethan Allen was furious. He excoriated the "Committee meeting" of "old farmers" at Dorset, who, "notwithstanding my zeal and success in my Country's cause," entirely neglected him when they chose officers for the regiment of Green Mountain Boys. Allen believed that "officers of the Army" as well as the "young *Green Mountain Boys*" supported him. "How the old men came to reject me, I cannot conceive, inasmuch as I saved them from the encroachments of *New-York*."[12]

Allen's incredulity over the decisions made at Dorset revealed just how oblivious he was to the tenuous nature of his alliance with men like Clark, Fassett, and the majority of those who voted against him. Staunch advocates of New Light religious doctrines, these men, like Allen, wanted not only to republicanize governmental authority but to subject it completely to local control.[13] Moreover, they were every bit as determined as Allen to defend their land titles and to support the colonial cause. Nonetheless, as devoutly religious men, they had no intention of surrendering leadership of the Grants to individuals as profane and reckless as Ethan Allen and his favorite captains. Political democrats yet social conservatives, Clark and his supporters envisioned the creation of a communal culture on the Grants — a New Light brotherhood. They shared deep misgivings about the sort of socially fragmented and aggressively individualistic society that Ethan Allen appeared to represent, and for this reason they placed the new regiment in the hands of men who shared their beliefs. Raised within a devout Congregational family, Seth Warner worshipped at Bennington's First Church and had been elected to responsible positions in Bennington's town government.[14] Samuel Safford, the eldest son of Deacon Joseph Safford, was a full church member and had served as a selectman eleven times prior to being chosen major of the new regiment.[15] Both men fully identified with the communal society of Bennington.

The regiment itself did not form for some time. This delay resulted from the need to recruit outside the Grants in order to enlist enough men, a dispute between Warner and Allen caused by the latter's intense desire to command the regiment, and Schuyler's tardiness in delivering the commissions for the field officers.[16] Schuyler's hesitancy to sign these commissions reflected the delicacy of the political situation in his own colony, where even members of the Revolutionary government were not enthusiastic about granting official sanction to a regiment composed primarily of rebels against New York authority. This distaste on their part prompted bitter feelings on the Grants and rekindled old suspicions of New York officials.[17]

In late September Warner and his regiment finally joined Gen. Richard Montgomery in his campaign against Montreal. The city fell on November 13. Seven days later Montgomery discharged the Green Mountain Boys, who, as volunteers, were not equipped for a long winter campaign. Two months later, though, when the American forces became desperate for additional men, Gen. David Wooster, who had replaced the fallen Montgomery, called upon Warner to raise another regiment. He complied.[18]

The new regiment bore little resemblance to the old one; in fact, it was the merest shadow of Ethan Allen's original band of Green Mountain Boys. Of those individuals who served as captains under Allen only Weight Hopkins and Seth Warner remained; none of the enlisted men in the new regiment had been members of Allen's old companies.[19] As an organized entity the Green Mountain Boys no longer existed. After the capture of Ticonderoga and Crown Point the rank and file had disbanded and returned to their homes, where they occasionally participated in local militia companies. Some of the original cadre of leaders disappeared from the Grants: Remember Baker died during a scouting expedition for General Montgomery in August 1775; Robert Cochran left to become an officer in the Continental line; Ethan Allen fell captive to the British in September 1775 while serving under General Schuyler. Others, like Heman and Ira Allen, Micah Vail, James Mead, Benjamin Cooley, and Matthew Lyon, returned to their local communities, where they served as delegates to the political conventions that became increasingly frequent on the Grants. It was in this civil capacity that the ethos of the Green Mountain Boys persisted.

The first convention to gather subsequent to Warner's election as colonel of the regiment met at Dorset on January 16, 1776. Chaired by Joseph Woodward, a New Light militia officer from Castleton, with

Jonas Fay as clerk, this meeting requested that a committee led by Fay and Heman Allen compose a petition to bring the case of the Grants before the Continental Congress.[20] The petition reiterated the relations between settlers on the Grants and "the Monopolizing Land Traders of New-York" and related the military efforts made by inhabitants on the Grants to further the "General Cause." In addition, it expressed a willingness to continue fighting for that cause under the Continental Congress but not under the Provincial Congress of New York, particularly "in such a manner as might in future be detrimental to our private property." The petition specifically requested the Continental Congress to allow individuals on the Grants to serve as inhabitants of the New Hampshire Grants and not as residents of New York.[21]

The convention's efforts were inconclusive. Heman Allen delivered the petition to Congress in late May, but the committee charged with hearing it recommended that inhabitants of the Grants submit to the government of New York for the duration of the struggle against Great Britain. At the same time, members of the committee stated that this submission should neither prejudice the land claims of the settlers nor affirm the political jurisdiction of New York over them. The final determination of such issues would be left until peace could be established.[22] Meanwhile, Allen ascertained that the New York delegation, like the Provincial Congress of that state, was under the influence of James Duane, the Livingstons, and other large landholders.[23] Worse still, other members of Congress appeared to be in sympathy with these men. Realizing that Congress might not support his petition, Allen withdrew it.[24]

Following Allen's return to the Grants, a large convention gathered at Dorset on July 24. Joseph Bowker, a New Light militia captain from Rutland, chaired the meeting, and Fay again served as clerk. With only a single dissenting vote, the delegates voted an appeal to the residents of the Grants to form themselves into a "separate District."[25] Then, with but a single abstention, the delegates pledged themselves, as an "Association of the Inhabitants of the New Hampshire Grants," to defend the "United American States" against the British. They resolved that all "friends to the liberties of the United States of America" residing on the Grants should subscribe to the association and that those residents signing associations circulated by the Provincial Congress of New York or by any counties in that state would be considered "enemies to the Common Cause of the N. Hampshire Grants." The convention then appointed a committee of appeals that included Fay, Bowker, Woodward, and Thomas Chittenden to enforce the association.[26]

On September 25 another convention met in adjourned session at Dorset. Although Bowker and Fay again served as chief officers, this meeting differed from the previous one in a vitally important way: it included delegates from east of the mountains.[27] Led by radical whigs such as Benjamin Carpenter, Reuben Jones, Leonard Spaulding, and Ebenezer Hoisington, the majority of these delegates zealously opposed New York authority.[28] In addition, their leaders were New Light enthusiasts to a man.[29] An immediate bond formed between these men and their western colleagues, providing solid support for separating the Grants from New York. As a result, a resolution to form the Grants into a separate district passed in this session without a dissenting vote.[30]

Once unanimity had been reached on the principle of separation from New York, all else followed easily. The delegates accepted a compact written by a committee that included Fay, Moses Robinson, Hoisington, Jones, and Chittenden. The document stated that because they expected "a continuance of the same kind of disingenuity" — the "illegal, unjustifiable and unreasonable measures" taken by the New York government to deprive settlers of their property by means of "fraud, violence and oppression" — the inhabitants of the Grants felt that they had every right to form themselves into a separate district. The delegates pledged themselves to adhere only to the resolutions of conventions elected on the Grants "by the free voice of the Friends of American Liberties, that shall not be repugnant to the resolves of the honorable Continental Congress relative to the General Cause of America."[31] Prior to adjourning, the convention made provisions for the enforcement of the Covenant and appointed a committee of war, led by Bennington residents Simeon Hathaway, Jonas Fay, and Nathan Clark, to oversee efforts to defend the Grants against the British.[32]

By the time the next session of the convention met in Westminster, on October 30, New York whigs had met in convention, written a constitution, and begun to disseminate a pamphlet reiterating New York's claim to the Grants and seeking to undermine support there for an independent state. In addition, the British had reclaimed superiority on Lake Champlain and were menacing Ticonderoga. Because of the latter threat, few attended the meeting at Westminster. Those who appeared called Bowker to the chair and elected Ira Allen clerk. The delegates voted to have a response to the New York pamphlet prepared

as soon as possible and to publish a manifesto immediately that explained why they chose not to ally themselves with New York.[33] The
manifesto accused the government of that state of exacting discriminat-
ing quitrents from the Grants and flaunting the principle that all free
people had a right to be represented in whatever legislative councils
were responsible for governing them. It also accused New York authorities of "breaking of *Sabbaths*, neglect of public worship, etc," and requested that the Continental Congress investigate the dispute between
New York and the Grants.[34]

Responsibility for the larger pamphlet fell to Ira Allen, who was not
able to complete the task by the time the convention reconvened in
Westminster on January 15, 1777. Even so, the delegates, after again
electing Bowker chair and Allen clerk, called for the Grants to become
a "new and separate state" and appointed a committee to draft a declaration to that effect. This committee, chaired by Nathan Clark, declared unequivocally that "whenever protection is withheld, no allegiance is due, or can of right be demanded." And since the "lives and
properties" of those on the Grants had been threatened by the government of New York for many years, "necessity requires a separation."[35]

The declaration, prepared for the press by Heman Allen and Clark,
rested upon the Declaration of Independence, pronounced by the Continental Congress on July 4, 1776. Extrapolating from that document,
which proclaimed arbitrary acts of the crown null and void, the people
of the Grants nullified the king's 1764 decision to extend New York
jurisdiction over the Grants. Consequently the Grants were "without
law or government, and may be truly said to be in a state of nature";
thus, "a right remains to the people of said Grants to form a government best suited to secure their property, well being and happiness."
Choosing to exercise that right, the delegates declared "NEW CON-
NECTICUT" a free and independent state and pledged the support of
the new state to the cause of the United States of America.[36] The
convention then prepared a petition to the Continental Congress that
outlined their complaints against the "land-jobbers" of New York from
the time of the king's edict of 1764 to the decision made by the constitutional convention of New York for that state to continue collecting all
the quitrents previously owed the king. Fay, Chittenden, Heman Allen,
and Reuben Jones were to lay the petition before Congress. The convention adjourned, to reconvene in Windsor the first Wednesday in
June.[37]

Prior to the opening of the session in Windsor two fresh pamphlets

provided the delegates with strong arguments in support of independence for the Grants. One, written by Ira Allen, recited the standard
litany of New York's tyrannical actions toward the Grants from 1764
through the state constitutional convention of 1776.[38] As always he
expressed the ardent desire that the entire controversy be resolved by
the Continental Congress. Then, however, Allen shifted his argument
away from a bill of particulars to a more abstract mode of thought, one
that spoke to those who were simultaneously advocating the American
cause against Great Britain and their own independence from New
York. For these people the two movements sprang from a single source,
because "God gave mankind freedom by nature, and made every man
equal to his neighbor, and has virtually enjoined them to govern themselves by their own laws."[39] Drawing upon the authority of John Locke,
Allen declared that individuals "must consider what state all men are
naturally in." This was "a state of perfect freedom to order their actions, and dispose of their possessions and persons, as they shall think
fit, within the bounds of the law of nature, without asking leave or depending upon the will of any other man." Such a condition was also one
"of equality . . . no one having more than another, there being nothing
more evident than that creatures of the same species and rank . . .
should be equal, one amongst another, without subordination or subjection."[40] Such thoughts resonated powerfully with the visceral feelings of Green Mountain Boys and New Lights alike.

   The People the Best Governors struck a similar chord.[41] Written by an
anonymous New Light author,[42] this pamphlet too revealed the affinity
of political thought uniting the coalition of New Lights and Green
Mountain Boys that had assumed leadership of the conventions on the
Grants. After making straightforward suggestions regarding the form a
government might assume, the author, like Allen, rested his case on the
belief that "God gave mankind freedom by nature [and] made every
man equal to his neighbor."[43] He then applied this egalitarian concept
to the matter of representation. No portion of the legislature should be
based on wealth, because such a requirement would create "an inequality among the people and set up a number of lords over the rest." Nor
should representatives be required to be worth a certain amount of
wealth; "such a notion of an estate has the directest tendency to set up
the avaricious over the heads of the poor, though the latter are ever
so virtuous."[44] In addition, suffrage should be open to any free male
twenty-one years of age once he had resided in a town for at least a year.
All that distinguished the author of this pamphlet from Ira Allen was

the insistence that all officeholders possess "a belief of one only invisible God, that governs all things; and that the bible is his revealed word."[45]

On June 4, 1777, the seventy-two delegates gathered at Windsor chose Joseph Bowker their chairman. Jonas Fay served as secretary.[46] In order to avoid confusion with a district in Pennsylvania known as New Connecticut, the delegates voted to change the name of their state to Vermont. They issued a list of complaints against New York and called for delegates to a constitutional convention at Windsor on July 2. They named Jonas Fay, Thomas Chittenden, Heman Allen, and Reuben Jones a committee to draft a constitution for the state.[47]

Aaron Hutchinson, a New Light pastor from nearby Pomfret, opened the Windsor meeting with a passionate sermon in which he melded devotion to Christ and resistance to Great Britain and New York into an indistinguishable whole. Not only did Hutchinson expound upon "a *British* junto, laying a plot to enslave *America*," but he dealt at length with the fact that the "rulers" of New York "hate us, are strangers to us, stand aloof from our sore, have forged chains for us, and lift up themselves above us, not owning us as their brethren." There could only be one response: "We are obliged by the allegiance we owe to Christ, to discard all usurpation, and tyranny among men." Every professing Christian had "a divine warrant to resist a tyrant and oppressor, not only in the oracles of truth, but by that light and law of nature, by which we resist a thief or robber." And, since the "law of nature was put into us by our great Creator . . . not to resist in such a case, is the way to receive to ourselves damnation."[48]

At the conclusion of Hutchinson's sermon the delegates joined in singing a hymn by Isaac Watts, "The Universal Law of Equity," then rose to their feet and sang the Doxology. They once again summoned Bowker to the chair and elected Fay secretary, then promptly turned their attention to the draft. Several months earlier, members of the drafting committee had returned from Philadelphia with encouraging words from Ethan Allen's old friend Dr. Thomas Young.[49] Claiming to have talked with prominent members of Congress, Young assured the inhabitants of Vermont that all they had to do to be accepted as a new state was to write a constitution and petition Congress for admittance. Young even provided them with a model — the constitution of the state of Pennsylvania — which he believed firmly established "the people at large [as] the true proprietors of governmental power."[50] This document was, in fact, the pattern for the constitution drafted by Fay and his committee.

At first glance the Vermont constitution appeared to be little more than a copy of Pennsylvania's. Both established a unicameral legislature, created an executive and an advisory council, and subjected the constitution and the constitutionality of legislation to periodic review by a council of censors. Many provisions in the Vermont constitution were taken verbatim from that of Pennsylvania.[51] There were, however, important differences between the two documents. Most significantly, Vermont's constitution abolished slavery, eliminated all property qualifications for voting, and called for the governor, lieutenant governor, and twelve councilors to be elected by the people rather than appointed by the legislature as they were in Pennsylvania. Unlike in Pennsylvania, moreover, Vermont's governor and council had the power to review legislation before it became law.[52]

The departures from the Pennsylvania model revealed that the delegates gathered at Windsor took seriously the idea that all men were "born equally free and independent" and that their constitution should actually rest upon the sovereignty of the people. When they called for a governor and an advisory council elected by the people, they did so out of a belief that government should be kept as close to the people as possible. They adhered to the principle articulated by the author of *The People the Best Governors* that the people "themselves are the best guardians of their own liberties."[53] As a result, they accepted that author's reasoning against a council appointed by the legislature, "for the representatives to appoint a council with a negative authority, is to give away that power, which they have no right to do, because they themselves derived it from the people." If an advisory council were to be created, it should "be but few in number, and chosen by the people at large" so that its members would be "virtually the representatives of the people, and derive just so much authority from them as will make up the defect of the others [legislators], viz., that of confirming."[54] Accepting this reasoning, the authors of Vermont's constitution created a form of government in which all elected officials — legislators, the governor, members of an advisory council — were agents of the people; the people themselves remained the source of all governmental authority.

This perspective permeated the convention at Windsor. As a result the Vermont constitution, rather than being a slavish imitation of Pennsylvania's, was actually an amalgam of that covenant and the prin-

ciples and plan of government set forth in *The People the Best Governors.*
By integrating a radical whig document with a New Light tract, the
authors of the Vermont constitution managed to incorporate within a
single compact the principal beliefs of the two groups most responsible
for the creation of an independent state: New Light elders and leaders
of the old Green Mountain Boys. In the process, they created the most
democratic constitution produced by any of the American states.

Not surprisingly, a combination of New Lights and Green Mountain
Boys made up the powerful Council of Safety appointed by the convention to manage affairs until a state government could be officially organized under the auspices of the new constitution. Thomas Chittenden, a close associate of the Allens and a committed democrat, served
as president of the council, with support from Nathan Clark, Jonas
and Joseph Fay, Moses Robinson, Heman and Ira Allen, and Matthew
Lyon. The convention also appointed Ira Allen to serve as trustee of a
loan office established to support the fledgling government.[55]

The Council of Safety immediately confronted serious problems.
Preeminent among these was the matter of defense. Ticonderoga had
fallen to the British even before the convention adjourned, and General
John Burgoyne was advancing southward with a British army of more
than ten thousand men. Seth Warner's regiment, defeated at Hubbardton on July 7, had fallen back toward Manchester to regroup. The
situation was critical. Unless more troops could be put in the field all of
Vermont lay open to the enemy. The council sent all the militiamen it
could muster to augment Warner's forces, organized a regiment of
rangers under Col. Samuel Herrick, and sent an urgent plea for aid to
councils of safety in New Hampshire and Massachusetts.[56] The latter
responded with alacrity: within a month a militia company from Berkshire County, Massachusetts, was in Bennington, and Gen. John Stark
came at the head of a brigade of New Hampshire militiamen.

Stark arrived at a propitious moment. Burgoyne had dispatched Col.
Frederick Baum with a force of five hundred Hessian regulars, augmented by two pieces of light artillery and several hundred Canadians,
tories, and Indians, to capture a large supply of goods stockpiled at
Bennington by U.S. commissary agents. By August 15 Baum had entrenched his forces on the banks of the Walloomsac River, less than
ten miles west of Bennington. The next day Stark attacked the enemy
with his New Hampshire and Massachusetts militia, Herrick's rangers,
and two militia companies commanded by Captains Elijah Dewey and
Samuel Robinson, which included nearly every able-bodied man in

Bennington.[57] After desperate fighting these men captured the enemy position. However, an additional force of British regulars supported by artillery soon appeared and renewed the fighting. Fortunately for Stark, Warner arrived with his regiment, and the Americans were able to defeat the enemy reinforcements as well. By the end of the day Stark's men had killed more than two hundred enemy soldiers and captured about seven hundred men, four artillery pieces, and several hundred small arms. Thirty Americans, including Nathan Clark Jr., John Fay, and Henry Walbridge, lay dead, and another forty suffered wounds.[58]

The battle of Bennington eased the military threat faced by Vermont, but the Council of Safety still had to confront a difficult political problem that predated the victory. New York authorities were attempting to subvert the creation of an independent state by distributing throughout Vermont a series of resolutions that had been passed by the Continental Congress. These resolutions disavowed having given any encouragement to the independence movement in Vermont and censured Thomas Young for his interference in the name of Congress.[59] Realizing the respect commanded by the Continental Congress throughout the state, the Council of Safety felt compelled to respond. Council members calculated that the best way to blunt the effect of the congressional resolutions was to keep Vermont citizens stirred up against New York authorities and to fuse opposition to that state with resistance to Great Britain. Consequently, Ira Allen published a short piece in October warning Vermonters against acknowledging the jurisdiction of New York. To accept the constitution of that state would mean that "all the spirited exertions the noble sons of freedom have made, and still continue to make against the tyranny of New York and Great Britain," would go for naught. Worse than that, every citizen of Vermont, "together with their numerous families, [would] be reduced to pinching poverty only to gratify the avaricious land-jobbers of New York in their unwarrantable claims to the lands and labors of the good people of the State of Vermont." Since it was unquestionably the right of all people to defend their liberties, "to appoint their own rulers, and be governed by their laws," settlers in Vermont, "with a firm reliance on the Supreme Arbiter of Right for the rectitude of their intentions, in defiance of the usurpation of New York, have declared themselves to be a free State." The inhabitants of Vermont also had a wonderful opportunity to protect the revered principle of self-determination by participating in the "ensuing elections" and by selecting only men of "virtue, business and known patriotism" to the new state government.[60] Thus, as Ira Allen skillfully put it, to be loyal to the independent state of Vermont was to support the inalienable rights for which the American states were struggling against the British.

Due to the turmoil within the region, members of the Council of Safety decided that it would be difficult to hold state elections in December as called for by the Windsor convention. They asked Joseph Bowker to reconvene that convention on December 24, which he did. The delegates postponed the election for state offices until the first Tuesday of March 1778. They also delayed the initial sitting of the General Assembly until the second Thursday of the same month and ratified a long preamble that had been added to the Vermont constitution spelling out in detail New York's transgressions against the citizens of Vermont.[61]

By early February 1778 sufficient copies of the constitution had been printed to be distributed to the various towns prior to the March elections. Voters throughout Vermont responded in different ways to the constitution as well as to the call for elections on March 3. Those in Bennington objected to the constitution because it had not been subjected to a popular vote prior to the call to elect state officials.[62] Nonetheless, they cast their ballots for state officers and elected Nathan Clark and John Fassett to the General Assembly.[63] Freemen in other towns viewed March 3 as a day not only to elect representatives but to ratify the constitution itself. Residents of a few towns, particularly those with Yorker leanings, in the southeastern portion of the state, rejected the process altogether.[64]

On March 12, less than two weeks after the town meetings, the first General Assembly of the state of Vermont convened in the meetinghouse in Windsor.[65] The representatives elected Joseph Bowker to chair their organizational session, heard an election-day sermon, and named a committee to receive, sort, and count the ballots for state officers. Thomas Chittenden received an overwhelming vote for governor, but since there were no clear majorities for lieutenant governor or treasurer, the assembly elected Joseph Marsh and Ira Allen to these positions. The assembly also ratified the election of twelve councilors. Upon discovering that Bowker had been elected to the council, the assembly named Nathan Clark to be its speaker. After all the representatives had taken their seats and the executive officers had been named, it was clear that Vermont's government rested firmly in the hands of those groups who had pressed the hardest for independence: New Lights and men who had either served with the Green Mountain Boys or were sympathetic to their social and political principles.

Two months after the first meeting of the Vermont Assembly the inner circle that had been instrumental in creating an independent state lost one of its central figures: Heman Allen died on May 18 from a lingering illness contracted at the battle of Bennington. Less than two weeks later, however, his brother Ethan, having been exchanged for a British officer, received a hero's welcome in Bennington. To celebrate Allen's return and to express their excitement at the prospect of joining the union, the townspeople saluted him with fourteen rounds from the old iron cannon that he himself had ordered up from Fort Hoosick to defend the town against Governor Tryon six years earlier.[66]

Soon after his return Ethan began to play a large role in support of the fledgling state government. In his first week home his old friend and associate Thomas Chittenden appointed him to act as state prosecutor in the case of a notorious tory who was subsequently tried and hung in Bennington.[67] Because of his unwillingness to acknowledge the "divine inspiration" of the Bible or to "own and profess the protestant religion," as the Vermont constitution required of all officeholders,[68] Allen could not hold an elective office. Nonetheless, he became an unofficial adviser to Governor Chittenden and participated in sessions of the council, the General Assembly, and even the state courts at his pleasure. In addition, Chittenden often called upon him to serve as an official emissary of the state and entrusted him with delicate negotiations with the Continental Congress and other state governments. It was in a military capacity, however, that Allen performed his most notable service for the state. Having been appointed brigadier general of the Vermont militia by Governor Chittenden, Allen occasionally commanded special military expeditions to put down pockets of local resistance to the authority of the newly formed state government.[69]

Not long after his return to Vermont Ethan took up the pen as well as the sword to bolster support within the state for an independent government. In two widely circulated pamphlets he attacked the character and credibility of New York authorities — the greatest single threat to the sovereignty of Vermont — while defending the independence of his state in terms of natural law. The first essay, *An Animadversory Address to the Inhabitants of the State of Vermont*, maintained that New York "could almost vie with *Great Britain* in the art of vassalaging common people, and in erasing every idea of liberty from the human mind, by making and keeping them poor and servile."[70] To combat this the people of

Vermont must "maintain inviolable the supremacy of the legislative authority of the independent state of *Vermont.*" Such supremacy, "at one stroke, overturns every *New York* scheme which may be calculated for our ruin, makes us free men, confirms our property, 'and puts it fairly in our power to help ourselves.' "[71]

In his second essay, *A Vindication of the Opposition of the Inhabitants of Vermont to the Government of New York, and of Their Right to form an Independent State*, Allen drew an even sharper parallel between the governments of Great Britain and New York. If Great Britain's claim to an exclusive right to tax Americans would have eventually led to "abject slavery," Allen claimed, then New York had taken "a more direct and immediate method, for at one blow they struck at the landed property of every of the inhabitants of *Vermont.*" Thus, while Parliament's mutilation of the charter of Massachusetts was a "high handed stride of arbitrary power, and struck the very nerves of liberty," it was not nearly "so fatal as though they had appropriated the soil of the colony to new adventurers." Nothing was "capable of so effectually inslaving [a people] as the monopoly of their lands." Once this happened, "it is idle for them to dispute any more about liberty; for a sovereign nod of their landlord, cannot fail to overawe them, and by degrees erase the natural images of liberty from the mind, and make them grovel out a contemptable and miserable life."[72] Given New York's "unnatural and unjust" conception of equity, it should be unthinkable for any sensible inhabitant of Vermont to submit to the laws of that state.[73]

Both of Allen's pamphlets stressed that the inhabitants of Vermont had a right "received from nature" to form their own government. Once the Declaration of Independence had nullified the king's jurisdictional decision of 1764, the people of Vermont had "reverted to a state of nature." Consequently, they existed "as free as is possible to conceive any people to be; and in this condition they formed [a] government upon the true principles of liberty and natural right."[74] To question their right to do so would be to question the legitimacy of all the American states.

While Allen contrasted the hardy nature of Vermont settlers with the effete character of New York gentlemen in his *Animadversory Address* and *A Vindication*, he made no effort in either piece to amplify the yeoman persuasion that he had begun to articulate several years earlier. This was not the case, however, with *A Narrative of Colonel Ethan Allen's Captivity*, published in 1779.[75] In this little book he interwove his own experience as a prisoner of war with that of Revolutionary American

society so skillfully that his portrayal of self reflected his perception of
society in such a manner as to cast the egalitarian ethos he believed to
underlie the Revolution into particularly sharp relief.[76]

Although Ethan dramatized his personal torment at great length
throughout the *Narrative*, the book was more than simply an account
of his own desperate effort to survive; his story became the story of
an entire people struggling to transform themselves and their society.
Thus, in Allen's florid prose British prisons became metaphors for an
oppressive Old World culture dominated by aristocrats, in which social
and political prominence resulted from birth rather than from talent.
In stark contrast, American prisoners formed "little commonwealths,"
egalitarian communities characterized by a spirit of democratic cooperation in which no man deserved or expected to be treated better than
any other.

Throughout the *Narrative* Ethan challenged the assumption that
there was anything natural or ineluctable about a monarchical or aristocratic society. He considered all cultures to be man-made, the inven-
tion of those who held power within them. Consequently, ordinary
individuals should never accept the feelings of inferiority imputed to
them in a hierarchical society dominated by aristocratic gentlemen. To
demonstrate that gentlemen themselves were not intrinsically superior
to any other man, Ethan stripped the British and tory officers in authority over him while he was a prisoner of all honor, integrity, or character.
He portrayed Sir William Howe, commander of the British forces in
America, and Joshua Loring, a tory jailor in New York, as cruel, hypocritical men totally devoid of honor. Sir William personally oversaw
a "doleful scene of inhumanity" in which American prisoners were
treated in an "inhuman and barbarous manner."[77] And even though
Loring showed "a smiling countenance" and seemed "to wear a phiz of
humanity," he was actually "the most mean spirited, cowardly, deceitful, and destructive animal in God's creation."[78]

If British gentlemen lacked nearly every redeeming human quality,
American officers were courageous defenders of a noble cause, men
who gallantly endured unspeakable suffering and gross indignities to
uphold democratic principles. Allen recounted his own refusal to accept a bowl of punch a British gentleman ordered his servant to give
him; to establish himself the equal of any man, Ethan would drink from
the bowl only after the gentleman handed it to him personally.[79] Another time, huddled with many others in a crowded prison ship, he had
insisted on taking only an equal share of the meager provisions even

though he was an officer in order to "set an example of virtue and fortitude to our little commonwealth."[80] A fellow officer who was held for four months in a dungeon "with murderers, thieves, and every species of criminal, and all for the sole crime of unshaken fidelity to his country" had refused to go over to the other side. Instead, "his spirits were above dejection, and his mind unconquerable."[81] This same fortitude and natural strength also characterized the common soldier. In contrast to the "slavish Hessian," American soldiers, "undisciplined heroes" armed only "with their long brown firelocks . . . without bayonets," stood as positive proof that any people "not directed by virtue, wisdom and policy, never fails finally to destroy itself."[82] The natural strength of Americans could not help but carry their society to victory over its decadent counterpart.

The *Narrative*, published at a low point in Americans' morale, offered them hope; with perseverance and fortitude, they, like Ethan Allen, could overcome adversity and triumph over British tyranny. At the same time, Allen's captivity narrative presented a clear picture of the kind of society such a victory would establish. To prevail over the British would be to dissolve the senseless calibrations of rank and degrees of dependency and unfreedom that pervaded a traditional culture based on hierarchy. In its place would spring a fresh, new society resting on the idea of equality, a society in which no man was better than any other. If the aristocratic gentleman epitomized Old World society, the ordinary citizen emerged as the symbol of the new.

The *Narrative*, while widely read throughout the Northeast, spoke most directly to the inhabitants of Vermont.[83] Allen's emphasis on an egalitarian, democratic society of independent producers in control of their own lives and governments resonated with the political instincts of New Lights and Green Mountain Boys who had defied New York authority, supported the Revolution, and created an independent state. Since these same people made up the majority of Vermont's population when he published the *Narrative*,[84] Ethan's ideas enjoyed considerable influence throughout the state.[85]

Even at this time, though, Ethan's egalitarianism faced determined resistance in Vermont because of striking demographic changes taking place throughout the state. By 1780 Vermont was in the midst of a veritable population explosion.[86] Over the course of the previous decade the number of residents in the state had swelled from 6,132 to more than 20,000.[87] Although migration into Vermont continued at this accelerated pace well beyond 1780, its character underwent a decided shift after that date. Migrants from centers of Old Light strength in eastern Massachusetts and western Connecticut came to Vermont in such numbers that they overwhelmed New Light majorities in some townships and seriously contested their control in many others.[88] In addition, this tide of immigration brought an influx of gentlemen. Many were college-educated lawyers; all firmly believed in a traditional social and political order in which common people exhibited an unquestioning deference and respect toward their superiors.[89] These gentlemen and the Old Light migrants viewed the egalitarian attitudes of the New Lights and the Green Mountain Boys with utter disdain. Town after town in Vermont became fractured by a struggle between residents with conflicting cultural values.

Bennington did not escape such a confrontation. Its church became the focal point of conflict as divisions within the town grew particularly bitter. Such strife was not immediately apparent, however. As late as 1780 First Church appeared to be prospering, despite the loss of Jedediah Dewey, its pastor of fifteen years, who had died in December 1778. Membership had increased from its original 56 believers to more than 130, and the society had grown at an even faster rate.[90] More important, the rift caused by allowing the society to participate with the church in decisions regarding support for the pastor had healed. Dissidents were back in the fold, and on January 27, 1780, they came together with their fellow members to consider the church covenant, "it being very much shattered and torn." Joining in a spirit of Christian love and harmony, all members renewed their "Covenant with God and one with another."[91] This same meeting appointed a committee led by John Fassett to examine the principles of Rev. David Avery, who had been asked to preach at First Church as a first step toward giving him a call to settle in Bennington.[92] When they adjourned, the brethren had every reason to be optimistic regarding the future of their church; peace and unity reigned among its members, and prospects appeared excellent for securing a settled pastor.

A month later church members reassembled and issued a call for Avery to settle among them. At this gathering they also chose a committee to examine the Cambridge Platform and to "lay before the church their view of the same."[93] When this committee, chaired by Fassett, made its report to the church the following week, the members voted that the "decisive power in cases of discipline" rested "in the Body or Brotherhood" rather than with the pastor or a ministerial association.[94] This decision clearly indicated that even though a great many who were not Strict Congregationalists had been admitted to the society during Rev. Dewey's ministry,[95] church members remained steadfastly loyal to the Cambridge Platform and to their Strict Congregational heritage.[96]

Devotion to these principles caused increasing numbers of church members to become alienated from David Avery following his installation as pastor on May 3, 1780. These people simply could not abide Avery's arrogance, his exalted view of the power of the pastor over matters of church discipline, his acceptance of the authority of the presbyter, and the complex New Divinity principles he propounded in his sermons. Fassett opposed Avery from the moment the minister refused to allow the brotherhood to lay hands upon him at his installation.[97] Within a year Simeon Sears declared openly in a church meeting that Avery's preaching was "a perversion of the gospel of Christ" and that the church was guilty of "iniquity" for keeping him in the pulpit. Sears believed Avery was leading the church away from the gospel and deceiving the people; the church could expect no "union, harmony, and peace" so long as Avery was its pastor, he said.[98] Fassett and Sears, who had remained doggedly loyal to First Church throughout its earlier disputes and had held the church together following Dewey's death, withdrew from communion, shunned worship services, and refused to contribute to Avery's salary. Instead, they and a growing number of others gathered on Sundays to hear the preaching of Ebenezer Wood, one of their own brothers and a devout Separate.[99]

It was not only Avery's ministerial behavior that troubled so many church members; his genteel affectations proved equally offensive to people accustomed to simple living. Avery made no effort to conceal the fact that he considered himself a gentleman and expected to be treated like one. He wore a wig and sported silk handkerchiefs, cutaway coats, velvet breeches, and silver buckles on his shoes. Soon after taking up residence in Bennington he began constructing an elaborate house and imported a variety of plants and shrubs for his gardens. He married an affluent Massachusetts lady, who brought an impressive array of silks, satins, fine furniture, and china to her new home.[100] If this ostentatious display shocked Avery's plain-living parishioners, the fact that the couple walked to church arm in arm scandalized them.[101] Avery and his wife did not, however, walk to church often once he purchased his chaise and a matched set of horses.[102]

The manner in which Avery related to the inhabitants of Bennington did nothing to ease the tensions within the church resulting from

his pretentious behavior. Whether by accident, circumstance, or design, the settlement pattern in Bennington village had assumed clear
cultural manifestations by the time of Avery's arrival. Those committed
to the values of a simple life of rough equality had established their
homes and places of business in the "Up-Hill" section of the village,
known as Courthouse Hill; more cosmopolitan, genteel families resided in the "Down-Hill" area, commonly referred to as Meetinghouse
Hill.[103] The Fays, Robinsons, and Fassetts, the backbone of the church,
lived uphill; an influx of recent migrants to the town, young gentlemen
such as Isaac Tichenor, Col. Nathaniel Brush, Col. Joseph Farnsworth,
and Noah Smith, settled in the downhill region. These men, joined by
Jedediah Dewey's eldest sons, Elijah and Eldad, became the dominant
figures in the society of First Church. They contributed the largest
sums when it became necessary to form a voluntary society to pay
Avery's salary.[104] It was with these men of affluence, who were thoroughly committed to a graduated or hierarchical society, that Avery
associated most closely from the very moment of his installation. He
and his wife clearly favored their company over that of the more ordinary parishioners.[105]

Avery did little to conceal his own conviction that a great gulf separated gentle from simple folk. After a good many church members
abandoned his services for those of Ebenezer Wood, Avery characterized Separates as individuals who "think little & pay nothing."[106] When
he initiated plans to establish Clio Hall, a private academy, in Bennington, he turned to "Gentlemen of influence," since most townsmen
were, in his opinion, "people of rude taste & manners."[107] As Avery's
plans for the school went forward, he observed that a "number of *very
uneasy* men" opposed the venture.[108] He did not, however, acknowledge
the source of this uneasiness: Avery was actively promoting the creation
of a private school for young gentlemen at a time when the village still
had no common schools to educate the children of ordinary citizens.

By April 1783 Avery had offended so many members of the church
that a large number of them demanded that a conference of Strict
Congregational pastors be called to scrutinize his ministry. Allowing
"the indignity of this low ceremony of jealousy" to pass without comment, Avery called a meeting of the church to discuss the matter. At this
gathering Avery's friends "were overpowered by numbers," and a call
went out to a number of Strict Congregational ministers, who gathered
in Bennington on May 26.[109] After two days of prayerful consideration
these men absolved Avery of all specific charges relating to his inter-

pretations of the Bible. However, recognizing that he had lost the trust of the church, they recommended that Avery resign. He complied.[110]

Avery's resignation clearly revealed the cultural divisions emerging in Bennington. Men like John Fassett, who believed the town should remain a simple brotherhood of equals, rejoiced in Avery's departure. Others, like Isaac Tichenor, resented the measures of the "opposing party" and regretted that the people of Bennington would be left to listen to the preaching of ordinary men rather than "real ministers of God," men of dignity and education.[111] In his parting address Avery forcefully attacked the "levelling" tendency that affronted Tichenor and so many other members of the society. From Avery's perspective, adherents of equality, by denying their inferiority to any man, confounded "the distinctions which nature has made, and which time immemorial has sanctified, between members of society, on the account either of their age or rank." A spirit of equality, he warned, "disrobes public characters of that dignity and honour which God has conferred upon them for the good of others." As a result, "it renders useless their administrations, whether it be in church or state, exactly in proportion as they are brought down from the eminence in which their offices place them above others." Eminence, order, and deference were essential to any respectable society. For this reason the "daring, levelling spirit of the times" must be resisted at all costs, even if it meant that Avery himself must become a martyr to the cause of dignity.[112]

If Isaac Tichenor and other gentlemen believed eminence to be important in the ministry, they considered it absolutely indispensable in government. Elected officials should be men of property, independence of mind, firmness, and education and should command a wide knowledge of history, politics, and the laws of their society. Most important of all, they must be entirely disinterested; a gentleman always placed the public welfare before his own private concerns.[113] These beliefs caused Tichenor and the others to be particularly chagrined at the cadre of common, ordinary men that had dominated Vermont's state government since 1778. Foremost among them were Thomas Chittenden, elected governor every year since the formation of the state; Ethan Allen, brigadier general of the state militia and unofficial adviser to Chittenden and the council; Ira Allen, who simultaneously occupied the positions of councilor, treasurer, and surveyor general; and Matthew Lyon, the group's leader in the assembly as well as clerk of the powerful Court of Confiscation. Of this crowd only Chittenden, a backbencher during several sessions of the Connecticut General Assembly, had any previous governmental experience at all. None had had more than the most rudimentary common school education. The governor himself was nearly illiterate, and the others displayed all the affectations and egregious blunders common to autodidacts.

While the lack of sophistication of those in power offended the sensibilities of a gentleman like Tichenor, he was most disturbed by the apparent venality of these men. None seemed to be above using his official position to further his own interests. Through their control of the sequestration and confiscation of tory land and personal property these officials not only had created a powerful faction that enabled them to dominate the political life of the state[114] but had personally benefited by buying up choice plots of land as a consequence of the sequestration program.[115] The same was true of the manner in which the group awarded land grants within the state, becoming proprietors of hundreds of new townships created under their own administration.[116] Ira Allen, for one, had grown particularly adept at manipulating the laws of the state to his own economic benefit. His careless way of keeping the treasurer's accounts always seemed to accrue to his personal benefit. In addition, Allen took advantage of his office as surveyor general by taking his salary in land, amassing by war's end more than one hundred thousand acres in more than fifty townships in the northern part of the state.[117] Beyond that, prospective proprietors soon learned that they could greatly enhance their chances of obtaining a choice grant of land merely by giving Allen a "handsom Reward."[118]

Tichenor and his supporters became even more upset when Ethan and Ira Allen in the fall of 1780 entered into negotiations with General Frederick Haldimand, military commander and governor of Quebec, that lasted a year and one-half.[119] Although the Allens undertook these discussions with the full knowledge and support of Governor Chittenden and the Council of Safety and also managed to keep Haldimand from invading either Vermont or New York while the talks were under way, Tichenor and Nathaniel Chipman cried foul. These two men, always suspicious that the Allens were promoting their own speculative interests in the northwestern quadrant of the state, accused not only the Allens but Chittenden and the seven members of the Council of Safety of treason. Tichenor, Chipman, and their supporters did everything in their power to damage the reputation of their political opponents by implicating them with the "treason" of the Haldimand negotiations.

In September 1781 the citizens of Bennington gave Tichenor a chance to play a role in the governance of the state by electing him to the state legislature. Immediately upon taking his seat in the October session of the assembly Tichenor became embroiled in the bitterly divisive problem of land titles. This issue had a long and complex history: overlapping New Hampshire and New York land grants, combined with the confiscation and sale of tory lands by the Court of Confiscation and the great number of new land grants made by the state of Vermont, resulted in a quagmire of conflicting land claims. That surveys had been made by a variety of private individuals and that the state had no map or plan of its own surveys or even records of the deeds it had issued greatly complicated the matter. So, too, did the practice of the proprietors of vast tracts of land comprising overlapping or conflicting land grants. These men sold off small parcels as rapidly as they could find buyers. The purchasers, assuming that they held valid title to their property, proceeded to settle on the land and to bring it under cultivation, only to face, at a later date, ejection at the hands of those who could prove a clear title in a court of law.[120]

The first several legislative assemblies attempted to deal with the problem of land titles in as fair and as equitable a manner as possible. These men, representative of the coalition of New Lights and Green Mountain Boys that had brought Vermont into being, were particularly conscious of the plight of actual settlers and took whatever measures they could to protect these people. Thus, after adopting the English common law and establishing a court system capable of confirming legitimate titles to bona fide landowners, they provided relief for the great number of settlers who had purchased and improved land for which they held no legal title. They accomplished this by prohibiting trials involving land titles until appropriate legislation could be passed to protect individuals who had "undergone innumerable hardships in settling farms" in the honest belief that they held legitimate title. In the minds of the legislators, to "disposses them [now], would be cruel and unjust."[121] The judges of the state supreme court, none of whom were attorneys, were happy to oblige.[122]

This leniency reflected the attitudes of men entirely unfamiliar with the strict requirements of the law, men more interested in following principles of natural justice and fairness than the tenets of William Blackstone. Many recent immigrants to the state, however, felt otherwise. When, for example, the legislature asked Nathaniel Chipman's advice on a bill regarding confiscated estates during its March 1780 session, the young attorney's response led to a confrontation that revealed tensions beginning to build between old and new settlers. Following common-law principles, Chipman reported in favor of those individuals whose property had been confiscated by the state. Soon thereafter Matthew Lyon declared to Chipman that no man "with a spark of honesty" could have made such a report. Offended by the "rude manner" in which Lyon had addressed him, Chipman responded by calling his adversary "an ignorant Irish puppy." Enraged by this comment, Lyon grabbed Chipman by the hair, breaking the comb that held the young gentleman's coif in place. Chipman and a friend immediately grabbed Lyon by the arms and legs, carried him across the room, and, laughing at him all the while, dumped him unceremoniously in a corner.[123] Shortly after this altercation Lyon managed to gain a measure of revenge by scoring a victory over Chipman and his associates in the legislature. He successfully added a proviso to an act prohibiting unlawful settlement on unappropriated lands. Lyon's addendum stipulated that the legislation under consideration could not be construed in such a manner as to prevent "any person or persons from recovering pay for labor, settlement, etc, where it can be made to appear that such settlement was made through mistake, or on a supposed legal title."[124]

The encounter between Chipman, the college-educated attorney, and Lyon, the former indentured servant, symbolized sharp divisions beginning to emerge within the Vermont legislature. Chipman insisted that all persons be held strictly accountable to the very letter of the law regardless of their circumstances. Lyon, on the other hand, demanded justice for those who had actually settled and worked the land. At the October 1780 meeting of the legislature, Governor Chittenden, a man with a strong sense of justice and an equally pronounced sympathy for the common man, entered the fray by suggesting that measures be taken "as will in equity quiet the ancient settlers."[125] Finally, during the October 1781 session of the assembly, an act allowing dispossessed settlers to recover "of the person or persons in whom the legal right shall be found by such judgment, so much money as shall be judged equitable" passed without a division of the house.[126] The preface to this bill clearly articulated the feelings of men such as Chittenden and Lyon. Reminiscent of Ethan Allen's prewar diatribes contrasting hardworking yeomen with idle Yorker aristocrats, this document maintained that a great many individuals had "purchased supposed titles to land" in the state and had "made large improvements on the same." Nonetheless, "if the strict rules of law be attended to," these people would be dispossessed of the property they had improved "at great

labor and expense," while "others who have wholly neglected the settlement of the country, will enjoy the benefits of their labor."[127]

The so-called Betterment Act was a victory for Governor Chittenden and like-minded individuals in the legislature. It did, however,
meet with determined opposition from people like Isaac Tichenor and
Nathaniel Chipman. As attorneys these men took offense at Chittenden's gross ignorance of fundamental legal principles. Knowing full
well that the common law "makes every man a trespasser who enters on
the land of another without license, and subjects him to damages for the
tresspass," Chipman, in exasperation, exclaimed that the Betterment
Act "would compel the legal owner to pay [the trespasser] a bounty for
his trespass."[128]

With the passage of time, Tichenor and Chipman assumed greater
influence in the assembly. In fact, the legislators who gathered for the
new session in October 1783 elected Tichenor speaker of the house.
From that point on, power within the state government began to shift
inexorably toward the assembly, where the attitudes of Tichenor, Chipman, and their supporters gradually gained predominance. This shift
became clear when Matthew Lyon attempted to pass another betterment act during the October 1784 session. In this bill Lyon none too
subtly pitted hardworking yeomen against idle gentlemen by drawing a
sharp line between early settlers, who had struggled to bring a wilderness under cultivation, and latecomers, who would tear it away from
them by means of legal niceties. His resolution noted that "strict rules
of law" often dispossessed individuals who had, through their own
strenuous physical labor, raised the value of the land they occupied.
This allowed others, "who have neglected both the defense and settlement of the land, [to] unjustly enjoy the benefits of their labors." To
prevent such a "manifest evil and injustice," Lyon proposed to award
those stripped of their property the difference between the real value of
the land at the time they settled on it and its true value at the time of
their ejectment.[129] The bill failed by a vote of 33 to 45.[130] There was
such strong popular pressure for this measure, however, that its opponents had to acquiesce to a public referendum on the issue. Still, despite
a 756–508 popular vote in favor of the bill, the emerging majority
within the assembly again defeated the measure 31 to 29 at the June
1785 session of the legislature.[131] During that same legislative session a
second betterment act, written by Nathaniel Chipman, passed by a vote
of 34 to 29.[132] This bill halved the amount dispossessed individuals
could collect for improvements they had made to their property. Ever

so slowly, then, Chipman and his supporters chiseled away at the populist measures espoused by Lyon, Chittenden, and their associates.
Chipman's success in the legislature resulted from a number of factors. Most important, the bulk of his support came from legislators east
of the Green Mountains, where Old Light immigration had been the
heaviest. Traditional supporters of established order, these people had
great respect for "strict rules of law," especially those relating to property. In addition, many New Lights living in the eastern part of the state
abandoned the longstanding alliance with their counterparts in the
west and began to support Chipman's positions. The close association
of western New Lights with the Green Mountain Boys, particularly
Ethan and Ira Allen, was largely responsible for this shift in allegiance.
As a result of the Haldimand negotiations, with their distinct hint of
treason, a great many eastern whigs, whether New Light or Old Light,
grew suspicious of the Allens. In fact, these people were eager to accept
Ethan's resignation as brigadier general of the state militia when he
offered it in a fit of passion after his character had been questioned
during an investigation of the Haldimand matter.[133] Not only was Ira
Allen tainted by that affair but Tichenor and Chipman had been attacking his integrity as treasurer and surveyor general for several years.
Indeed, by this time Ira's public image was such that a clever wag could
insert *The pleasant Art of Money Catching reduced to Practice*, by "I.A.," in
a list of books advertised for sale in the *Vermont Gazette* and no one
wondered who the author might be.[134]
    As long as transgressions by the Allens could not be fully authenti-
cated many eastern New Lights gave them the benefit of the doubt and
remained loyal to the old coalition. That became increasingly difficult,
however, after the publication of Ethan Allen's massive *Reason the Only
Oracle of Man* in the fall of 1784.[135] In this book, the most radically
democratic of all of his works, Allen supported a natural religion resting
upon man's reason rather than the revealed religion based upon the
Bible and the hierarchy of ministers that held sway throughout New
England. In place of a fearsome Calvinist deity, Ethan offered a benevolent god who allowed each person, through the use of intelligence and
conscience, to judge between right and wrong. In essence, Allen democratized religion, just as he had democratized all other social and political aspects of his culture. Unlike his earlier publications, however, his
attack upon the Bible predictably brought the wrath of clergymen down
upon his head. Timothy Dwight, for example, referred to *Reason* as the
"contemptible plagiarism of every hackneyed, worn out, half-rotten

dogma of the English deistical writers."[136] Others were even more zealous in their criticism. Thus, with the publication of this book Ethan forfeited his support among most New Lights living in eastern Vermont, who became increasingly receptive to the appeals of Tichenor and Chipman.

By the fall of 1786 residents of Vermont, regardless of their religious views or place of residence, had more to worry about than religious dogma. Difficult economic times had befallen them. Because of the depressed prices they had to accept for their produce, as well as the extreme shortage of hard currency in the state, vast numbers of settlers who had purchased land on credit were unable to pay their debts. Creditors, in turn, had no recourse except to foreclose on farm after farm. Cries for relief erupted throughout the state. Distressed citizens deluged the legislature with petitions calling for reforms in judicial procedures, the issuance of paper currency, and changes in the tax structure of the state.[137] Individuals from Rutland, for example, contended that the laws "as they now stand doth admite of attornys harrising the People without being under any sort of Restrant" and "admit of a number of Depety Sheriffs which prove Burdensom to the Good people of this State."[138] From Tinmouth came the charge that the "present mode of taxation" was a "very great and real grievance" because it was "manifestly unequal and impolitic." The tax burden fell too heavily upon "the poor and middling class of people." In addition, taxing only improved lands and products was "in fact no other than to tax industry skill and economy."[139] All petitioners agreed that they needed fewer sheriffs and attorneys, less frequent meetings of the courts, and the issuance of paper currency by the state.

Governor Chittenden sympathized with their plight. Prior to the meeting of the assembly in October 1786, he acknowledged that "for a remedy one cries a Tender Act, another a bank of money, and others, kill the lawyers and deputy sheriffs." The governor recommended a small bank that could loan paper money to the people. In his mind, an ample currency would drastically reduce the great numbers of lawsuits that so troubled the people and might, as a result, force the "pettifoggers" to earn an honest living.[140]

When the General Assembly convened in October, pressure immediately built to pass a tender act that would oblige creditors to accept goods in lieu of money in payment of all debts. In addition, a great many members favored the creation of a bank that could issue paper currency; others desired legislation that would place restrictions upon lawyers, sheriffs, and the courts with respect to the collection of debts. Such measures appalled Nathaniel Chipman, who believed that those begging for relief had only themselves to blame for their distressed condition. Their own shiftless habits—the idleness and dissipation so characteristic of the lower classes—not the legitimate work of sheriffs and attorneys, were responsible for the plight of these people.[141] So certain was Chipman in this opinion that he published a poem ridiculing the illiteracy, ignorance, and unrestrained passion of a crowd of poor farmers who gathered at a convention in the town of Wells to protest their depressed economic condition.[142]

Bolstered by his convictions, Chipman took the lead in opposing any measures that would afford relief to embattled debtors. The stratagem finally employed by Chipman to blunt the demand for relief involved a masterful use of popular rhetoric for essentially conservative ends. In consultation with like-minded men in the assembly, including Elijah Dewey, who had replaced Isaac Tichenor as Bennington's representative, Chipman devised a plan to stall action on a bank of currency and various tender acts until the popular demand for them had subsided. In this way they might keep the acts from ever becoming law. Chipman and his associates pressed for a popular referendum on a bank and tender laws. Claiming that the suffering of the people had become so great that relief was absolutely essential, Dewey and others exclaimed that the people themselves were the best judges of what laws were truly necessary and that therefore any legislation involving a bank or other relief measures should be submitted to a vote of the people. Dewey then proposed just such a resolution. Even though the proponents of relief immediately saw through this ruse, they found themselves on the horns of a dilemma. The resolution had been written in such a populist style—its proponents had so carefully aligned themselves with the cause of the people—that to oppose it would be to deny all principles of democracy. The resolution passed easily.[143] Much to their chagrin, the cadre of egalitarian democrats entrenched in the executive branch of Vermont's state government found themselves outmaneuvered by elitists like Chipman; ironically, the latter's ever-expanding power base lay in the assembly, that branch of government intended by the creators of Vermont's constitution to be the very embodiment of egalitarian principles.

Subsequent to the close of the assembly Thomas Chittenden and his supporters faced even greater frustrations. Unfortunately for them, the course of events played into the hands of Chipman and his colleagues before the referendum on relief measures could be held. As early as October a band of armed men attempted to close the courts in Windsor County in order to prevent foreclosures on their farms; then, throughout November these same people threatened to break into jails to free fellow rioters and anyone imprisoned for debt. The insurgents dispersed after a force of more than six hundred militiamen took the field.[144] A similar outbreak occurred in Rutland on November 21, when a band of "Regulators" disrupted court proceedings there. It required an even larger militia force to quell this disturbance.[145]

The insurgency in Rutland, involving hundreds of armed men, caused Governor Chittenden great anguish. Gentlemen associated with the courts contemptuously depicted the rioters as "boys and men of low character" who had been "misguided by a few persistent demagogues,"[146] but Chittenden knew better. Convinced that "whenever people were oppressed they will Mob," the governor sympathized completely with the men who attempted to close the courts.[147] He knew that the Regulator leaders included Col. Benjamin Cooley and Col. James Mead, who had been captains in Ethan Allen's original Green Mountain Boys, and others who had served as officers throughout the war in Seth Warner's regiment. Most of their followers had also been Green Mountain Boys or had fought under Warner. Beyond that, their political leader, John Fassett's son Jonathan, had just been elected to a fourth term in the Vermont Assembly. It disturbed Chittenden terribly to see so many who had been instrumental in the very creation of the state of Vermont now being pilloried in its courts as shiftless malcontents and irresponsible demagogues.

Regardless of the governor's compassion for the rioters, these outbreaks had a chilling effect upon voters throughout the state. Prior to the January 1, 1787, referenda on relief measures a call went out for a convention of "distressed" and "oppressed" inhabitants of the state to meet in the town of Ira. There committees and clerks of the Regulators of Vermont were to consult over the steps necessary to put "an immediate stop to Tyranny and Oppression" within the state.[148] In the wake of the disturbances in Windsor and Rutland, however, such a call was futile. Not only was the meeting of no consequence but the referenda suffered resounding defeats at the polls.[149]

Even before the newly elected assembly convened in Bennington on February 15, 1787, still another outbreak of violence had occurred. A rebellion of distressed farmers led by Daniel Shays had embroiled central and western Massachusetts in turmoil since the previous summer.[150] Finally, on February 3 the Massachusetts state militia routed a large force of insurgents commanded by Shays at Petersham. A great many Shaysites fled into Vermont. The Massachusetts government immediately dispatched Royall Tyler as an official emissary to the state of Vermont to request the aid of that government in capturing the fugitives. Tyler himself met with Governor Chittenden and the council, and Isaac Tichenor presented Tyler's petition for assistance to the Assembly.[151]

Tyler received conflicting responses from the executive and legislative branches of government in Vermont. Chittenden remained decidedly unsympathetic to Tyler's mission. Still disturbed that so many poor Vermont men who had risked their lives at the battle of Bennington and elsewhere were now indicted as rioters, he refused to aid Massachusetts in punishing similarly oppressed people from that state. Ethan Allen was a good deal more outspoken. He declared that "those who hold the reins of government in Massachusetts were a pack of Damned Rascals and that there was no virtue among them."[152] At the same time, though, Tyler's petition enjoyed quite a favorable reception in the assembly, where a special committee recommended that Chittenden issue a proclamation denouncing the "horrid & wicked rebellion" in Massachusetts, forbidding citizens of Vermont from harboring fugitives from that insurrection, and calling on all justices within the state to issue warrants for the apprehension of Shays and his followers.[153] When the governor and the council refused to cooperate with the assembly on this issue, the legislators promptly passed a resolution requiring Chittenden to issue the proclamation.[154] Four days later the representatives voted unanimously to support Elijah Dewey's resolution to strip Jonathan Fassett of his seat in the assembly.[155]

Chittenden and his supporters realized that they must cooperate with the majority in the assembly if they were to maintain any semblance of power in the government. Consequently, Matthew Lyon offered a resolution on March 2 praising members of the state militia, "whose spirited exertions crushed the late daring insurrections against Government in the Counties of Rutland & Windsor."[156] Clearly, those loyal to a conservative social order were gaining the ascendancy in Vermont's assembly.

Even before this meeting of the legislature, however, the power of the Chittenden-Allen faction was on the wane. The previous September Ira Allen had failed to be reelected to the council. Even though Chittenden appointed him secretary to that body, thereby enabling him to attend meetings, Allen's influence was seriously weakened. In addition, his hold on the treasurer's office became increasingly precarious. Having failed to gain a popular majority in 1784 and 1785, he had been elected in both these years only by a joint vote of the council and the assembly. Since that time, though, he had come under heavy fire from committees appointed by the assembly to audit his accounts and from private citizens who aired their suspicions of his actions as treasurer. Even more damaging, the Council of Censors, called for by the state constitution, in February 1786 issued a public statement critical of the council "for the appointment and continuance of persons in office of great public trust, who did not keep regular books."[157] In the face of such attacks Allen felt compelled to defend himself, which he did by publishing a lengthy "Treasurer's Address" in the *Gazette*.[158]

Allen's response only increased the opposition building throughout the state to his remaining in the treasurer's office. Nathaniel Brush of Bennington, who was an auditor of the treasurer's accounts, declared Allen's efforts mere "political puffs, formed to answer certain sinister purposes of his."[159] "A Plain Man" exclaimed that Allen would "not again deceive the people." "Rustick" openly wondered if the character and integrity of prominent state leaders were "unblemished by any little tricks to forward their private emolument." For their part, "Rustick" and his friends announced that many of "those now in office . . . will not answer our turn again."[160] These sentiments ultimately prevailed. In the September 1786 election Allen once again failed to gain a majority of votes for treasurer, and this time the legislature replaced him. Not only that, they named yet another committee to audit his accounts.

During the time that Allen was defending himself as treasurer, his activities as surveyor general also came under close scrutiny, especially his practice of accepting grants of land in lieu of a salary. As early as October 1785 the General Assembly had passed a resolution annulling and discontinuing Allen's surveys. Even though Chittenden and the council managed to postpone passage of this act in a joint session,[161] criticism of Allen would not die. "A Friend to Justice" pointedly inquired, "Where is the justice that the Surveyor General be allowed three times as much for his service in surveying an inhabited country, as the Surveyors appointed by Congress to survey the western wilderness?"[162] Expressing his suspicions of Allen and his close associates, a prominent political leader from east of the mountains asked, "Does any gentleman suppose, because the whole state has from its formation been assisting them to make an independent fortune, that they have a right to command the purses and properties of all its subjects?"[163] Chittenden's efforts to defend Allen's activities as surveyor general elicited bitter attacks upon the governor himself. "Lycurgus" declared that the "arts of a politician are like the dress of a harlot, both are calculated to deceive." He then proceeded to "undress the prostitute production" of Chittenden. At this same time "The Last Struggle" accused the governor of being an "artful politician."[164] When a man as popular as Chittenden suffered such criticism for defending his surveyor general, it was clear that Allen's days were numbered. Finally, in October 1787 the assembly named a new surveyor general. For the first time since 1778 Ira Allen held no elected position in the Vermont government.

Allen's questionable activities touched more than just his own reputation; they soon began to haunt his close friend and political associate Thomas Chittenden. Two years after Allen lost his position as surveyor general, Chittenden failed to be reelected governor. This resulted from a scandal involving a lapsed township charter that Chittenden had granted to Allen in payment for his services as surveyor general but had failed to clear with the legislature. When the assembly unearthed this transaction, public outcry became so strident that Chittenden failed to garner a majority of votes in the gubernatorial election of 1789. The assembly promptly named Moses Robinson to replace him even though he had received only 746 popular votes to Chittenden's 1,263.[165]

Chittenden's defeat in the assembly revealed that a growing number of citizens, following the lead of Tichenor and Chipman, had serious questions regarding the ability of Chittenden and the old guard to lead the state. In 1786 the Council of Censors had expressed gratitude "to that Being who is wisdom, and by whom a few husbandmen, unexperienced in the arts of governing, have been enabled to pilot the ship through storms and quicksands, into the haven of independence and safety."[166] Now, three years later, many of Vermont's new political leaders, no longer willing to rely upon providential intervention, meant to take government out of the hands of those "unexperienced husbandmen." With the removal of Chittenden and Ira Allen, the impeachment of Matthew Lyon for refusing to turn over the records of the Court of Confiscation, and the death of Ethan Allen in February 1789, this task, which once had appeared so formidable, now seemed within the grasp of Chipman, Tichenor, and their allies.

In Chipman's mind the best way to effect this transfer of power was to court the supporters of the new federal constitution and to bring Vermont into the union under their auspices. He initiated a correspondence with Alexander Hamilton that culminated in a convention held in Bennington on January 6, 1791, to ratify the U.S. Constitution.[167] Although Chittenden, who had been reelected governor in 1790, chaired the convention and Ira Allen attended as a delegate from Colchester, Nathaniel Chipman was the driving force of the meeting. The composition of the convention showed how radically things had changed. Only 5 of the 110 delegates had been members of the convention of July 24, 1776, which had initiated the movement for a separate state.[168] The coalition of New Lights and Green Mountain Boys that had brought the state into existence had given way to a nearly even mix of Old Lights, New Lights, egalitarian democrats, and those committed to a hierarchical view of government and society.[169]

Following Vermont's entrance into the Union on February 18, 1791, these same groups continued to contest one another for social and political dominance within Bennington and throughout the state. After statehood, though, the battle lines became ever more sharply drawn, the conflict increasingly bitter.

6. Divisions throughout the Town

At the time of Vermont's entrance into the Union, Bennington, with a population of 2,350, was the second largest town in the state and the most influential west of the Green Mountains, where it assumed a position of central importance.[1] Its strategic location at the intersection of major east-west and north-south thoroughfares helped make the village the hub for economic activity in the region. The opening of the stone post road to Albany in March 1791 gave the town's farmers easy access to the markets of Albany and, ultimately, New York City and enabled Bennington merchants to strengthen their position as the essential middlemen for an extensive agricultural hinterland. The *Vermont Gazette*, the only newspaper printed west of the mountains, further augmented the town's economic strength and political influence. The Vermont Assembly validated the town's political stature when it gathered for the eighth time in the meetinghouse at Bennington on January 10, 1791. In addition, whenever the state supreme court met west of the mountains, it convened in the courthouse in Bennington, which was also the center of land and probate activities in the area. The town gained additional stature from the fact that it was home to prominent federal officeholders: Noah Smith, the newly appointed collector of internal revenue for the state, resided in the village, as did Moses Robinson, the first man elected to the U.S. Senate from Vermont. Little wonder, then, that Bennington was the only town in the state visited by Secretary of State Thomas Jefferson and Congressman James Madison during their northeastern tour in the summer of 1791.[2]

As political activities centering upon Bennington intensified and as

the region served by the town experienced increasing commercializa-
tion, the village itself underwent marked changes. By the time of statehood many new homes and public buildings graced the hills overlooking the Walloomsac. In addition to the Catamount Inn, nine other
taverns served patrons in Bennington. The State Arms Tavern, located
opposite the courthouse, on the militia green, had become the social
center for the uphill section of the village; Elijah Dewey's commodious
inn situated near the meetinghouse assumed that function for downhill
people. Six merchants sold a wide variety of mercantile goods, and
numerous artisans practiced their trades in shops throughout the village. In addition to wheelwrights, goldsmiths, tailors, watchmakers,
and blacksmiths, those serving the townspeople of Bennington even
included a hairdresser and a wigmaker. While the saw and gristmills of
the Saffords, the Walbridges, and the Henrys continued to meet their
essential needs, town residents could now purchase finished iron products from an iron forge and blast furnace that had begun operations on
the eastern fringe of the township. They could also draw on the professional services of the town's three doctors and four attorneys. If their
physicians, including Jonas Fay, the first president of the newly formed
Vermont Medical Society, were self-educated, their attorneys were not.
Noah Smith and Isaac Tichenor, the town's most successful practition-
ers of the law, were graduates of Yale and Princeton, respectively. Such
sophisticated gentlemen appeared eminently qualified to deal with the
dynamic new world of politics and business facing the townspeople of
Bennington and the inhabitants of the infant state of Vermont.

     While the village proper teemed with activity and change, the sur-
rounding countryside had taken on a distinctly settled appearance.
During the last decade of the eighteenth century, when Vermont experienced the highest growth rate in the nation, Bennington's population
had already stabilized.[3] This was not only because the town was one
of the oldest in the state but because of its initial settlement pattern
as well. Since Bennington's original proprietors were also among the
town's first settlers, they were able to use the power of the proprietary
for their own economic advancement. Consequently, certain families —
the Robinsons, the Fays, the Deweys, the Saffords, and others — controlled most of the best land in the township from the outset.[4] Their
initial advantage grew exponentially over time. Because they owned so
much property, these families were able to reap large profits when land
values rose as a result of increased migration into the township. It was
they who had excess land to sell to newcomers. In addition, income

from such sales enabled them to outbid others for land sold at public auction, land they could then afford to hold for speculative purposes and thus further advance the cycle of profit.[5]

At the same time that these early settlers were buying and selling land, they were also improving their own farms. This enabled them not only to ship crops to market in Albany but to dominate the lucrative trade in provisions purchased by newcomers in the area as well as by the constant stream of migrants passing through Bennington on their way north.[6] With the passage of time, then, the pattern of land and wealth distribution in the township became increasingly skewed; older families, particularly those that had been original proprietors, controlled a disproportionate amount of both.[7] A tremendous disparity existed between the amount of land owned by these men and the amount owned by individuals who settled in Bennington after the Revolution. It was not unusual for early settlers to own more than four times as much land as a man who came to the area after 1791.[8] In addition, early settlers dominated the important positions in town government during the last decades of the eighteenth century.[9] Thus, by the time Vermont entered the Union on March 4, 1791, Bennington was already a stable, settled community.

First Church too exhibited every outward sign of stability on the eve of statehood. The divisions caused by David Avery's dismissal appeared to have healed. After his departure the church had not only survived without a minister but had actually thrived. Forty-seven new members owned the covenant during a 1784 revival tended by neighboring ministers.[10] Following that, a new spirit of cooperation pervaded the church. Swayed by this feeling of harmony, members of the church and the society joined together to give a call to Rev. Job Swift, whose installation as pastor took place in May 1786.

While unity within the church certainly contributed to the call given to Swift, other factors played a part in bringing a man so much like the recently dismissed David Avery to Bennington. The fact that the members of First Church could unite upon Swift reflected not only their commitment to have a settled minister among them but also the shortage of ordained ministers in rural New England.[11] In any event, Swift was cut from the same stamp as Avery: born to a family of moderate means, he had graduated from Yale, married a woman from a conservative Massachusetts family, served as a chaplain during the Revolutionary War, and been dismissed from several churches before coming to Bennington, and he was a firm advocate of the principles of the New

Divinity. He was also outspoken and pugnacious.[12] Unlike Avery, however, Swift was able to temper his religious doctrines to such an extent that he neither offended nor confused his parishioners. While only one person joined the church during Avery's ministry, thirty came into the fold under Swift.[13] Further, Swift was a family man; he arrived in Bennington with eight children, and his wife gave birth to six more during their tenure in the town. Throughout the course of Swift's ministry in Bennington, his home was open to any and all of his parishioners.[14]

Although the church did not experience any tension because of its minister, problems nonetheless developed shortly after his installation. On January 16, 1789, Daniel Harmon brought a charge against Simeon Hatheway for "being dishonest in his dealings and overreaching his brother by false representations." Following several months of labor during which three arbitrators failed to bring the men together, the church excommunicated Hatheway.[15] This did not bring the matter to a close, however; instead, what began as a simple dispute between two individuals mushroomed until it disrupted not only the church but the entire town.

This escalation did not stem from the simple facts of the case — a mistaken notation on a deed. The initial quarrel became caught up in the cultural tensions beginning to divide the townspeople of Bennington as well as the citizens of Vermont. The Harmons, ordinary farming people who had been among the first signers of the church covenant, maintained a strong belief in equity and fairness. They, like the majority of their fellow church members, placed far greater faith in common justice than they did in the strict letter of the law. In their view, simple fair-mindedness required that Simeon Hatheway change a deed that had mistakenly given him a tremendous advantage over Daniel Harmon. Hatheway, whose family's mercantile and industrial activities linked him to men such as Noah Smith and Isaac Tichenor, refused to comply on the grounds that, regardless of how unfair it might seem to church members, the law specifically prohibited him from altering a legal document. Not only did he refuse to revise the deed but he took his case to the public in a series of open letters published in the *Gazette*.[16]

Simeon Hatheway's legalistic defense and his deliberate flouting of the privacy traditionally associated with church discipline helped widen the growing division between uphill and downhill sections of the town. This tension between those espousing a simple, egalitarian communalism and those committed to a more cosmopolitan, hierarchical perception of society had festered in the town since the ministry of David

Avery. It worsened when Isaac Tichenor led the opposition to Thomas Chittenden's relief measures during the winter of 1786–87; then, by the fall of 1793, with Tichenor himself running for governor against Chittenden, the resentment of the uphill people finally boiled over. "A Farmer" warned the people of Bennington of the emergence of an "aristocratical party"; in fact, the "republican spirit" of the town was in danger of being eclipsed by a "patrician order." Even though the "genuine principles of good government" were neither complex nor mysterious and "men of common capacity [were] capable and better suited than others to be public officers," Tichenor's supporters — "lawyers and literary people" who had "imbibed all their political knowledge from books" — claimed that farmers and mechanics were "unacquainted with the principles of government" and thus "incapable of holding office." If allowed to succeed, Tichenor and his party would live in "idleness" while "the poor peasant and his family" toiled away in poverty to support the "splendor and luxury" created by a government of "energy and power." Devotion to "liberty, equality, and the rights of man" demanded that aristocratic politicians be brought down "on an average" with ordinary citizens.[17] Equality, not hierarchy, must remain the rule in Bennington.

Much to "Farmer's" relief, the election of 1793 resulted in yet another term for Governor Chittenden. Although Tichenor, commonly referred to by his uphill opponents as the "Jersey Slick,"[18] easily carried the eastern counties of the state, Chittenden's large majorities west of the mountains enabled him to prevail.[19] The results were the same in three subsequent gubernatorial elections. It was not until September 1797, following Chittenden's death in August, that Tichenor finally succeeded in being elected governor of Vermont. In the absence of the popular old governor, Tichenor also increased his support west of the mountains. For their part, though, the citizens of Bennington voted overwhelmingly against Tichenor in all these elections.[20]

The stubborn opposition to Tichenor sprang from a dogged loyalty on the part of most Bennington freemen to an egalitarian heritage rooted not only in the original foundations of the town and the church but also in the struggle against Yorker aristocrats that had united New Lights and Green Mountain Boys. During the Revolution Ethan Allen had grafted an exaltation of the ordinary yeoman to this opposition to aristocracy, an exaltation that became ingrained in the thought and language of Nathan Clark, John Fassett, Samuel Robinson, and other leaders of the Revolutionary movement within Bennington. With the onset of difficult economic times in the fall of 1786, this populist ethos led many townspeople to view certain recent immigrants, especially college-educated gentlemen and lawyers, as a threat to the natural republican order they so cherished. "Philo Justitiae" exclaimed that the machinations of attorneys led "honest farmers" to be "greatly distressed and their property unjustly extorted from them by designing men."[21] An old soldier, "Ephrim Shuwstrings," claimed to "have been through a tedius Wore fiting for liberty and Propurty and Seposing that [he] hadd Obtained it," only to return home to find the court "for Which [he] fought . . . fild up With theves, Cold By Som Parsons Lawyers." "Ephrim" considered attorneys "Law Lest Robers of the honest tillars of the Earth."[22]

Statehood, with its plethora of federal offices to be filled, intensified anxieties of the sort articulated by "Ephrim," "Philo," and many others. With the first election of representatives to Congress rapidly approaching, "Old Ethan" warned the freemen of Vermont to beware of aristocrats, who placed their own interests above the "equal freedom and happiness of the whole." In his mind, "brother Isaac [Tichenor]," "brother Noah [Smith]," and "brother Nathaniel [Chipman]" formed a combination that "ought to alarm *the old Greenmountain corps.*" Offended by such men's presumption that only gentlemen — sophisticated, cosmopolitan, and well educated — were capable of holding public office, "Ethan" declared "common sense and good natural powers" to be worth far more than "the flowers of oratory, the rhetoric of schools, or the duplicity of courtiers."[23] Urging the people to vote in the upcoming elections, "A Land-Holder" asked what class of people should be represented in Congress and the state assembly: "Who are the *great body* of the people? Are they lawyers — Physicians — Merchants — Tradesmen? No — they are a respectable *Yeomanry, Farmers.*" It was the yeomanry, then, who ought to be represented. Lawyers were a "necessary *evil* in society" and must, therefore, be kept in their proper place. They might be judges, generals, or even governors, but because they represented "a particular order of men, whose views, feelings, and interests, are by no means, the views, feelings, and interests of their constituents," they must never serve as legislators.[24]

These attitudes were not unique to the freemen of Bennington. They pervaded areas of the state in which the old alliance between radical New Lights and Green Mountain Boys had been particularly strong. A militia gathering in Benson in the summer of 1792, for example, first saluted the memory of Ethan Allen and then expressed the hope that America might "be long defended from inundation which is threatened by the increase of aristocrats, who wish for a rich metropolis, and a poor peasantry."[25] For his part, "A.B." declared that the interests of lawyers "and those of the respectable Yeomanry Farmers, or the great body of the people, are in direct opposition."[26] Enraged by the argument that only gentlemen possessed the rationality, intelligence, and education to serve as public officials, "Preceptor" asked, "Are colleges the only resort of genius and ability? Are blockheads no where to be found but at the plough? Are American farmers vassals?" "Preceptor" emphatically maintained that farmers comprised "the most independent of our countrymen. They are the supporters of the liberties of our country, and of the rights of man."[27]

Immediately upon entering the race in 1791 to represent Vermont's western district in Congress, Matthew Lyon was the lightning rod for this groundswell of popular emotions.[28] With Ethan Allen dead and his brother Ira beset by personal economic difficulties, Lyon became the principal spokesman of the emergent yeoman ethic.[29] In this capacity he helped mold commonly held yet seemingly inchoate convictions — beliefs that had long seemed too instinctive, and their outward manifestations too occasional, scattered, and ephemeral, to assume the strength of a coherent belief system — into a powerful social and political ideology.

From the time he first entered the race for Congress until he finally gained election to the U.S. House of Representatives over five years later, Lyon kept up an unceasing attack upon privilege and aristocracy. In Lyon's mind, privilege did not mean wealth; it connoted wealth gained by special advantage, without labor. Equal rights, which to Lyon required that every citizen enjoy equal access to all means of earning a living as well as equal access to public office, became his passion. The absence of such equality smacked of aristocracy, a social and political condition that had elicited blind rage in him since childhood. A successful entrepreneur himself, Lyon never begrudged a man his affluence.[30] He did, however, care deeply about *how* a man acquired that affluence. Wealth gained from an individual's own honest effort was one thing, wealth resulting from special advantage quite another. Thus, Lyon constantly pitted independent, hardworking, producers against idle, unproductive members of society.

With the passage of time Lyon sharpened his focus considerably. Prior to the election campaign of 1793 he began publishing a newspaper in Rutland, the *Farmer's Library*, with his son James as editor.

The first edition set the tone for the paper: an address by Thomas Paine advocating liberty throughout the world consumed the entire front page.[31] By this time Paine's *Rights of Man*, published the previous year, had become Lyon's bible; its principles filled both his rhetoric and the pages of his newspaper.[32] This was particularly true of Paine's egalitarian attack upon all forms of aristocracy, his advocacy of the natural ability of the common man, and his emphasis upon not only republican principles of government and society but democratic beliefs as well.[33]

Through the campaign of 1793 and thereafter, Lyon characterized Federalist supporters of Alexander Hamilton in Congress and their advocates in Vermont as "a set of aristocrats" intent upon subverting American republicanism. He accused Nathaniel Chipman, who had been appointed judge for the federal district of Vermont, of betraying republican principles in exchange for gaining "a share of the spoils of your country." By this he meant that Chipman had helped elect a man to Congress who would "concur with the secretary of the treasury, and the other nabobs," in "screwing the hard-earnings out of poor people's pockets" in order to pay "enormous salaries to idle judges" and a whole range of other useless public officials. There was little doubt in Lyon's mind that Federalists intended to create an American aristocracy at the people's expense.[34]

Believing that "the great body of the people themselves [should] undertake to watch over the government," Lyon praised the activities of Democratic-Republican societies, which had sprung up throughout the nation.[35] These groups, derisively characterized by Federalists as "self-created" societies composed of "butchers, tinkers, broken hucksters, and trans-Atlantic traitors," promoted the open discussion of political subjects by ordinary citizens and the careful oversight of elected officials by these same people.[36] Lyon acknowledged that these societies were "laughed at, and ridiculed" by Federalists, "men who consider the science of government to belong naturally only to a few families, and argue that these families ought to be obeyed and supported in princely grandeur." They thought that "the common people ought to give their earnings to these few, for keeping them under." Lyon sarcastically observed that ordinary individuals should be thankful to such gentlemen for "awing their poor commonality from destroying one another, which their savage nature would lead to, were it not for the benignity and good sense of the few superiors heaven has been pleased to plant among them."[37]

Lyon argued vehemently that town meetings in Vermont should

follow the lead of the Democratic-Republican societies by discussing public issues and public officials. Citizens should learn exactly how their tax money was spent and why; they needed to question the actions of their representatives in the General Assembly and to call them to task for all unpopular votes. Let the annual town meeting, which usually lasted only a matter of hours, take up several days if necessary. The citizens of Vermont must take responsibility for state government into their own hands. Such suggestions "will be despised by a set of gentry, who are interested in keeping the government at a distance from, and out of sight of the people who support it," but rule by effete gentlemen was, nonetheless, over. In place of their cosmopolitan sophistication "plain good Sense" must reign. From Lyon's perspective, this was entirely "sufficient for the government of a Democratic Republic."[38]

Several months after Lyon's strident defense of popular involvement in politics, citizens banded together and formed Democratic-Republican societies in Rutland, Chittenden, and Addison counties. Members of these clubs pledged themselves to support the "promotion of genuine republicanism," "the exaltation of human nature," and "equal liberty and the equal rights of man."[39] They took as their primary function the discussion of all political issues in Congress.

The appearance of Democratic-Republican societies alarmed Vermont Federalists. Nathaniel Chipman wrote an extensive and widely reprinted letter in which he contrasted the turbulence and chaos characteristic of "simple democracies" with the stability and good order of "representative democracies." From Chipman's perspective, these Democratic-Republican societies meant to "dictate" — to instruct representatives — how to vote on various measures before Congress. Nothing could be worse; popular discussion of public issues in "self created societies" rather than in traditional forums — organic manifestations of society itself — led by responsible individuals were "not merely useless, but mischievous and a very dangerous imposition." They were the very embodiment of simple democracies, with all the "turbulence, violence, and fluctuation" of that form of government. Chipman thought that long experience revealed ad hoc assemblies of common people to be "impatient of discussion," "fatally incapable of reasoning," and "highly susceptible of passions." The people in such assemblies easily fell prey to artful demagogues. There could be no stability, no good order; instead, "every thing is liable to be changed by the frenzy of the moment, or the influence of popular faction." Since most public measures were complicated, the people, "for want of information, for want of leisure,

patience or abilities," would be "wholly ignorant of the relative circumstances necessary to be known, in order to [reach] a just and proper
determination." Consequently, the ignorance of the people could result
only in "presumption, passionate zeal, and obstinancy" rather than in
the disinterested and rational judgment rendered by those with experience, education, and the leisure to reflect upon the public welfare.[40] In
Chipman's mind, then, only gentlemen gathered in well-established
representative assemblies could provide the kind of permanent security
for all promised by a republican form of government and society.

   Although the residents of Bennington County never formed a
Democratic-Republican society, many of the citizens of Bennington
Township took seriously Lyon's call for popular discussion of public issues. Thus, on Saturday, August 28, 1795, a large number of freemen
gathered at the courthouse to discuss Jay's Treaty.[41] After electing Samuel Safford moderator and having the document itself read, many spoke
out against the treaty. When no one responded to Safford's call for
discussion in favor of the treaty, the assembly unanimously declared
it to be unjust, partial, and dishonorable to the United States. The
group then chose Samuel Safford, Jonathan Robinson, Anthony Haswell, David Fay, and Joseph Safford to prepare critical resolutions,
which were discussed and passed the next Tuesday. They called for a
convention of all the towns of Bennington County to meet later in the
month to instruct their representative in Congress how to vote on the
issue and elected Haswell and Fay the town's delegates to the county
convention.[42]

   By this time the principles of Thomas Paine and the rhetoric of
Matthew Lyon had become a shaping influence in the thought of the
uphill people in Bennington. From the time Thomas Jefferson introduced the town's democratic leaders to Paine's *Rights of Man* during his
visit in the summer of 1791 an emphasis upon the "Natural rights of
Man" had assumed great importance for these men.[43] When, for instance, an eminent lawyer declared that individuals must be capable not
only of reading Jay's Treaty but of understanding it in the context of
other treaties before they could pass judgment on it, a local democrat
became livid. He compared such sentiments to the traditional idea
"which secured to the high born, *the right to rule; to the* well bred, *the
privilege of exclusive rights*, and *to the* well educated, *the supreme power of
judging and determining what is white and what is black.*"[44]

   These attitudes were not peculiar to residents of Bennington. Ordinary citizens throughout the western half of the state spoke out vig-

orously in favor of the natural abilities of the common man and against special privilege for gentlemen. "A Farmer," for example, expressed resentment toward the inequalities of Vermont's militia laws. Declaring that there had "ever been a combination of men in this state, who have strained every nerve, to fling this and every other unequal burden, on the poor and industrious part of the community," he asked, "Why are we the poor, the industrious poor, the only persons who are obliged to perform military service?" And then: "Why are not attorneys, who amass large fortunes, by encouraging litigation among their neighbors, called on to contribute to the general defence?"[45] For his part, "Green Mountain Boy" declared that every man had an equal right to speak on any and all issues. To those who claimed that a person must be bred as a scholar, a lawyer, or a statesman to offer an opinion on politics he asked, "Is this liberty?" Who, after all, were the supporters of government, if not the farmers and mechanics, who bore the greatest burden of governmental expense? In his opinion, the honest and industrious laborer had more merit than the "idle, let them be of what profession they will, whether divine, statesman, lawyer or physician." A farmer's thoughts on politics were superior to those of any of these men, certainly more candid and honest, because they were natural and thus without the bias resulting from formal education.[46]

Beliefs such as these were not, however, universal in Vermont. Many who lived in the eastern half of the state viewed such attitudes with contempt; in addition, growing numbers of citizens west of the mountains also opposed them. "Sound Policy," for example, supported Isaac Tichenor for governor in 1797 because there was "nothing of the scholar or gentleman" in his opponents, who were "as rude and rough as any man can wish." A governor should be a man of dignity, property, and independence, but most of all he should be educated and intelligent. Instead, Tichenor's opponents included individuals "who can scarcely read or write."[47] "A Friend to Order" declared that at a time when the nation faced "foes of order, religion and government from abroad" and "a turbulent, designing and execrable faction at home," it was necessary for every "friend of peace and morality" to stand against those who would undermine the peace and good order of their nation and state. The people of Vermont must oppose the election of Matthew Lyon.[48] "No Jacobin" supported Isaac Tichenor in 1798 against Moses Robinson and Gideon Olin. In his mind, it was "sufficient to say," of Tichenor's opponents, "*they are democrats.*"[49] In an impassioned address to the public, "Observer" claimed that citizens attached "to the federal government, to good order, regularity, the laws, and *our most holy reli-gion*" must stand together against the "base designs and artful intrigues of" the state's "worthless, degenerate, *Frenchified* citizens." Men such as Samuel Safford and Gideon Olin, "secret enemies to our country and our religion," were "base, irreligious, atheistical, disorganizers, and pretended philosophers, who will introduce anarchy, confusion, rapine and murder into this peaceable and happy country."[50]

Becoming increasingly exasperated by the success in Bennington of the political sentiments of their uphill opponents, downhill leaders, who were by this time proud to call themselves Federalists, vented their frustrations on July 4, 1798.[51] For the first time in the town's history two separate celebrations of the nation's birth took place in Benning-ton. While uphill folk gathered under a liberty cap and the American flag at the State Arms Tavern, downhill leaders assembled at Elijah Dewey's inn, where they enjoyed a sumptuous dinner and celebrated sentiments such as "The American character—May it wipe off the rust of Jacobinism and assume its native dignity" and "The essence of Republicanism—The acquiescence of the minority, in the decisions of the majority." Noah Smith, Eldad Dewey, Moses Robinson Jr., and others offered volunteer toasts: "May the friends of order move for-ward and the rest be allured to follow" and "A speedy downfall to modern democracy."[52]

Like so many other New England Federalists, the downhill people of Bennington supported a social ideal that stressed stability, harmony, dependence, and the common good.[53] More than anything else, they identified with established authority emanating from a hierarchical so-cial and political order. They esteemed their "betters" and felt obliged to guide and direct those inferior to themselves. They considered a stable, structured society to be an anchor of security and identity in a rapidly changing, chaotic world. They remained very much aware of inequalities in society and intended to maintain a governing elite sup-ported by the votes of the people by strengthening traditional habits and customs of deference through the family, the church, and energetic government.

Federalists, whether they resided in Bennington or Boston, felt that something deeply disturbing was at work in American society. The economic and social changes wrought by the Revolution and the cor-rupting influence of the French Revolution brought older standards of behavior under attack, new ones arising in their stead. Instead of quietly accepting their status in life, all sorts of people now struggled for material wealth and political prominence. Men who had always sought only the respect of their neighbors now clamorously appealed for the votes of the mob. What was worse, they had banded together to form a political party — the very bane of a republican government's existence — that aimed at nothing less than the total transformation of society. Courting all men regardless of their status or worth, the Democratic party intended to create the new man who would demand social, political, and economic equality with even the most genteel.[54]

Bennington's Federalists viewed unrestricted free speech in much the same manner. The notion that all free individuals should be allowed to voice their opinion, no matter how scandalous or abusive, left them incredulous. If this were true, they would be forced to accept the fulminations of Matthew Lyon and his supporters as not only legitimate but proper. This was intolerable; if any man symbolized all that was wrong with politics and society, it was Matthew Lyon. This former indentured servant, this "ignorant Irish puppy," not only had risen to become one of their state's leading manufacturers but had been elected to Congress in 1797. Worse still, he enjoyed the overwhelming support of Bennington freemen.[55] How fortuitous, then, when the Federalist majority in Congress passed the Sedition Law (1798) and a federal court found Lyon guilty of seditious libel under its provisions in October 1798 and sentenced him to four months in prison and a fine of one thousand dollars.[56]

Whatever pleasure Bennington Federalists enjoyed as a result of Lyon's imprisonment was short-lived. *The Scourge of Aristocracy*, a magazine printed by Lyon and his son in Fairhaven, kept up an unrelenting attack upon Federalist "aristocrats" while the prisoner served his sentence.[57] In addition, Anthony Haswell began to criticize Federalists as "church and state men, who preach Presidential instead of Papal infallibility."[58] Haswell also rallied to Lyon's defense, lauding the congressman while criticizing Isaac Tichenor. As a result of Haswell's editorials, the *Vermont Gazette* rapidly became the most forthright voice of democracy in the state. Far more irritating to Bennington Federalists, the editor became an outspoken champion of the common man — a thorn in the side of the "great" men of Bennington. A committed egalitarian, Haswell subjected the pretensions of the downhill leadership to constant criticism. After noting how the presence of a "common farmer" as their congressional representative was "truly a grievance to the great," for example, Haswell observed that throughout history the defense of civil and religious liberties in a republic had rested with "common men." He reveled in the distress the "sober men of Bennington" suffered whenever Congressman Lyon visited their town. The way these "literary men" carped about Lyon's abilities as a writer also amused him. He was not amused, however, when "our great men declare[d] lately, in public company, that none are fitted for offices of profit or honor, but such as have had a collegiate education."[59]

Haswell further outraged Tichenor and his associates upon Lyon's release from prison. Having been reelected to Congress while incarcerated, Lyon enjoyed a triumphant ride through Vermont upon gaining his freedom. He received wild accolades from his supporters in all the towns along the route he followed to take his seat in Congress. At the State Arms Tavern in Bennington a large group of Republicans serenaded him with a ballad composed for the occasion by Haswell that praised Lyon and ridiculed his Federalist opponents.[60] Haswell gave a stirring oration lauding the principles of the Revolution, the wisdom of Thomas Jefferson, and the fortitude of Matthew Lyon. He then asked his audience to "explore the tracts of truth, and follow the enthusiastic glow of liberty, till the minions of despotism tremble at the frown of democratic virtue, till the gewgaws of royalty cease to glitter in the western world, or levees and drawing-rooms cease to monkify the fashions of our rising nation."[61]

In light of such rhetoric, political tensions continued to increase in Bennington. Once again the townspeople held separate celebrations on July 4. This time, however, the Federalists made fun of the fact that John Fassett and Anthony Haswell, president and vice-president of the Republican celebration, could not take part in their party's procession through town because both were confined to the gaol yard for their inability to pay their debts. The Federalists crowed that the bulk of the Republican procession consisted of "boys and negroes." Haswell responded that the Federalist celebration included primarily "old tories who opposed our Revolution," "professed opposers of republicanism on the avowed principle that no people has virtue enough to support such a form of government," and men "who have sworn out of gaol to defraud their creditors." On the other hand, "real republicans, substantial farmers, veterans of our Revolution and youth who have embibed their sentiments" made up the Republican procession.[62]

Through the summer of 1799 Haswell kept up an unrelenting attack upon Federalism. At a Republican celebration on August 16 he delivered a devastating critique of Federalist transgressions, particularly the manner in which the Sedition Law restricted the people's right of free speech. During a lengthy oration commemorating the battle of Bennington he continually returned to a central theme, the sovereignty of the people. Republican governments rested on the principle that "the supreme power is, and forever ought to be, in the hands of the body of the people." Since "the supreme power itself can never be deputed, the actual sovereignty resides in the body of the people." Anyone who attempted to subvert this principle was a "traitor to the commonwealth of freedom."[63] Every true republican must "spurn the idea in its every shape, that when the people are assembled [to elect their representatives] they are omnipotent, but when they have appointed their servants, they have transferred their omnipotence and sink to nothing."[64] Even after "the people have deputed they are not defunct; the sovereignty is not annihilated."[65] Instead, the "public voice" must always "have a mode of expressing itself";[66] otherwise tyranny reigned supreme.

By the fall of 1799 Federalist authorities had had enough. On October 8 two deputy marshals arrested Haswell and escorted him to Rutland, where he faced indictments on two counts of violating the Sedition Law. U.S. Supreme Court Justice William Paterson bound him over to the May term of the court in Windsor and released him on bail. On May 5, 1800, a jury selected from the Federalist strongholds of Brattleborough, Putney, and Westminster found Haswell guilty on both counts. Four days later Judge Paterson sentenced the editor to two months in prison and fined him two hundred dollars and court costs.[67]

Knowing that Haswell was to be released on July 9, Republican supporters in the Bennington area postponed their Fourth of July celebration until that day. The moment Haswell left the Bennington gaol a free man, celebrants fired a salute with the old cannon on the parade ground. Several thousand strong, they escorted him through town to the tune of "Yankee Doodle." When they reached the State Arms, they began singing patriotic songs Haswell had composed for the occasion. Before the day was over more people had flocked onto the parade ground to celebrate the release of this martyr to liberty than had ever previously gathered in Bennington.[68]

While unity and harmony characterized the throng at the State Arms Tavern, this was anything but true within the town itself; citizens of Bennington were turning upon one another with fierce intensity. Political tension became so strident that the very institutions that had long been the sources of the community's cohesiveness fragmented into warring factions. Indeed, animosities assumed such bitterness in the Masonic lodge that it disintegrated altogether.

The demise of Temple Lodge was eloquent testimony to the divisive power of the political strains rending the communal fabric of the town. In Bennington as in many other areas, Freemasonry had provided a means whereby men caught up in the mobile, expanding society of Revolutionary America could unite in a fraternity pledged to furthering the principles of republicanism.[69] Believing that they were creating a voluntary community devoted to reconciling public and private interests in a free society, a diverse set of citizens had united in Bennington and throughout the nation.[70] Temple Lodge, chartered on May 18, 1793, joined together such unlikely coworkers as Noah Smith, Isaac Tichenor, Nathaniel Brush, David Robinson, Anthony Haswell, Joseph Safford, and Joseph and David Fay.[71] Within five years, however, political differences in the lodge became so intense that its members could not agree even on delegates to represent them at the annual meetings of the Grand Lodge.[72] By 1800, lodge meetings were impossible, and in 1809 the Grand Lodge declared Temple Lodge extinct.[73]

First Church also began to experience serious divisions. In fact, the church's pastor was rapidly becoming the focal point of discord not only within the church but throughout the larger community as well. It was not the Reverend Swift's theology but his political beliefs that created strife among his parishioners. Job Swift was an ardent Federalist. He shared the political dogma of his brother-in-law Theodore Sedgwick and other of the party's most extreme partisans in Massachusetts and throughout New England. Imbibing their social sentiments as well, Swift believed that society should be like a "well regulated family," an organic whole whose harmony resulted from "each one learning his proper place and keeping to it." The "better sort" should "rule" rather than "govern" in a political system held together by a deferential spirit.[74]

Swift often preached that an "all-wise God" had "established a beautiful subordination amongst men," which rested on "different relations and circumstances" and was "absolutely necessary to the harmony and well-being of society." It naturally followed that the modern "doctrine of liberty and equality" was "destructive to society, and subversive of the fundamental principles of religion and morality." When the Bible instructed Christians to honor their father and their mother, it "meant not only natural parents, but all superiors in age and gifts; especially, such as by God's ordinance, are placed over us in authority in family, church, or commonwealth."[75] Thus did Swift meld Christian theology with Federalist ideology.

That their pastor had become one of the most prominent "church and state" men in the community deeply troubled members of First Church, most of whom were loyal Republicans. To make matters worse, Swift quite pointedly slighted their most revered leader in his public prayers. While offering the customary supplication in support of the nation's president, he refused to recognize Vice President Jefferson as a Christian and therefore deliberately excluded him.[76] Worse still, Swift even began flaunting a Federalist cockade in public. When he entered First Church wearing this emblem, however, Moses Robinson arose and snatched it away from him. Following a brief scuffle, Swift regained the badge and proudly mounted the pulpit. Robinson stalked out and refused to return as long as Swift remained as minister.[77] Even though Swift maintained considerable support within the society, most members of the church sided with Robinson in what became an increasingly bitter feud. Longtime friends crossed the street to avoid speaking to one another, and church services became chilly affairs. Finally, on June 7, 1801, the church dismissed Job Swift.[78]

The political divisions affecting the fraternal and religious life of Bennington intruded into its courtrooms as well. During the summer and fall of 1802 the community experienced its first brutal killing and the subsequent trial of those involved. On Sunday evening, August 8, three farm laborers harvesting grain for Roswell Moseley became involved in a violent argument. Two of them picked up clubs and crushed the skull of the third man, who died two days later.[79] The case immediately assumed political overtones. Moseley, a prominent Federalist, took an interest in the fate of the deceased man, Stephen Gordon, a transient Indian, and had the other two men arrested for murder. This was the charge the grand jury, dominated by Federalists, brought against George Tibbetts and George Whitney. The defendants were from loyal Republican families of poor farm people in nearby Pownall and Stamford. Local Republicans immediately came to the aid of the two young men, raising enough money to hire Pierpont Edwards to defend them. Edwards, the youngest son of Jonathan Edwards, was a New Haven lawyer with a reputation for representing difficult cases. He was also one of the principal leaders of the Republican party in Connecticut and the driving force behind attempts to disestablish the Congregational Church in that state.

The trial, which was heard by the Vermont Supreme Court, opened in the courthouse in Bennington on November 4. Chief Justice Jonathan Robinson and Associate Justices Royall Tyler and Stephen Jacob presided. Following lengthy arguments by Edwards and State's Attorney Richard Skinner, the jury, made up of local Republicans, found the defendants not guilty of murder. They did, however, find the two men guilty of manslaughter. The verdict threw Justices Jacob and Tyler, both distinguished Federalist leaders in the state, into a rage. Jacob, a graduate of Yale and a trained attorney, lectured the jurors on the judicial statutes regarding murder. Tyler, a Harvard graduate and a trained lawyer as well, followed with a lengthy and erudite examination of the legal definition of manslaughter. Clearly, the commonsense approach taken by members of the jury exasperated both men; they demanded that the case be reconsidered in light of the legal edification they had just delivered. Chief Justice Robinson, a loyal Jeffersonian of little formal education and no legal training, returned the case to the jurors without commenting on the finer points of the law. He simply asked for their prayerful reconsideration. Once again the jurors returned the identical verdict. The following day Robinson sentenced both defendants to three months in prison, fined both men four hundred dollars, and required each of them to post a five-hundred-dollar bond to ensure their good behavior over the next ten years.[80]

The end of the trial did not, however, ease the town's anxieties. In the minds of many residents, the trial itself assumed quite a minor role in a much larger drama, a drama involving the very moral character of their town. George Tibbetts's pathetic warning against the evil tendency of breaking the Sabbath, offered spontaneously to the crowd gathered for Stephen Gordon's funeral, alerted those present to the moral deterioration enveloping their community.[81] Shortly thereafter Anthony Haswell pointed out the reasons for this decline: "The moral cause is the declension of religion; the natural cause, the prevalence of folly, and the introduction of frivolous amusements, gambling and Intemperance." Haswell was certain that if Bennington fathers and mothers would only "consider the consequences of permitting [their] sons to attend unlawful games, cards, dice, and billiards," they would recognize the evil consequences of these amusements: "In proportion as gambling and irregularity engage the mind of a man, female attractions and virtue lose their charms, and lewdness and inconstancy become less odious than formerly in their eyes." If such evils were not confronted, Bennington's sons would become "worse husbands and worse men," and its daughters "more lonesome and unhappy women."[82]

Haswell was not alone in his critique of Bennington. Following a visit to the town, Francis Asbury too "felt awful for this place and [its] people." In his opinion, the townspeople were "sinners, Deists, [and] Universalists."[83] A Congregational minister from Chelsea, Vermont, observed that "the degeneracy of Bennington was truly lamentable." He believed that the "depravity, infidelity, and heaven daring wickedness" of its people was "a subject of lamentation to the friends of Zion."[84] A young teacher who moved to Bennington in the fall of 1802 also noted the worldliness of most of its residents. Struck by the "greatness and grandeur" of the community, she felt that many "seemed marked with haughty ostentation" and did not take religion seriously. The teacher faced the threat of embarrassment whenever she went to her class since the room where she taught was directly above the shop of a man of "tremendous wit," who "usually turned [this wit] against religion."[85]

Members of First Church were all too aware of the moral declension their community had suffered since its founding as a New Light haven of Christian harmony and order. That the church was without a settled pastor did nothing to lessen these anxieties. Led by their deacons, Moses Robinson and Samuel Safford, members held regular Sunday services and attempted to maintain Christian discipline. Still, the church required a moral leader; not only First Church but also the larger community desperately needed revitalization. In the fall of 1802 the church sent out committees in search of pastors to lead a religious rebirth in Bennington. They returned with two Massachusetts ministers, James Davies from Mendon and Joshua Spalding of Salem. Neither man even faintly resembled Job Swift. Davies was an uncultivated, plain-spoken, and deeply earnest man of the people.[86] Spalding too was an unassuming egalitarian of little formal education, although he had attended a two-year school for ministers in rural Massachusetts.[87] Both were powerful evangelists who abhorred any manifestation of religious or social hierarchy and espoused an unflinching millennialism.

The two began their vigil in Bennington early in November and labored unceasingly through the following March. They initiated protracted three-day meetings in various parts of town, visited private homes, held prayer sessions in boardinghouses, established regular prayer meetings in the church on weekday evenings, and took charge of church services each Sunday. Their sermons, prayers, exhortations, and hymns combined images of free grace, a loving Jesus, and God's awful wrath on the day of vengeance.[88] Both men alternated between soothing descriptions of Jesus the Lamb and terrifying images of God the Avenger — between everlasting peace and total annihilation. Aroused to a fury, Spalding described the battle on the great day that preceded the millennium, when "the beast [would be] taken, and with him the false prophet that wrought miracles before him." Both would be "cast alive into a lake of fire burning with brimstone." The "remnant" would be "slain with the sword of Christ, which sword proceeded out of his mouth, and all the fowls were filled with their flesh."[89]

Such powerful language, with the emotional tension it elicited, had a profound effect upon many who attended the revival meetings. At one such gathering "an aged man came forward and declared what God had done for his soul." Soon after that "a ten year old girl in a manner most animating related her remarkable experiences." Such testimonials, combined with the Reverend Spalding's constant assertion of the power of God, led a young woman who had been attending meetings regularly for several months to exclaim that she felt herself to be "lost forever." With this confession, "my long pent tears flowed most rapidly; and while bursting sobs almost tore my heart asunder, I reviewed my wicked, desperately wicked exercises toward Him, whom I now saw to be just even in my eternal condemnation." Concluding that she most certainly deserved to be slain with the remnant, she "experienced such unusual convulsions of body, as induced me to take hold of a chair before me to keep my seat." Convinced that "my soul was taking its final separation from my body, I attempted to rise, in order to go into another room, but found it impossible." Writhing in agony, her spirit cried out, "Jesus, to thy dear faithful hand my naked soul I trust." Immediately "the thick clouds seemed to disperse, and give place to such a transporting view of the glorious Savior, as no words can express." She raised her head and saw the Reverend Spalding zealously urging others to believe in the righteousness of Christ, "but he seemed altered — he seemed wonderful — the whole congregation appeared joyful."[90]

The following day, when Spalding "preached in the most terrific manner" in order to reveal "the terribleness of Christ's coming to judgement," the young woman felt no fear. She trembled for others but personally felt a "joy unspeakable."[91] She experienced this same sense of peace when she and thirty others accepted the covenant and became full members of the church. On that day, during which "the child and the grey-beard, the illiterate and the learned, rich and poor, black and white, all became one in Christ Jesus," she rejoiced in the "impartiality of God, who is no respector of persons."[92] Thus did the traditional democratic egalitarianism of First Church experience a vigorous revitalization under the guidance of Davies and Spalding.

This renewal of the democratic foundations of the church resulted not only from the emphasis the two evangelists placed upon the equality of all believers but also from the fact that the majority of those who joined the church as a result of the revivals were related to old, established Bennington families composed of individuals who were already members of the church.[93] It was this particular group of people who felt the economic and social changes affecting Bennington the most keenly and who most deeply resented the influx of new residents, who threatened the traditional social and religious values of the community. These same people had been responsible for the dismissal of Job Swift. They had no intention of replacing him with a like-minded person. Along with the majority of freemen within the town, they gave Spalding a call to become Bennington's settled pastor.[94] To their particular chagrin, he refused.

Even though church members took delight in the democratic character of the revival, more practical concerns of the church gave them much less satisfaction. Participants at the same town meeting that issued a call to Spalding voted to build a new meetinghouse. Because it involved the manner in which money was to be raised to support the church, this decision opened a sore that had been festering for some time: the degree to which the church should be independent of civil authorities. The original meetinghouse had been built with the voluntary subscriptions of members of the church and the society. The same means had also been employed to pay the minister's salary. This had remained the case even after 1783, when the state allowed towns to tax their residents to support an established church.[95] For members of First Church to take advantage of this law, however, would have been to fly in the face of their original covenant, which had taken specific exception to the provisions of the Cambridge Platform calling for civil authorities to support the gospel. Committed to the voluntaristic, egalitarian principles of Strict Separatism, church members were determined that their church should remain pure. The faithful would give freely of their bounty to support the gospel; there would be nothing pretentious about either the church structure or its members. The building lacked even a steeple, and all worshipers — equal in the sight of the Lord — mingled freely within the sanctuary; no effort was ever made to seat the church by assigning pews according to status within the church or the community.

With the passage of time, however, these traditional beliefs came under increased strain. By 1790 voluntary subscriptions were insufficient to pay the minister's salary, so the townspeople voted to accept the state law regarding support for established religious societies.[96] Henceforth, despite the anguished public protest of old Nathan Clark,[97] all inhabitants of Bennington would be taxed to pay Job Swift's salary. By March 1792 dissatisfaction with the original meetinghouse had become so widespread among prominent members of the society that they demanded a new one. Finally, in December 1803, after a ten-year struggle, the town voted to erect a larger building.[98] To pay for it participants at a town meeting voted to raise $5,000 by means of a tax assessed on the polls and rateable estates of citizens who had not signed a certificate releasing them from such an obligation.[99] The meeting then elected a committee led by Isaac Tichenor and Moses Robinson Jr. to supervise construction.[100]

When it was finished in December 1805, the new edifice, complete with private pews, an ornate, raised pulpit, graceful columns and arches, and a magnificent steeple, replicated the meetinghouses constructed by the Old Light churches of Connecticut and Massachusetts.[101] The cost of such an impressive structure — more than $7,000 — created a terrible problem for the town. Since only a little more than $2,000 had been raised by means of a tax assessment, some other source of revenue must be found. Following extended and troubled debates, members of the church and the society finally decided to auction off the individual pews in order to raise sufficient funds to meet construction costs.[102] This approach proved wonderfully successful, and the meetinghouse was immediately solvent.

Auctioning the pews solved the financial crisis associated with the new meetinghouse, but it raised troubling problems regarding the church itself. Once the auction took place, a hierarchy had been established within the sanctuary; the most prestigious pews went to the wealthiest patrons. Even though this stratification resulted from shifting economic circumstances within the town rather than from any conscious design on the part of church leaders, First Church had been seated just as surely as if the elders had assigned the pews. Further, the rank order created within the meetinghouse mirrored the social structure that had emerged within the town over the last several decades. Of the 108 original proprietors of church pews, 80 were not members of the church; those same individuals accounted for $5,420 of the total of $7,725 raised by the auction.[103] These people, who had come to the community following the Revolution, were Federalists, pursued busi-

ness and professional interests rather than agricultural ones, held liberal religious views and cosmopolitan social attitudes, and had little, if
any, interest in joining the church. They did, however, become ensconced within the society. Ironically, the democratic attitudes cherished by church members, particularly their willingness to accept the
participation of members of the society in major decisions affecting
First Church, allowed these new families to gain increased authority
within the community. As their numbers increased, the power of the
downhill leaders to contest important issues and offices within the town
grew apace.

Try as they might, however, downhill people could not overcome
the determination of democratic elements within the town to keep a
man like Job Swift from being called to preach at First Church. While
the meetinghouse was under construction Joshua Spalding continued
to preach on an interim basis. Then in March 1805 the church and the
society extended an invitation to Rev. Daniel Marsh, a plain man of
little education, to preach in Bennington for a year.[104] He accepted, and
he delivered the dedication sermon for the new meetinghouse on January 1, 1806.[105] In March he accepted an offer to become the town's
settled pastor; an ecclesiastical council met in Bennington in May and
officially installed Marsh as minister of First Church.[106]

The majority of citizens in Bennington who opposed an elitist like
Job Swift were certainly pleased with their new minister. Daniel Marsh
was every bit as egalitarian in his social and religious views as Joshua
Spalding. Born in New Milford, Connecticut, on May 10, 1762, to a
poor farm family, Marsh did not attend common schools until after
the outbreak of the Revolution. Then he went to class only during the
time he was not serving in various state militia companies. After the
war Marsh settled in Rowley, Massachusetts, where he chopped wood
mornings and evenings in order to support his studies at the same two-
year ministerial school that Joshua Spalding had attended.[107] At Rowley
he came under the tutelage of Rev. Ebenezer Bradford, a fervent New
Light, advocate of emotional preaching, ardent democrat, and enthusiastic supporter of Thomas Paine. Bradford even went so far as to
preach that Paine's political sentiments were perfectly "consonant to
the nature, end and genius of all republican government, and not at all
inconsistent with the great principles of Revelation."[108] These ideas
caused the established clergy of the state to ostracize him as a "vandal"
and an "insurgent."[109] Nevertheless, Bradford stood firm in his dedica-

tion to Revolutionary principles and his loyalty to Jeffersonian Republicanism; his students left Rowley imbued with democratic social, political, and religious principles.

Daniel Marsh brought these beliefs to the pulpit of First Church. He
also lived the simple ideals that he preached. Being poor, Marsh and his
wife had to work a farm in order to augment his minister's salary.
Whenever his horses were in use on the land Marsh traveled about the
township on foot to attend prayer meetings, visit the sick, or bury the
dead. Such a lifestyle, which was a far cry from that of David Avery, with
his elegant chaise, or the dignified demeanor of Job Swift, offended
many downhill people. So, too, did Marsh's constant willingness to
open the pulpit at First Church not only to Rutland's black minister,
Lemuel Haynes, but to itinerate evangelists, including even young and
inexperienced Free-Will Baptists.[110] Still, Marsh continued to preach
the simple love and equality of the Lord and to laud the common man.
In a sermon at an August 16 celebration of the battle of Bennington,
Marsh celebrated the "wonders" of the ordinary American militiaman
in his battle against the professional troops of the British army. No
matter what the "skill of the enemy in military tactics, their experience
in the arts of war; their former successes, and their great bravery in
facing danger," none of these had enabled them to overcome the natural strength of "the yeomanry of America."[111]

Downhill people began to complain shortly after Marsh settled in
Bennington. It was not merely the minister's message of equality but
his very commonness that offended them. Within two years after his
installation serious confrontations began to take place within First
Church over whether Marsh should be allowed to remain. Finally,
Jonathan Robinson took such a strong stance in support of Marsh, even
threatening to vote against any other minister who might be brought to
Bennington, that the downhill people did not press the issue.[112] But
their dissatisfaction remained.

This discontent found another outlet, namely, politics, which offered both downhill and uphill people abundant opportunity to vent
their spleen. By this time the fierce partisanship affecting state and
national politics had permeated even Bennington's annual town meeting. Early each March cadres of local political leaders caucused in order
to agree on a slate of candidates for the major offices to be filled at that
year's meeting. Moses Robinson Jr., Jonathan Hunt, Elijah Dewey,
Noadiah Swift, Micah J. Lyman, Aaron Robinson, and Isaac Tichenor
led a small gathering of Federalists to decide whom they would support

for offices such as moderator, clerk, and the all-important posts of selectmen. At nearly the same time David Fay, Jonathan Robinson, O. C. Merrill, David Robinson Jr., and Samuel Safford played leading roles in the Republican caucus. Bitter conflict often erupted once the town meeting began. Divisions became so heated and meetings so tumultuous that it was impossible to continue the tradition of voice voting; paper ballots now became necessary. Violent confrontations broke out when adherents of one party questioned the voting qualifications of individuals from the other, even of those who had actively participated in town meetings for years.[113] The competition often grew so fierce that it became necessary to cast repeated ballots for each office before a clear majority could be established. It was not unusual for annual meetings to last far into the night, sometimes adjourning to meet a second day.

The same was true at annual freemen's meetings. On the first Tuesday of September voters in Bennington assembled at the courthouse to cast ballots for federal and state officials. The state organizations of both the Republicans and the Federalists had developed to such an extent by this time that each party offered a full slate of candidates and voters simply had to pick up a ballot for one or the other party's nominees. Town officials immediately sealed up these ballots and sent them on to the state legislature to be counted at a later date. There was, therefore, little cause for confrontation. This was not true, however, of the selection of the town's representative to the General Assembly, which had to be decided before the meeting adjourned. Tempers flared as members of both parties exerted great pressure on undecided voters. So acute was party feeling that David Fay declared at a Republican caucus that he was absolutely certain that most "of the leading characters on the federal side, were for taking the government out of the hands of the people."[114] For their part, men like Isaac Tichenor and Moses Robinson Jr. were equally sure that Democrats threatened the very fabric of society. Thus, election day in Bennington ofttimes degenerated into fractious quarreling.

Political excitement in the village was not limited to town meetings and election days; in fact, the partisanship on these days paled in comparison with that manifested at the annual commemorations of July 4 and August 16, when emotions ran so high that the two parties had to stage separate celebrations. Naturally, the party faithful inevitably took the opportunity not only to praise the principles of their own cause but to impugn those of their opponents.

While Federalist gatherings, with their emphasis upon an organic society based on order and hierarchy, were generally simple and decorous, Republican celebrations tended to be larger, more exuberant affairs. Independence Day began at sunrise with the discharge of the cannon on the parade ground. At midday a crowd of five to six hundred men would gather in front of the courthouse, form a procession, and, accompanied by the town band, march to the meetinghouse. There they listened to anthems sung by the church choir, a sermon by Daniel Marsh, and a reading of the Declaration of Independence by Anthony Haswell. Following these ceremonies, the participants marched to the State Arms Tavern, where they enjoyed a copious banquet and drank toasts until well into the night.[115] Republicans supplemented this routine when commemorating the battle of Bennington by incorporating military maneuvers by their local militia regiments into the festivities.[116]

Very often Republicans staged elaborate symbolic tableaux during their celebrations. It was not at all unusual for young children to play a part in their festivities. During one Independence Day ceremony "a number of amiable little masters and misses" entered the meetinghouse while the choir was singing "Hail Columbia." The little girls, dressed in the purest white, had wreaths of flowers and evergreens in their hair and carried sprigs in their hands to represent the "peaceful olive." The choir immediately stopped singing in order to listen to the children, who, with "easy mien and lively voices keeping exact step to their own music," proceeded up the middle aisle. After the first couples gave way to the left and the right upon reaching the front of the sanctuary, the final couple presented the Declaration of Independence to the speaker of the day.[117] On another occasion a procession of "young Masters and Misses" entered the meetinghouse. Once again the girls were dressed entirely in white. This time, however, a small boy bearing the Declaration of Independence led the entourage; behind him came a young lady dressed as the "Genius of Liberty" accompanied by two young men bearing her spear and liberty cap, which was decorated with the olive branch of peace. After Anthony Haswell received and read the Declaration, "Liberty" approached her seat only to discover that the "crown of royalty and the mitre of priestcraft had daringly usurped her place." Then, "with peculiar dignity the beauteous Nymph removed the encumbrances, set them at her feet and seated herself to preside over the exercises of the day."[118]

At Republican celebrations of the battle of Bennington an ornate bower was often placed in front of the State Arms Tavern to signify the meaning of the day. On one such occasion an American flag flew from a large pole in front of the bower. At one side stood the image of an eagle swooping down to drop an olive branch in the midst of the assembled throng. On the other side a full-length representation of the "Goddess of Liberty," complete with flowing robes, loose ringlets, and a wand bearing her liberty cap, seemed to descend from heaven in order not only to preside over the bower but to envelop all those present in her aura of harmony and love.[119]

At this celebration in August 1809 Anthony Haswell read a letter from John Stark that incorporated the symbols Republicans held most dear: the eagle, the goddess of liberty, the American flag, and the sturdy, independent yeoman. Stark recalled that he had commanded "American troops" at the battle of Bennington, men who had neither learned the "ART OF SUBMISSION" nor been trained in the "ART OF WAR." His incredible success taught all "enemies of liberty" that "UNDISCIPLINED FREEMEN" were in all ways superior to "veteran slaves." Stark wanted the citizens of Bennington to understand that he remained as always the stalwart friend of "the equal rights of men, of representative democracy, of republicanism, and the declaration of independence." He wanted every free man in America to know that a "DANGEROUS BRITISH PARTY" lurked in their midst, a party more dangerous than all of America's foreign enemies.[120] If loyal Americans did not band together to resist this party, which everyone present knew to be the Federalists, everything gained by the Revolution would be sacrificed.

Over the years Bennington Republicans toasted hundreds of principles, ideals, and individuals at their annual celebrations. They did, however, repeat particular toasts in one form or another at nearly every gathering. Certain concepts — republicanism, equality, democracy, American womanhood, agriculture, and domestic manufacturing — assumed a profound saliency for them. It was the figure of the independent yeoman, however, that dominated their public declarations of faith. Bennington's Republicans believed in the innate wisdom of the common man. All else followed from this. "Tim Scribble," for instance, declared that all "mankind are endowed with a moral perception, an intuitive notion of justice, and a natural sagacity, which enable them to discern merit, corruption, or weakness with an acuteness beyond what many are willing to allow."[121] Echoing these sentiments, "A Vermont Farmer" observed that republicanism "delights in simplicity — that is, in a kind of simplicity in the governing, by which every man of common abilities may be able to clearly understand every mea-

sure of government."[122] Given such assumptions, it was easy for Republicans to see two principles of government struggling for ascendancy: "one is for the establishment of government *over* you, composed
of a few of your most cunning and ambitious characters, rendered as
independent of you as possible; the other is for the perpetuation of a
government, flowing *from* you, and its agents continually accountable
to you, and removable at your pleasure."[123]

"Democratic Farmer" agreed that the confrontation between Federalists and Republicans was essentially "a contest between the rich
men and men of professions on one side, and the common farmer and
mechanic on the other." Put another way, it was "a conspiracy of the
indolent against the *industrious.*"[124] Americans were divided into two
classes: "those who gain a livelihood by their own industry and those
who get it by art or strategem, . . . by what is commonly called head
work." Farmers, mechanics, and manufacturers made up the first class;
judges, lawyers, priests, and merchants the second. It was merchants,
however, who were the most invidious. By manipulating prices, credit,
and the flow of goods, they were able to exploit the industrious farmer.
By running hardworking people into debt and then holding them to the
letter of the law, merchants supported a whole cadre of lawyers, sheriffs, and judges, men who "live by the sweat of your brows, and ride in
their carriages, and strut and puff about the street, and call you the
vulgar and rabble."[125] These observations of "Farmer" revealed the
essential core of Republican thought in Bennington, a belief that America's productive classes were locked in a struggle for survival against idle
nonproducers.

Bennington's Republicans thought that the answer to the machinations of the merchant was local manufacturing, whether in the home or
in the mills beginning to appear along the Walloomsac and its tributaries. Their own spinning wheels would free farm families from dependence on the foreign goods sold by local merchants, while new
woolen mills not only provided a market for farmer's wool but produced cloth, which further released them from the grasp of merchants.
Republicans thereby recognized a dynamic relationship between manufacturing and the independence of the yeoman. It was for this reason
that they toasted domestic manufactures as well as agriculture at their
annual holidays. Indeed, they often combined the two by celebrating
"Agriculture and Manufactures—one in political sympathies."[126] For
this same reason, Bennington's Republican newspaper offered constant
encouragement to manufacturing.[127] Anthony Haswell proclaimed that

the honest working classes could free themselves from dependence upon local merchants if they would produce and manufacture raw materials into finished products themselves. Then the yeomanry of America, "this great and useful class, would not as now be the *servants* of a less numerous and useful class of men: they would then have no speculating *masters* to make the whole contract: no supercilious whitefaced gentry to say, sirs, we give you so much for your produce, and no more, half cash, and half gewgaws at *our price.*"[128]

The uphill folk were certain they knew the source of this "whitefaced gentry." "Franklin" observed that students came out of college "with no other direction and no other object in view than to rise on the necks of the people." In addition, "these young nobles are manufactured into priests and lawyers with astonishing facility, and *clod hoppers* and *geese* are their usual phrases when speaking of the people."[129] "Metellus" also considered college education a primary source of the pollution of republican simplicity: "A man that goes to our little Burlington and Middlebury colleges can scarce mix with common people after having gotten a Diploma all written in Latin from the President." College graduates might generally be "very much improved in Greek and Hebrew," but they were "very much impaired in every thing else."[130]

Hiram Harwood, a descendant of one of Bennington's original settlers, expressed similar resentment toward college graduates during an election of militia officers in which Moses D. Robinson carried the day over his Republican opponents. Robinson turned the election in his favor only after making quite a "handsome, short speech." In disgust, Harwood exclaimed, "And why couldn't he do *that,* when everybody knows he had been to college where all sorts of speeches are learned."[131] Harwood resented even more the manner in which the newly elected militia officer's father, Moses Robinson Jr., Bennington's most prominent merchant, "amass[ed] wealth in his skinning way."[132] Harwood himself was content to be with Republicans at their annual celebrations, where he would mix only with "the enemies of aristocracy and monarchy — and the friends of the rights of man."[133]

Like many other Republicans in Bennington, Hiram Harwood gained increased precision of language and greater clarity of thought regarding the condition of American society from prominent Republican newspapers such as the *Philadelphia Aurora* and the *National Intelligencer,* which he and his political associates borrowed from local subscribers.[134] In this way Bennington's uphill people integrated their own thoughts, feelings, and circumstances with those of Republicans throughout the

nation, thereby unself-consciously assimilating a powerful social ideology—Jeffersonian Republicanism—that gave increased meaning and
legitimacy to their own yeoman persuasion.

The Jeffersonian concepts absorbed by Bennington Republicans
rested on Revolutionary principles long familiar to the great majority
of Americans.[135] These ideas integrated a strong commitment to John
Locke's insistence on the protection of property and the good of the
people as the only legitimate end of government with a libertarian fear
of power and of the enslavement of the people at the hands of corrupt
officeholders. Jeffersonianism also emphasized that humanity was capable of unbounded improvement. Such improvement was possible,
however, only in the least constraining civil, political, and religious
environment. Progress resulted not from the benevolent paternalism of
an elite but from the separate efforts of free and equal citizens. Since
individual rights as well as popular control of government were essential to achieve such progress, Jeffersonian leaders believed they must
effect two integrally related revolutions, one economic and one political. Both rested on the idea of equality. The first could be accomplished
only by expanding commercial opportunities for a larger number of
people in such a way as to promote greater prosperity and equality of
opportunity. The other demanded the destruction of an elitist, deferential politics in favor of one that fostered the active participation of
all men.

Within its broadest parameters, then, Jeffersonianism held out to
Americans the promise of autonomy as economic individuals and the
right to equal political participation as individual citizens. Believing
that industrious, self-reliant citizens represented the natural economy
of America, Jeffersonians made the commercial prosperity of ordinary
individuals the primary economic base for a democratic, progressive
nation. A dynamic economy that incorporated the majority of citizens
would release the human potential long held in check by artificial governmental restraints. This belief underlay the Jeffersonian Republican
conception of a democratic republic, a fusion of economic freedom and
political democracy. Fortunately for Jeffersonians, the worldwide demand for grain that emerged in the early national period provided a
practical material base on which to build this vision of America. Rising
prices held out the promise of a flourishing trade in the American food-
stuffs produced on family farms. Rather than stagnating in subsistence
farming, the independent husbandman could partake in the spreading
economic prosperity, and the prosperity of the ordinary farmer could

become the basis for a democratic, progressive America. Free land, free trade, and scientific advances in agriculture spelled progress and prosperity for all Americans, not just a special few.[136]

To achieve such a political economy, Jeffersonian leaders intended to promote the free competition of individual citizens in an open, competitive marketplace. Again, their hope that ordinary people might free themselves from economic and political subservience to their social superiors rested on the bright promise of commercial agriculture. Jeffersonian Republicanism thus integrated the virtuous-yeoman ideal of classical republicanism with Adam Smith's concept of the self-interested individual to form a radical new moral theory of government and society. Fragmenting society into its individual human components, it endowed each with a fundamental economic character and a natural capacity for personal autonomy. In addition, its proponents invested the independent producer with the moral qualities long associated with the virtuous citizen extolled by classical republicanism.

Once the principal beliefs of Jeffersonian Republicanism had been thoroughly absorbed by Bennington Republicans, their own yeoman persuasion finally assumed the character of a coherent social philosophy. Having achieved legitimacy through association with similar ideas being articulated by an increasingly powerful national movement, its primary concepts took on a life of their own with the potential to shape thought and social behavior. Ironically, at the very time when the persuasion assumed such power, its major proponents were no longer yeomen. Men like David Robinson Jr., O. C. Merrill, Jonathan Robinson, and David Fay had long since become commercial farmers or professionals. This was true of the great majority of Bennington's Republican leadership. Since the original settlement of the town, the most successful families — those that persisted over the years — had gradually, quite imperceptibly, and perhaps even unconsciously become embedded in market production. They concentrated on growing staple crops for distant markets, relied exclusively upon hired labor to tend these crops, become entirely dependent upon merchants for most of their essentials, and formed political organizations to protect their interests against all competitors. No longer independent subsistence farmers, they had become petty capitalists deeply enmeshed in regional and national market forces. In the process their communal egalitarianism was transmuted into an emphasis upon individual success and popular control of government. The old fear that higher authority would erode local customs gradually gave way to a personal distrust of all social and political distinctions that might impede their quest for profit and status.

And yet uphill leaders clung to their yeoman beliefs long after these concepts had been drained of all social and economic reality. Propelled by forces over which they had little control and of which they had, perhaps, even less understanding, their language became increasingly disembodied from a rapidly changing social reality. Their cries of equality and their salutes to the independent yeoman, the "Goddess of Liberty," and the "American fair" became ever more insistent at the very time when they restricted women to a limited economic and political sphere and created an increasingly stratified commercial society. Their ideology, however, allowed — even impelled — them to view themselves as committed to equality and communal well-being while actively creating a competitive, materialistic, and highly structured society. The result was, of course, a violent war of words with their Federalist counterparts, men whom they identified as *the* preeminent threat to yeomen independence and equality.

This war of words became increasingly violent. In Bennington, unlike in the rest of the nation, the triumph of Thomas Jefferson in 1800 did not inaugurate an era of Republican ascendancy and Federalist decline. In fact, just the opposite occurred, in large part because of demographic changes that had taken place in Bennington over the two decades since Vermont's entrance into the Union. During that time Bennington's population had remained static.[137] Its composition, however, had changed dramatically: the number of attorneys in the village had increased by 600 percent, while the number of merchants had risen by nearly 500 percent. These two groups assumed increasing influence throughout the county.

The success of Bennington's commercial elements in the years following statehood led to a dramatic change in the composition of the town's most affluent and influential citizenry. A core of families remained within Bennington and assumed positions of leadership within the town.[138] While men involved in agriculture dominated this group prior to 1790, this was not the case by 1812. Many members of the old agricultural families remained, but their numbers had not increased over the years because of the transient nature of the agricultural population in Bennington County. After 1791 farmers who came to Bennington found themselves without access to good land; most moved on shortly after their arrival. Those who chose to remain failed to acquire enough wealth to enter the town's leadership ranks. This was not true

of merchants and lawyers; indeed, members of these two professions —
the majority of whom were Federalists — enjoyed a good deal of stability as well as upward mobility during the two decades after statehood.[139] With each passing year, then, the authority and influence of
the downhill people in Bennington steadily increased at the expense of
their old antagonists on Courthouse Hill. Consequently, the political
strife that had permeated Bennington for so many years showed no
signs of slackening. Indeed, the divisions throughout the town appeared more intense than ever by the time Vermont and the nation
began to gird themselves for war with Great Britain. It was during this
time too that a new generation of leaders emerged in Bennington.

PART THREE: A DIFFERENT VILLAGE

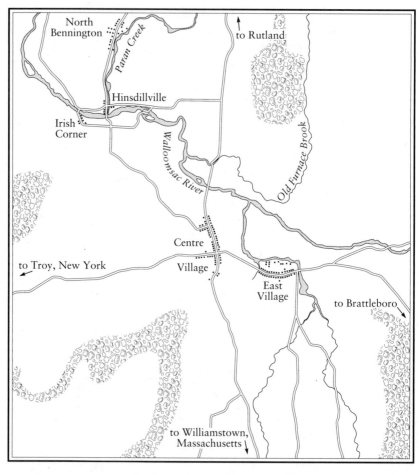

Bennington and its environs in about 1835 showing the matrix of roads serving the
town and the communities that surrounded it. (Adapted from Joseph Hinsdill's map of
Bennington by William L. Nelson)

7. The Next Generation

The state of our society proclaims, loudly, that the enemy is here. And shall I be your enemy, if I tell you the truth on this painful subject? I am not, "for God is my record how greatly I long after you all in the bowels of Jesus Christ." And so far as I know my own heart, it is from feelings of the deepest and most cordial friendship to your best interests, that I "cry aloud and spare not" to "shew my people their transgressions, and the house of Jacob their sins." The subject is painful to my soul. Self-love, selfish friends, and perhaps some timid christians, would say to me, in these circumstances "Spare thyself." Ambition, love of praise, and aversion to the cross, would say, "Spare the rich and powerful." But God says, "Lift up thy voice like a trumpet, and spare not; but reprove, rebuke, with all long suffering and authority." I must, for my souls sake, and for my people's sake obey God rather than man.

Let me tell you then, my hearers, the enemy has come upon us like a flood. Infidelity, and opposition to the happiest and most benevolent movements of the church, have been openly and loudly advocated in our streets. — Profaneness grates harshly upon the ear of the passing traveller, while the reelings and the belchings of intoxication, have sometimes met his eye at every corner of the streets. The ordinances of God are neglected by the great mass of our inhabitants, while publick and lawless sports are pursued on the sabbath of the Lord, and that too, within sight of this sanctuary. And, since the sitting of yesterday's sun, and the dawning of this holy morning, upon what has the eye of Jehovah fallen in our own village? Oh, brethren! Who can contrast the small number, now in this house, with the thousands that have thronged our streets, and traversed our fields, during the week that is past, and not be convinced that the enemy has come in like a flood? The Gaming-house, the Theatre, and the Horse-race, in defiance of the wisdom of the laws that govern us, have called together a greater multitude, than we have ever seen assembled here, at this house of

God, at any one time. Why, bretheren, I have seen men travelling away to these
scenes of dissipation, with weeds on their hats, who lately wept at the funeral of some
dear friend, and over whose dead bodies, after a little while, perhaps, other mourners,
without hope, will shed floods of tears. Now they can sport themselves at the gambols
of a dumb animal.

Let me here relate a single fact, which, in a most melancholy manner, illus-
trates our position. In the course of the last week, I was called to attend the burial of
an aged and very respectable inhabitant of this town. At the hour appointed, a little
group of women assembled at the house of mourning. But, Oh, how heartrending
and doubly mournful was that occasion, when it was found that there were hardly
men enough present, of suitable age, to bear her body decently to the grave! while it
was conjectured that, at that very time, there were four or five thousand citizens and
strangers, assembled in this same town, to witness — What? the speed of a horse! How
much better, thought I, for all that multitude to have gone to the house of mourning,
than to that cruel and lawless sport! "For this is the end of all flesh, and the living will
lay it to heart." "A horse," with all his speed and activity, "is a vain thing for safety,"
but "godliness is great gain, having the promise of the life that now is, and of that
which is to come."

I am aware that, by this remark, I may have made myself "a prey." It may
become the subject of sport and ridicule in our streets, and of "the song of the
drunkard." But, my dear hearers, should you ever invite me, as your pastor, to visit
you in your last sickness, or to pray over you, when the soul is just about to leave the
body, you will then confess to me, that it contains a most important and infinitely
momentous truth.[1]

For Absalom Peters, preaching the "infinitely momentous truth" of
God's grace held the key for reforming the lives not only of those in his
own congregation but of all of the inhabitants of Bennington as well.
Indeed, for him evangelical reform was essential for the well-being of
all of American society. Piety, not politics, would preserve the American
experiment in republicanism and renew its bright promise in an age of
decadence and decay.

When Peters first arrived in Bennington early in August 1819 to
take the place of Daniel Marsh, he viewed religious life in the town as
"comparatively stagnant and unprogressive." He perceived the church
to be "sadly riven by political and other parties." Even so, he believed
that "excellent materials existed for a substantial reform" and immediately set out to "sacrifice all my popularity there on the altar of duty,
to accomplish the desired reform."[2] He never hesitated to speak out
against whatever signs of moral decay he discovered in Bennington.

"Sportsmen" who built a track in sight of the meetinghouse and raced their horses on the Sabbath received the full brunt of his indignation, as did those who attended the races and the authorities who allowed them to take place. He castigated a theatrical troupe that rode through Bennington's streets on a Sabbath morning "with much indecent noise, and unhallowed merriment." Even more alarming, the town authorities had allowed these "lewd actors" use of the courthouse, where they presented their theatricals until nearly midnight every evening for a week.[3] No one escaped the Reverend Peters's sharp eye.

The moralistic fervor that Peters brought to his ministry in Bennington sprang from years of careful nurturing. Born September 19, 1793, on a farm in Wentworth, New Hampshire, he grew up in a household composed of "Puritan stock," and his parents adhered diligently to the principles of their ancestors. In the absence of established pastors in this newly settled region, Absalom's parents undertook the religious training of their family. With the aid of the *New England Primer* and the Bible, they ingrained a "strict observance of the Sabbath," "the cardinal principles of a religious life," and "a conscience towards God" in all their children. It was primarily Absalom's mother, though, who shaped the moral lives of the children; through the "ever-consistent" example of her kindness, affection, and moral integrity, she guided them away from the "careless living" and "vices" of their "rude and unorganized" surroundings.[4]

Until the age of sixteen Absalom labored on the family farm, where his father inculcated habits of industry, self-discipline, and strict economy in all his children. Along with his eight brothers and sisters, Absalom attended district school during the winter months, but, like them, he owed most of his early education to his father, who was a graduate of Dartmouth College and far better educated than the local schoolmasters. Under their father's guidance, all the Peters children received a solid elementary education. The five boys enjoyed further advantages: when they reached the age of sixteen, their father, who was a successful farmer, a state legislator, brigadier general of the state militia, and county sheriff, allowed them to choose a career and then provided whatever additional education that choice might require.

Young Absalom's first inclination was the military, which followed a family tradition. His father was a leader in the state militia and had served as a captain in the Revolutionary War; one of his older brothers, a recent graduate of West Point, was an officer in the U.S. Army. Hoping to pursue the same path as his brother, Absalom wanted to attend West Point. His father received assurances from the proper authorities that his son would have the next available appointment. In the meantime, Absalom went to Troy, New York, where he worked as a clerk in the store of his eldest brother and underwent a change of heart. The earnest entreaties of his mother and his own regular participation in Baptist church services in Troy led him to set aside time each day to study the Bible his mother had given him when he left home. This and the fervent ministry of his Baptist preacher filled him with "a sense of ill-desert and of religious obligation." Finally, after he suffered "much conflict of spirit," he experienced "divine grace." His only desire now was to devote his life to the service of God. Filled with this new-found purpose in life, he returned home anxious to attend Dartmouth and prepare himself for the ministry. To ready himself for the college's entrance examination, he enrolled in a preparatory course at Moor's School in Hanover, New Hampshire, during the fall of 1810.[5]

Eighteen months after entering Moor's School, Absalom gained admission to Dartmouth, where he followed the same course of instruction offered at Harvard or Yale. While the curricular requirements of the college were formidable, its scholastic standards were much less exacting. If members of the student body, made up primarily of ill-prepared young men drawn from the hill towns of New Hampshire, Vermont, and western Massachusetts, did not leave school for pecuniary or disciplinary reasons, they invariably advanced from class to class with little difficulty.[6] More than any other factor, poverty shaped student life at Dartmouth. So many students could not afford to pay a steward that the college abandoned any attempt to provide communal dining and living facilities. Even within the college's classrooms students had to supply their own firewood throughout the bitter cold New Hampshire winters. Such conditions prevented the emergence of a rigidly hierarchical environment such as prevailed at Harvard or Yale. In fact, the rules requiring strict deference between the classes had been abandoned at Dartmouth as early as 1795.[7]

Like other colleges populated by young men living on the edge of poverty, Dartmouth adjusted its winter schedule to allow its students to teach in common schools throughout the region. Peters and most of his classmates took advantage of this opportunity to augment their income. Peters had been teaching in the district school near his home since the age of sixteen. He considered his qualifications, "though poor enough," to be "probably equal to the usual standard in the neighborhood." The greatest problem he faced as a teacher was maintaining control over pupils who were nearly full-grown men. His father removed this obstacle for him by working out an arrangement with the local school committee to "insure the good conduct of the larger scholars." This left Absalom responsible "only for the government of those of my own size and smaller."[8]

Throughout his college career Peters stood apart from his classmates only in his religious zeal. At a time when very few of his colleagues were professing Christians, he joined the Congregational church in Hanover as a full member;[9] his faith seemed to grow rather than diminish during his college years. Fortunately, he was able to further his religious training after graduating from Dartmouth in 1816. In the fall of that year, following a brief experience as a teacher in New York City, Peters, with the help of "generous friends," entered Princeton Theological Seminary. At last he could devote himself wholeheartedly to the study of Christian theology.[10]

During the three years he spent at Princeton he became immersed in the seminary's principal mission, which was to establish a learned defense of the Christian faith and counteract the rampant wave of infidelity that the school's trustees felt was rapidly spreading through American society. The seminary curriculum required first-year students to concentrate on the analysis of natural and revealed religion as well as the study of mental and moral science. Second- and third-year students focused on the exegesis of the Old and New Testaments, the composition of sermons, and the study of theology and church history.[11] The mission of the seminary actually went far beyond simply producing well-educated ministers. The school had been founded in 1812 in reaction to the emergence of Unitarianism and the ascendancy of Jeffersonian Republicanism.

The appointment of Henry Ware to the Hollis Professorship of Divinity at Harvard College in 1805 set off a furor among orthodox Congregationalists all over New England. To these people, Harvard's choosing Ware, a liberal who promoted the doctrines of Unitarianism, meant that it was no longer a fit place to train ministers. New Divinity and Old Calvinist Congregationalists united in the creation of the Andover Theological Seminary as a bastion of Congregational orthodoxy. Four years later Presbyterians led by Ashbel Green established a divinity school at Princeton intended to serve the same purpose for their denomination. Ministers trained at the Princeton Theological Seminary would be entirely free of any taint of Unitarianism or other forms of religious liberalism.[12]

For most orthodox Calvinists, Thomas Jefferson's election to the presidency in 1800 brought terrible consequences that threatened the very moral fiber of American society. The triumph of Jefferson and his supporters portended the spread of deism, unrestrained popular democracy, and social chaos throughout the republic. Supporters of Princeton bemoaned the age as "a time of great degeneracy and distress." The votes of "the deluded Multitude," so supportive of "anarchy and confusion," had helped bring about "the present awful state of the country."[13] Elias Boudinot, a senior trustee of the college, exclaimed: "When I see so many, who have rec[eive]d the best Education, under the most pious Instructors, turn out the greatest opposers of the kingdom of Christ in the World, I am fully convinced of the truth of the Gospel, that our sufficiency must be in Christ."[14]

Boudinot's observation that "our sufficiency must be in Christ" revealed much about Princeton's response to the crisis. For those in the Princeton circle the answer to the nation's problems lay not in politics and government but in the renewal of piety and the revitalization of morality among the people. The trustees of Princeton did not intend to rely on elected officials; instead, they meant to promote proper ministerial education, religious revivals, and the creation of voluntary agencies to help instill proper moral values in the people of the United States. Only in this way could they create the pious, self-restrained, and morally upright citizens necessary to save the nation from its present degenerate course. To further these high purposes, Boudinot and many of the younger Princeton trustees played a central role in the formation of such reform societies as the American Bible Society, the American Tract Society, the American Home Missionary Society, the American Sunday School Union, and the American Society for the Promotion of Temperance.[15]

When Ashbel Green simultaneously became president of both Princeton College and the board of directors of the new theological seminary in 1812, he took immediate steps to implement the ideas of Boudinot and the other trustees within both the college and the seminary. Convinced that the rampant immorality in the larger society promoted communal disorder, Green was certain that only strenuous moral exertion could reestablish social stability. Properly trained individuals should, therefore, help reform others. Consequently, Green set out to instill appropriate values in both his Princeton undergraduates and his seminary students. He urged these young people to organize their own voluntary societies in order to disseminate religious literature, to form

Sunday schools in their local churches, and to aid in the education of the poor.[16]

When Absalom Peters left Princeton as a licensed Presbyterian minister in May 1819, he took with him an enthusiasm for the principles and techniques learned at the seminary. For several months he labored as a minister for the American Home Missionary Society, and under its auspices he preached in destitute communities in upstate New York that had no settled pastor. Then in August he received an invitation to come to First Church in Bennington. Filled with the evangelical spirit of the various reform societies that had been formed while he was a seminarian, Peters commenced his Bennington ministry "under impulses awakened by these purely philanthropic and nonsectarian institutions." Animated by the faith and optimism that sustained these organizations, he fully intended to implement the progressive reform techniques of these agencies in Bennington.[17] Absalom Peters had in mind nothing less than the moral reformation of the entire village.

TUESDAY SEP *1.st. [1835]*

Made ready in season to ride with father & Mr. Wight to town. The latter did not take part in the Election. The candidates for Assembly were John S. Robinson (Jackson) & Jed'h Dewey (Anti-Jackson). The former as a man *was my favorite, but being of a very different political faith from me — conceived it not proper to vote for him — therefore cast it for the latter. The friends of R, some of them, endeavored to persuade me, & likewise my father, to go for him — but it was of no avail. We stuck* to our *party just as* they *ever have done to theirs. In* this *we copied the manner of the opposite party. It pained me to be obliged by an imperious sense of duty to vote in opposition to so fine a man as John S. There was nothing of ill will, nothing personal in this — Just so with my father. We* loved *&* respected, *but could not support him for Rep. to Assembly. In voting we must be independent of all little personal impartialities — these should all give way to what we may conceive to be most for the Public Good. At any rate it was a warm contest — at one time they came close upon having a riot, but it soon calmed down and nothing of the kind ensued. A very great number of freemen attended & near sunset it was proclaimed that Dewey was elected by 104 majority.*[18]

John Staniford Robinson had served two consecutive terms in the Vermont Assembly, during the years 1832–33. This seemed fitting, since the townspeople of Bennington had elected a member of the Robinson family in twenty-four of the fifty-five years that they had been sending representatives to that body.[19] In 1834 and again in 1835, however, Robinson had been defeated for the post. His name alone was no longer sufficient; no matter how much his fellow citizens might respect him as an individual, they simply would not support him unreflectively as a political candidate. New party loyalties were beginning to take shape in Bennington, and John Robinson, like others of his political persuasion, had to face the unpleasant reality of repeatedly finding themselves in a minority at the polls.

The Robinson family had not remained cohesive, much less harmonious, over the years. As early as 1808 one observant neighbor noted that the "Robinsons are in a quarrel among themselves — and will probably be the means of their own fall."[20] Born to Nathan and Jerusha Staniford Robinson on November 10, 1804, John grew up amidst a great deal of family dissension. His father, the youngest son of Governor Moses Robinson, was a lawyer of modest means and a loyal supporter of Thomas Jefferson. His uncles, Moses Robinson Jr. and Aaron, however, were wealthy merchants, large landholders, and prominent leaders among Bennington's Federalists. Bitter political rancor poisoned relations between the families of Governor Robinson's children until Nathan's death in 1812.

Following the death of her husband, Jerusha sent young John to be educated first in her hometown of Windham, Connecticut, and then in Hartford. Then, following the example of David Robinson Jr. and Jonathan E. Robinson, the first members of the family to attend college, John entered Williams College in 1820. By that time the school had three buildings and a faculty of four. Although both the entrance requirements and the curriculum remained the same as they had been when his cousins matriculated there in 1793, one very important change had taken place: Edward Dorr Griffin had become president of the college in 1821. One of the most powerful evangelists of the day, Griffin took charge of the senior recitation room on Fridays and treated his students to a demanding course in the principles of rhetoric. In this class students, confronted by Griffin's constant, exacting criticism, learned how to prepare and deliver effective original orations.[21]

The college itself, however, as well as the composition of its student body, had changed very little over time. While Williamstown had become slightly less isolated by 1820 — a stage passed through the town on a regular basis — the college still attracted the relatively untutored boys of western Massachusetts and southern Vermont. Even a decade after John Robinson graduated, Nathaniel Hawthorne considered Williams students to be "a rough-hewn, heavy set of fellows, from the hills and woods in this neighborhood. — great unpolished bumpkins, who had grown up farmer-boys." He described those receiving diplomas as "country graduates, — rough, brown-featured, schoolmaster-looking, half-bumpkin, half-scholarly figures, in black ill-cut broadcloth. — their manners quite spoilt by what little of the gentleman there was in them."[22]

John Robinson returned to Bennington following his graduation from Williams in 1824. He immediately began to study law in the office of David Robinson Jr., who had read law under John's father, Nathan. Following a brief apprenticeship, John set out on his own; he was admitted to practice before the Bennington County Court in August 1827 and the Vermont Supreme Court in February 1832. Although they were never actually partners, John and David Robinson Jr. maintained a close professional and personal relationship after John established his own law office. Their homes and offices were next-door to one another on Courthouse Hill.

When John first began to establish himself as an attorney the legal profession in Bennington was undergoing important changes. In its earliest years the practice of law had been crude and informal. A stranger happening upon a court might well have had difficulty determining whether or not it was in session. He most certainly would have been at a loss to identify the judges. Such was the case with a traveler in 1808 who entered the courthouse in Rutland, where he observed "about a hundred persons, shabbily dressed, standing, sitting, and reclining on the benches and tables." It appeared to him that the court was in recess; it was not. Finally, he concluded that a small group of men who were dressed like everyone else except that they were bareheaded were the judges. These men, along with the attorneys for the prosecution and the defense, sat around a table covered with a green cloth. Several casual spectators sat on this same table with their backs to the court.[23]

The vast majority of cases that came before justices of the peace or the superior court in the early years involved debt or trespass.[24] Before the advent of sufficient paper currency, most merchants and private individuals engaged in barter. This meant keeping extensive records of credit and, of course, giving over considerable time to the collection of debts. Lawyers could earn a great deal of money by prosecuting debtors. Standard practice called for a lawyer to bring a debtor to court, get a judgment against him, and have him committed to jail. No sooner would the man be placed in jail than he would post a bond, which he immediately broke. A new suit would ensue upon the bond, which would lead to judgment, commitment, and a second bail bond, breach, and suit. Village lawyers often brought as many as several hundred such suits yearly. Although each judgment brought only a small collection fee, the end result could be a handsome living for the most successful lawyers.[25]

By the time John S. Robinson began legal work in Bennington, court practices had become more formal, and both judges and attorneys were somewhat better versed in the law. Issues regarding the protection of property remained the central concern of the lawyer and his clients, but the scale of these issues had changed dramatically. In place of some local blacksmith demanding payment of a bushel of wheat stood the Bennington Furnace, the Norton pottery, Stephen Hinsdill's company store, or one of the cotton or woolen factories emerging along the Walloomsac and its tributaries. Much larger sums of money were involved.

From the time he first returned to Bennington after graduating from college, John Robinson's personal and political associations harmonized nicely with his legal affiliations. He became closely allied with the more democratically inclined members of the Robinson family in Bennington, particularly members of the branches headed by David, Jonathan, and Samuel Robinson Jr. These men and their sons formed the central core of the old Republican party in Bennington and later of the Democratic party that emerged with the advent of Andrew Jackson on the national scene. Indeed, Gen. David Robinson, a veteran of the battle of Bennington, became the patriarch of the Bennington County Democracy. The general, along with his sons David and Heman, at all times forthrightly championed democratic principles. At the same time, though, John Robinson's uncles, Moses Robinson Jr. and Aaron, stood firmly with the old-line Federalists in the village. John had extensive business dealings with these men, including Aaron's son Phineas, who owned one of the largest cotton textile mills in the county, but he remained adamantly opposed to their political principles.

John's initial involvement in the political tensions that were building within Bennington came on August 16, 1827, at the fiftieth-anniversary celebration of the battle of Bennington. Following the traditional festivities, some townspeople offered volunteer toasts. After several salutations to Bennington's Revolutionary past, R. H. Blackmer, a prominent local attorney and influential member of the old Federalist faction in town, saluted the administration of John Quincy Adams. John S.

Robinson, the twenty-three-year-old attorney who had just been admitted to the county bar, responded with a toast to Andrew Jackson. Soon after that Isaac Doolittle, superintendent of the Bennington Furnace, rose from his seat and proclaimed, "May military talents, and military celebrity never be considered as a sufficient passport for the Presidential Chair." Finally, someone closed the celebration with a toast to "General Andrew Jackson — The Hero, the Scholar and the Statesman — to him are we indebted, let us improve the first opportunity to discharge the debt, by elevating him to that station to which his talents and services entitle him."[26] Clearly, Andrew Jackson was becoming the focus for political divisions within Bennington, just as he was throughout the nation.

As political differences between the Democratic-Republican supporters of Andrew Jackson and the National Republican followers of John Quincy Adams began to emerge in Bennington, John S. Robinson became one of the town's most outspoken supporters of Andrew Jackson's candidacy for the presidency. Following the Old Hero's election to the White House, Robinson served on the county Democratic-Republican committee, whose members staunchly referred to themselves as "friends of the administration."[27] In July 1830 county Republicans chose Robinson to attend a district convention called to nominate a candidate for Congress.[28]

In order to help the freemen of Bennington County better comprehend the vital importance of the pending congressional election, Heman Robinson, as convention chair, gave a public address in which he traced the origin and contemporary state of political parties in the nation. In his mind, two parties, one republican and the other monarchical, had emerged during the administration of George Washington. The former respected the specific enumerated powers written in the Constitution and felt that these delineated the outermost boundaries of national power. The latter, constantly seeking to expand the powers of the central government beyond its constitutional limits, threatened to transform the republican society of America into a class-ridden culture much like that of England. When John Adams came to power the monarchical party enjoyed free rein; a "wild and unchastened exercise of powers without Constitutional limits" ensued. Only the election of Thomas Jefferson and the resultant strict adherence to constitutional limitations saved the republic from the decadence and degeneration that would inevitably have followed from the unconstitutional actions of the Adams administration. Fortunately for the nation, Jefferson's successors James Madison and James Monroe proved to be the same friends of the Constitution as the Sage of Monticello. This was not the case, however, with John Quincy Adams. Under his administration "the same class of engines were in operation, which were in action in the days preceding the restoration of the Constitution under Jefferson." Thankfully, after eighteen months in office, Andrew Jackson had been able to bring the federal government back within its legitimate constitutional limits.[29]

Following his history lesson on the origin and development of political parties, Heman Robinson asked the voters whether they favored the Constitution or "the assumption of aspiring ambition." If the former, they should align themselves with the Democratic-Republican candidate for Congress; this was the only way to show their support for the Constitution as well as Andrew Jackson's efforts to protect that document and the nation against the encroachments of those who would corrupt the federal government for their own benefit. Just as in the vital early days of the republic, the choice now lay between aristocracy and democracy.[30]

After John S. Robinson and his colleagues at the district convention nominated O. C. Merrill for Congress, they supported his candidacy in much the same terms that Heman Robinson had employed in his address to the freeman of Bennington County. Only Merrill's election would safeguard "the principles of the Revolution." The differences between the candidates could not be more sharply drawn: "*Mr. Hunt has Money. Merrill has Talents.* Hunt is a well *known federalist and purse proud Aristocrat.* Merrill is a REPUBLICAN OF THE JEFFERSON SCHOOL, and is the candidate of the Republican Yeomanry of his district." Once the voters clearly understood these distinctions, Merrill would be their only choice and "the Constitution will be sustained at the coming crisis."[31]

Such ideas constituted the foundation of the political persuasion espoused by John S. Robinson and his Democratic colleagues. Uel M. Robinson swore that "Jacksonism must be right as it favored the poor & contended against the rich."[32] Merrill maintained that the common people supported the Jackson administration because it was truly "Democratic" and its opponents were "Aristocratic." This was particularly telling, since Merrill believed that political parties "were now divided as formerly on the same principles — Federal or Aristocratic & Democratic." In his mind, Jackson, the great democrat, had done more to establish freedom in the country than even Jefferson himself simply by destroying the National Bank.[33]

As political partisanship became increasingly heated in Bennington, John S. Robinson intensified his involvement in the activities of the Democratic party. Applying his abundant forensic talents to full advantage, he repeatedly served as a delegate to the party's county conventions, filled elected offices at those gatherings, played a prominent role in the party's annual celebrations of July 4 and August 16, and served on the Democratic Committee of Vigilance for the town of Bennington.[34] As a reward for his efforts he gained his party's nomination for Congress in 1834 and 1836. After suffering defeats in both these contests, Robinson succeeded in being elected to the state senate in 1839 and again in 1840.

In all of these campaigns Robinson ran as the champion of egalitarian democracy, a true old-school republican. In 1836, for example, his supporters called for every freeman to give their vote to Robinson, the candidate of the "Anti-Monopoly Democratic Ticket" for Congress, on the grounds that he was a "sterling Republican." They attacked his opponent, Hiland Hall, not only because he had recklessly opposed every one of Andrew Jackson's measures but also because his continual reelection went against the principle of rotation in office. No man should be elected to office for life, particularly when "there are hundreds of equal talents in the district." More important, Robinson supported a specie currency rather than the paper-money system advocated by "the monopolists of the Banks," who "make their *twelve to thirty per cent.* out of the industrious hard working part of the community." Hiland Hall, on the other hand, "advocated the *rag-money-monopoly-system* in Congress, and ridiculed the idea of a specie currency as only fit for '*Semi-Barbarians, Tartars, or Despots!*'" Voters had a clear choice between "a specie currency and a rag and shaving monopoly system." If they favored the former, they should vote for Robinson; if, however, they preferred a "privileged ragmoney monopoly system," they should cast their ballot for Hiland Hall.[35]

The same populist appeal characterized Robinson's race for the state senate in 1839. The editor of the *Vermont Gazette* declared "Equal Rights and Privileges" to be the rallying cry of the Democracy. For him, no matter how the issue might be disguised by the opposing party, the senate race was "emphatically a contest between the Banks and the People; Between the rich monopolist and wealthy stockholder and the great mass of community." The editor dramatically asked how "the farmer, the mechanic, or the day laborer [could] give his suffrages in favor of souless and irresponsible corporations, simply because his own party have seen fit to nominate men in favor of exclusive privileges, to office." No matter how the "designing leaders of the Bank party" might strive to keep the power and influence of banks and large corporations in the background, every "opposition [Whig] farmer, mechanic, and laborer, has the same interest in this question, as the Democrat." Only the election of loyal Democrats would serve the interests of all the people, not just those of a privileged few.[36] With such a message, John S. Robinson, scion of one of Bennington's most influential families — a true representative of the town's old elite — offered himself as the people's candidate.

Mr. C. was happy, in devising means for blessing the dear people of his charge. The revival had no sooner subsided, than he began to contemplate with a melancholy interest, the ravages which Intemperance had made, and was still making, in the town. At that time his people had not the light which has been shed by the present Temperance Reform, to guide him. Even good men had labored hitherto under the mistaken notion, that a moderate use of alcoholic drinks is not only not hurtful, but beneficial. Mr. C. felt, however, that something could, and must be done, to stay the ravages of the destroyer. He came forward with this proposition, "Let the name of every individual in the town be obtained, who is willing to report faithfully, what amount of distilled liquor he has used in his family during the current year." Strange as it may seem now, only twenty-five persons, among a population of about four thousand, could be induced to go even that length. As loose, however, as this compact was, it still resulted in great good, for it demonstrated, what had not yet been found out among this people, that total abstinence from ardent spirit was a practicable thing. The year came round. None! was appended to the names of eight out of twenty-five. This result was both surprising and encouraging. The second annual report was still more gratifying. The Society now numbered more than one hundred members, most of whom had wholly abstained from the use of distilled liquors. The sale of liquors in the town had been reduced by nearly one-half. At this meeting the Society ventured to advance another step. It was accordingly resolved to practice total abstinence from distilled spirit. This, at that time, was thought to be a very ultra measure, and stirred up the united wrath of the rum-drinkers and rum-sellers of the place. And here commenced, permit us to state, the first organized, settled opposition to Mr. C. in Bennington — an opposition which was severe and unrelenting — but which only served to inspire him with increased zeal and energy in carrying forward the cause of his Master. The Society now went steadily forward, increasing in num-

bers and in usefulness. They have now adopted the total abstinence pledge, and numbers over twelve hundred members, and is one of the most thorough and efficient societies that we are acquainted with in any part of the country. With all this before us, we cannot help remarking that the day of small things is not to be despised.

One fact, in connection with the Temperance Reform in Bennington, we cannot refrain from stating, as it is an illustration of Mr. Clark's manner of unmasking error, and of his boldness in preaching the truth. The temperance cause having advanced so far as to admit of a question whether professors of religion ought to be engaged in the traffic or not, a Church meeting was called to discuss the subject. At that time we had a very worthy Deacon who was trafficking in the poison, who came forward, and in a labored argument, tried to convince the Church, that, as the sale would go on, it had better be confined to conscientious persons, who would be more decent about it than others. The Deacon had no sooner resumed his seat, than Mr. Clark arose, and replied in substance, as follows: "Strange doctrine this! The argument of my brother goes too far. It would prove that all the theatres, and brothels, should be kept by conscientious men, that sinners might be guided down to hell the more decently. No! no! If it must be sold, I would place at the tap the same old lying serpent that handed Eve the apple, that it might appear to be the very infernal traffic that it is."[37]

The two Bennington gentlemen who described Rev. Daniel Clark's efforts to promote the cause of temperance also provided a vivid portrayal of his pastoral experience in their village. Describing Clark as a "bold, original, pungent, direct" preacher, they noted that he gave "no quarter to sin, in any shape or form, in high places or low." Nothing, no matter how formidable, "could daunt him, or divert him a moment from his purpose." At all times, "whatever *was truth,* he would advocate it, no matter what the opposition."[38] Others observed that when Clark was thoroughly aroused, "which he often was," he would deliver his message "from the pulpit with herculean force." At these times Clark, "self-trained to great terseness of expression, and by nature intense," would manifest "the fierceness of the lion rather than the gentleness of the lamb." His strident manner and the certainty with which he held his convictions caused him to aim "deadly blows at intemperance, Sabbath-breaking, dancing, card-playing, [and] covetousness." Indeed, "if there was an infidel-club in the town, he discovered it, and poured his hottest fire into it." Clark, "like Sampson, . . . was willing to pull down the temple of Dagon upon himself as well as the Philistines, if, otherwise, he could not destroy them."[39] Clark knew with certainty that only God's saving grace could redeem man's heart and change his nature. Any other doctrine was false and encouraged the degeneracy that existed in Bennington and throughout the nation.

For Clark, "men, in all countries and ages, and under every variety of customs and manners, have had, and continue to have, naturally, the same moral character." Every unregenerate man had a "deformed and polluted character" no matter what his rank or status in society. Clark advised anyone who questioned this "to look around him, and within him, and see how the human heart belches forth its moral corruption, poisoning domestic and social joy, and contaminating every district of this unfortunate and ruined world." Let any doubter "attend our courts of justice, and see how men will perjure themselves; let him read the catalogue of divorces; let him spend an evening in the grog-shop; let him stop a moment at her door, whose 'house is the way to hell;' let him enter one of our criminal prisons; let him penetrate once into the secrets of his own heart, and stay there till the light is let in." He thundered at his congregation that "when God takes off those restraints that now make unholy men differ, they will be so much alike that none will impeach his justice when he assigns them all the same outer darkness, the same gnawing worm, and the same quenchless fire." At that instant, "he that has stolen his neighbor's property, and died a felon, and he who has concealed the article found in the street, or the mistake made in his favor, or has purposely become a bankrupt, to escape the obligations of honesty, will appear too much alike in the judgment to require any material diversity in their final sentences." On the day of judgment "the same perdition will suit them both, though one drops down to hell from the gallows, and the other is borne there on a downy bed."[40]

Clark's most fervent supporters believed their minister was surrounded by a "mass of infidelity and ungodliness" in Bennington. In their minds, no reasonable person could, therefore, suppose that "his bold and fearless course would awaken no hostile feelings." Rather, his relentless "exposure of iniquity, both out of the church and in, were [simply] too glaring to be endured in silence." Consequently, soon after Clark's arrival in town following Absalom Peter's resignation in December 1825 to join the American Home Missionary Society "the elements of wrath began to combine for his overthrow and removal."[41] Naturally, the pious rallied to his defense. Rancor and divisiveness spread throughout Bennington.

The intense self-righteousness with which Daniel Clark pursued his ministry in Bennington and which helped to account for its tumultuous nature had characterized his conduct long before he came to town. A belief in his own moral rectitude had marked Clark's behavior from the age of fifteen, when he had undergone a conversion experience that initiated a year of emotional turmoil in his life.

Born in Rahway, New Jersey, in 1779, to an indulgent father and a devoutly pious mother, Clark spent his early years in a "wicked and thoughtless" manner. His mother attempted to raise him according to the strictures of the Bible, but he detested her for these efforts. When he was fifteen she barged into a dance he was attending against her wishes and ordered him home. He obeyed but wished her dead. Silently cursing her, he hoped that something might free him from her. It appeared that his wish might be granted when his father made arrangements to apprentice him to a "very wicked" though quite successful man of business. Before going to live with his employer, however, Daniel attended a revival meeting in nearby Elizabethtown. Planning to "fix myself in a corner of the pew, and during the sermon take a nap," the boy became transfixed by the minister's words. Although he longed to join those who gave themselves to Christ that day, he obscured himself in the pew "till the sacrament was over, pouring out one constant flood of tears." After that he tried to hide "from my merry companions, with whom I felt that I could never again have communion, unless they were regenerated."[42]

Following this experience Daniel believed that his father should have fostered his "growth in grace." Instead, his father sent him to live with the "evil" businessman. This situation, which Daniel had formerly anticipated with much delight, became unbearable for him. He lived amidst the "oaths and curses" of men who "laughed at my seriousness, and tried many ways to make me dishonor religion." During the daytime, he often felt compelled to "leave the wicked throng which surrounded me, that I might spend a few moments alone." Many evenings were "spent in tears" or in reading the Bible. After a year of this ordeal, he joined the church and "took [his] seat among the followers of the Lamb."[43]

Upon completion of his apprenticeship Daniel decided to devote his life to the Christian ministry. In 1802, at the age of twenty-three, he went to live and study with a pastor in Basking Ridge, New Jersey, to prepare himself for Princeton College. Three years later he returned home briefly to his mother's deathbed. As he watched her die in peace, she spoke only of the great joy she found in God's countenance. Daniel finally realized that as "a child of prayer, he knew a mother's worth."[44]

In the same year that his mother died, Daniel gained admission to

Princeton, where his academic preparations enabled him to enter the second-year class. Shortly after arriving on campus he joined the Clio-sophic Society and became fully involved in the traditional life as well as the traditional curriculum of the college. This was not, however, a normal time for Princeton. Under the presidency of Samuel Stanhope Smith, a staunch Federalist, the college's administrators and faculty assumed a decidedly reactionary posture following Thomas Jefferson's election. Since Princeton drew a large proportion of its student body from Southern families who were ardent Jeffersonian Republicans, Smith's stance did not bode well for the peace and tranquility of the college.

President Smith, a believer in "the universal science of history," maintained that nations prospered only so long as their citizens maintained their virtue; decline inevitably followed "the corruption of morals, and the disorder of public manners." For this very reason Jefferson's election greatly disturbed Smith. The triumph of the Democratic-Republicans meant that the social and political chaos that had ruined France would soon pollute American society as well. He constantly warned his students that the cause of France's ruin — unrestrained democracy — would bring about the same results in America: impiety, the dissolution of public manners, and the breakdown of social order. They, like all other citizens of the United States, must guard against "the spirit of equality . . . carried to an extreme." The best way to promote "the tranquility, order, and happiness of society" was to instruct "every class of the people" in their proper moral and social duties.[45] Smith intended to begin with the students in his charge.

Fearful that the social ferment they perceived all around them might envelop Princeton, Smith and the college trustees took strict measures to maintain good order on the campus. This resulted in a student petition of protest and then a revolt against the administration that resulted in the suspension of over a hundred students.[46] Daniel Clark would have no part in this unrest.[47] He believed that an anti-Christian dissoluteness, not an attachment to republican principles and personal honor, underlay the student rebellion.[48] The true republicanism of the Revolution supported Christian faith and good order, not individual willfulness. During his years at Princeton Clark did not deviate from the God-fearing course he had marked out for himself and others. Shortly after the rebellion he begged his aunt and uncle to allow "a young pilgrim [to] admonish you to keep your eyes fixed upon your ascended Redeemer." For Daniel Clark, "to serve Christ is the whole business of life."[49]

During his last year in residence the Princeton board of trustees underwent a transformation that brought the school much more in line with the aspirations of pious students like Clark. Ministers now made up over one-fourth of the board, and their influence became increasingly dominant in that body's decisions. Education at Princeton became sharply focused on the preparation of Presbyterian ministers trained in the efficacy of voluntary agencies and religious revivalism. Evangelical Presbyterianism assumed precedence over Revolutionary republicanism; from the perspective of the new trustees, the salvation of the nation depended upon the moral reform of its citizens by well-educated ministers rather than upon the political actions of voters swayed by demagogic office seekers.[50] Clark graduated thoroughly imbued with these beliefs.

After leaving Princeton Clark went to Newark, New Jersey, where he studied theology under the guidance of Edwin D. Griffin, pastor of the First Presbyterian Church of Newark and one of the most effective revivalist preachers of the day. In May 1809 Griffin left Newark to become professor of public eloquence at Andover Theological Seminary. He took Clark and several other ministerial students with him.

At Andover Clark found everything he desired: a bastion of orthodox Calvinism comprising pious professors and serious students intent upon spreading the word of Christ.[51] Having studied with Griffin, he was so well prepared in Biblical studies—the focus of first-year students—that he entered the second-year class, which concentrated on theology. In their final year students touched on church history, but they devoted most of their time to the art of writing and preaching sermons.

Life at Andover assumed the quality of an ascetic religious commune. The students lived together in Phillips Hall, shared spartan meals in the commons, and procured their own drinking water and wood to warm their rooms. The dining hall remained unheated even through the coldest months of winter. All students became members of the Society of the Brethren and called one another "brother." The Brethren formulated all regulations touching upon the communal life of the student body. Thus, seminarians, acting in common, set their own study hours and established the rules that governed their behavior at Andover.

Many Brethren, particularly the founding members, devoted themselves to the creation of foreign missionary societies and other voluntary associations. Very soon such activities became popularly associated
with the student body at Andover.[52] Clark, however, devoted most of
his time outside the classroom to revivalistic activities. He and several
of his classmates led a religious revival in the town of Andover during
their fall break in 1809. Then Clark, who had often prayed to be where
God "was pouring out his Holy Spirit," found that place in Beverly,
Massachusetts, where he spent six weeks tending a revival during the
summer of 1810. The experience moved him deeply: he now longed
always to be "where God reveals his gracious name . . . to have every day
some view of his face, to feel every morning and evening the same
fervent glow of affection."[53]

In the fall of 1810, prior to leaving Andover, Clark passed an examination administered by the Presbytery of New Jersey and received his
license to preach. He spent a short time as interim preacher in Port-
land, Maine, and then, on January 1, 1812, was ordained as a minister of
the gospel and installed as pastor of the Congregational Union Church
of Braintree and Weymouth, Massachusetts. That same year he married Eliza Barker, whom he had met while preaching in Maine.

Clark's years in Weymouth were not easy. He complained that few
among his congregation would pray for a revival and that a great many
took grievous offense at his preaching, including many who failed to
measure up to his exacting standard of piety. Others simply could not
stand his constant attacks upon their lack of religious fervor, their covetousness, or their proclivity for cardplaying, gambling, or dancing.[54]
Certain that his vision constituted the Truth and the Light, Clark
refused to compromise with any who differed with him.[55]

The church at Weymouth dismissed Clark in the fall of 1815, setting
Clark and his wife off on a peripatetic course. First they traveled to
Hanover, New Jersey, where he helped lead a revival. Then in January
1816 he accepted a position as pastor of the Congregational church in
the isolated village of Southbury, Connecticut, where he also taught
school. Four years later he was installed as pastor of the Congregational
church in Amherst, Massachusetts. By November 1823 that church had
appointed a committee to bring charges against him; the following
April the committee asked Clark to take a dismissal. He refused. Three
months later the church called for an ecclesiastical council. In the
meantime, church members notified Clark that they did not wish him
to remain in the pulpit while his dismissal was pending. With the coun-

cil's support, the church dismissed Clark in August 1824. Nevertheless, the council gave Clark an excellent recommendation as a minister of the gospel.[56] Two years later his old friend and mentor Edward Griffin, now president of Williams College, preached at the ceremony installing Clark as pastor of First Church in Bennington. Daniel Clark would now offer his message of reform and repentance to the good people of Bennington.

Wednesday Octo. 22, 1834 — The Church met agreeable to notice given by their Pastor last Sabbath — by the request of some of the Brethren living in the north-west part of the Town. meeting opened with Prayer. When Dea. Hinsdill presented the following request, to wit, "We as a Committee & our associates ask this Church to grant us the privilege of establishing the Gospel, & organising a Church in the northwest part of the town at S. Hinsdill Chappel." a motion was made — that the request of the committee be granted — which was put & decided against the request, — Dea. Hinsdill then in behalf of the Committee made a Verbal request, that the Church would unite with them in calling a mutual Council to decide this matter. — when a Motion was made, that the request of the Committee be granted & a mutual Council be Called, which was put & decided in favor of the request.[57]

When the church council met on October 29 its members advised that Deacon Stephen Hinsdill's petition be granted. One week later members of Bennington's First Church met and formed a committee to help establish the new church and to settle with Deacon Hinsdill. Two days after that seventy-five members of First Church asked for and received letters of dismissal; these individuals formed the core of the Hinsdillville Presbyterian Church.[58] At first the new church assembled in a chapel located in a large room in one of Hinsdill's factory buildings. Then late in the fall of 1835 the congregation occupied a stone church constructed by Deacon Hinsdill. This impressive edifice stood near several rows of tenements that housed workers employed in Hinsdill's extensive cotton and woolen mills.

Hinsdillville had been appropriately named. Stephen Hinsdill owned four of the six cotton mills and the only woolen mill located in the village that bore his name. He also owned the single store and most of the houses there.[59] Under his guidance the village had grown and flourished. Without the advantage of its location at the confluence of Paran Creek and the Walloomsac River, however, Hinsdillville could never have prospered. The abundant water power supplied by these streams operated the spindles of the factories located along their banks. These factories, in turn, attracted a population large enough to support its own church.

Hinsdillville was no anomaly; it was, in fact, an integral part of social and economic changes that were transforming Bennington Township. The power and authority of the old village of Bennington was slowly eroding. Located high on a hill overlooking the Walloomsac valley, and thus totally without water power, old Bennington languished while settlements located along the banks of Paran Creek, Roaring Branch, and the Walloomsac steadily gained in population and productive capacity. Signs of the original village's diminishing influence abounded. In 1833 inhabitants of both the North Village, located along the upper reaches of Paran Creek, and the East Village, spreading out around the confluence of Roaring Branch and the Walloomsac, asked the selectmen of Bennington to lay out and establish the limits of these communities.[60] Implementing this request accorded two areas of the township official recognition of what had previously been only informal custom: selectmen should be elected from each of the distinct geographic districts of the township.

If the political coherence of Bennington was beginning to fragment, so, too, was the town's religious unity. Baptist and Methodist congregations built churches in the East Village in 1830 and 1833, respectively. Episcopalians organized a parish there in 1834 and erected a church two years later. Then in 1836 a Congregational church colonized from the old First Church formed in the East Village, and a group of Methodists constructed a church building at Irish Corner, less than a mile down the Walloomsac from Hinsdillville. In that year a Universalist congregation also erected a house of worship in North Bennington. Thus, within a year of the formation of the Hinsdillville church, Bennington's First Church, which had been the only organized congregation in the township for over half a century, found itself forced to share its religious authority with seven other churches, which had come into being within a single decade.[61]

Stephen's nephew Joseph N. Hinsdill recorded the changing realities of the day when he published a detailed map of Bennington Township in 1835. No longer did the old village on the hill bear the name Bennington; instead it had assumed the title Centre Village and taken its place alongside North Bennington, East Village, and Hinsdillville. Contemporary gazetteers brought the shifts taking place in Bennington Township into even sharper focus. Zadock Thompson, for one, considered old Bennington "a place of considerable capital and business." However, "having been begun on high ground, a portion of the business, of which it would otherwise have been the centre, has departed to more fortunate locations on the streams." His summary of vital statistics confirmed this observation. Bennington Centre, with a population of nearly four hundred, had seventy-five homes, one church, two academies, the county courthouse, a jail, a post office, a bank, three taverns, five stores, seven law offices, a printing office, and a variety of mechanics' shops. By comparison, East Village, with a population of more than seven hundred, had 140 houses, four churches, one academy, a woolen factory, two wadding factories, two iron furnaces and manufactories, three tanneries, an extensive pottery, a brick factory, a great many mechanics' shops, a gristmill, a sawmill, an oil mill, eight stores, three taverns, a printing office, and three law offices.[62] Thompson's figures left little doubt that East Village, long referred to derisively by folks on the hill as "Algiers," was rapidly outstripping old Bennington.[63]

At the same time that these physical changes were occurring, family names long associated with the original village were beginning to appear in increasing numbers in the competing communities. This was particularly true of East Village. Rev. Jedediah Dewey's son Eldad established several mills on the Walloomsac and settled nearby. His sons Jedediah and Stephen, who worked ochre and iron ore beds near the river, also resided in East Village. The Saffords, following the lead of Joseph Safford Sr., operated grist- and sawmills on the Walloomsac and became leading members of the East Village community. The same was true of the sons of Captain John Norton, who moved the family pottery works there in 1833. The Robinson family also experienced this dispersal: Gen. Henry Robinson became East Bennington's first postmaster, and Phineas Lyman Robinson moved to North Bennington, where he became one of the most successful cotton manufacturers in the township.[64]

From earliest childhood Stephen Hinsdill was closely associated with the manufacturing that drew so many individuals away from the agricultural focus of old Bennington. His father, Joseph, came to Bennington in 1772 from Canaan, Connecticut, where his family had been involved in weaving and dressing woolens. Joseph married Hannah Bingham and purchased a large farm near Irish Corner, in the northwest part of town.[65] During the Revolution Capt. Samuel Robinson's militia company elected him ensign (second lieutenant).[66] At the close of hostilities Joseph expanded his economic endeavors: in 1786 he

formed a partnership with his neighbor Ebenezer Walbridge, and the
two took over a paper mill located on the falls of the Walloomsac; then
he assumed a proprietary interest in an iron forge being erected near
Eldad Dewey's gristmill, in the eastern part of the township; shortly
after that he opened clothier shops in Bennington, Manchester, and
Arlington, where he employed workmen skilled in the use of dyes; and
at the same time he became a proprietor in extensive land grants in
Canada.[67] Prior to his death in August 1800, Joseph involved his five
sons in his business affairs as much as possible, but only Joseph Hinsdill
Jr. and Stephen carried on their father's interest in cotton and woolen
manufacturing.[68] By September 1808 Stephen was advertising homespun woolens and cloth of various kinds at a factory he had constructed
on Paran Creek. He offered to card wool and dress cloth at this same
establishment.[69] A year later he advertised the addition of more machinery to enable him to weave a better grade of cloth.[70] By 1810 the
two brothers had formed a partnership and opened the Bennington
Woolen Factory,[71] and soon they were building and selling machinery
for carding wool, spinning thread, and weaving cloth.[72] As their venture
on Paran Creek prospered, the partners expanded their facilities, produced more machinery, sold large numbers of machine cards for dressing wool, leased out former operations, and took on a great many
apprentices and workers.[73]

Even while his partnership with Joseph thrived, Stephen busily constructed cotton mills of his own along the lower portion of Paran
Creek. Because of such efforts he was the wealthiest man in Bennington
at the time of his brother's death in 1822.[74] Following Joseph's death,
Stephen devoted himself to business with increased intensity.[75] Within
a year he had constructed a large canal along the Walloomsac that
delivered a powerful flow of water to an extensive new woolen factory
that he had constructed.[76] The increasing number of workers, machine
shops, and factories that appeared in the area created a bustling village
at the confluence of Paran Creek and the Walloomsac. It was there,
near the east bank of Paran Creek, that Stephen Hinsdill built the large
home where he and his wife Hannah raised five daughters.

While he devoted much time and attention to his business ventures,
he was not single-minded in his attachment to them. After he under-
went a religious experience at the age of twenty-nine and joined First
Church in May 1816, he worked arduously to further the cause of
Christ in any manner he could. He and his family strictly observed the
Sabbath, and he chartered a four-horse team to bring whichever of his

factory workers or neighbors wished to accompany his family to worship on Sundays. It was not long before he had become a pillar of the
church; in May 1822 the members of First Church elected him to be
one of their deacons.[77] Deacon Hinsdill soon became one of the most
influential figures in the religious life of the township.

Hinsdill's prominence in the religious affairs of Bennington did not
involve him in town government. Despite their long residence in the
township, the Hinsdills had rarely been called to positions of authority
by the annual town meeting. Joseph Hinsdill Sr. had served several
times as a selectman; otherwise he and his eldest sons had assumed such
minor positions as fence viewer, surveyor of highways, or juryman.[78]
That they neither resided in the old village nor were members of First
Church severely handicapped whatever political ambitions the elder
Hinsdills may have entertained. Neither of these factors, however, affected Stephen; geographical representation within town government
had become accepted custom by the time he gained prominence in the
larger community, and he was certainly a solid member of the church.
Still, he served only three times as a petit juror, twice as a tithingman,
and once as a surveyor of highways.[79] Clearly, other considerations kept
a man like Stephen Hinsdill from holding important town positions.

Except for a brief flurry during which he professed the Jeffersonian
ideals that had long been ingrained within his family's political lore,
Hinsdill showed very little interest in politics. In 1816 at a particularly
rancorous town meeting he suffered defeat at the hands of a Federalist
after he had been nominated to be selectman from the northwest part
of the town.[80] Then in July 1818 participants at a Republican rally
elected him to serve on a committee with David Robinson, O. C. Merrill, David Fay, and several others to arrange for the August 16 celebration of the battle of Bennington.[81] This was the full extent of his political involvement.

Whatever order, harmony, purposefulness, and improvement Hinsdill wished for Bennington, he did not look to politics to achieve them.
He thought that political parties could never foster the self-control,
rationality, industriousness, and social order essential to a republican community. For him, the best way to bring about the changes so
desperately needed in Bennington and throughout America was not
through the political process, but rather through an amalgam of evangelical religion, voluntary associations, and economic development.

Hinsdill began this process of redemption, appropriately enough, in
his own factory village, where he personally fostered piety, family val-

ues, and industrious work habits. Envisioning Hinsdillville as an extended family and himself as its benevolent patriarch, he preferred to hire families that had three to six females "well recommended for sobriety, morality and industry."[82] He housed them in company lodgings, supplied them from the company store, taught them disciplined work habits in his mills, and provided for their spiritual well-being in the factory chapel.[83] In addition, he led periodic religious revivals among his workers. Despite his disdain for politics, at election time he even provided wagons to carry his male workers to the courthouse to vote.[84] In Hinsdill's view, then, factories and factory villages not only promoted economic development but were of tremendous moral benefit to society because they fostered human redemption by promoting honesty, sobriety, industriousness, and self-restraint.

By no means did Hinsdill restrict his reform energies to his own company village. He was deeply involved in attempts to shape the religious lives of poor people throughout the county. He became a director of the Bennington County Bible Society at that organization's original meeting in October 1819,[85] and from then on he served not only as a director but also as the society's general agent for Bennington County.[86] In the latter capacity he assumed responsibility for distributing Bibles to the destitute of the county.

Following the arrival of Absalom Peters in August 1819, Hinsdill grew even more enthusiastic in his support of voluntary reform agencies and other collective efforts to promote the common good. The young pastor's enthusiastic promotion of temperance, Sabbath schools, education, and moral reform struck a responsive chord in the devout industrialist.[87] Education was an essential foundation of the reform impulse Peters brought to Bennington, and Hinsdill, who became one of the pastor's most earnest disciples, served on the board of directors of the Bennington Academy, which had been created at the urging of Peters. When the academy opened in 1822, Hinsdill and his fellow directors pledged that the school would instruct its students in academic subjects and "nourish the moral culture of youth" as well.[88]

When Daniel Clark replaced Peters as pastor of First Church, Hinsdill became his strongest advocate and warmest friend. He fitted out a large room in one of his factories as a chapel, where Clark held a weekly religious service, and Clark often stayed with the Hinsdill family afterwards. When Clark's preaching sparked a religious revival in Hinsdillville in the fall of 1826, Hinsdill did all he could to help. On the day Clark appointed for fasting and prayer Hinsdill set aside an entire factory building in order to accommodate one of the largest crowds ever assembled in Bennington.[89]

Hinsdill supported Clark in all his reform efforts, but he took a special interest in education. When his son-in-law, James Ballard, offended many prominent members of the community and lost his position as principal of the Academy, Hinsdill constructed a new building, where Ballard opened the Bennington Seminary. Along with Daniel Clark, Hinsdill served on the seminary's board of directors, and he gave it his earnest public endorsement.[90] At about this same time he became a life member in the northwestern branch of the American Educational Society, an organization devoted to raising funds to support the education of indigent young men who wished to enter the ministry.[91]

Hinsdill's close relationship with Ballard and the Bennington Seminary brought him into contact with another young reformer who had recently moved to Bennington. William Lloyd Garrison, brought to Bennington in the fall of 1828 by supporters of John Quincy Adams to edit the *Journal of the Times*, roomed in the boardinghouse that Deacon Erwin Safford constructed for resident students of Bennington Seminary. Garrison, Ballard, and Clark soon became intimate friends.[92] Garrison's enthusiasm for temperance and other moral reforms blended nicely with those of Ballard, Clark, and Hinsdill. It was, however, the young editor's passion for antislavery activity that most profoundly affected Hinsdill. At first he, like Garrison, supported the colonization of blacks and became a manager of the Bennington Probate District Colonization Society.[93] Gradually, however, his antislavery beliefs intensified. In December 1833, when a number of Bennington's most prominent political leaders prevented Orson Murray, an agent of the New England Antislavery Society, from speaking at the meetinghouse on the hill, Hinsdill opened his factory chapel to Murray.[94] Following this incident Hinsdill became more fully committed to abolitionism; within three years he was serving on the board of managers for the Vermont Anti-Slavery Society.[95]

While he was becoming involved in moral reforms such as abolitionism, Hinsdill was also a committed advocate of economic development. He was an active member of the Bennington County Agricultural Society.[96] Out of this association emerged several other groups to which Hinsdill gave his full support, including an association of farmers and manufacturers and one for wool growers and manufacturers. Hinsdill not only joined the efforts of these groups but helped articulate their beliefs in memorials addressed to the public. These resolutions always stressed the natural affinity between agriculture and manufacturing; indeed, one statement that Hinsdill helped formulate claimed that a union between these two formed "the fountain of national prosperity, wealth, knowledge and distinction." Consequently, to allow "the over-grown capitalists of Europe to glut and control" America's markets would be "impolitic, and unjust to our own people." Only the passage of a strong tariff could prevent such a travesty.[97]

Strong tariff protection became the central economic reform called for by Hinsdill and many other manufacturers. Whereas the "great men of the last generation" achieved the "political redemption" of America, it fell to the present generation "to rescue increased and increasing millions of freemen from a thraldom and degradation, chilling to the vital, moral, and productive energies of a rising empire, and to guide them to a condition of independence and prosperity unsurpassed" in the annals of civilization. Only increased tariffs could protect the "reward claimed by honest industry at home." The federal government must, therefore, follow the example of England and other European nations by nourishing and protecting native industries. Only in this way could American "virtue, prosperity and happiness" be promoted.[98]

In 1828 Hinsdill became involved in yet another economic organization, one that would help provide the capital needed to foster economic growth in the Bennington area. When the Bank of Bennington received a charter from the Vermont Assembly and opened its doors to the public in 1828, Hinsdill, who owned a majority of the bank's stock, became a member of the board of directors.[99] While he was a director the bank became closely linked with manufacturing corporations in the community.[100] In Hinsdill's view, banks, like tariffs, were essential to the economic development of Bennington.

Hinsdill's advocacy of moral reform, religious regeneration, and economic development gradually developed quite unself-consciously into a single coherent perception of social progress. Best described as "Christian capitalism,"[101] his mind-set rested on the belief that the capitalistic enterprise, when conducted with honesty and sincerity, was a sublimely creative endeavor in perfect harmony with the doctrines of Christianity that bestowed great benefits upon the entire human community. The capitalist's primary economic motive in such a system became the stewardship of wealth for the good of all mankind — to promote social reform and Christian benevolence — not the maximization of his own private gain. For Hinsdill, all groups within society, whether agriculture or manufacturing, capital or labor, existed in harmony with one another. Completely interdependent, each prospered or languished with the others; none truly gained at another's expense. In order for the system to work in a naturally harmonious manner, however, government must protect it from the disruptive intrusion of foreign goods. Tariff protection would allow native industries to thrive, and increased economic growth would naturally follow. Such growth would not only improve every person's material well-being but foster their social, moral, and spiritual condition as well. All citizens would be able to reach that station in life to which their natural abilities, moral attributes, and willingness to work entitled them. The end result would be a true Christian commonwealth, the kind of virtuous republic envisioned by the Founding Fathers.

In the belief that he was striving toward just such a goal, Stephen Hinsdill worked to reform and redeem Bennington in every way he could. At the time that he owned and operated the largest manufacturing complex in the area, formed the Hinsdillville Presbyterian church, constructed the Bennington Seminary, and served in various capacities for the Vermont Anti-Slavery Society, the Vermont Bible Society, the Bennington Agricultural Society, and the Bank of Bennington he was at the height of his ability to bring about the changes he so desired. Surely he should be able to shape Bennington into a Christian capitalist community.

The efforts of the Gazette within this county have been often felt by the republicans, and acknowledged by aristocratic enemies. The steady republican ascendancy of the county, is testimony in its favor. Five times has this press been assailed and its ruin meditated, by attempts to establish aristocratic opposition papers, and five times have the friends of the establishment rallied around and sustained it. We trust republican principles, and the republican interests of the county will continue to sustain it.

It is, however, our duty to state that the old enemy is again upon the alert, to anti-republicanise the county, and put down this press. The first Editor of this paper, who suffered in the republican interest, every thing almost but burning at the stake, said there was then a political party "who rose and throve by lying." And there is a set of men at the present day, who make most wretched constructions of our views, and "monstrous versions" of our principles.

The agents of federal papers printed in adjoining counties, with the aid of young federal lawyers, and young and old federal men resident among us, are busily at work to obtain a circulation of these papers, in various towns in the county. This would be nothing alarming to the republicans of this county, if the price and terms, did not prove it must be something more serious than the strife of printers to vend what papers they could; for we might afford to print as cheap as they, and perhaps bear to lose as much; but when it is found they proffer to sell these papers for one *dollar a year, there is good reason to suppose there is a monied combination in favor of their papers, and a political concert to prostrate the republican standing and character of this county; this is a cheaper way to put down the* Gazette, *than the establishment of a local press. We call upon republicans to reflect upon the probable result, and consider what is to be the probable condition of this county, if success attends this plan of operations.* We have only a common interest. *We rely not upon our own strength, we make no pretence, and are aware "many of the fathers have fallen asleep."* [102]

This editorial, published in the *Vermont Gazette* in February 1828, resembled those written by the paper's original editor, Anthony Haswell. It exuded the same moral indignation against Federalists, aristocrats, and "monied combinations" and preached the same belief in a common interest of the people that must constantly be nurtured and protected.

The similarity between this editorial and those of Anthony Haswell was hardly coincidental. In fact, its author, Orsamus C. Merrill, had served as Haswell's apprentice more than thirty years before. Born in Farmington, Connecticut, on June 18, 1775, Merrill migrated with his parents into Vermont in the spring of 1791. When the family stopped in Bennington, James Merrill took the opportunity to apprentice his sixteen-year-old son Orsamus to Haswell; James and the others then continued on to Castleton, where they settled on a small farm.[103]

Whenever Haswell needed help with the *Gazette* or his printing business, he advertised for an "active young republican" or a person "of the republican principles of 1776."[104] When young Merrill became his apprentice, Haswell was in the midst of a struggle to defend Governor Thomas Chittenden, Matthew Lyon, and the yeomanry of Vermont against the aristocratic pretensions of men such as Isaac Tichenor and Nathaniel Chipman. The fiery editor aggressively defended the rights of all men; he would not brook government by or for a privileged few. The lessons of the master were not lost on the apprentice. Haswell's republicanism—his egalitarianism and his strong advocacy of democratic principles—became thoroughly ingrained in the consciousness of the impressionable young man. Thus, by the time Merrill had completed his apprenticeship and served for a time as an independent printer he had become a loyal Jeffersonian Republican with a deep-

seated commitment to the principles of republicanism.[105] He retained
these same values after reading law with Andrew Selden and gaining
admittance to the Bennington bar in June 1804.

Merrill's enthusiastic support of the Jeffersonian cause and his talent
for public speaking made him a popular figure with local party leaders.
They often called upon him to serve as speaker of the day at party festivities such as their Fourth of July celebration.[106] On such occasions Merrill lauded the character and integrity of Thomas Jefferson, praised the
actions of his administration for promoting republicanism throughout
the nation, and attacked Federalists as "a coalition formed against the
liberties of America" and an "anti-republican confederacy" threatening
the very sovereignty of the American people.[107] The central theme of all
his speeches, however, was the need to nurture and protect "liberty"
from the forces of "tyranny." Liberty to Merrill meant freedom of
thought and action; it implied such things as freedom of the press and
freedom of religion, but most of all it meant the freedom of the individual to live and work untrammeled by the kind of social, political, and
economic restraints imposed on the common citizens of Europe by
their social superiors. Tyranny stood for the loss of such freedom. It
meant special privilege for the few at the expense of the many, the
ability or opportunity for some individuals or groups of individuals to
shape the lives of others. Where liberty reigned, government acted as a
"shield" to protect the interests of all the people; whenever tyranny
emerged, government became a "sword" to serve the interests of the
few.

Two months after Merrill began to practice law in Bennington
County, he married Mary Robinson, the only daughter of Jonathan
Robinson, the youngest son of Samuel Robinson Sr., the founder of
Bennington. His marriage to "Polly," therefore, brought Orsamus into
close contact with a man of wealth, power, and influence in Bennington
and throughout the state. At the time Merrill married his daughter,
Robinson was chief justice of the Vermont Supreme Court. In 1807 he
resigned this position in order to take a seat in the U.S. Senate, where
he became a staunch supporter of Thomas Jefferson.[108]

Despite his personal prominence, Jonathan Robinson displayed no
aristocratic affectations. Personally committed to democratic political
principles, he strove to live by such standards himself and insisted that
all members of his family do the same. One Sunday morning, when the
Robinsons were preparing to attend church, Polly appeared in an expensive silk dress that her mother had purchased for her. Jonathan

immediately exclaimed: "Take it off, and put on your calico dress, or you shall not go to meeting with me; when your mates have silk dresses to wear, then you may wear one."[109]

Merrill's relationship with his father-in-law not only reinforced the egalitarian ideals he had formed in association with Haswell but also linked him to the intense localism that permeated the old democratic elite of Bennington. These men, intent upon maintaining the values and institutions of their own community, were loath to surrender control over their lives to others, especially to a hierarchy of men unlike themselves. They were highly suspicious of individuals or groups outside their community, who might attempt to restrict or shape their lives. Above all, they believed that every citizen in Bennington should be able to pursue his interests free of all restraints except those traditionally imposed by the common good of the community.

In addition to instilling a strong sense of localism within his son-in-law, Jonathan Robinson helped Merrill's career in important ways. Because of the great number of lawyers practicing in Bennington County, Merrill did not enjoy immediate success at the bar.[110] Consequently, when Robinson went to the Senate, he used his influence to have Merrill named postmaster for Bennington. Upon the outbreak of the War of 1812, Senator Robinson, who had considerable influence in the Madison administration, aided in having his son-in-law commissioned a major in the regular army. Before the war's end Merrill had been promoted to lieutenant colonel. After Robinson left the Senate in March 1815 he became a judge of the state probate court. In that capacity he managed to have Merrill appointed a register of probate in 1815 and then a clerk of the court in 1816. Finally, with the support of his father-in-law and other local Republicans, Merrill gained election to the U.S. Congress in 1816.[111] He was reelected in 1818 but lost his seat to an opponent who contested the election on the grounds of irregularities in the recording of the votes of several Vermont townships.[112]

By the time he returned from Congress Merrill was a fixture in the local Democratic-Republican organization. A regular speaker at party celebrations, he served on committees to organize these festivities, helped compose the formal salutations to be offered there, and always stood to offer his own voluntary toast, often a salute to "the people."[113] As a former congressman and regular army officer with a commendable war record, Merrill enjoyed considerable status in Bennington. Townsmen elected him corresponding secretary of the Bennington County Agricultural Society, and he served on the resolutions committee of a

local meeting of farmers and manufacturers.[114] Election to political
office was quite another matter. In 1819 Isaac Tichenor defeated him
for moderator of the annual town meeting. Then in 1820 and again in
1823 he lost to Moses Robinson Jr. in races for the state assembly. His
only successes came in 1822, when, after three ballots, he gained election to the state legislature, and in 1824, when he succeeded in being
elected to the state council. A Republican-dominated state legislature
did appoint Merrill a probate judge in 1822 and a state's attorney for
Bennington County in 1823.[115] Otherwise his political fortunes were
unspectacular. Neither his experience in Congress and the regular
army nor his close association with the Robinsons could guarantee him
success at the polls.

Merrill's repeated disappointments at the hands of the Bennington
freemen were not unique to him. Republicans suffered increasing political difficulty; indeed, as early as 1815 several staunch party members
calculated their majority in town at only sixteen.[116] Two years later,
after repeated Federalist victories in town races, one of these frustrated
Republicans observed that no matter how many elections "terminated
federally, our democrats held up the idea that a majority of this town
were democratic, but owing to inertness, want of spirit and organization, it could not be brought into action." Finally, however, he sadly
admitted that with "this election I gave it up that the town was federal."[117] He was correct. While the period following the War of 1812
may have been an "era of good feelings" in Vermont state politics, this
was anything but true in Bennington. Political contests there remained
bitter, hard-fought affairs between two clearly delineated factions. Bennington was no longer the Republican town it had been since the time
of Thomas Chittenden; it had become a tension-filled political community in which Republican successes were increasingly rare.[118]

The political changes taking place in Bennington were part of larger
demographic, social, and economic transformations affecting both the
town and the state from the time of their initial settlement. At first
Vermont's population had grown at a fantastic rate. So many people
migrated there after 1791 that it was the fastest-growing state in the
Union during its first decade of existence. After 1810, however, the
state's growth rate fell off steadily; in the decade after 1850 Vermont's
population declined.[119] Long before that time, though, the state's thin
soil and depleted natural resources had led to massive outmigrations to
the more fertile regions of western New York, Ohio, and Michigan.[120]

Most of the growth within the state after 1820 took place in areas like Bennington, which had been able to make the transition from subsistence agriculture to prosperous commercial farming and manufacturing. The growth rate of these towns noticeably outstripped the average for the entire state. In fact, most Vermont townships either stagnated or declined in population. Their plight worsened because of towns like Bennington, whose very success caused them to act like magnets, drawing citizens away from the less prosperous towns and villages, which gradually fell further behind.[121] This was precisely the relationship that emerged between Bennington Centre and the East Village, where the majority of growth that occurred in the township after 1820 took place. That so many of Old Bennington's Federalist leaders allied themselves with the manufacturing interests of the East Village in large part explained the political eclipse of the Democratic elite, who remained firmly rooted on Courthouse Hill.

As some Vermont towns prospered and others declined, a social distance developed between their citizens.[122] The same process took place within the successful towns themselves, where a distinctly hierarchical social structure gradually but surely emerged. Bennington was no exception.[123] With the passage of time it too became an increasingly stratified community, one in which leaders of the opposing parties, regardless of their political differences, were themselves an integral part of the town's persistent core of affluent citizens. The social distance between them and the transients who made up the bulk of Bennington's population within any given year grew steadily wider.

Like most citizens of Bennington, Merrill may well have been unaware of the precise nature of the transformations being wrought by the social, economic, and demographic forces present in his community. He was, however, quite conscious of certain changes taking place during the year 1820. In the summer of that year Merrill strengthened his ties with the old village and its leading family when he formed a partnership with Uel M. Robinson, grandson of the town's founding father, Samuel Robinson, and the two opened a law office in the courthouse.[124] Of wider significance for the entire community, a dissatisfied element within the society at First Church led by Isaac Tichenor and other of the more refined members gained the dismissal of Rev. Daniel Marsh, their plainspoken, egalitarian, minister of sixteen years. In his place they managed to install Absalom Peters, the articulate young graduate of the Princeton Theological Seminary, a man who clearly meant to bring about the moral reformation of the town. Even before his ordination as Bennington's pastor, Peters established Sabbath schools throughout the community to serve as "a powerful restraint on human conduct."[125] He immediately began to preach against dancing, horse racing, the theater, traveling circuses, and similar entertainments. Rather than simply accepting a district school in the recently constructed brick academy building, he agitated for a sophisticated private school that would shape the moral character of its students.[126] He also actively supported a wide range of state and national moral reform agencies.

From Merrill's perspective, there seemed to be no end to the young preacher's efforts to establish voluntary societies of every sort in order to promote proper conduct. To Merrill, however, these organizations seemed anything but voluntary: they pressured all members of the community to behave in a certain manner; they were, in a word, coercive. While men like Peters, who valued order over freedom, were perfectly willing to restrict the behavior of others to instill discipline within society, Merrill placed a premium on liberty. He valued the liberation of the individual from all artificial restraints; it was his belief that citizens of a republic must never allow their behavior to be regulated by others.

Peters and other moral reformers offended Merrill's traditional social instincts, but their intrusions into the lives of his own family stirred far more personal animosity. Beginning in the fall of 1823 the Reverend Peters initiated proceedings in the church against Polly for the sin of intemperance. He pursued the case relentlessly and even appointed a day for public prayer and fasting because of the "low state of religion" that Polly's behavior indicated. Finally, after more than a year of ceaseless labor by Peters, church members followed the lead of their pastor and voted to cut Polly off from communion.[127] Two years later the Merrills suffered an additional public humiliation at the hands of yet another zealous moral reformer. This time James Ballard, principal of the Bennington Academy, expelled their son for attending a theater in Bennington.[128] Even though the boy lived at home and attended the theater after school hours with his parents's permission, Ballard took it upon himself to assume moral authority over the youngster's behavior. Such self-righteous interference infuriated the Merrills.

By the time Ballard expelled his son, Merrill had taken over the editorial duties of the *Vermont Gazette* and Daniel Clark had replaced Peters as pastor of First Church.[129] Allied with James Ballard, William Lloyd Garrison, Stephen Hinsdill, and old Federalist leaders such as Isaac Tichenor and Noadiah Swift, Clark began his own concerted effort to redeem the citizens of Bennington by instilling proper standards of morality, restraint, and self-control. Like Peters before him, Clark meant to achieve this redemption through his own evangelical efforts and by promoting as many voluntary agencies as possible. Representatives from organizations such as the American Colonization Society, the New England Tract Society, the American Bible Society, the American Education Society, the American Home Missionary Society, and the American Antislavery Society appeared in increasing numbers in Bennington.

The activities of Clark and the various reform agencies upset Merrill enormously; their constant intrusions into the lives of others offended his basic belief in the free individual's right to shape his own life. Equally disturbing, their growing influence flew in the face of his commitment to localism. Whatever problems a community faced should be addressed by its traditional structure of leadership — men long familiar with the local people and their customs — not by a cadre of strangers with little understanding of, or true concern for, the area. Clark and Peters were outsiders. Worse than that, they had close ties with large, well-coordinated regional and national organizations with a vast network of impersonal auxiliaries and agencies. None of these people had any respect for established customs or traditional leaders, and yet they all believed it to be their prerogative to shape the lives of the citizens of Bennington.

Merrill interpreted the actions of Clark and his reform associates from a traditional point of reference. Viewing these people and their organizations as part of a resurgence of aristocracy in America, Merrill repeatedly warned of the threat they posed to republican values. Thus, when Clark organized the town's Fourth of July celebrations in 1827 and 1828, Merrill took offense. He objected to processions of Sunday school classes instead of town leaders and war heroes; the delivery of moral reform sermons rather than lectures devoted to republican political principles greatly offended him; and the substitution of effusive praise for the abolitionist stance taken by the government of Great Britain in place of traditional patriotic eulogies particularly rankled him. The American people, he thought, must constantly be on guard against the "views and intents of modern origin to regulate society."[130]

The "views and intents" that Merrill considered most dangerous emanated from what he and others termed the "Christian Party in Politics," or the "Pioneer Party."[131] These people were strict Sabbatarians and zealous moral reformers who wished to impose their principles upon everybody else. For Merrill, Daniel Clark and James Ballard epitomized the type. He hoped to reveal the subversive nature of their actions in the *Gazette* when he declared: "The idea of the teachers of youth 'controlling the amusements and holidays' of our children has an *important* meaning, when we annex to it the idea of inculcating in their tender and susceptible minds an attachment for the 'church and state' government of England, and in preference to our own." Unfortunately, this had been "most daringly commenced on the 4th of July last in this town, under a cloak of piety."[132]

To oppose the "Christian party," Merrill became a dedicated follower of Andrew Jackson. From his perspective, Jackson had been "called from his Hermitage, like Cincinnatus from his farm to the Presidential chair." And like that simple ancient hero, Jackson behaved with independence, simplicity, and courage. His messages to Congress and the people "breath[ed] the pure spirit of republicanism uncontaminated by aristocracy or consolidation." He insisted upon "economy instead of extravagance, strict accountability of the servants of the people instead of frauds and defalcations, rotation in office, instead of permanency, industry instead of idleness."[133] He was truly the Old Hero, the man who could save the nation from those who would sap it of its republican virtue.

This emotional attachment sprang from the association Merrill drew between Jackson's political battles on the national level and his own local confrontations with the Pioneer party. He fully identified with Jackson's posture toward the Whig party: to be taken in by the Whig economic and financial system was to surrender individual independence to banks, corporations, and a network of autonomous, impersonal institutions with little understanding of local needs and relationships. Merrill also applauded Jackson's belief that the active, complex government demanded by his Whig opponents restricted rather than enlarged the sphere of human freedom by promoting special corporate privileges for a few. In its place the president offered a limited and frugal democratic government modeled after that of Thomas Jefferson. Moreover, Jackson contended that, left to themselves, the "real people," those independent yeomen republicans engaged in plain and useful toil who made up "the bone and sinew of the country," would enforce a natural moral discipline free of aristocratic privilege and irresponsible social and economic enterprises.[134] Few political principles were closer to Merrill's heart than this belief in a self-regulating natural order.

His fervent editorials in support of Jackson helped Merrill become a prominent figure in the local and state Democratic party. Twice party members nominated him for Congress; twice he went down to defeat at the hands of fellow Bennington attorney Hiland Hall. He received the party's endorsement for the state senate in 1836, lieutenant governor in 1839, and presidential elector in 1840. Locally, he served as president of the celebration that town Democrats organized to observe the anniversary of Jackson's victory at New Orleans and in the same capacity at several annual commemorations of the battle of Bennington.

Election campaigns and commemorative festivities served as vehicles for Merrill and his Democratic colleagues to articulate their political principles. When Merrill ran for office, his supporters stressed their candidate's lack of wealth, his devotion to the traditional republicanism of Thomas Jefferson, and his determined opposition to "*pioneer* measures."[135] Merrill, along with a great many others, continually emphasized that the republicanism upon which the nation rested required a dedication to liberty, equality, and local control. Their emphasis upon equality, however, gradually became transmuted into an attack upon wealth. Indeed, the antipathy to men of wealth and their privileged corporations became so strong within the Vermont Democracy by 1836 that its statewide candidates ran on an "Anti-Monopoly Democratic Ticket." Candidates on this ticket included David Robinson Jr., John S. Robinson, and Merrill.[136]

In 1840 Merrill accepted his party's nomination to serve as an elector for Martin Van Buren in his campaign for the presidency against William Henry Harrison. In Merrill's mind, the Democratic party was the only means to protect the values of Thomas Jefferson's republic against the political decay being fostered by the Pioneers in Bennington and their Whig allies throughout the state and nation. He refused to abandon his old republican principles. They were too deeply ingrained in his political and social conscience, and they alone made sense of the changing environment in which he found himself.

Fellow Citizens

We are met on the top of our native Mountain, overlooking and taking in, as it were, at a single glance, all our variously diversified interests. Our Head Quarters is a building which above all others is suitable to the business in which we are engaged. It was the log cabin that furnished a shelter to our fathers when they made the first lodgment in the Green Mountain wilderness. It was within the log cabin that were planned and executed those bold and decisive measures which protected the early possessions of our fathers from the grasp of the land jobbing government of a powerful neighboring Province. It was from log cabins that issued that fearless band of volunteers who on the morning of the 10th of May '75, within the walls of Ticonderoga, thundered at the door of the commander of the fortress, and demanded the surrender in the name of the Great Jehovah and the Continental Congress. It was log cabins that sent forth the men, who in their hunting packs & with their blue barrel guns without bayonets, stormed the works of the British & German regulars at Bennington and handed back on the foe the tide of success which until that day threatened to overwhelm our country. . . .

To the distinguished Senator who honors us with his presence on this occasion, I claim on behalf of ourselves a revolutionary log cabin relationship. I am not mistaken in my historical recollections. The father of Daniel Webster, then the tenant of a log cabin among the hills of a neighboring state, stood side by side with our fathers at the battle of Bennington, with them scaled the walls of the Hessian redoubt and received the submission of its dying commander.

Fellow Citizens I congratulate you — I congratulate you on the relationship.

Thanks to the Aristocratic Office-holder who taunted us with presenting a log cabin candidate for the Presidency. It has waked up the true whig revolutionary spirit, a spirit that will carry in triumph to the Presidential Chair the great log cabin defender & protector of the west, the soldier, the statesman, the honest man, William Henry Harrison.[137]

With this oration, Hiland Hall opened an immense assemblage of Whigs gathered in convention on July 7, 1840. Delegations from townships all over Vermont's First Congressional District had streamed into a huge natural amphitheater formed by the dense forest of Stratton Mountain. Some carried banners, others marched to martial tunes played by their town bands, and all looked forward eagerly to hearing America's most illustrious orator, Daniel Webster. They were not disappointed. Webster, the great defender of the Constitution, pointed out the true meaning and intent of that document and expounded at great length on the manner in which Whig principles supported and protected it. He pleased the crowd even more by announcing his intention to camp that night with "the Green Mountain boys on the summit of their far famed hills."[138]

For Hiland Hall the Stratton Convention was a particularly momentous occasion. Not only did the delegates nominate him for a fifth consecutive term in Congress but they accorded him the signal distinction of introducing the Great Man. The son of a barely literate, debt-ridden farmer, Hall could take great pride in assuming a place of honor

next to Daniel Webster. He had earned it. Years of hard work, moti-
vated by a powerful determination to improve himself, had preceded
his appearance on the speaker's stand at Stratton Mountain. For Hall,
then, the log cabin — the image that permeated his own speech as well
as those of other Whigs in 1840 — represented far more than simply an
empty campaign slogan or an attractive party emblem. It symbolized
progress, Hall's own personal progress as well as that of so many others.
In his view the log cabin was the perfect image for American society. It
expressed not permanent poverty but rather the dynamic march of
civilization from subsistence to commerce. It embodied the ability of
the individual, through his own initiative and effort, to improve his
station.

Hall's personal odyssey began on July 20, 1795, on a farm near Sage's
City, a small hamlet in northern Bennington Township.[139] His parents,
Nathaniel and Abigail, raised him and his seven brothers and sisters in a
plain, hardworking, religious household. On weekdays and Saturday
mornings everyone worked at tasks about the farm. Then on Saturday
afternoons the entire family attended meetings at the Baptist church in
nearby Shaftsbury, where Nathaniel was a deacon. Sundays meant a
strict observance of the Sabbath. On that day Nathaniel hitched his
team to a double wagon equipped with extra seats so that he could carry
the aged and feeble of the neighborhood, as well as his own family, to
church. So regular was he in this ritual that people living along his
route could tell the time even though the church in Shaftsbury had no
bell to call its worshipers to services.[140]

Nathaniel and Abigail were simple, unaffected people. Universally
respected by their neighbors as honest and reliable, they hardly ever
had dealings with anyone beyond their neighborhood. Nathaniel was
so reserved that he rarely spoke in public. Although a deacon, he would
not lead the congregation in prayer, nor would he offer a prayer among
his own family or even ask a blessing at table. Neither Nathaniel nor
Abigail had more than a rudimentary education. Nathaniel had great
difficulty keeping the accounts of his limited dealings with workmen
and neighbors, and the only books he ever read were the Bible and Isaac
Watts's *Hymns and Spiritual Songs*.[141] And yet both he and his wife
wanted their children to be better educated than they were.

This commitment to education meant that during the winter
months, when their labor could be spared from the farm, all the Hall
children attended the local district school. By the age of nine, Hiland
had made such progress in his studies that a new teacher, hired from

outside the town, felt that the boy should be introduced to grammar. After Nathaniel obtained a grammar book while trading wheat in Troy, Hiland and an older student began to study the subject. Their fellow students, curious about this new branch of learning, carried home confusing terms — *verb, adjective, noun* — that they overheard the teacher and his two prize students discussing. This jumble of foreign-sounding words disturbed many parents, some of whom were already upset that a teacher from outside the district had been hired in the first place. A meeting of concerned citizens met, dismissed the teacher, and voted that grammar should not be taught in the school. By the next year, however, more reasonable minds prevailed and the district hired a well-qualified instructor to teach grammar to all students.[142]

Hiland, the eldest of the Hall children, proved to be a precocious student and a voracious reader. Although he was most interested in history and biography, he would borrow whatever books he could from neighbors. Because farm work consumed most of his daylight hours, Hiland often read at night. And then, since candles were a luxury in the household, he had to make do with the light from an open fireplace.[143] While necessarily frugal in their own lives, Nathaniel and Abigail supported Hiland's interest in learning as best they could. Their final contribution to his education was to send him to the Granville Academy in Salem, New York, for a three-month term in the summer of 1811. There he studied Latin grammar and took courses in surveying and astronomy.[144]

For several years after returning home from Granville, Hall alternated between helping his father on the farm and teaching school during the winter months. In December 1811 he became the first teacher in a new schoolhouse constructed in Sage's City. At the end of that term he returned to the farm, and in June he rode on horseback to Michigan's Upper Peninsula, where he made final payment on a piece of land his father had purchased. As a result of this investment, which coincided with consecutive crop failures, Nathaniel Hall fell into debt and remained in that condition for over twenty years.[145]

Upon his return from Michigan, Hiland resumed his work on the farm. That winter he taught in the same Shaftsbury district school he had attended as a youngster. After completing the term, he worked on his father's farm through the summer and then used the money he had earned as a teacher to attend a three-month session at an academy in White Creek, New York. Following that he taught the winter term again in Shaftsbury. By the spring of 1814, realizing that farming in

Vermont no longer held out much promise of prosperity, Hall decided to go into the mercantile business by opening a store in Sage's City. To prepare himself for the undertaking, he took a clerk's position in the factory store of the Paran Creek Manufacturing Company.[146]

Even before beginning this new job, however, Hall had become involved in a local organization that diverted his attention from his personal future. On September 5, 1813, he had joined with a number of other ardent young Jeffersonian Republicans at the State Arms Tavern to form an association, a "band of Brothers," to support the war against Great Britain. During the next several weeks he had helped write the constitution of the Sons of Liberty. At their first meeting twenty-eight charter members had subscribed to this constitution and elected Hall their treasurer.[147]

Over the next several years membership in the Sons of Liberty swelled to well over one hundred. Each of these men, required by the constitution to be between sixteen and thirty, wore a special cockade in his hat and participated in monthly meetings that staged debates over such matters as capital punishment, divorce, temperance, and the relative benefits of commerce versus manufacturing. They agreed to debate the liquor question even though their constitution prohibited any beverage except water from being served at their gatherings.[148] Many arguments presented in these debates were hyperbolic and convoluted, but one brother particularly remembered that Hall's were always "concise, plain, and simple."[149]

The association promoted brotherhood and stimulated intellectual discussion, but its primary purpose was to support Vermont's troops and to promote patriotic enthusiasm for the administration of James Madison. The brothers accomplished the former by forwarding socks and mittens knitted by Bennington women to the soldiers on the northwestern frontier.[150] They strove for the latter by organizing mass rallies on the Fourth of July, where the young men mixed with such elder statesmen as O. C. Merrill, David Robinson Jr., and Jonathan Robinson. Their toasts lauded the principles of Jeffersonian Republicanism and excoriated "the Washington-benevolent, federal-republican peace party — How various are the names that vice assumes! How different are the garbs that she puts on! To deceive mankind, and thus to pass for virtue!"[151]

When the War of 1812 ended and the activities of the Sons of Liberty concluded, Hall faced an unclear future. Still planning to become a merchant, in September 1815 he moved to Lansingburgh, New

York, where he became a clerk in a large mercantile firm in order to
gain business experience. During the fall of 1815, however, commercial
prices fell precipitously; times were difficult throughout eastern New
York and Vermont, forcing Hall to reevaluate his future. He abandoned
hope of becoming a merchant and enrolled in the Lansingburgh Academy to broaden his education. He also began to read law in the office of
a local attorney. Residence in Lansingburgh proved to be unbearably
expensive, however, and Hall returned to the family farm, where he
lived while studying law with David Robinson Jr. A little over a year
later he moved into the old village of Bennington, boarded with the
Fassett family, and clerked in the post office. Then in the spring of 1817
he took up residence in Samuel Young's household while reading law in
Young's office. The following year he studied law with Marshall Carter.
By this time he had acquired sufficient knowledge and experience to
assume a share of Carter's practice before the various justice courts of
Bennington County.[152]

In the same year that he began to work with Marshall Carter, Hall
married Dolly Tuttle Davis. Financially strapped, the couple rented
rooms in another family's home and took in Mr. Carter as a boarder. In
December 1819 Hall gained admission to the Bennington County Bar
and became a full partner with Carter. Carter died the next year, whereupon Hall formed a partnership with William White, a young Dartmouth graduate who had just been admitted to the bar. This partnership, which lasted a year, ended when White moved to Philadelphia
to become a teacher.[153]

From the time Hall began practice in Bennington he steadily built a
reputation for personal integrity and solid professional skills, and the
citizens of Bennington increasingly called upon him to fill positions of
public trust. He served two years as the register of probate, represented
the town in the state assembly, and filled the position of clerk for the
county and supreme courts. In addition, the state legislature appointed
him state's attorney for Bennington County for four consecutive terms,
from 1829 to 1833.[154]

Although Hall's practice grew along with his reputation, he did not
prosper financially. His own generous nature prevented him from refusing those who needed his assistance but were unable to pay him. At
the same time, he did all he could to provide his family with every
comfort. Taking out a large mortgage, he built a house in old Bennington for Dolly and their five children. This, combined with a sizable
mortgage he assumed for his law office, opposite the Bennington Acad-

emy, put him deeply in debt.[155] Hall knew firsthand the need citizens had for credit if they were to improve their position in society.

The means by which Hall chose to advance his own fortunes and those of his family helped shape his political behavior; indeed, his political beliefs reflected his own life experience. Committed to self-improvement through education and hard work, Hall believed that everyone who practiced a similar self-discipline would be able to better his life. In his mind, improvement in people's condition was the proper order of things in a republican society. The key to improvement was always, however, opportunity. No matter how industrious and hardworking a man might be, if he lived in a society devoid of opportunities for advancement, he would stagnate. For Hall, this was the essential difference between a subsistence environment and a commercial one. At the same time, he realized that the mere presence of a prosperous market economy was not sufficient; individuals must have the means to take advantage of opportunities presented by the market. They must have access to credit, a readily available and secure currency, protection from unfair foreign competition, and the means to get their goods to market.

His awareness of such economic needs led Hall to become a strong supporter of John Quincy Adams, casting his presidential vote for him rather than for Andrew Jackson in 1824.[156] While a regional identification may have initially drawn him to Adams, the latter's actions as president solidified Hall's political loyalty. When Adams claimed in his first annual message that "the spirit of improvement is abroad upon the earth" and that the "tenure of power by man" in America should be exercised "to improve the condition of himself and his fellow-men," he gave voice to Hall's personal feelings.[157] When the president advocated Henry Clay's "American System" — government support for a national bank, internal improvements, and protective tariffs — he provided Hall and many others with a substantive program to stimulate opportunity throughout the nation.[158] Hall had already worked to foster a more dynamic market environment in Bennington when he led a successful effort in the Vermont Assembly in 1827 to charter the Bank of Bennington.[159] By the election of 1828, then, Hall was a confirmed National Republican and again cast his vote for Adams.

Hall's adherence to the National Republicanism of John Quincy Adams separated him politically from many of his former colleagues in the Sons of Liberty. William Haswell, Uel M. Robinson, and numerous other brothers had become loyal supporters of Andrew Jackson's Democratic-Republicanism. Hall found himself allied with many of Bennington's longtime Federalist leaders, such as Isaac Tichenor, Aaron Robinson, Noadiah Swift, and the numerous descendants of Jedediah Dewey. Loyalty to National Republicanism also brought Hall into close contact with men such as Daniel Clark, James Ballard, Stephen Hinsdill, and William Lloyd Garrison. His association with these men was, however, always uneasy. Not a moral reformer by temperament, Hall assumed a more practical and pragmatic attitude. He wanted to create an environment within which people could improve their station in life. If they chose not to take advantage of whatever opportunities might be created for them, he would not attempt to change their minds; he most certainly would not attempt to change their character. Hall was far more interested in improving a man's economic condition than in saving his soul.

This utilitarian outlook did not lead Hall to shun all reforms. Although a proponent of both temperance and colonization, he did not approach either of these from a moralistic perspective. Rather, he adopted a more moderate, pragmatic approach. Thus, while never taking a drink himself, Hall did not advocate eliminating all sources of alcohol in Bennington. Instead, he maintained that town authorities should take their responsibilities seriously by licensing only respectable taverns and forbidding groceries and other stores from dispensing alcohol. In this way drinking could contribute to community cohesiveness but would not degenerate to such an extent that it might inhibit productive citizenship.[160]

Hall's advocacy of the American Colonization Society was equally practical. He made it quite clear that the Constitution of the United States left the matter of slavery to the states and that he did not favor altering the Constitution. He pointed out the miseries of slavery but never attacked the slaveholder. To do so would be to "proscribe many of our ablest statesmen and purest patriots." Hall simply believed that the black would be injured rather than aided by being given his freedom within the United States. "Pressed down till debasement becomes a habit, he has grovelled till the desire of rising out of the dust is lost." Without the initiative to improve himself, the freed slave had no place in a competitive, mobile society like the United States. He could only become "what he is found to be, indolent, dissolute, indigent and depraved." Blacks could, however, prosper in a colony such as Liberia, where their American experience would be a boon. For this reason the philanthropic efforts of the colonization movement deserved support.

There was another singularly important reason for supporting colonization: it would shrink the proportion of blacks to whites in the southern states and thereby lessen the possibility of a revolution similar to
the one that had shaken the foundations of society in St. Domingo.[161]

For Hall, education constituted the principal means for intelligent,
industrious citizens to improve themselves. It was "the moving force in
Anglo-Saxon civilization," fostering progress and enhancing lives.[162]
Consequently, he believed that his own children should receive the
best education possible. Even though his family constantly faced financial difficulties, Hall insisted that his son Nathaniel attend Bennington Academy because the boy might "lose his ambition at a District
school."[163] His wife agreed; even in the face of rising tuition, Dolly
declared that "our children *must* go to school, they might be ruined if
they stay at home so much." To provide a private education for her
children, Dolly took the academy principal as a boarder in exchange for
tuition.[164] So intense was Hall's belief in learning that he advised one
of his older sons not to take time away from his business to dabble in
party politics. Instead, he should devote his spare time to reading history, especially Plutarch's lives or Goldsmith's histories of England and
Rome.[165]

Hall's devotion to education, like his advocacy of temperance and
colonization, was always pragmatic rather than idealistic or moralistic.
He believed that a teacher's primary function was to provide students
with the skills to compete in a market society, not to shape their moral
character. This attitude put him at odds with some of his National
Republican colleagues in Bennington. In particular, it brought him into
conflict with Clark, Ballard, and Hinsdill.

The clash with these men stemmed from the original construction
of the brick academy building in 1820, when a group of Bennington
citizens pooled their resources to build the structure. Although just
starting his law practice, Hall felt strongly about the need for better
education in Bennington and contributed as much as he could to the
enterprise. He became one of the proprietors of the building and by
1829 was chairman of the committee of trustees and thus responsible
for overseeing the operations of the Bennington Academy, a private
school established in the building in 1823. While Hall chaired this
committee, James Ballard, the principal of the academy, dismissed several students for attending a dancing school in town. In addition, he
raised the quarterly tuition. In neither instance did Ballard consult with

the committee; in fact, he refused to recognize their authority. The result was that they dismissed him and hired a new principal.[166] Ballard started another school, the Bennington Seminary, with the help of his father-in-law, Stephen Hinsdill, and the full support of the Reverend Clark, Isaac Tichenor, Noadiah Swift, and other prominent National Republican leaders, but Hall remained doggedly loyal to the Bennington Academy. Not only did he send his children to that school but he remained on the committee that supervised its operations. This stance aligned him with such Democratic leaders as David Robinson, Merrill, and Uel M. Robinson.[167]

Because of his utilitarian outlook toward education and other reforms, Hall had little in common with the fervent moral reformers in his party. Even though Dolly became a member of First Church while Daniel Clark was its pastor[168] and he attended services there, Hall was increasingly alienated by Clark's moral zealotry. As a result, he joined David Robinson Jr. and other members of the Congregational society to discuss the best way to rid themselves of Clark.[169] When the church finally dismissed its pastor, Hall heartily concurred with Hiram Harwood's relief that Clark's "tyrannical career" had come to an end.[170] This was not the only source of agreement between Hall and Harwood, another faithful member of the Sons of Liberty who had become a National Republican for practical rather than moralistic reasons. Both men detested James Ballard.[171] Hall could also relate to Harwood's feelings when the latter confessed that he could not sympathize with Stephen Hinsdill "as I should with one who appeared to be guided by the plain rules of Common sense." As for Hinsdill, Harwood could only exclaim: "Away of your ambition of setting up Seminaries — Instituting, organizing & establishing new Religious Societies & Churches, building meeting houses etc. etc."[172] Economic progress, not moral reform, appealed to men like Harwood and Hall.

By 1832 Hall was in a position to advocate just such progress. In June delegates to a countywide meeting called Isaac Tichenor to the chair and elected Hall their secretary. In addition, he served on the committee that drafted resolutions to express the sense of the meeting. Resting upon a belief in the mutual interdependence of agriculture, commerce, and manufacturing, these resolutions enthusiastically supported federal tariffs to protect home industry. Hall personally drafted a resolution claiming that cotton and wool manufactories in the county furnished a market for farmers' produce, supported laborers and mechanics, and

gave "life & energy to every business." Naturally, any action that jeop-
ardized this industry would be "deeply felt & deplored by every class of
our community."[173]

Such a strong stance in favor of protective tariffs, as well as his belief
in the dynamic relationship between business and the economic well-
being and progress of all members of society, gained Hall the support of
many local National Republicans.[174] A Bennington County convention
chaired by Aaron Robinson met in June 1832 and nominated Hall to fill
the unexpired congressional term of Jonathan Hunt.[175] The voters of
the First Congressional District elected him over his Democratic rival,
O. C. Merrill.

While Hall had little in common with the moral reformers in his
party, he was not entirely sympathetic with the views of men such as
Isaac Tichenor and Aaron Robinson either. These men certainly believed in economic progress and the power of the market to bring about
change, but they remained stubbornly elitist in their outlook. Not so
Hall: he favored a distinctly egalitarian form of capitalism, one in which
the market offered opportunities for all men rather than simply those
with money to invest. This became apparent once he took his seat in
Congress.

The most difficult issues Hall faced in his first sessions of Congress
related to Andrew Jackson's attack on the Bank of the United States, his
insistence upon a specie currency, and his disdain for those who lived
on credit. Skeptical of Jacksonian rhetoric on these matters, Hall was
particularly disturbed by terms such as "Monied Aristocracy," "Monster," and "Monopolies." As always, he took a practical stance toward
the Bank of the United States and banking in general. Confessing that
his "notions about a National bank do no[t] arise from any love towards
institutions without souls, but from the fear of a general derangement
& apathy of business without one," Hall feared that it would be easier
for people swayed by Jackson's emotional language to pull down an institution accused of "dangerous powers" than to get along without it.[176]

Loyal to these beliefs, Hall rose in the House of Representatives on
May 5, 1834, to present a memorial from his constituents that opposed
President Jackson's war on the Bank of the United States and his criticism of paper money and credit. Hall specifically defended a resolution
to the effect that "the declaration of the President, that 'any man ought
to break who trades on borrowed capital,' is a foolish and wicked assertion." Like his memorialists, Hall believed that "borrowed capital"
rested entirely upon good credit established only by "the industry and

integrity of the borrower." Thus, Jackson's statement was an "insult to honest enterprise." Hall stated unequivocally that while the idea that men should live without credit might be true "on the banks of the Potomac," it was false in the Green Mountains.[177]

Warming to his subject, Hall defended the citizens of Vermont for being "as purely republican in their habits and notions" as any people in the country. In their minds, as well as his own, a reliance upon credit was clearly "in accordance with their republican principles." Indeed, it was credit that "enabled the poor but enterprising citizen, who has established a character for integrity and skill, to commence life with some prospect of raising himself to the level of his neighbor who derives his capital from the gains of his ancestor." Credit placed "worth on something like an equality with wealth, and enables honest poverty to outstrip and conquer riches on the fair field of honorable competition."[178]

Hall had nothing but disdain for the remedy that Jackson recommended for the nation's economic troubles, namely, hard money. For Hall and his constituents, specie currency was a "humbug." He believed instead that a "well-regulated paper medium, founded on a specie basis," was more fitting for the transaction of business in an "improved state of society." A "hard-money system" might be appropriate for "Arabs," "Tartars," or other "semi-barbarians," but it made no sense for a "modern free people." According to Hall, "Congress might as well undertake to carry the people of this country back from the canal to the forest horse-path, from the steamboat to the scow with its setting poles, from the railroad car to the handbarrow, as to expect to legislate them back to a 'hard-money system.'"[179]

In both Washington and Bennington, Hall championed a progressive, democratic form of capitalism in which government—local, state, and federal—fostered economic opportunity for all citizens by supporting institutions such as banks and manufactories. He could not understand the continued Democratic attack on banks and banking even after the destruction of the National Bank. The *Gazette*'s vitriolic denunciations of the Bank of Bennington and paper money could only make it more difficult for that bank to maintain public confidence. Without such trust it could not sustain its credit and would soon go out of business. Thus, Hall inquired of a Democratic constituent, "If we fight down the bank, what show of business are we to keep up in our village, except a few days in court time?"[180]

Repulsed by the vision of Bennington as a sleepy village huddled around its courthouse, Hall did not wish to force either his own community or the nation at large back to the age of the horse path, the scow, and the handbarrow. Instead, he envisioned a dynamic partnership between government and private enterprise that would create economic opportunities for every person willing to take advantage of them. In this way America could become a society in which each individual could, through his own hard work and perseverance, become a capitalist. It was this vision that Hall championed when the participants at a huge Whig rally held in Bennington on July 4, 1840, called him to the chair.[181] Having risen to prominence through his own initiative and determination, Hall wanted all citizens to have the same chance to improve that he had enjoyed. To ensure this, the Whig party must prevail not only in Bennington but throughout the state and the nation. It was to this end that Hiland Hall, the fervent democratic capitalist, devoted his most strenuous efforts.

8. Tensions Persist

The War of 1812 brought significant political changes to Vermont. Opposed to the war and frustrated with commercial restrictions imposed upon them by the Republican administration in Washington, a majority of voters in the state turned to the Federalist party.[1] In 1813 that party gained control of the Vermont Assembly for the first time in the nineteenth century. And since no gubernatorial candidate had a clear majority, this assembly elected Martin Chittenden, a Federalist congressman, to that position. In addition, twelve of the thirteen men elected to the Council of Censors that year were Federalists. Isaac Tichenor, the last Federalist governor before Chittenden, presided over this body. The following year brought even more Federalist triumphs. Once again the party enjoyed a majority in the legislature; once again its members elected Martin Chittenden to the governor's office. The assembly also selected Isaac Tichenor to replace Jonathan Robinson in the U.S. Senate. Completing the Federalist sweep, all six of Vermont's congressmen chosen in 1814 were Federalists.

By the time voters went to the polls in 1815, however, political perceptions were changing. In September 1814 Vermont militiamen had fought at the battle of Plattsburg, in which American land and naval forces under Gen. Alexander Macomb and Capt. Thomas Macdonough had soundly defeated a British attempt to gain control of Lake Champlain. That effort, combined with the spectacular victory of Gen. Andrew Jackson's Kentucky and Tennessee militia over British regulars at New Orleans in January 1815, seemed to revitalize Vermonters' faith in the ordinary citizen and renewed their allegiance to the Republican

party. The voters returned Jonas Galusha, four-time Republican governor from Shaftsbury, to office by a slim majority over Martin Chittenden and gave Republicans control of both the council and the assembly. The following year, Galusha enjoyed an even larger majority
over Gen. Samuel Strong, the commander of Vermont troops at Plattsburg. In addition, Republicans increased their numbers in the council
and the assembly, and the state's voters replaced all six Federalist congressmen with Republicans. In an attempt to halt their political slide,
Federalists nominated Isaac Tichenor for governor in 1817. Galusha,
however, easily defeated the senator, and Republicans maintained their
dominance in the legislature. In 1818 Federalists failed to offer a slate
of candidates for statewide offices, and the following year Galusha and
his fellow Republicans ran entirely unopposed. By that time many
prominent leaders of both parties throughout the state had put aside
their political differences and coalesced in support of reform movements such as temperance, colonization, and evangelical religion.[2]
Tranquility rapidly displaced the rancor that had characterized Vermont politics since the 1790s. Indeed, state politics gave every appearance of having entered an era of good feelings.

The same was certainly not true of political life in Bennington,
where fierce partisanship persisted long after the conclusion of the War
of 1812. Such intensity resulted primarily from the fact that Federalist
power in the town, rather than waning with the dissipation of wartime
passions, continued to grow.

In Bennington as in other townships throughout Vermont, the initial signs of Federalist success appeared simultaneously with the outbreak of war in 1812. In September of that year voters elected Elijah
Dewey to the General Assembly.[3] Then at the annual town meeting the
following year they elected Isaac Tichenor moderator, Aaron Robinson clerk, and five other Federalists as selectmen.[4] The editor of the
Bennington News-Letter, a Federalist newspaper established in 1811,
crowed that the "Friends of Peace" had prevailed in the annual March
meeting "by a very handsome margin." Not only had they elected
Tichenor, Robinson, and all five selectmen but they had chosen the
town constables and assessors and delivered healthy majorities to the
Federalist candidates for the Council of Censors as well.[5] Elijah Dewey
subsequently gained reelection to the General Assembly at the freeman's meeting on September 7, 1813. Far more important, though, at
that meeting a majority of Bennington's freemen — for the first time in

the town's history—cast their ballots for the Federalist candidate for governor.[6] This was a crushing blow to local Republicans. Even more upsetting was the identity of the successful gubernatorial candidate, Martin Chittenden. That old Tom Chittenden's son had "embibed the poison of aristocracy" by becoming a Federalist had long troubled Bennington Republicans.[7] For him to be elected governor, however, particularly with the aid of Bennington voters, was even more disturbing. It was an ominous sign of the times.

Chittenden's election was indeed a precursor of things to come.[8] In 1816 and again in 1817 voters in Bennington supported the Federalist candidate for governor over Jonas Galusha. In addition, during the war and in its immediate aftermath (1813–19) the town chose a Federalist for the Vermont Assembly four times, while it sent a Republican only twice.[9] During these years Bennington Federalists also dominated town offices, choosing the moderator of the annual town meeting and all of the selectmen every year between 1812 and 1820.

Clearly, in Bennington, unlike at the state and national levels, Federalism was not dying out. It was not simply that it had experienced a brief resuscitation during the War of 1812; rather it enjoyed bountiful good health quite apart from the special circumstances of that conflict.[10] The reasons for this lay deeply embedded in the culture and the political economy of Bennington. The prolonged life of Federalism in Bennington did not involve the persistence of a political party nearly so much as it did the perseverance of cultural attitudes that predated the existence of party. The cosmopolitan beliefs of Bennington's downhill people were the stuff of which Federalism was made. More important, the economic and demographic forces that lay behind the ascendancy of the downhill people in Bennington during the first two decades of the nineteenth century accelerated rapidly in the postwar years. As the economic and social structure of the town became increasingly stratified, the power of the old agricultural interests weakened considerably. Conversely, as economic activity in Bennington became more and more commercialized as growing numbers of people shifted from a subsistence to a market focus, the power and influence of local merchants grew ever stronger.[11] This was particularly true during the years following the Embargo of 1807, a time when Moses Robinson Jr., Elijah Dewey, Jonathan Hunt, Micha J. Lyman, Lyman Patchin, and Noadiah Swift provided much needed stability to the merchant community in Bennington. These men, Federalists all, emerged from the

War of 1812 firmly in control of local trade. Indeed, the authority of the downhill people in Bennington had never been so pervasive as it was during the years following the War of 1812.

While Federalist leaders in Bennington could take pleasure from the authority they wielded as town officers and from the parity they had achieved with their Republican adversaries in state and national elections, they could not fully enjoy their new status while Anthony Haswell remained editor of the local newspaper and Daniel Marsh occupied the pulpit at First Church. Long an affront to the sensibilities of downhill leaders, these two men were constant irritants to Tichenor, Moses Robinson Jr., Swift, and other Federalist leaders. Haswell's outspoken Republicanism and Marsh's egalitarian manner seemed to mock the achievements of the downhill people, to rob them of the full satisfaction that should have accompanied their recent victories.

It was easy to understand Tichenor's and others' displeasure with Haswell. Throughout the war with Great Britain Haswell kept up a constant attack upon Federalists in Bennington, the state, and the nation. In the summer of 1812, for example, he warned his readers that a "wicked faction" was attempting to deceive the people of Vermont and to turn them against their own national government. Haswell did not hesitate to name Tichenor as the leader of this faction or to accuse him of being more loyal to the "nation of New England" than to the United States.[12] Men like Tichenor "abjure[d] democracy!" Indeed, the government of their own "democratic republic" was for them an object of scorn.[13] Prior to the annual freemen's meeting in September 1813, the editor warned his readers that the coming election would "either be the means of producing a bold attempt to raise an aristocracy in the New England states, or of blasting the hopes of the enemies of union!"[14] As the war continued, Haswell exclaimed that the "enemies of equal liberty are playing a deep game" and tried to alert the people to Tichenor's "duplicity."[15]

The cessation of war did not quiet Haswell. He launched a diatribe against Tichenor and Vermont's six Federalist congressmen for accepting a fifteen-hundred-dollar pay raise passed by Congress, claiming that such legislation was "dangerous to the principles of liberty and economy, so essential to republicanism." It demonstrated that Vermont's representatives had succumbed to personal selfishness, that they had become "money speculators instead of representing the wishes of the people."[16]

Shortly after the appearance of this editorial, Anthony Haswell fell silent; he died on May 22, 1816, at the age of sixty. Darius Clark, owner and publisher of the *Green Mountain Farmer*, immediately took over Haswell's editorial duties. Even though Clark restored the paper's original name — *Vermont Gazette* — and maintained it as the leading voice of Republicanism in the state, something had been lost. Clark was every bit as loyal to Republicanism as Haswell; nonetheless, a vital link with the past had been broken. Born to an earlier era, Haswell had a visceral attachment to Revolutionary principles. Clark was of another generation.

Like Haswell, Daniel Marsh, that other irritant to Federalist sensibilities, was a child of the Revolution. And from the time of his installation as pastor of First Church in 1804 he too displeased downhill Bennington. His plain dress, coarse speech, lack of wealth, poor education, and rough egalitarianism offended most of these people. In a word, he was a democrat. It was not long after his arrival, therefore, before debates took place in church meetings about whether Marsh should remain as pastor. Such gatherings generally remained calm except when "party feeling could not be suppressed."[17] Regardless of Marsh's efforts to remain neutral in the party battles of the time, the downhill people always identified their pastor with their uphill opponents.[18] Discussions about Marsh, whether relating to his salary or to his tenure as the town's minister, therefore always led to "warm speeches, savoring of political division."[19] Prominent Republicans supported him; leading Federalists opposed him.[20]

Isaac Tichenor never made a secret of his opposition to Marsh. He spoke disdainfully of the minister's "want of talents" and charged that he was a bad speaker.[21] Downhill folk began to stay away from church services in large numbers. Finally, emboldened by his enhanced status in town during and after the War of 1812, Tichenor promised to donate a bell for the still empty belfry if the church settled a minister "who should fill the meetinghouse."[22] Such agitation brought results in the summer of 1819. Exhausted by the constant opposition to his ministry, Marsh resigned his charge in July and agreed to consider dissolving his relationship with the church. Ironically, the church's own democratic egalitarianism — its willingness to allow members of the society to participate with church members in decisions regarding the minister — doomed Marsh. On January 31, 1820, the church met and voted to take steps to dismiss its pastor.[23] Then at a church council convened on

April 25 the society, dominated by Tichenor and other downhill folk, resolved "that from the peculiar circumstances of this Society, Mr. Marsh's usefulness in this place is at an end."[24]

His relationship with First Church dissolved, Marsh left Bennington to take up ministerial duties in New York. His departure did not, however, leave the town without a pastor. The previous August the church had hired Absalom Peters as a temporary replacement for Marsh. The new minister proved to be an immediate success. His youthful enthusiasm and fervor attracted great numbers to the meetinghouse for Sunday services.[25] The presence of a vibrant young pastor such as Peters, combined with the church's desperate desire for unity, brought a fresh sense of harmony to the community at the dawn of the new year.

For the first time in years peace reigned at the March 29 town meeting. Unlike the previous annual meeting, fraught with acrimonious contests between the foremost leaders of the opposing parties,[26] townspeople on this occasion calmly elected men not prominently associated with either party. And they did so by the old consensual method of voice voting rather than paper ballots. Thus, they selected William Henry, a veteran of the battle of Bennington and a tavern keeper, farmer, and mill owner from Irish Corner rather than the old village, to be moderator and filled the remaining town offices with men noted for moderate good sense rather than political partisanship.[27]

This same accord permeated First Church. In early April, by a unanimous vote of the church and "the almost entire assent of the congregation," Absalom Peters received a call to succeed Daniel Marsh as Bennington's settled minister.[28] Peters accepted on the condition that he be allowed to retain his ministerial connection with Presbyterianism and be granted the freedom to attend meetings of that denomination's various judicatories. In return, Peters promised members of First Church that he would govern their church according to Congregational forms of discipline, "so long as this is the mode of your choice."[29] The church accepted his terms and formed a committee to make the necessary arrangements for his ordination. The very composition of this committee, which included David Robinson, O. C. Merrill, Moses Robinson Jr., Aaron Robinson, and Jotham French, testified to the unity that prevailed within First Church.[30] Then on June 20, amidst demonstrations of "pomp and joy" throughout the town, workers raised a magnificent brass bell and hung it in the church belfry. Isaac Tichenor, true to his promise, had purchased the bell in nearby Troy and donated it to the church.[31] Two weeks later the bell rang out to celebrate the installation of Absalom Peters as the new pastor of First Church.[32] Peace, gaiety, and good fellowship appeared to be the order of the day in Bennington.

Even before the installation of Peters, another venture appeared to bode well for the peace and harmony of the village. Ground had been broken for an academy building to be constructed on the slope between Courthouse Hill and Meetinghouse Hill. Not only the midway location between the uphill and downhill sections of the village but the composition of the proprietors — prominent leaders from both political factions as well as many not identified with either group — indicated a desire by Bennington's leading citizens to put their differences behind them. The same hope for unity that drew the community together behind the Reverend Peters characterized the campaign to construct the academy building.

As the structure neared completion, however, the question of exactly what sort of school would inhabit their building confronted the proprietors. Should it be open to all students at minimal cost, or should it cater to a more exclusive set of scholars? In a learned essay, "Amicus" advocated the creation of an academy of higher learning. He claimed that a true academic education would not only foster religion but exert a stabilizing effect upon the political and civil life of the community. Academies carried students beyond the elementary subjects taught in common schools to a true appreciation of the history of their nation, which was an absolute necessity if a republican form of government were to survive in the United States. This vital understanding of the nation's past could be accomplished only "by means of schools . . . of the higher kind." Overcrowded common schools that met only seasonally under the tutelage of young and inexperienced instructors who were barely able to teach even the most rudimentary branches of learning were entirely inadequate. Instead, "it requires men of considerable science and experience to teach history to advantage." For this reason, "it is in academies and in them only, that suitable provision can be made for these objects."[33]

By the time the annual town meeting convened in March 1821, disagreements over the academy had begun to develop throughout the community.[34] These differences were not, however, sufficient to disrupt that gathering, which one participant described as having "very little if any politics about it." Only the election of town clerk, in which William Haswell defeated Aaron Robinson, necessitated voting by ballot; there were no divisions over any of the other offices. William Henry again served as moderator, and, with a single exception, the townspeople chose the same selectman who had served the previous year. As in the previous year's meeting, "all was conducted harmoniously."[35]

The same could not be said of the freeman's meeting that met six months later. Although the offices of governor, lieutenant governor, and treasurer caused no problems — Republican candidates ran unopposed for these positions — the struggle within the town to select a representative to the General Assembly "was a real hard one." Moses Robinson Jr. and O. C. Merrill were the principal candidates, and their supporters did all in their power to influence undecided voters; "every kind of appetite was tampered with among the mean characters to carry the day." One disgruntled voter observed that "liquor, pork & meal & all the good things of this world were said to be plentifully distributed by the great movers among the federalists." Despite such strenuous efforts, however, the meeting ended at eleven o'clock that night without a clear majority for any candidate.[36]

Once again the town was so divided that it would not be represented in the General Assembly. Terrible hostility had built up since the town meeting in March because of the Bennington Academy, destined to be located in the recently completed brick academy building. Many townspeople believed that this institution epitomized the elitist ideas of "Amicus." "One of the Subscribers" expressed these anxieties on the eve of a meeting of the building's proprietors to discuss tuition. "Subscriber" feared that after the great effort made by so many townspeople to construct an impressive building for the education of their children, "one or two persons shall presume to establish the prices of tuition so high, that none but the rich can give their children an education." In his mind this was equivalent to telling "the middle and poorer class of citizens, STAND BACK, 'for we are holier than thou. Education will be a damage to your children, — none but the children of the rich shall be admitted into this institution.' "[37]

Despite such arguments, the Bennington Academy opened in December 1821. As president of the board of trustees, which included Moses Robinson Jr., Noadiah Swift, and Stephen Hinsdill, Absalom Peters proudly announced that it was his goal to "build up an institution, more elevated in character than most of the Academies in our country." To accomplish this, the board named a tutor from Dartmouth College as principal and hired an assistant to help him teach the various courses offered at the academy. Members of the board also set tuition rates at five dollars per quarter for the upper-division courses and four dollars for courses at the lower level. The school opened with over seventy scholars in attendance.[38]

No sooner had the Bennington Academy opened its doors than citizens began either to attack or defend the school in the pages of the *Gazette*. Its supporters assumed a decidedly superior tone and derided the ignorance of their opponents. Those opposed to the academy argued that the "circumstance of wealth, ought not to confer superior privileges, so far as it respects common education." In their minds "the perfection of the distribution of privilege, in this respect, would be that all should be equal."[39]

Soon divisions in town grew much more serious. By the time of the annual town meeting in 1822, tension had escalated considerably. Although voting for the principal town offices went smoothly, Jedediah Dewey gained the post of collector only after "foul play was used on both sides." A fellow Republican bragged to Hiram Harwood that he had spent twenty dollars on the election. Harwood presumed that that amount "would fall far below what Capt. R. [Moses Robinson Jr.] distributed in drams & otherwise." For his part, Harwood viewed the whole proceeding as a "disgrace of this town & of human nature." What made the process so distasteful to Harwood, a lifelong Republican, was the fact that "the giving of drams & gifts" had not been restricted to Federalists. Harwood, who had always "boasted of the correct principles of my party," sadly confessed that many of its members had "departed from the good old rules which governed our ancestors."[40] Serious divisions again plagued the inhabitants of Bennington.

Following the March meeting, uphill leaders, particularly Uel M. Robinson, David Robinson Jr., and O. C. Merrill, took the lead in attacking both the academy and its leading proponent, Absalom Peters. Their object was to have a district school share the building with the academy. They organized school meetings in which "party spirit pervaded all their doings" and "voted down the minister throughout."[41] Finally, they succeeded, and a district school taught by two young Bennington women opened early in May 1822 in rooms specifically set apart for this purpose. Tuition was one dollar per quarter.[42]

Locating a common school in the academy building did not satisfy the uphill leaders; these men wanted to wrest full control of the academy building away from Peters and his board of trustees. They gained their object at a bitterly divisive meeting early in January 1823 at which David Robinson Jr. and Merrill, on the one side, and Peters and Moses Robinson Jr., on the other, "accused one another of many vile intentions & actions." In the end, Robinson and Merrill emerged victorious. Outright ownership of the building passed to all proprietors in common; they, not the board of trustees of the Bennington Academy, now had full control over the building and all that went on within it.[43]

Learning of this bitter confrontation, Hiram Harwood exclaimed in disgust that he considered "colleges and academies [to be] nurseries of monarchy & aristocracy." In fact, he believed that "the money laid out for education there might do much greater service to the public to be put into a vast fund for the support of our common schools."[44] Such sentiments became a veritable litany for Darius Clark, whose editorials in the *Gazette* effusively praised common schools. If such schools declined, he warned, "society languishes in all its relations, in its morals, in its republican manners, in its securities, and in its general economy." Common schools "diffuse[d] that intelligence which is the life of liberty."[45] For Clark, then, "*academic* instruction, brought under popular control, and chastened as are our *common schools*, by annual checks and shaped to the uses, and within the reach of the *many*," stood beside freedom of the press as the great bulwark of American republicanism, and "any artificial expedients to aid and abet inequality in this is unprincipled warfare with the just rights of man."[46]

By the time Clark wrote these editorials he was embroiled in a bitter feud with Peters. The issue dividing the two was, ostensibly, the academy, but their differences actually ran much deeper. They emanated from the way each man perceived the individual and society. Clark supported common schools out of a commitment to equal opportunity, not because he believed they should or could reshape human nature. He stubbornly maintained that every man should be free to live as he saw fit; society for him was simply a collection of autonomous individuals pitted against one another in a competitive effort to improve their stations in life. The competition must, of course, be equal for all participants.

If Clark desired the liberation of the individual from societal restraints, Peters hoped for the redemption of the individual through moral suasion. Human nature was malleable; it could be shaped by schools, benevolent societies, and evangelical religion. Society for him was an organic whole that could be improved by altering the environment in which Americans lived and worked. He would not hesitate, therefore, to change the lives of others for the better. In fact, he felt a moral obligation to do so. The means Peters employed to shape that culture were, however, the very ones that Clark attacked as "artificial expedients to aid and abet inequality." Further, what Peters considered moral suasion, Clark viewed as social coercion — the attempt by a minority to inhibit the natural freedom of the individual to act in his own best interests, to provide special benefits for a few at the expense of the many. Little wonder, then, that Clark and Peters were at loggerheads not only over the academy but also over the pastor's attempts to foster moral reform within Bennington.

From the moment he arrived in the community, even before he was installed as pastor of First Church, Peters actively promoted moral reform societies in the village and throughout the county. In June 1820 he organized the Bennington Sabbath School Society. By early the next year young Peters had been elected secretary of the Bennington County Bible Society. He could hardly contain his excitement at the prospect of melding this local organization with the Vermont Bible Society, the American Bible Society, and other national Bible societies as well as their thousands of auxiliaries throughout the world. He exuded this same enthusiasm for the activities of the American Foreign Missionary Society, the American Domestic Missionary Society, and the American Education Society. Such organizations were instrumental in bringing about the moral reformation so badly needed not only within his own country but throughout the world. Consequently, he opened the pulpit at First Church to their agents and personally solicited funds for these benevolent organizations from that same platform. It was this zeal for missionary activity that brought Peters into open conflict with Darius Clark.

In the March 26, 1822, issue of the *Gazette*, Clark published a letter from a subscriber who maintained that all classes of society subsisted on the hard labor of farmers. Even so, those whom farmers supported never hesitated to denigrate and exploit them. This was particularly true of missionaries — "beggars in velvet." Indeed, these people were by any calculation "the most able financiers" of all. They taxed the people "by mites, by cents, by dollars — by male, by female, foreign and domestic, in publick, in private, by spiritual & temporal promises, by tracts, magazines, pamphlets, gazettes, by catchpenny Almanacks. &c. &c." So grasping were missionaries that if they could "not be present when we die, they publish *correct forms* of wills, by which we can give our property to them, all for the poor heathen in *foreign* countries."[47]

For missionaries to be dubbed "beggars in velvet," and their fundraising activities publicly ridiculed, incensed Absalom Peters. He attacked the offending letter in two successive sermons devoted to the good works of missionary societies. When Clark refused to condemn either the offensive letter or its author, Peters canceled his subscription to the *Gazette* and urged others to do the same.[48] Clark promptly declared that he did not feel obliged to pay his portion of Peters's salary so long as the pastor discouraged subscribers from taking his paper.[49]

Harsh words about the young pastor's moral zeal began to circulate among uphill folk.[50] Soon a spirited dialogue erupted in the pages of the *Gazette*. Clark's supporters lamented the "pontifical persecution" he suffered at the hands of Peters and excoriated missionaries as conspirators intent upon fashioning a tyrannical union between church and state like those found in Europe. One correspondent even wondered how long it would be before "designing men under the garb of Religion, would become perfect masters of every man's property, both personal and real."[51] Another exclaimed that the "predominating influence of the clergy enslaves the people."[52] Those defending the pastor considered such sentiments not only "apt to attract the attention of the giddy multitude" but "aim[ed] at the destruction of every means to disseminate the tenets of religion" and therefore dangerous to the stability and well-being of society.[53]

Finally, on September 29, 1822, the Reverend Peters mounted the pulpit at First Church and assaulted the forces of evil that he saw everywhere around him. Taking his text from Isaiah 59.19, he declared that the enemy had "come upon us like a flood." Profanity, infidelity, drunkenness, and "opposition to the happiest and most benevolent movements of the church" were being "openly and loudly advocated" in Bennington. Many townspeople had attended the theater that performed in the courthouse until midnight every evening the previous week. Many more patronized a horse track that had recently been constructed in the East Village, where races took place on the Sabbath in full view of the meetinghouse. Never doubting that "every soul around us is in jeopardy," Peters asked those in attendance if they suspected "that our neighbours are there; or our children, or our backsliding breathren in the church." He entreated the congregation to "offer prayers, and intercessions, according to the number of all our neighbours, all our children, and all our brethren, who will not pray for themselves."[54] The righteous inhabitants of Bennington must exert a moral authority over their unrepentant neighbors; this alone could ensure the peace and good order of the town.

Peters's sermon outraged individuals throughout the uphill community,[55] and their response was immediate. Tuesday's *Gazette* included an

anonymous attack upon the pastor. Its author wondered why "the industrious hard labouring part of society, the farmer and mechanic on
whose labours all the idle classes live," should be told that they "cannot
have a day's — an evening's relaxation from their labour without crime."
Knowing that Peters had been away from Bennington for several weeks,
he observed that "we see people whose whole life is a holiday exemption
from labour, . . . leaving their flocks — days and weeks journeying in
style and leisure to a commencement." Such people did not "leave their
business and travel in haste, perhaps on foot and return to increased
labour like the farmer and mechanic." Instead, "they ride at ease — no
stop in salary — tarry perhaps within a day's journey of home a day or
two previous and during the Sabbath, leaving their flocks destitute."
While Peters ignored such delinquency, he was quick to attack "the man
who laboured hard during the year, or perhaps even the day previous, to
gain time and earn money to go an evening to a theatrical performance." For the *Gazette*'s outraged correspondent, this was "straining
at a gnat and swallowing a camel." Even worse than Peters's hypocrisy
was the presumptuous misuse of his office. When ministers "descend
from their high calling to criticise a theater or determine the merits of a
horse race on the Sabbath . . . or even to destroy the liberty of the Press
during the other part of the week," there was no doubt that "the friends
of morality have much to fear."[56] Individual freedom would soon give
way to the demands of a privileged few.

Shortly after the appearance of this letter, Clark wrote an editorial
expressing similar misgivings about the direction the church appeared
to be taking in Bennington. He regretted that just as party animosities
were disappearing throughout Vermont "a division should have arisen,
far more intolerant and persecuting than that of federal and republican." It was disconcerting that this "most revengeful and unchristian-
like spirit, should *mask* itself under the cloak of *religion.*" Clark refused
to censor letters attacking Peters or missionary societies; their authors
were sincere and honest men who had the best interests of society at
heart. Their judgment that missionary activities and theological seminaries were "anti-christian" — the surest means of "destroying pure
good old fashioned religion" — deserved to be heard. He would not
close his paper to them.[57]

By the time of the September 1823 freemen's meeting the relationship between the church and politics in Bennington appeared to have
strengthened considerably. When Moses Robinson Jr. defeated Merrill
for the General Assembly seat, Hiram Harwood attributed the out-

come to a "strong Church party backed up by the real old federalists."[58] While the very existence of a "church party" indicated a significant change in the political life of the town, the fact that members of this party aligned themselves with longtime Federalists was even more striking. The church in Bennington had, from its very founding, always espoused a sturdy egalitarianism.

What had happened? Why had First Church abandoned its democratic heritage? "A Friend to Religious Liberty" thought he understood what lay behind the transformation. Recent attempts "to trample on the rights of the Church, and to palm upon congregations, presbyterian rules, and aristocratical government and discipline" were entirely responsible for changes at First Church. Citing a recent history of England that contrasted the "intolerant spirit" and "clerical aristocracy" of Presbyterianism with the "benevolence" and "universal toleration" of Congregationalists, "Friend" left it to his readers to decide whether the system of government being imposed upon First Church was consistent with "liberal and enlightened views."[59]

For all his hyperbole, "Friend" did reveal an essential truth: First Church had in fact assumed a Presbyterian form of government. From the time of his installation Absalom Peters had worked to tighten the internal organization of the church as well as the discipline it exerted over its members. In addition, he had attempted to draw First Church under the jurisdiction of the Presbyterian Church. Thus, within two weeks of his installation he had not only reorganized the church records but drawn up new articles of faith and a new covenant for the church.[60] By October of the following year church members agreed to observe the day of fasting appointed by the presbytery of Troy.[61] Six months after that they discussed the importance of having some ecclesiastical connection with other churches.[62] Then on May 10, 1823, the church voted to send a delegate to the meeting of the Troy presbytery.[63] Two years later the membership, after reviewing the original records of their church and portions of the Cambridge Platform, agreed that no obstacles stood in the path of their desire to consociate with other churches. In fact, they discovered that consociation seemed to be "distinctly contemplated in the Platform." They voted to join the Rutland Consociation of the Congregational Church.[64] With this decision, whatever semblance of its origins as a bastion of New Light separatism First Church might have retained over the years vanished entirely.

As part of his effort to transform the governmental structure of First Church, Absalom Peters also managed to obtain unanimous acceptance of the rules of discipline that he had drawn up.[65] These rules laid out precisely how members of the church were to fulfill their pledge in the covenant "to watch over one another." According to the rules of discipline, members of the church truly became their brothers' keepers, as the Merrill family discovered on the very day the church accepted the rules. On that day, December 25, 1823, Absalom Peters brought the charge of intemperance against Polly Merrill that resulted in her public humiliation.[66] Peters and the majority in First Church considered the action taken against Polly Merrill and others like her to be absolutely necessary if they were to regenerate their community. In their view, church discipline encouraged individual self-restraint through moral suasion. The Merrills of course viewed church discipline from quite a different perspective. In their minds it represented an onerous intrusion upon their privacy, a gratuitous restriction of their freedom to govern their own lives.

While "A Friend to Religious Liberty" identified the structural changes taking place in First Church, his explanation for these alterations was not only incorrect but obscured important permutations taking place within the membership of the church itself. Men like Governor Moses Robinson no longer served as deacons. Those stalwart champions of democracy had been replaced by Jotham French, Calvin Bingham, Erwin Safford, and Stephen Hinsdill, men who were ardent supporters of Peters and allies of downhill political leaders such as Tichenor and Aaron Robinson. First Church, like Bennington itself, was undergoing change. The social and economic forces affecting the larger community were transforming the membership of the church. Thus, by no stretch of the imagination were Presbyterian rules, discipline, and governmental structure "palmed off" on the congregation. The majority of church members not only acquiesced in such changes but welcomed them with enthusiasm. They willingly discarded the church's traditional concern for democratic individualism in favor of promoting sufficient institutional strength to effect the moral redemption of their community.

At the same time that downhill influence was beginning to assert itself in First Church, Tichenor and others took steps to create yet another institution to exert moral influence in Bennington. Actually, these men revived an old institution: the Masonic lodge. On October 7, 1823, the Grand Lodge of Vermont, in response to a petition from Tichenor and a number of his close associates, chartered Mount Anthony Lodge in Bennington.[67] Unlike old Temple Lodge, which had

included men from all political factions in town, the new lodge consisted entirely of traditional Federalists and young men like David
Henry and Hiland Hall, second-generation Bennington residents who
were beginning to form political alliances within the downhill community. The composition of the new lodge did nothing to lessen the tensions building within the village.

The fact that no uphill leaders nor any of their younger colleagues
belonged to Mount Anthony Lodge stood as mute testimony to the
increasingly polarized nature of life in Bennington. And yet these tensions, however pervasive, did not prevent the factions from agreeing on
economic matters. Three months after the formation of the new lodge,
uphill and downhill leaders joined together at a meeting of farmers,
manufacturers, and mechanics at the courthouse on January 10, 1823,
to discuss the economic future of their town. David Robinson Jr. served
as secretary for the group, and the twenty-man committee chosen to
draft resolutions included Merrill, Moses Robinson Jr., Stebbins Walbridge, and Stephen Hinsdill.[68] Perfect unanimity characterized this
committee's deliberations; its report, delivered at an adjourned meeting
a week later, expressed a consensus that pervaded not only the committee but all participants at the convention. Their demand that Congress
pass higher tariffs in order to protect home manufacturing rested on a
belief that agriculture and manufacturing shared inseparable interests.
In the opinion of committee members, the time had arrived "when placing 'the manufacturer beside the agriculturist' " had become the age's
"great moral and political desideratum."[69] Their memorial to Congress
stoutly maintained that "the union of manufactures and agriculture, has
invariably increased commerce, and been the fountain of national prosperity, wealth, knowledge and distinction." Only a stronger tariff policy
could guarantee the future of such a union. Realizing this, "the *cultivators of the soil* require the measure."[70]

That committee members such as Hinsdill, Walbridge, and Erwin
Safford should conflate the interests of farmers and manufacturers in
order to support high tariffs was not at all surprising. They operated
flourishing wool and cotton factories. It was not these men, however,
who most passionately linked agriculture and manufacturing. Uphill
leaders had been offering a single toast to "Agriculture, Commerce, and
Manufacturers" at their celebrations of the Fourth of July and the battle
of Bennington for years.[71] And Merrill gladly joined Hinsdill and others
at a convention of wool growers and manufacturers in sending a memorial to Congress proclaiming that "the union and mutual cooperation of

manufacturing and agricultural industry and enterprize, have invariably
been the source of positive national wealth, resources, knowledge &
distinction."[72] Indeed, Bennington's most outspoken critic of Absalom
Peters, missionaries, and academies was also the town's foremost champion of farmers, manufacturers, and high tariffs. "Z" repeatedly contended that "all classes of society" subsisted on the "hard-earned labours of the FARMER." And yet the very people whom farmers "clothe
and feed, have at all times tried to disgrace their calling, and tax their
industry."[73] Those exploiting farmers included lawyers, ministers, merchants, politicians, and "beggars in velvet," but, importantly, not manufacturers. Manufacturers held the key to the independence and prosperity of agriculture. Farmers required the local markets that domestic
manufacturers provided. These manufacturers, in turn, must be protected from unfair foreign competition if they were to survive. Farmers
must, therefore, "encourage our own mechanicks and manufacturers";
they must "assist one another as brethren" if they were to prosper.[74]

Thus, in their exaltation of the farmer's independence, traditionally
believed to be a vital element in the preservation of a republican social
order in America, "Z" and his uphill colleagues inextricably linked
the farmer with the manufacturer. In the process they quite unself-
consciously integrated the yeoman persuasion of Ethan Allen with the
Christian capitalism of Stephen Hinsdill. As a result, they helped ensure that manufacturing entrepreneurs like Hinsdill shared with tillers
of the soil the mantle of republicanism's independent citizen. It had
been supposed since the time of the Revolution that the independent
yeoman's small freehold joined his interests to that of the larger commonwealth; now the entrepreneurial establishments of Hinsdill, Walbridge, and others also were considered vital to the common good of
society.[75]

At nearly the same time that uphill leaders were praising the republican independence promoted by an alliance between agriculture and
manufacturing, another group in Bennington offered quite another
perspective on the subject of liberty and property. On July 4, 1822,
while uphill leaders toasted the Revolution for banishing "tyranny and
oppression" from American society, debtors lodged in the Bennington
gaol offered a distinctly different toast: "*The United States of America* —
the boasted land of freedom. The slavery of the blacks in the south —
the imprisonment of the poor and unfortunate in the north — foul blots
upon our national character." While celebrating "Our land of freedom," the imprisoned debtors observed "how strange, that liberty

should be subservient to property—that the worshipers of Mammon should be permitted to ravish from us the sacred boon, and not permit us to till and tread its soil."[76]

These sentiments, redolent with the egalitarian spirit of Thomas Chittenden and Matthew Lyon, failed to strike a responsive chord with the current generation of uphill leaders. For all their rhetorical allegiance to the equality, virtue, and independence of the yeoman, men like David Robinson Jr., John S. Robinson, Merrill, Uel M. Robinson, and Heman Robinson were not farmers, much less independent yeomen. They were lawyers, with a much greater affinity to business entrepreneurs than to the mill workers and tenant farmers who formed an ever larger proportion of Bennington's population. If their rhetoric voiced the egalitarianism of an earlier era, their actions fostered an increasingly unegalitarian present. Although they launched an occasional attack on imprisonment for debt,[77] these men gave most of their time and attention to promoting and protecting the interests of the entrepreneurial institutions that were springing up around them. Indeed, they treated these organizations with the same solicitude that they had always reserved for the independent yeoman. As a result, they applied to businesses the same principles that they had long advocated for private individuals: the unbridled pursuit of self-interest was in the long-term interest of the entire community and should be encouraged in every possible manner.

The willingness of uphill and downhill leaders to join together in support of manufacturers and a higher tariff did nothing, however, to lessen their disagreements over the Reverend Peters, the academy, and moral reform. Noadiah Swift found it increasingly difficult to collect the tax rate to pay Peters's salary,[78] and David Robinson Jr. made that task all the more difficult by placing every possible legal obstacle he could in Swift's path.[79] Robinson and Merrill battled Peters over whether the district school should be allowed to continue in the academy building and over what facilities the common school should enjoy while located there. Partitions dividing students from the separate schools came down only to be put back up.[80] Peters wanted to incorporate Bennington Academy in such a manner as to gain control of the building itself, but Robinson and Merrill led a victorious movement to block this effort.[81]

By early November 1825, however, there were signs that the tension might be lessening. Peters announced that he had been asked by the United Domestic Missionary Society to become its corresponding secretary and that he very much wanted to accept the post.[82] Even though a great majority of church members opposed his dismissal, a council of churches met on December 14 and decided in favor of Peters.[83] Within a matter of days he delivered his farewell sermon and left Bennington. Taking note of Peters's departure, Darius Clark hoped that "*all* [might] profit by our past experience" and that "He who governs all things, again unite the hearts of this people as they were once united." But Clark, unable to stifle his resentment of moral coercion, added, "May He send us one, who shall not only be willing to inculcate the precepts, but to follow the *examples* of our meek and lowly Saviour."[84]

Whether Clark's hopes would be realized rested in large part with the committee chosen to find a new pastor. Given the composition of this committee, which was divided evenly between members of the church and members of the society, Clark's fears must have been stronger than his hope; all six men were either prominent downhill leaders or closely associated with them.[85] Six months later, following a unanimous call from both the church and the society, installation ceremonies took place for Rev. Daniel A. Clark as pastor of First Church.[86] Hope for peace and harmony throughout the community blossomed. One observer enthusiastically suggested that the "perfect unanimity" of the church and society might "betoken well of the prosperity of Zion among us." Darius Clark celebrated the event in an editorial glowing with goodwill toward all who participated in the service. Then, cleverly employing the biblical figure of Absalom, he pointed out the disservice done whenever ministers "should be so lost to duty, as to descend from their elevated station, and to sit in the gate sowing the seeds of dissention and sedition and expressing desires to ambitious temporal rule."[87]

While only time would tell whether the Reverend Clark's presence in Bennington would bring unity or discord, the community basked in the goodwill of the installation ceremonies through the summer and fall of 1826. Leaders from the town's uphill and downhill factions joined to organize the fiftieth-anniversary celebration of the nation's independence.[88] On July 4 a procession formed on Courthouse Hill and marched to the meetinghouse. The Reverend Clark opened the ceremonies with a prayer, following which Merrill delivered a patriotic oration and a spirited reading of the Declaration of Independence. At the conclusion of services, the celebrants marched in procession to the State Arms Tavern. There, after a blessing by Reverend Clark, they enjoyed a dinner provided by Uel M. Robinson, who had recently become proprietor of the old tavern. After dinner they joined in toasting various luminaries as well as "Agriculture, Manufactures, Mechanic arts and Commerce — Mutually advantageous, sources of national wealth, prosperity and happiness." So convivial was this gathering of old political rivals that soon after joining Darius Clark in a toast to Thomas Jefferson they all raised their glasses as Pierpont Isham paid tribute to the memory of Alexander Hamilton.[89]

Meanwhile, the new pastor was devoting himself to fostering religious meetings throughout Bennington. So successful was he that by October a religious "stir" permeated the entire township.[90] Then in December, with the enthusiastic cooperation of Deacon Stephen Hinsdill, Clark led a massive revival in Hinsdillville that led to the conversion of a great many factory workers.[91] On a single Sabbath morning sixty of these converts became members of First Church.[92] Clark's evangelical efforts were so fruitful[93] that genteel church members began to worry that First Church was being "espionaged" by its new converts.[94]

While the results of Clark's evangelism created concern among some church members, the stridency of his message and the arrogant and disdainful manner with which he treated common folk began to antagonize increasing numbers of townspeople. Whether addressing a massive revival, smaller religious meetings, or individual families, Clark made it unrelentingly clear that there was no middle ground between the salvation he preached and eternal damnation. So frightful was his message during a private visit to the Harwood household that he reduced the women to tears.[95] On another occasion, when he arrived at a neighborhood religious meeting only to find it sparsely attended, he belittled the "backwardness" of the people, grilled several individuals, uttered "some pretty frightful comments," and rode off in a rage.[96] As instances of such behavior multiplied, one offended parishioner retaliated by girdling the young maple trees that Clark had planted in front of his home.[97]

If the individual who committed this act of vandalism believed he might deter the pastor from the moral path he had chosen for himself and for the community, he was badly mistaken. Clark took it upon himself to organize the annual Fourth of July celebration in 1827. And what a different celebration it was! Children attending Sabbath school convened in the meetinghouse with their parents to hear Clark deliver a sermon against slavery. Then, following a collection taken up for the American Colonization Society, the students, their parents, and Sabbath school superintendents and teachers formed a procession and marched to a grove of trees near the courthouse, where they enjoyed a picnic lunch provided by the families. The repast was entirely free of ardent spirits. After lunch the procession reformed and marched to the meetinghouse, where Merrill and Hiland Hall delivered patriotic addresses. Following a benediction by Clark, the crowd dispersed to their homes, well before sunset.[98]

Although the celebration of Independence Day did not follow its accustomed routine, it was, nonetheless, a day of harmonious unity in Bennington. The same was true of the festivities marking the fiftieth anniversary of the battle of Bennington. Organized by a mixture of uphill and downhill leaders,[99] the ceremonies—in the absence of the Reverend Clark, who was in Amherst, Massachusetts—opened with the firing of guns and the ringing of the meetinghouse bell. A procession marched from the courthouse to the meetinghouse, where the participants listened to an oration by Pierpont Isham. Following that, they paraded to the State Arms Tavern, where they enjoyed a banquet provided by Uel Robinson and drank toasts to the heroes of Bennington and the republic. While there were contradictory toasts offered to Andrew Jackson, perfect unanimity prevailed in favor of the American System. One toast hailed "Agriculture, Commerce, & Manufactures—The 'American System'—Equal, and adequate protection to them all—graduated on the scale of their wants." Another derided any in the next Congress "who may oppose the American System of encouraging domestic industry—protecting the Farmers and Manufacturers." The clearest sign of good feeling came when old Isaac Tichenor rose and lauded Governor Thomas Chittenden and the Council of Safety for steering Vermont through the Revolution. Perhaps none who were present were old enough to remember the vitriolic and partisan way Tichenor had attacked Chittenden and every member of the Council of Safety for their actions during the Haldimand negotiations in 1781. Or perhaps the spirit of joviality kept them silent.[100]

Unfortunately, the harmony did not last much beyond the conclusion of these festivities. Several factors were responsible for the new disruptions. First, Reverend Clark resumed his moral zealotry. For some time the focus of his attention had been a dancing school conducted in the ballroom of the State Arms Tavern. By constantly demanding that this "barrier" to moral purity be eliminated, he transformed the school—an institution with a long and uneventful history in Bennington—into a divisive public issue.[101] Many church members took up Clark's cause and attacked dancing and ballrooms as the work of the devil. Convinced that "wherever our Blessed Lord makes his appointment it makes the place awful and solemn, banishes all merriment and vanity and changes their musick into notes of praise," they challenged the people of Bennington to consider whether "a Ball Chamber was a suitable place to prepare for eternity."[102] Others believed that preaching against dancing only turned young people away from the church and promoted "hatred to *religion* itself." In their opinion the "canting, persecuting, hypocritical conduct of the presbyterians in the time of Oliver Cromwell" should not be revived. Religion no longer consisted of "putting on a long face, and damning all those who do not agree in deed, and doctrine." Instead, "true religion produces a cheerful heart, and a forgiving temper."[103] Rather than mediating differences, however, the Reverend Clark exacerbated them by his intolerant crusade against all who disagreed with him.

Local politics also contributed to a growing unrest in the town. The previous year Charles Hammond, president of the Bennington Furnace, had been supported for the General Assembly by Tichenor and his downhill associates but had needed three ballots to be elected. Opposition had come primarily from men like Hiram Harwood, who objected to being urged to vote for Hammond simply because the man "belonged to a company that had located itself here & was annually expending large sums among us."[104] The hardworking farmer feared that "with property any man having ambition could rule Bennington at will — only throw out the bait & fishes enough could be taken."[105] Now, with the annual freeman's meeting approaching and Hammond again being supported by the downhill leadership, the same issue was before the voters. Uphill leaders did all they could to exploit the natural fear or envy of a manufacturer's wealth that existed within the agricultural sector of the community. In fact, whenever Gen. David Robinson went out on the hustings he spoke forthrightly "against supporting these great capitalists for office."[106] His son, David Jr., also argued "against Hammond & [the] Factory influence" whenever he encountered local farmers.[107] The result was a close victory for Hiland Hall in an election in which the "old parties" became terribly "worked up." Indeed, the "minds of the people . . . were highly wrought upon about this time."[108]

The minds of a great many people continued to be "wrought upon" even after the votes had been tallied because of the tactics adopted by Hammond and his supporters. For the first time in the history of Bennington elections, the ballot for one candidate — Hammond — was distinctive from all others. Workers from factories around Bennington arrived at the freeman's meeting with orange ballots bearing Hammond's name. Following the election Hammond dismissed those of his employees who cast ballots of a different color. This immediately led to charges that local manufacturers might "raise up into 'knots of little aristocracies' " and that all laborers might become "dependents, subject to their masters good will or displeasures, and in little better condition than the colored slaves of the south."[109]

These charges placed uphill leaders in a difficult position. Although they were personally opposed to Hammond, they did not want to foment resentment against the manufacturing establishments they considered so essential to local prosperity. Making full use of traditional republican maxims, they declared that American workers could never become a dependent class: they were "too well informed through our common schools"; they were as "necessary to the capitalists, as the capitalists [were] to the workmen," since both looked to "individual *profits* to themselves, and both are equally beholden to the other"; in addition, the larger community would simply never allow any group in American society to destroy another's "independence of opinion, and freedom of individual action." In fact, it was "really absurd" even to suggest that it might be attempted "in the year of our Lord, 1827, to violate, in republican America, freedom of popular opinion, and the solemnities of the oaths of freemen." Even though there had been some dismissals, there could be no doubt that every "agent, clerk and workmen that remain[ed]" would freely testify that neither such dismissals nor special ballots affected "personal freedom of opinion and action." Any who thought otherwise were clearly "opposers of the manufacturing interests, and the *protecting* system."[110]

Tensions resulting from Hammond's actions simmered through the fall. Then in December James Ballard brought moral issues once again to the fore. Ballard, who had taken over as principal of the academy at the first of the year, expelled a number of boys, including the sons of Merrill, Darius Clark, and Heman Robinson, for attending plays put on by a theater company performing nightly at the courthouse.[111] Ballard, an ordained Congregational minister and close associate of Daniel Clark, believed that the academy, like Sabbath schools, should instill self-restraint within the youth of the village. This task assumed even greater urgency for him when parents proved unwilling or incapable of performing such a vital duty. In such cases he had no doubt that his own moral authority must take precedence over that of the student's own father and mother.

Parents of the aggrieved students were, of course, outraged. A call went out for the proprietors of the academy building to meet in order to consider forming a committee to assume supervision over the academy.[112] The proprietors immediately decided in favor of such a committee. They did, however, make every effort to keep old political differences to a minimum by selecting an even mix of uphill and downhill leaders, with Hiland Hall as chair.[113]

Shortly after the proprietors' meeting adjourned, tensions within the town lessened considerably. The formation of the supervisory committee calmed some frayed nerves, the theater troupe moved on to its next stop, and Ballard readmitted the expelled students. By the time of the annual town meeting in March 1828 most townspeople had quietly settled back into their normal routines. Although some still resented Hammond's dismissal of workers following the September election[114] and voted against Joseph Hinsdill "on account of a certain weight it was feared might be added to the establishments of the Furnace & Hinsdill's Works," the meeting moved along swiftly with "much harmony & good feeling."[115]

The amicable relations lasted only until July 4, 1828. On that day the Reverend Clark again organized the local celebration of Independence Day. Once again it consisted of Sabbath school students, their parents, and their teachers sharing a picnic lunch and listening to a moral reform speech by Clark. This time, however, the minister took the opportunity not only to speak in favor of temperance but to deliver a vitriolic attack upon the traditional manner of observing the day. He castigated past celebrations for encouraging sin, vice, dissipation, intemperance, the spirit of party, and a wasteful use of money that could be used to help the needy around the world. Reverend Clark saved his most powerful invective, however, for the manner in which traditional celebrations nurtured a continuing hostility toward Great Britain. He waxed eloquent about the "impulses to science, virtue, and benevolence" that Americans received from that nation. Beyond that, Great Britain, "the fairest spot in Europe," was "pouring forth upon a miserable world an influence to evangelize and render it happy, beyond the whole residue of that continent." Instead of recognizing the old mother country's beneficence, however, "thousands of puerile orations" kept alive the Revolutionary hatreds.[116]

The pastor's message infuriated Merrill. When Clark had taken charge of the Independence Day celebration the previous year, Merrill, who had just assumed the editorial duties of the *Gazette*,[117] had portrayed the ceremonies respectfully. After the pastor's performance this year, however, this was simply not possible. Rather than discuss the festivities, Merrill wrote an editorial bemoaning the fact that Bennington did not celebrate the Fourth in the "manner of our fathers." Ostensibly, abandonment of the old ways stemmed from a desire to promote temperance, a cause Merrill considered "praise-worthy." But "to extirpate one crying evil" by introducing a great many others "which sap the vitals of liberty, and the simple purity of republican principles, is unwise." Moreover, to set apart the anniversary of the Declaration of Independence for the purpose of "*eulogizing the British government, where the tremendous and infidel union of church and state is in its vigor,*" indicated that subversive forces were at work in Bennington. "Let any particular class of men regulate the national songs and festivals, and they will rule the nation." Furthermore, "let the manner of our national jubilee be changed from the custom of our fathers, and their principles will be changed also." Citizens of Bennington had to recognize Clark's ceremonies for what they were: an "attempt to effect a revolution of public opinion, by certain would-be great men and lords *spiritual*, by eulogizing foreign importations, and advising the importation of wisdom from the old European school" in order to undermine America's republican form of government and society.[118]

By the end of the summer, advocates of moral redemption and their opponents were verging on a public confrontation. Then late in September William Lloyd Garrison arrived in Bennington to become the editor of the newly established *Journal of the Times*. In his first editorial Garrison pledged unequivocal support for temperance, the gradual emancipation of slavery, and the cause of national peace. He also advocated education, the American System, and the presidential candidacy of John Quincy Adams.[119] But it was not long before Garrison began to attack the *Gazette* in order to punctuate his reform goals. Within three weeks after his arrival he had initiated an unprovoked war upon the *Gazette* and its editor.[120] Nothing was beyond Garrison's purview; he criticized the local militia system, the way justices of the peace were chosen, and the absence of a lyceum. It was Garrison's intrusion into the academy issue, however, that proved most divisive.

Upon settling in Bennington, Garrison took up residence in the boardinghouse Deacon Erwin Safford had recently established for out-of-town students attending the Bennington Academy. Having sanc-

tioned the boardinghouse without the permission of the supervisory
committee, Ballard was again at odds with its members. Tichenor,
Swift, Daniel Clark, and Hinsdill took the opportunity to endorse both
the boardinghouse and James Ballard's leadership of the academy. Ballard himself defiantly promised "perpetual oversight of students in
their walks and recreations" while at the academy, vowing to give special attention to the taste and morals of all students; "the low vices of
the common schools" would be entirely excluded from the academy.[121]
Garrison not only printed Ballard's pronouncements but gave the man
a ringing endorsement in the next issue of his paper.[122]

The academy controversy came to a head shortly after the beginning
of the year, when Ballard raised tuition at the school without consulting
the supervisory committee. When committee members requested that
he meet with them to discuss the matter, he refused on the grounds that
they had no authority over him. The committee promptly met and
dismissed Ballard as principal of the academy. Both Ballard and the
committee immediately wrote long letters outlining their respective
positions. Ballard's defense appeared in both the *Gazette* and the *Times;*
Garrison, however, refused to print the committee's letter.[123] Instead,
he attacked the committee's conduct as "extraordinary" and "unwarrantable" and asked the townspeople how they could tolerate such
"domination."[124]

Although both the committee and Ballard mentioned the issue of
tuition, it was clear from their statements that it was Ballard's insistence
upon exercising complete moral authority over his students that was
truly at stake. He simply would not relinquish his prerogative to exercise total control over the "amusements and holidays" of any and all
children while they were enrolled in his school.[125] Members of the
committee acknowledged that Ballard should have "exclusive control"
of students "from the moment of their starting from home in the
morning until their arrival at home at night." They could not, however,
delegate him the power to regulate the behavior of children while not
in school, for the simple reason that they themselves had not been
granted this authority by the proprietors. Further, they considered a
student to be "nearer and dearer to his parent than he possibly could be
to his teacher." Therefore, while it was possible "that some parents
would err in the government of their families; yet . . . it was better, upon
the whole, to leave each parent to the individual control of his children,
and risk his failure, than to attempt a uniformity by placing the control

in the hands of another."[126] No clearer statement could have been made by those opposing the moral reforms of Daniel Clark, James Ballard, and William Lloyd Garrison: individuals must be free to control their own lives.

Shortly after his dismissal, Ballard opened a new school, the Bennington Seminary, which met in Erwin Safford's boardinghouse, while Hinsdill had a classroom building constructed next-door. In the meantime, the supervisory committee hired a new principal and teacher for the Bennington Academy. Each school had its champions: Reverend Clark, Tichenor, Hinsdill, and Swift publicly endorsed the seminary; Heman Robinson, William Haswell, and Hiland Hall stood by the academy. The seminary drew its student body primarily from old downhill families and nonresidents, while the academy served mostly children of uphill folk.[127]

With the emergence of the two academies, cultural divisions in Bennington began to assume much greater clarity and cohesion. Those who favored the liberation of the individual from the control or influence of others and supported greater participation for the ordinary citizen in the decision-making process of their society rallied to the support of the academy. The seminary drew its support from townspeople who favored the redemption of others by means of moral suasion and by coercion if necessary. That Garrison and the *Times* supported the seminary, while Merrill and his correspondents in the *Gazette* defended the academy, only exacerbated these differences.

Other disagreements emanated from the cultural divisions within the town, especially over temperance, peace, slavery, and Bible societies. Second only to the matter of the academies, though, was Sabbatarianism. Garrison, Ballard, and Clark all opposed Sunday delivery of the U.S. mail and just as ardently supported the Pioneer Line, a stage line running from Albany to Boston, which did not operate on Sundays.[128] They maintained that people should not be compelled to observe the Sabbath but, by the same token, they should not be forced to break it either.[129] Garrison, therefore, attacked the editorials of the "Gazette blockhead" and letters written by his rival's supporters as the "belchings of a deceitful and *unsanctified* heart."[130]

Merrill, his loyal readers, and other opponents of the moral reformers stood by the "Old Line," the stage company that had been traveling daily between Albany and Boston for years. They were convinced that the "Pioneer system of compulsion" would not end with preventing the delivery of the Sunday mail; the mail was but "*one item* of the system." Moral coercion would subsequently be applied to "our presses, our schools, and Academies, our dealings with merchants, and mechanics, and our social intercourse in neighborhoods." It was "*this system* that the Roman Catholics adopted with so much success, and which is now attempting to be established in this town."[131]

The vitriolic conflict between the *Gazette* and the *Times* came to an end on March 27, 1829, when Garrison published his valedictory address. He left for Boston shortly thereafter to help Benjamin Lundy edit the *Genius of Universal Emancipation.* His opponents in Bennington could barely contain their joy. Reflecting the tremendous resentment against moral coercion that had built up among many townspeople, "Yankee" wished "My Lloyd," that "great egotist" who had set himself up as the "pattern of morality and decency" in Bennington, a fond farewell.[132]

Garrison's departure left Clark and Ballard to bear the brunt of the antipathy displayed by "Yankee." Both men were unrelenting in their efforts to bring about the moral redemption of the community. Their self-righteousness — their moral authoritarianism — offended an ever-growing number of townspeople. Feelings ran so deep that when Ballard related his saving experience to church members, David Robinson opposed receiving him as a member of First Church. Robinson brought a list of charges against Ballard's moral character to a church meeting, but the members voted not to allow them to be presented. Then, by a nearly two-to-one margin, church members voted to propound Ballard for admission to the church at the next communion ceremony.[133] On Sunday, July 4, 1830, when First Church welcomed Ballard as a member, David Robinson and his supporters walked out of the service.[134] They were, however, a distinct minority. Robinson no longer held sway over the church his father had founded. Perhaps nothing so clearly illustrated the changes First Church had undergone over the years than this humbling of the patriarch of the Robinson family.

Just as the majority of church members stood by Ballard, so, too, did they attempt to defend Daniel Clark from a rising storm of criticism. This was not an easy task. In fact, the day before Clark administered communion to Ballard, a number of townspeople, frustrated because no festivities had been planned for Independence Day, held an ad hoc ceremony of their own. After the party ended, several celebrants broke out windows in Clark's home and trampled a portion of his garden.[135]

Such vandalism resulted from the anger so many townspeople harbored against Clark. For well over a year previous to this incident he
had been criticized by a wide range of people in the pages of the *Gazette*. These people simply would no longer listen to Clark's charge that
they were incapable of hearing the truth he was delivering with such
force and clarity. The time had passed when "the hypocritical tear
could cleanse the clerical robe, or the cry of 'persecution for righteousness sake' could heal the deep wound of the church, occasioned by
clerical arrogance."[136] One citizen accused Clark of "secretly advising
and contriving the ways and means to sustain a school in opposition to
the old Academy" as well as repeatedly declaring "that none but his
immediate supporters and flatterers belong to respectable society —
and that the lines ought to be drawn — and the sooner there is a division
the better."[137] Still another accused Clark of "intrigue for a high aristocratic school, in which the offspring of the poor were not to enter
unless through the back-door of charity." When told that such a plan
would "breed permanent quarrels and ruin our village academy if it
succeeded," Clark only "snuffs at the idea as trivial, and perseveres."[138]

The bitterest charges resulted from the efforts of David Robinson
Jr., who corresponded with members of the churches Clark had served
before coming to Bennington and was only too happy to share this correspondence with anyone who might be interested.[139] Thus, "A Friend
of the Church" quoted freely from these letters, inquiring whether any
minister could be held in good standing "who has been publicly accused, of being 'neither an honest man nor a man of truth' of 'cheating
the widow,' of 'taking property unlawfully,' of 'dividing society' and
that 'he would wholly break them up,' and who has been several times
dismissed?"[140] By the summer of 1830 discontent in the society of First
Church had risen to such an extent that some action had to be taken. A
committee was formed by the society to inquire into the difficulty
between the pastor and his congregation. Its composition revealed
how widespread the discontent with Clark had become, for it included
not only Heman and Uel M. Robinson but Hiland Hall and the old
downhill stalwarts Jonathan Hunt, Stebbins Walbridge, and Solomon
Safford.[141]

A struggle immediately ensued between members of the church and
members of the society when the committee's report directly attacked
Clark's character. Church members simply refused to entertain any
criticism of their pastor until the committee threatened to publish its

report, complete with the letters from Clark's former parishioners.[142] Finally, on October 12, 1830, a council of clergy and deacons met in Bennington and voted unanimously in favor of Clark's dismissal.[143] Hiram Harwood surely expressed the feelings of many when he exclaimed that the council's action finally "closed this man's tyrannical career in this place."[144] And yet the division between advocates of liberation and proponents of redemption persisted. What would become of this tension remained unclear as the townspeople of Bennington looked forward both to a new year and to a new minister.

9. Paeans to the Green Mountain Boys

If residents of Bennington hoped that Daniel Clark's departure in October 1830 might help quiet the turmoil disrupting their town, they were sadly disappointed. By mid-November dissension had become so intense that members of First Church held special meetings to discuss "the unhappy division in the church."[1] Energized by the friction between David Robinson and James Ballard, factions in the church reflected the conflict rending the larger community. This discord finally grew so acute that church members voted to call a council of churches in the hope that some peaceful solution might be found to the issues driving them apart.[2]

The council met in mid-December, and its members held the church in error for not fully discussing the charges Robinson brought against Ballard. They also declared that Ballard's admission to the church should have been delayed until such a discussion had taken place. In addition, council members maintained that Robinson and his supporters had been wrong to withdraw from communion. Believing that no satisfaction should be exacted from either party to the controversy, though, the council advised all concerned to "return to brotherly courtesy and communion." In closing, the visiting clergy admonished First Church to keep all matters of a "worldly nature" out of their "sacred pale."[3]

Despite the wisdom of the council's recommendations, its efforts came to naught. Five months later First Church continued to be torn by conflict. Acutely aware of the "luke-warm state of the church" and the "want of brotherly love among the brethren," members knew that something must be done to calm the state of feelings between Robinson and Ballard. The church therefore appointed a committee to see whether the differences between these two men could be mediated. The effort proved fruitless.[4] It seemed that nothing could bring peace to First Church. Then in the summer of 1831 Rev. R. W. Gridley of Williamstown began to preach in Bennington.

The Reverend Gridley brought to town many of the "new measures" associated with revivals conducted by Charles Grandison Finney.[5] He favored protracted meetings (revival sessions lasting from three to five days), prayer meetings extending until dawn, intense family devotionals, public prayer by women in mixed audiences, neighbor-to-neighbor canvassing by the faithful, praying for individuals by name, and the open humiliation of sinners who had been driven to the anxious seat or bench by the intense pressure of the moment. Such practices brought sinners into intimate public contact with ardently professing Christians. Most important, they transformed prayer and the conversion experience from a private into a distinctly public affair. Conversion no longer resulted from the arbitrary grace of God, prolonged solitary encounters between individuals and their souls, or even intellectual choice; it came, instead, from the deliberate actions of fellow citizens. The collective regeneration associated with Finney's techniques also rested on the concept of free moral agency. Individuals were free to accept salvation or to remain eternally damned; the choice was theirs.[6]

Finney's revivals were simple, urgent affairs that generated fresh hearts in thousands of individuals. They produced feelings of complete trust and common purpose. Religious excitement invariably began with the rededication of church members and then spread to their immediate families. The evangelism of intensive week-long revival meetings and evening services lasting through the night, however, generally could not be contained; instead, it spilled over into the larger community, where it lay the groundwork for a unified Christian community.

When Reverend Gridley began to preach in Bennington during the last week in June, Deacon Hinsdill read a "peace making letter" to the church and the society in which he called for all to "throw by their dissintions [sic] and unite in prayer." Soon thereafter, a "great awakening seemed to prevail in various parts of the town."[7] By September a committee charged with examining all those who wished to join First Church had determined that 131 recent converts had given sufficient evidence of a change of heart to be admitted as full members. Since the church was still without a pastor, Absalom Peters returned by special invitation to serve communion and to admit these people into the church. He also performed the sacrament of baptism for the 76 who had not been baptized at birth.[8] By the time he finished his work, Gridley was responsible for the admission of 168 new members into First Church. These included old political rivals such as Merrill, Pierpont Isham, and Noadiah Swift, as well as many members of traditional church families such as the Robinsons, the Harwoods, and the Henrys. A majority of new members, however, came from the factories of Stephen Hinsdill and other local entrepreneurs.[9]

When Gridley left Bennington to return to Williamstown, he left behind a far more peaceful community than he had found. The trust and common purpose so essential to the success of his revival persisted long after his departure. Indeed, the residual effects of his protracted meeting lingered so long that no festivities whatsoever took place on Independence Day because the people "had their mind raised to higher objects."[10] So pervasive was this sense of communal peace that when First Church met on January 10, 1832, members of the church and society were able to join together in a unanimous call to Rev. Edward W. Hooker to settle among them as their pastor.[11] Eight months earlier these same people had been torn by bitter and seemingly irreparable factionalism.

Whether Edward Hooker was the appropriate person to continue the work of Reverend Gridley—to maintain the peace and harmony of the village—was not immediately apparent. In some ways he closely resembled Daniel Clark. A graduate of Middlebury College and Andover Theological Seminary, Hooker was a Congregational minister who believed in the power of evangelical religion and moral reform. In fact, he had left a position with the American Temperance Society to assume the pulpit in Bennington.[12] There, however, all resemblance to the much reviled Clark ended. A mild man with a sunny disposition, Hooker celebrated life. There was simply no trace of Clark's narrow self-righteousness in his character. Thus, residents of Bennington could enjoy circuses, dancing schools, or theaters without heavy burdens of guilt. Hooker even allowed the town's singing school to hold a recital in the meetinghouse. Not only that but during the performance Hooker descended from the pulpit and performed "masterly" on the German flute before resuming his place in the pulpit to deliver a sermon on how music could enhance the religious experience.[13] Such behavior endeared Hooker to his parishioners and soon gained him the universal admiration of the larger community as well. Unlike his predecessor, Hooker had a wonderful ability to draw people together.

One clear manifestation of the unity being forged within First Church came on September 15, 1832. On that date prominent members of the community, drawing their authority from the eighteenth-century state law that allowed residents of a town to form themselves into a religious society in order to create a tax-supported church, formed the Congregational Society of Bennington. This new organization collapsed the traditional distinction between the church and the society and placed complete control of the affairs of First Church in the newly formed Congregational Society. The initial meeting of the Congregational Society, which was restricted to those individuals who were willing to be taxed up to fifty dollars annually, elected Isaac Tichenor president, Noadiah Swift vice president, Heman Swift treasurer, and Stephen Hinsdill to the board of trustees. These men served with the full approval of David Robinson and his uphill supporters.[14]

By forming the Congregational Society, leaders of the uphill and downhill factions in Bennington closed ranks in order to keep control of the church from passing into the hands of the nearly three hundred new converts who had joined First Church over the previous six years. Membership in the church no longer carried with it the right to an equal vote in all decisions concerning the church. Fundamental decisions regarding First Church had been taken out of the hands of church members altogether. Whether they would admit it or not, members of the Congregational Society had abandoned the traditional principles of equality and democracy upon which First Church had rested for so many years. Not to have done so would have meant surrendering control to the common working people of Bennington, who now made up the majority of First Church's membership.

In other ways too uphill and downhill leaders came together. This became readily apparent during an extended religious revival led by the Reverend Hooker in December 1833. Hooker established nightly prayer meetings in various districts, or "circles," throughout the town; then, with the assistance of Rev. Horatio Foote, he conducted a protracted meeting lasting eleven days. Employing all of Finney's "new measures," Hooker and Foote packed over 250 new converts into an overflowing meetinghouse on the final day of the revival.[15] During his sermon, Foote, an ardent advocate of temperance, asked all those in the sanctuary who were members of a temperance society to stand, whereupon a "vast multitude" responded. Then he requested everyone present who was friendly to the cause of temperance to rise, and a "great majority" came to their feet.[16]

The scene in the meetinghouse offered graphic testimony to the wide appeal of the temperance movement in Bennington. It was, however, a more moderate form of temperance than the total abstinence so vigorously demanded by Daniel Clark. This moderation resulted from the demise of the Pioneer Line, which had drained the Sabbatarian issue in Bennington of its moral intensity. The absence of Clark's moral authoritarianism also allowed the townspeople, both uphill and downhill, to draw together in support of a less divisive form of temperance. Supported by men such as David Robinson Jr., Hiland Hall, and Noadiah Swift, town authorities began to limit the number of alcohol licenses issued in Bennington. By restricting such licenses to a few respectable taverns, the selectmen eliminated the "grog shops" that had sprung up in so many grocery stores in town.[17]

Quite unwittingly, Horatio Foote helped unify the leadership of Bennington on another pressing moral issue: slavery. In this instance, though, Foote served as a powerful negative reference. His vehement support of radical abolitionism during the protracted meeting helped galvanize uphill and downhill leaders in support of the colonization of blacks rather than the immediate emancipation of all slaves. Less than two weeks after Foote preached to a packed meetinghouse, Bennington's most respectable leaders denied an outspoken advocate of immediate abolition the privilege of speaking in the building.[18]

On Friday, December 20, 1833, Orson Murray, an agent for the New England Antislavery Society, arrived in Bennington and asked Reverend Hooker if he could use the meetinghouse the following Monday evening to deliver an antislavery address.[19] Hooker granted him permission and announced the time and subject of Murray's intended lecture in church that Sunday. When Murray entered the meetinghouse at the appointed time on Monday, he discovered a large group of men engaged in earnest conversation. Bennington's political leaders had called a meeting of concerned citizens to discuss whether the town should allow Murray the use of the building. After listening to a number of impassioned statements supporting the American Colonization Society and opposing William Lloyd Garrison and his "fanatical co-agitators," the group decided to close the house to Murray. Deacon Hinsdill offered his factory chapel as an alternative meeting place, and Murray delivered an abolitionist lecture there on Christmas day.[20]

The Murray incident isolated Hinsdill and Ballard from other prominent citizens of Bennington on the issue of slavery. These two remained staunch abolitionists, but the majority favored the sentiments expressed at the meeting of December 23: abolitionism would agitate the South and cause the destruction of the Union; blacks were better off under slavery than they would be if they were suddenly emancipated; and the gradual process of colonization would allow blacks to adjust to freedom with a minimum of disruption to southern society or the nation at large. Therefore, the citizens of Bennington should give their full support to the American Colonization Society.[21]

Both uphill and downhill leaders subscribed to these beliefs. When, for example, First Church considered appointing a new deacon, Lyman Patchin, a prominent merchant and longtime leader in the downhill community, spoke out forcefully against choosing a man adhering to "the principles of Foote and the Abolitionists," who could only disrupt the community and destroy the church.[22] David Robinson, William Haswell, and Heman Robinson were officers of the local colonization society. It was John C. Haswell, though, who most clearly articulated the town's attitude toward the issue of slavery. As editor of the *Gazette*, Haswell repeatedly attacked Garrison and others for being counterproductive.[23] They would bring violence and the destruction of the Union. When asked what kind of antislavery advocates resided in Bennington, Haswell responded vehemently, "Not immediate abolitionists." Citizens of Bennington would become abolitionists only when "a plan of safety is first devised for our white brethren at the South and a plan of sustenance for our black brethren in the same region."[24] Nor did anyone at First Church speak out against the "negro pews" installed at the time the new meetinghouse was constructed. Instead, all were content to require blacks, whether full members or not, to be segregated during church services.[25]

Bennington's leading citizens presented the same united front on the subject of public education. Whenever they gathered to celebrate Independence Day or the battle of Bennington, they invariably toasted common schools. They lauded "common education" as the "life of Liberty . . . the moral, and sure defence, against the enemies of freedom."[26] In such encomiums, common schools constituted the very "life and happiness of society, the only safeguard of Republican Government."[27] The *Gazette* too praised common schools, describing them as the "foundation upon which all our institutions . . . depend."[28] Not only did these schools constitute the "stamina of liberty" but they contributed to the "general prosperity and moral dignity of a community, in a greater degree than any other single medium."[29]

And yet, Bennington's principal leaders sent their own children, not to the common schools, but to the town's academies.[30] They also steadfastly refused to distribute the proceeds of the town's school fund to the district schools. Had they done so, students attending these schools would not have been responsible for any fees whatsoever and the children of families working in Bennington's mills would have been able to attend. Instead, led by their most prominent citizens, the townspeople of Bennington repeatedly voted to keep the school fund intact, to allow it to accumulate and to accrue interest.[31] Thus, unfortunately for the majority of citizens, town leaders simultaneously glorified and demeaned common schools. Paying lip service to the glories of common education helped unify Bennington's uphill and downhill communities at little or no cost to themselves. This growing gap between rhetoric and reality took a toll on common schools as well as on those children who might benefit from them.

A similar dynamic shaped the relationship between Bennington and its poor. Town leaders were as quick to attack imprisonment for debt as they were to laud common schools. The *Gazette*, which opened its pages to discussion of the matter, considered imprisonment of debtors an "unequal and an unjust tax" that "visits the poor," while "the rich are exempt."[32] Branding slavery and imprisonment for debt a "cloud thick and black in the horison [*sic*] of our enlightened Republic," a participant at a celebration of the battle of Bennington asked that the "wisdom and genius of our country put forth an energy, such as did our fathers in the purchase of liberty" to abolish these antirepublican institutions.[33]

Since imprisonment for debt was state law, its abolition did not rest with the citizens of Bennington. Still, unlike their behavior regarding tariffs to protect local manufactories, they did not gather in conventions to memorialize Congress or their state legislature on the subject. Nor did they instruct their representatives to broach the issue; consequently, none ever did. Local authorities did, however, have the power to deal with poor people living in the township. But here too, just as in the case of common education, a disjunction appeared between the language and the actions of Bennington's leaders. The town had a real opportunity to promote the yeoman independence these men extolled. It might have followed Reverend Hooker's suggestion that it purchase a farm where the town poor could work off their indebtedness.[34] Under his plan, the profits of the farm would accrue to the town and the poor would have an opportunity to work their way out of poverty. Instead, following the advice of their most influential citizens, voters routinely chose to follow custom: town authorities auctioned off Bennington's poor to the highest bidders at annual vendues.[35] Thus, private individuals, not the community, profited from the labor of the poor, who remained bound by debt. Whether by circumstance or by design, leaders of the uphill and downhill communities benefited from this practice. Not only did they avoid the taxes necessary for purchasing a poor farm but they retained a cheap source of labor. Once again, only the town poor suffered.

By this time such an affinity of economic interests bound the leaders of the uphill and downhill communities together that both groups welcomed a steady supply of inexpensive and cooperative labor. What few ties uphill leaders had with agriculture involved large farms dependent on transient farmworkers and tenants. The ancient division between uphill agricultural interests and downhill commercial ones had long since dissolved. David Robinson Jr., for example, was not only one of the town's most successful attorneys but served on the board of directors of the Bank of Bennington, was a proprietor of the Paran Creek Manufacturing Company, and represented the most influential factory owners in the area.[36] Along with his cousin John S. Robinson, he had been retained to handle the legal affairs of Stephen Hinsdill's enterprises. This involved great sums of money. Indeed, John Robinson stood to gain by more than fifty thousand dollars from one transaction alone.[37] With the passage of time, then, business corporations, rather than ordinary individuals, constituted the majority of the clients handled by the Robinsons and their associates. John's cousin Uel M. Robinson became the local representative for the Vermont First Insurance Company.[38] Uel's law partner, O. C. Merrill, represented first the Springfield Fire Insurance Company and then the Ascutney Fire Insurance Company.[39]

While they did not subscribe to all the tenets of Stephen Hinsdill's Christian capitalism, these men did consider a prosperous business environment essential for the community's well-being. This, in turn, required a sober, hardworking labor force. Men such as Merrill and David Robinson Jr. joined with Hinsdill and Aaron Robinson in melding the interests of the free laborer and the manufacturer. The rhetoric of both uphill and downhill leaders accorded the virtues of the independent yeoman — so essential to the continued existence of a republican society—to both the mill owner and his workers. The employer's ownership and control of property linked him with the good of the commonwealth, while the employee, through hard work, discipline, and a common-school education, retained the personal independence required of a free republican citizen.[40] Bennington's leading citizens quite naturally, therefore, accepted popular maxims calling for individuals to "pledge [their] purse, [their] time, and [their] influence, for the preservation of order, intelligence, morality, and religion in the community," as well as for all citizens to "identify [themselves] with the interests of the community." Common citizens must adopt a regime of personal industry, temperance, discipline, punctuality, and honesty.[41] They should, in short, become good workers.

Slowly, then, the intense factionalism that had divided Bennington for so long began to fade.In the absence of Daniel Clark, uphill and downhill leaders began to find common ground; quite unselfconsciously they moved toward a consensus on a variety of cultural issues. Such a union gave them tremendous influence and authority in the township. So powerful was their position that any challenge to their leadership would have to come from outside the community. The death of William Morgan in neighboring New York during the summer of 1826 and the subsequent rise of the Anti-Masonic movement triggered just such a threat. By 1832 Anti-Masonry had become the most divisive force in the state of Vermont.

The first sign of Anti-Masonic sentiment in Vermont emerged in the town of Randolph in 1827.[42] Five years later Anti-Masonry dominated the state; the party organized the General Assembly from 1831 to 1835 and elected the governor from 1831 through 1834. In 1832 Vermont was the only state in the Union to cast its electoral votes for William Wirt, the Anti-Masonic presidential candidate. In addition, the movement disrupted town and county elections throughout Vermont. In many areas cadres of longtime officeholders found their power and influence shattered by the Anti-Masonic insurgency. So great was the turmoil caused during these elections that a Manchester editor bemoaned the "violence and recklessness of spirit" that characterized the Anti-Masonic movement. Even the "ties of consanguinity have not been able to stay its remorseless hand." Instead, the movement "has separated brother from brother, and thus planted daggers in the bosom of kindred affection."[43]

Anti-Masonry's core appeal in Vermont was the fervently antiaristocratic persuasion articulated throughout the state by its strongest advo-

cates. These men pictured Masons as ambitious, self-aggrandizing perpetrators of an antirepublican conspiracy that threatened to envelop
Vermont and corrupt the entire nation. The initial Anti-Masonic meeting in Randolph in May 1827 denounced Masons for establishing "an
unnatural and unwarranted distinction, a species of favoritism and aristocracy, derogatory to the equality of a free and independent people."[44]
Exclaiming that the "freemen of Vermont" were jealous of the privileges "so dearly purchased at Bennington and so bravely defended at
Plattsburgh," an Anti-Masonic editor hoped that the "noble exertions
of those opposed to secret societies" would ultimately emancipate the
state from "an institution which has so long intruded upon the equal
rights of the people."[45] Delegates to the Vermont Antimasonic Convention of 1830 attacked Freemasonry as "an aristocratic and monopolizing" institution that granted special privileges to the few while making "direct war upon the rights of the rest." By raising up an elite
without the consent of the common people, Freemasonry undermined
the basic principles of the Vermont constitution, principles that placed
"every individual in a perfect level with his neighbor as to the enjoy-
ment of all the rights and immunities" of society.[46]

The Vermont Anti-Masons focused their attacks upon "Village Aristocracy." They believed that in nearly every township of any size or
importance an "aristocracy" had emerged. If allowed to continue, these
village elites "would end in nothing short of despotism." As it was,
they constituted virtual "treason against republicanism" and should be
"made punishable by law."[47] Short of passing laws to eliminate aristocracy, however, the citizens of Vermont could band together to destroy
Freemasonry. Without the unfair advantages gained from this secret
order, village aristocracies would disappear.

This rhetorical appeal resonated with the fears and anxieties of a
great many Vermont voters caught up in the uncertainties of wrenching
change. Most areas of the state either had passed from self-sufficiency
to commercial agriculture and manufacturing or were in the process of
doing so. Some towns accomplished this transition successfully and
prospered; a great many others declined. The latter slipped further
behind the successful and prosperous townships. The same was true of
individuals and groups throughout the state. Those who were experiencing failure or a comparative loss of wealth and power searched desperately for an explanation. Many found it in Freemasonry. It seemed
to them that members of this secret sect gained unfair competitive
advantages because of their access to influential Masons in govern-

ment, who granted them special privileges. Such clandestine favors extended to business as well. It was all too clear why some prospered and others failed in what should have been a free and fair economic environment. Anti-masonry therefore spread rapidly but unevenly across the state. It did particularly well in areas experiencing decline.[48]

Those who opposed Anti-Masonry lamented that "all at once the confidence of thousands seems to be withdrawn from men of the purest lives, the brightest talents, and the most tried integrity and bestowed upon the uncertain, the discarded, and the insignificant."[49] A prominent Mason declared that he detected "a strong affinity between the prejudices of the lower classes, and the absurd declamations with which the anti-masonic publications are filled."[50] The editor of the *Burlington Sentinel* even went so far as to describe leaders of the Anti-Masonic movement in Vermont as "a mass of stupidity — a collection of individuals hardly qualified for *hog-reeves.*"[51]

The initial reaction in Bennington to the emergence of Anti-Masonry was calm and reasonable. When the editor of the *Gazette* was asked to publish the proceedings of an Anti-Masonic convention held in Manchester in late February 1829, he did not hesitate. He did, however, take the opportunity to explain that he was publishing the proceedings as "an article of news" and not from "any partiality to anti-Masonry, or approval of the popular excitement sought to be aroused." In addition, he claimed that until "further enlightened" the *Gazette* would refrain from "intermeddling in quarrels we do not understand." Intending to do "equal and exact justice to all," the *Gazette*'s editor promised to be careful neither "to inflame on one hand, nor wound on the other."[52]

Six months later the editor of the *Gazette*, apparently now "enlightened," denounced the "anti-masonic excitement" as "deplorable" and "preposterous." The only event to which he could compare it was the "persecution and hanging of persons imagined wizards and witches" in seventeenth-century Massachusetts. Far too many members of the "*black coated* gentry [ministers]" had become involved in the movement for anyone to give credence to its "proscriptive projects."[53] What disturbed him most, however, was that Anti-Masonry was assuming a "*political* character." The movement had become a "'war, famine and pestilence' project for political ascendancy"; it was little more than a vehicle for ambitious men to gain office, a means by which dissatisfied outsiders might displace responsible leaders throughout the state.[54]

By the time John C. Haswell took over as editor of the *Gazette* in January 1832, such suspicions of Anti-Masonry had been reified into political certainties. Haswell was convinced that the "enlightened yeomanry" of Vermont would soon unmask the "shallow and rotten hearted pretensions" of Anti-Masonic leaders. The "pure and patriotic" principles of "primitive" Anti-Masonry had been abandoned and utterly forgotten by the party's present leaders in their single-minded quest for power. These men cared little about Masonry; they simply made it a "cat's paw to obtain office, office, office!"[55] Haswell finally delivered his most damning opinion: "Federalism under the garb of Anti-masonry has crawled up under their wings and has sucked their very life blood."[56]

Such intense language, triggered initially by Anti-Masonry's phenomenal success at the polls, escalated as the influence of the movement spread throughout the state. Haswell witnessed traditional leaders, men accustomed to holding local office year in and year out, being replaced in town after town. No longer did the same prominent men perennially serve as selectmen; new individuals also began to act as moderators, constables, and collectors. The same was true of county positions. Once Anti-Masons gained control of the General Assembly, they were able to appoint sheriffs, states attorneys, and justices of the peace, and several counties experienced complete turnovers in these important positions.[57] It was little wonder, then, that Haswell became increasingly distraught; the entire established order in Vermont seemed to be in danger of imminent destruction at the hands of men for whom he had little respect. The editor called for Vermont's freemen to unite and "redeem the State" from the "imbecile and intriguing" Anti-Masons, who, "under a feverish excitement," had been "thrown upon the surface."[58]

If Haswell feared an Anti-Masonic insurgency in Bennington, he need not have been concerned. Both the uphill and the downhill leadership were solidly against the movement. When William Wirt carried the state in the 1832 presidential election, Bennington County gave him only 18 percent of the vote.[59] The townspeople of Bennington cast no votes for him.[60] Two years later the town gave the Anti-Masonic candidate for governor one-fourth of its ballots, but the party's congressional candidate received fewer than 3 percent of Bennington's votes.[61] Members of the Anti-Masonic party made no inroads at all in Bennington's town government. Throughout the period from 1820 to 1840 the board of selectmen remained remarkably stable. Three men served as first selectman twenty of these twenty-one years, and rarely did more than one of the other four positions change from year to year.

One man, William Henry, served as moderator of the town meeting fourteen times during this period.[62] In Bennington as in other success- ful commercial centers in the state — towns in which well-entrenched elites had emerged within an increasingly stratified social and eco- nomic environment — the "village aristocracy" held firm.[63]

Nor did First Church suffer disruptions as a result of Anti-Masonry. The divisions there stemmed from the rift that continued to simmer between James Ballard and David Robinson. Tensions within First Church ceased, however, when Hinsdill organized the Hinsdillville Presbyterian Church in November 1834. Ballard immediately with- drew from First Church and joined the congregation formed at his father-in-law's factory village. With his removal, the old church came together as one body.

Like problems in the church, cultural strains in Bennington dur- ing these years did not result from Anti-Masonry's ascendancy in the state. They stemmed from persistent divisions between supporters of the Bennington Seminary and advocates of the Bennington Academy. These tensions came to an end in February 1837, with the failure of Stephen Hinsdill's business enterprises. Grossly overextended, Hinsdill could not withstand the economic depression that settled on the nation during the winter of 1836–37. Outstanding debts of well over $150,000 forced him to liquidate his property in Bennington.[64] Immediately after Hinsdill's default became public, Ballard closed Bennington Semi- nary,[65] and Ballard and Hinsdill moved their families to Michigan.[66] Within a matter of months Bennington Academy also closed. Only Union Academy remained; this school, like the East Village, where it was located, continued to grow and prosper.

Just as the children of uphill and downhill families came together at the Union Academy, their fathers ceased battling over issues that had long divided them. Nearly every citizen of the old village attended a "Union Meeting" held on March 2, 1837, to discuss important prob- lems facing the community. Prompted by the speeches of David Robin- son Jr., Dr. Heman Swift, and others, "Union" became "the order of the day." Inspired by this spirit of cooperation, those in attendance agreed to tax themselves in order to make much-needed alterations to the meetinghouse, repair the courthouse, build a new stone jail, re- model the old jail building so that it could be used as a "town house," and establish a female seminary in the building recently vacated by Ballard. So cordial was this assembly of old rivals that Hiram Harwood left the meeting convinced that there was to be "No *Old Line* nor

Pioneer—No *up Hill* nor *down Hill* hereafter." In his opinion, "The era of good feelings" had finally come to Bennington.[67]

At the same time that uphill and downhill leaders reached an accord on local matters, though, they were vigorously attacking one another over political issues affecting the state and the nation. Editor John Haswell dubbed Hiland Hall the "Panic Candidate" for Congress in 1836 and upbraided him for being "the advocate and supporter of the measures of a reckless opposition" and an advocate of the "*rag-money-monopoly system* in Congress."[68] When Pierpont Isham and Martin Deming ran for the state senate in 1839, Haswell exploded that no two men in the state were "so totally federal in all their opinions and sentiments." Neither had "one principle or feeling in harmony with republicanism, a drop of democratic blood never warmed their hearts." Both men were "aristocrats, who would make money the only evidence of worth or respectability."[69] The following year, the *Gazette* questioned whether Noadiah Swift was a suitable candidate for the state senate. After all, the people expected bank reform from their senators, but Swift had been president of the Bank of Bennington for years. In addition, the *Gazette* accused him of transferring bank stock to his son previous to being nominated so that he could campaign for office free of the charge of being a stockholder in a bank.[70]

This intense partisanship resulted from the political alliances that formed in Bennington following Andrew Jackson's election in 1828. Uphill leaders became ardent followers of the Old Hero and his Democratic party, while the leadership of the downhill community fervently supported Jackson's opponents, the National Republicans. Since Jackson's election came at the height of the fight over Rev. Daniel Clark, these political divisions seemed entirely appropriate. The egalitarian rhetoric of the Jacksonians resonated with the yeoman persuasion cherished by uphill leaders. So, too, did the Jacksonian emphasis upon republicanism and the party's laissez-faire social and economic attitudes. If the uphill leaders' intense localism and desire for individual autonomy drew them to the Democratic party, the cosmopolitanism of the downhill leadership, as well as a belief in moral suasion that emanated from their more organic view of society, led the downhill community to support the National Republicans.

By the mid-1830s, when uphill and downhill leaders were reaching a consensus on fundamental community issues, the rhetoric of the competing political parties set their respective advocates against one another with a vengeance. It was as if political ideas had taken on a life of

their own — an autonomous power — that shaped people's consciousness and behavior quite independent of their own will. Thus, Jacksonians in Bennington, taking their cues from the national press, railed
against banks, corporations, internal improvements at federal expense,
monopolies, paper money, and aristocracy, while stoutly affirming their
allegiance to equal rights, republicanism, democracy, and the people.[71] Bennington's National Republicans stood behind the Bank of the
United States, internal improvements, tariffs, paper money, corporations, and support for manufacturers; they vehemently opposed the
independent treasury, the Specie Circular, and executive authority.[72]

 Actually, the exigencies of the national political dialogue placed Bennington's uphill leaders in an increasingly tenuous position. Previous to
Jackson's election they had supported banking, internal improvements,
manufactures, high tariffs, and even the American System as essential
for the growth and prosperity of their community.[73] During the 1830s,
however, these principles became the stock and trade of the Whigs, the
party label assumed by National Republicans in the 1830s. This left the
uphill people in Bennington with little more than rhetorical issues
stemming from their emotional attachment to the Jacksonian attack on
aristocracy. Thus, when a convention of Bennington County Whigs
called on the "yeomanry of the country" to oppose Jackson's veto of the
Bank of the United States, the editor of the *Gazette* labeled this assembly a collection of the "rich gentry" of the county. He was certain
that the freemen of Bennington County would ignore such "dictation"
from the area's "nobility." He declared that every National Republican
believed it was "of more consequence to sustain the U.S. Bank than it
is to sustain the liberties of our country"; that it was right and just that
"rich speculators of our country should have the privilege of investing
their money where it will make 12 per cent and be free from all taxation"; and that "every owner in rich manufacturing establishments
ought to make a clear profit every day of at least 100 dollars without
reference to the capital he has invested."[74] The *Gazette*'s Democratic
editor grew increasingly shrill. In his opinion, Whigs in Vermont must
be voted out of power because they "have shingled the State over with
BANKS AND CORPORATIONS, which, like putrid canker sores, are gnawing upon the vitals of the body politic — consuming the wages of Labor,
eating up the profits of Industry, and making THE RICH RICHER and
THE POOR POORER."[75]

 Bennington Whigs too became embroiled in the passions of the day.
Two of their party's leaders, Isaac Tichenor and Isaac Doolittle, de-

nounced Andrew Jackson as an "assassin, duelist, horse racer and anything but a statesman."[76] Caught up in the rhetorical warfare raging
throughout the state and nation, a convention of Bennington County
Whigs declared that when "the patronage of the government is pros-
tituted for the purposes of party aggrandizement" and the "institutions
of government are polluted by the very hands which should preserve
them pure and unsullied," the people should "fearlessly meet such ag-
gressions upon their rights, and award to the violators, the punishment
which the law places in their hands." It was the duty of all freemen in
the county "professing the Whig principles of the revolution" to "resist
the introduction into this state of the office holder's system of politics."
All true Whigs must oppose the effort to "perpetuate the principles of
Gen. Jackson" — to "fasten upon the country the despotism of a party,
having for its object, not 'the benefit of the governed,' but 'the spoils of
victory.' "[77]

    Democratic emotions reached a fever pitch during the annual cele-
bration of the battle of Bennington on August 16, 1840. After electing
Merrill president of the day, a massive gathering of the party faithful heard ex-governor Cornelius Van Ness articulate their most visceral feelings. Insisting that political confrontations in all governments
"have been the *few* struggling against the masses of men, and usurping
their rights," Van Ness linked his Whig opponents directly to aristocratic Federalists such as Alexander Hamilton and John Adams. For
him, the Whigs' use of the log cabin prophesied "the future condition
of the masses of men," in which the many would be "reduced to log-
cabin habitations for themselves and their families." Van Ness charged
that Whig policies, rather than securing the fruits of their labor to
hardworking yeomen, merely transformed plain citizens into "beasts of
burden" forced to serve the interests of the "grasping avarice, venality,
and rapacity of the few." In order to make the mass of citizens "manage-
able," the Whigs considered it "necessary to make them poorer, and
the rich, richer." This was, in fact, the logical outcome of the "anti-
republican tendencies" of the Whig party. Only the staunch republicanism of the Democratic party could save the state and the nation
from such degradation.[78]

    Despite such Democratic efforts, the election of 1840 confirmed
what had been apparent for some time, namely, that the town of
Bennington and the state of Vermont had become bastions of Whig
strength. Vermont delivered William Henry Harrison the largest majority in proportion to the number of votes cast of any state in the

Union.[79] All five of Vermont's congressmen and both of the state's U.S. senators were Whigs. The party's gubernatorial candidate won in a landslide and enjoyed large majorities in both houses of the state legislature.[80] In Bennington, Whig presidential electors triumphed by a comfortable margin, Hiland Hall won his congressional race easily, and the Whig candidate for the General Assembly won by a wide margin.[81]

While there was no doubt of Whig dominance in Bennington by 1840, the party had changed over the years. The Bennington Whigs who celebrated William Henry Harrison's victory were very different from the town's National Republicans who had supported John Quincy Adams over a decade before. Stephen Hinsdill, James Ballard, William Lloyd Garrison, and Daniel Clark had moved away; Isaac Tichenor, Aaron Robinson, Elijah Dewey, and Moses Robinson Jr. were dead. In their absence the moral authoritarianism and elitism of the party gave way before the more utilitarian perspective of men such as Hiland Hall and Hiram Harwood, second-generation residents who had been raised within the Jeffersonian Republican tradition. The democratic capitalism of Hiland Hall, rather than the cosmopolitan elitism of Isaac Tichenor or Aaron Robinson, permeated the language of these new Whigs.

Hall always considered himself a man of the people, a true Jeffersonian. He invariably emphasized traditional values such as the "vigilance of freemen" as the primary means for retaining a republican government and society. In America the people were sovereign, but only through "intelligence & vigilance" could they retain "the privileges & preeminence of free men."[82] In Congress he lauded the "purely republican" habits of Vermonters, the way they judged governmental actions in "accordance with their republican principles." It was just such principles that caused the people of Vermont to oppose measures that promoted "the aristocratical accumulation and transmission of wealth in particular families."[83]

In Hall's mind, Andrew Jackson, by assaulting the Bank of the United States "under color of attacking "aristocratical monopolists," was actually "waging a destructive war upon the labor and business of the country." Because of Jackson's war on the national bank, ordinary citizens — farmers, manufacturers, mechanics, and laborers — saw their fortunes declining. Unless stopped, Jackson's actions would "transfer a large share of the property of the country into the hands of capitalists, and leave in poverty and want a great portion of that class of society which is below them in wealth." Placing himself in that "lower class,"

Hall entered a solemn protest against the war on "aristocrats" that the president was inviting him to join. It was perfectly obvious to all who would see that at the end of Jackson's war, "the 'aristocrats' will bear off the 'spoils' and the 'glory,' and 'all the blows will fall upon us.' "[84]

To emphasize his own opposition to "aristocracy," Hall associated himself with the egalitarian tradition of Ethan Allen and the Green Mountain Boys. On July 4, 1840, while introducing Daniel Webster to the Stratton Mountain convention, Hall skillfully linked the Whigs' log cabin with "the names & deeds of our Chittenden, our Allens, our Warner and of all those who as the fathers of our state we love dearest & prize highest." Then in a burst of passion he exclaimed that any "son of the Green Mountains who would discard the log cabin as an unfit emblem of his patriotism & love of liberty, would voluntarily dishonor the memory of his fathers & shake hands with the slanderer of the mother that bore him."[85]

This was not the first time that Hall linked himself and the Whig party with the Green Mountain Boys. In fact, he did so regularly in his speeches on the floor of Congress and during local party celebrations of the Fourth of July and the battle of Bennington. On one of the latter occasions he characteristically arose to toast "Thomas Chittenden, and the Seven farmers of Vermont" as men whose "diplomatic skill, during two years, defended the northern frontier against an army of 10,000 men."[86] Once, while speaking in Congress, he exclaimed in no uncertain terms that while Jackson's actions might be acceptable in Washington, D.C., they would be renounced in Vermont. Quoting Ethan Allen, Hall declared that "the gods of the valleys are not the gods of the hills." Then he boldly predicted that the "sons of the whigs of '75," those brave men who were "the first in the land to proclaim the authority of the 'Continental Congress' within the walls of a fortress of the Crown," would not "tamely submit to see the rights of that Congress, or any portion of it, trampled under the foot of prerogative power." While Hall did not want his listeners to suppose that "the 'Green Mountain Boys' [would] resort to any violent or illegal measures," he did want them to know that the proud citizens of Vermont would certainly "unite with their brother whigs throughout the Union" to overthrow executive tyranny by means of the "peaceable, constitutional, truth-telling, power-enlightening ballot-box."[87]

Bennington's Democrats were not to be outdone. They too praised the sovereignty of the people, lauded the egalitarian values of the Green Mountain Boys, and attacked aristocracy. John C. Haswell wondered in

the *Gazette* what had become of "that sterling independence, that ab-
horrence and detestation of tyranny, exhibited by our forefathers." Was
it possible, he asked, that "descendants of Ethan Allen, and his copatri-
ots should have become so debased, so servile, as to cringe and fawn
around the palace of a monied aristocrat?"[88] In another attack on Vermont's Whig congressmen, the fiery editor asked if it were "possible
that the enlightened Green Mountain Boys can approve of the conduct
of the Bank."[89] This identification with past heroes became standard
fare at Democratic celebrations, where participants repeatedly toasted
the wisdom and diplomacy of "the eight Farmers of Vermont. Gov.
Chittenden and his associates" and the courage and character of the
Green Mountain Boys.[90] David Robinson Jr., O. C. Merrill, and John S.
Robinson spoke passionately against the "Monied Power." They too
saw the "great conflict between the democracy and monied interests of
the country." They too warned the townspeople of Bennington against
being "robbed of your birthrights by a monied aristocracy."[91] The great
question of the day for Bennington's Democratic leaders was, "Which
shall be master, the Banks or the People?" Elections for them became
battlegrounds "between the Banks and the People; Between the rich
monopolist and wealthy stockholder and the great mass of community."
For these men, then, nothing could be clearer: the Democratic party
represented "Equal Rights and Privileges" for all citizens, while Whigs
fostered wealth and special privilege for the few at the expense of the
many.[92]

The similarity between Whig and Democratic appeals revealed the
emergence of a new political culture in Bennington. No longer did
the dialectic between uphill egalitarianism and downhill elitism shape
the town's political dialogue. Now both parties espoused the democratic ethos of the uphill community. Whig and Democratic leaders
alike championed the ideals of equality, opportunity, individualism, and
free enterprise. In essence, these men competed with one another in
their efforts to embrace the yeoman persuasion of Ethan Allen, Matthew Lyon, and Anthony Haswell. By so doing — and by attacking one
another as enemies of the yeoman — they obscured the similarity of
their own social and economic interests.

The triumph of the yeoman persuasion in Bennington was, however,
more symbolic than real; it represented a victory of rhetoric over reality. Far from being an egalitarian community, Bennington had become
a hierarchically structured, economically stratified town in which the
extremes of inequality increased with each passing decade. A core of

relatively affluent families controlled a disproportionate share of the land, wealth, and power in the town, while great numbers of landless poor passed through the area during any single year.[93] By 1840 two distinct populations, one stable, the other highly mobile, resided within the town limits at any given time.[94] Bennington had become a town in which the great majority of its inhabitants — transient day laborers, tenant farmers, and mill workers — enjoyed very little of the equality or the opportunity being praised so ardently by Whigs and Democrats alike.

That Bennington was not a community of equals — that some residents had a great deal more than others — did not particularly disturb either the town's Whig or its Democratic leaders. Inequality seemed quite natural to them. Their equanimity stemmed from the yeoman image they embraced so passionately, an image that had undergone subtle transformations since Ethan Allen and the Green Mountain Boys thwarted New York authority more than a half-century earlier. Then the figure of the yeoman had symbolized equality, the displacement of an aristocratic society of special privilege with an open, competitive one composed of common citizens. By the 1840s, however, the image of the yeoman had become far more libertarian. The attacks by Matthew Lyon, Thomas Chittenden, and others upon artificial barriers to equality had not led to social or material equality. Instead, their principles eventually supported the idea that every man should enjoy equal opportunities to establish superiority over his competitors. The egalitarian ethos underlying their actions had gradually been transmuted into a belief system that not only justified inequality but embraced it as morally acceptable.

Far from diminishing or eliminating inequalities in their society, the yeoman persuasion espoused by Hiland Hall, David Robinson Jr., and others helped perpetuate them. It was not that these men lacked Matthew Lyon's or Anthony Haswell's deep commitment to equality. They embraced the concept with identical fervor. Equality to them, however, meant equality of opportunity, and equality of opportunity presumed a vast array of differences in talents and abilities. If some prospered while others failed, it was only because they worked harder or had greater ability than their less successful colleagues. All that was required of any society was fairness; each person must have an equal chance to compete with all others. Where such equality of opportunity existed, effort and talent would naturally create distinct differences in social status.

In a truly free society, then, inequality was not only legitimate, it was ethically justifiable. To believe otherwise was to doubt the validity of the yeoman persuasion itself—to doubt the individual initiative, personal autonomy, and free enterprise upon which a truly republican society rested. None of Bennington's political leaders raised such a question. How could they? To doubt these principles was to doubt the very meaning and identity of their own lives. It was little wonder, then, that they accepted without reflection the premise that Bennington actually was a fair and open society. The town's Whig and Democratic leaders never doubted that the son of a tenant farmer or a mill hand had the same opportunity to make something of himself as one of their own children. After all, he had access to the town's common schools, was free to vote in town meetings, and could find gainful employment on their farms or in their factories.

Even though they were united in their confidence in the equitable nature of their community, Bennington's leaders did experience significant divisiveness following the elections of 1840, when many of the longstanding changes affecting the town intensified greatly. East Village continued to outstrip the older community on the hill in population, prosperity, and commercial opportunity. Serious tensions resulted from this growing inequality.[95] The first overt indication of strife came when the courthouse burned on October 26, 1846. Citizens from the East Village immediately began an earnest and persistent effort to have the state government place the new courthouse in their community. The legislature appointed a committee to determine the location of the new building, and in January 1847 committee members held a public hearing in Bennington. Residents of both communities crowded into old First Church to hear A. P. Lyman support the claims of the East Village and John S. Robinson argue in favor of the original site on Courthouse Hill. Much to the chagrin of East Village residents, the committee decided in favor of the old village. The new building would not, however, be built on Courthouse Hill; instead, the committee chose a site opposite the First Church cemetery.[96]

Whatever relief residents of the hill felt as a result of retaining the courthouse soon turned to consternation. Within a month after the legislative committee's favorable decision, John C. Haswell moved his printing office and the *Vermont Gazette* to the East Village. Being postmaster, he quite literally took that office with him as well. Since he owned the building that housed the post office, Haswell simply placed it on skids and had it pulled down the hill by a team of oxen. Hundreds of East Village residents turned out to cheer the appearance of the building, and church bells rang out in joyous observance of the occasion. This celebration did not last long, however. David Robinson, John S. Robinson, and Benjamin Fay traveled to Washington, D.C., and demanded that Postmaster General Cave Johnson replace Haswell as postmaster and return the post office to their village. Johnson did not remove Haswell, but he did require that the office be returned to its original site.

Returning the office to the hill did not end the strife between the two communities. Angry over the removal of the *Gazette*, several men in the old village began publication of a new newspaper under the same name. A bitter struggle ensued between the editors of the two papers. Haswell had a distinct advantage: as postmaster he controlled all mail addressed to both newspapers. Soon the editors of the new *Gazette* began to encounter certain difficulties. Important material meant for them was often lost or delivered to their competitor. The aggrieved editors complained to the postmaster general, who replaced Haswell as Bennington's postmaster on January 25, 1848, and later that year Haswell emigrated to San Francisco. Even without competition, the newspaper on the hill could not survive. In October 1850 the *Vermont Gazette*, the voice of the Democratic party in Vermont for over half a century, fell silent. The *State Banner*, a Whig paper published in the East Village, was now the community's only newspaper.

By the time the *Gazette* closed, the post office was back in East Village. It was a sign of the times: East Village was rapidly eclipsing Old Bennington. The village on the hill contained barely four hundred inhabitants, the courthouse, First Church, four stores, and several mechanic's shops.[97] Its competitor had a population of nearly four thousand, four churches, a great many stores, quite a number of flourishing artisan's shops, and numerous streets lined with private dwellings.[98] Several iron foundries, as well as numerous cotton and woolen mills, occupied choice sites along the town's streams. In addition, rows of two-story structures fronted these establishments to house the ever-growing number of workers required to operate the spindles and other machinery so essential to the town's prosperity. On July 12, 1849, the inevitable occurred: the postmaster general awarded the venerable old name of Bennington to East Village, renaming the old village West Bennington. In response to a fervent petition from residents on the hill, however, the postmaster general changed the name of the latter to Bennington Centre.

Bennington in 1850 was a very different place from the village founded nearly ninety years before. Once composed of self-sufficient farmers with a strong attachment to the land, now less than 13 percent of the town's male population owned any real estate at all.[99] The decennial increase of population came largely from an influx of young Irish men and women, who worked in the mills for a season or two and then moved on.[100] Still, the emphasis upon an independent yeomanry remained. The town's leaders continued to trumpet the principles of liberal individualism. The church, the home, and the common school, they insisted, produced solid republican citizens — well-informed, self-reliant persons who jealously guarded their own freedom of action. As the social and economic stratification of the town intensified, so, too, did the fervor with which its most prominent residents glorified ideals such as initiative, individualism, personal freedom, and independence. From their perspective, individual freedom and choice characterized the community, because every citizen of Bennington enjoyed the same social and economic opportunities. Ordinary folk had only to apply themselves and self-discipline and hard work would bring sure rewards.

With the passage of time, then, the egalitarian community envisioned by Bennington's New Light founders had become a liberal democracy — materialistic, utilitarian, aggressively individualistic, and inequitable. Under the pressure of rapidly changing socioeconomic conditions the independent yeomen, the sturdy mainstays of an egalitarian communalism, gradually became the ambitious, self-made men who set themselves against neighbors and community alike. Simultaneously, however, the yeoman persuasion persisted; it continued to foster a rhetoric of selfless virtue that obscured the direction in which Bennington society was moving. By indirectly promoting the desire for unrestrained enterprise, through an appeal to popular virtue — the reification of an independent yeomanry — Bennington's Whig and Democratic leaders helped produce a society of capitalists who were oblivious to the spirit of their own enterprise. Thus were they able to define their purpose as the promotion of traditional communal values, while actually hurling themselves into the desperate pursuit of individual material gain. Over the years Samuel Robinson's independent yeoman had become Hiland Hall's democratic capitalist. Yet few in Bennington perceived the difference. The strength of the yeoman persuasion was such that, like a veil, it obscured all actions or circumstances that might contradict it. Ironically, the Green Mountain Boys assumed a central role in this process.

Partisan attempts to associate either the Whig or the Democratic party with Ethan Allen and his stalwart band became increasingly wide-spread. Such tremendously popular appeals resonated with a vague but nonetheless deeply felt uneasiness in a great many Vermonters. These people sought to escape the hyperbole and hypocrisy associated with such vitriolic conflicts as those raging between advocates of the Pioneer Line and the Old Line, between supporters of the seminary and the academy, or between the editors of the *Gazette* and the *Times*. For his part, Hiram Harwood found refuge from these disputatious clashes in the correspondence between Governor Tryon and "the real old Green Mountain Boys whose answers and statements were unvarnished, fearless, energetic, and powerful."[101] Harwood was not the only one to feel the appeal of the Green Mountain Boys, who were perceived as common, ordinary men of true integrity and character. Many of his fellow townspeople, longing for relief from the unsettling changes of their own day, also identified with these figures from a simpler and seemingly more forthright past.

Such longings gave force to Whig and Democratic claims to be the true heirs of Ethan Allen and the Green Mountain Boys, men whose reputation had gone into virtual eclipse following the Federalist victories during the War of 1812. These claims were, however, merely political manifestations of a much larger phenomenon that swept the state throughout the 1830s and 1840s. During this time an outpouring of popular literature transformed Ethan Allen and the Green Mountain Boys into cultural icons, symbolic figures who helped ease or even obscure the anxieties and contradictions accompanying the emergence of a liberal democratic culture.

Zadock Thompson's *History of the State of Vermont* (1833) gave many readers their first glimpse of Vermont's past. This slender volume told of plain and simple pioneers on the New Hampshire Grants who overcame countless hardships to carve productive farms out of a trackless wilderness. Having accomplished this, however, Thompson's intrepid settlers found themselves facing expulsion at the hands of New York aristocrats. At this point the Green Mountain Boys, forced to become outlaws to protect what was rightfully theirs, arose to defend their fellow settlers from avaricious New York officials. Commanded by the "bold, ardent and unyielding" Ethan Allen, the Green Mountain Boys were successful.[102] Then, according to Thompson, the outbreak of the American Revolution inspired this same band of ardent whigs to enlist gallantly in the American cause. Led by steadfast patriots like Ethan and Ira Allen, Thomas Chittenden, and the Council of Safety, Vermont not only gained its own independence but protected the northern border of the United States from a British invasion. In fact, these "sagacious and daring individuals, secured, by their negotiations and management [the Haldimand negotiations of 1781–82], the extensive frontier of Vermont, which was exposed to an army of ten thousand of the enemy."[103] Thompson's portrayal of Vermont subsequent to its admission into the Union was one of steady adherence to republican principles by a sturdy citizenry composed of independent husbandmen.

A year after Thompson's book appeared, Jared Sparks provided Vermont citizens a nearly identical narrative of their state's early history in his biography of Ethan Allen. Here too readers encountered settlers on the New Hampshire Grants, "at home on the soil, which they had subdued by their own labor," uniting in common cause against autocratic New York officials bent upon ejecting them from their homes so that wealthy speculators might take control of the land. So unified were these settlers, however, that "to drive one of them from his house, or deprive him of his hard-earned substance, was to threaten the whole community with an issue fatal alike to their dearest interests, and to the rights, which every man deems as sacred as life itself." Banding together, these people created committees of safety "organized on the strictest republican principles, being created and constituted by the people themselves, acting at first voluntarily in their individual capacity, and agreeing to be controlled by the voice of a majority."[104]

The leader of these stalwart republican bands was, of course, Ethan Allen. In fact, Allen became a representative figure in Sparks's narrative of the Revolutionary epoch in Vermont. Admitting Allen's "roughness of manners and coarseness of speech," his "presumptuous way of reasoning upon all subjects," and his "religious skepticism," Sparks attributed these flaws to a "want of early education" and to "habits acquired by his pursuits in a rude and uncultivated state of society." He believed that Allen merited a "charitable judgement" despite these handicaps. Describing him as "brave, generous, and frank, true to his friends, true to his country, consistent and unyielding in his purposes, seeking at all times to promote the best interests of mankind, a lover of social harmony, and a determined foe to the artifices of injustice and the encroachments of power," Sparks contended that "whatever may have been his peculiarities," Allen stood as the foremost figure in the creation of the state. An honest, self-sacrificing man of the people, Ethan Allen exemplified the best qualities of the yeomanry of Vermont.[105]

Among those writing about their state's past, none was as popular as Judge Daniel P. Thompson. His two historical novels, *The Green Mountain Boys* (1839) and *The Rangers* (1851), went through dozens of editions, to the great delight of Vermonters, who were captivated by the figures out of their state's past that peopled Thompson's romantic sagas. The initial settlers on the Grants, "a generation of no ordinary men," emerged in these pages as "a crop of hardy, determined, and liberty-loving men." Opposing the powerful government of New York, they stepped "boldly and confidently forth for some extraordinary enterprise, of which the hazard and difficulty are so great, that nothing but an uncommon union of courage and strength can accomplish it."[106] Following their success in that venture, these same men gathered together at Windsor in 1777 to create a civil government "suited to the genius and necessities of an industrious and frugal people."[107]

Thompson believed that it was on the battlefield at Bennington, however, that Vermont's first citizens truly proved their mettle. On that day in August 1777, "every man in the ranks of freedom, though frequently wholly untrained, and in battle for the first time in his life, at once became a warrior, fighting as if the whole responsibility of the issue of the battle rested on his own shoulders." Wherever one looked, "deeds were performed by nameless peasants rivalling the most daring exploits of heroes." At one point, "a company of raw militia might be seen rushing upon a detached column of British veterans, firing in their faces, and, for want of bayonets, knocking them down with clubbed muskets." At another location, "old men and boys, with others who, like them, had come unarmed and as spectators of the battle, would spring forward after some retreating band, seize the muskets of the slain, and engage, muzzle to muzzle, with the hated foe."[108] Everywhere, "the plain and hardy sons of liberty, unflinchingly engaged face to face, and often arm to arm, in deadly strife with the gorgeous and disciplined bands of their outnumbering foes" until victory was theirs.[109]

Ethan Allen, a "chivalrous" man of "many high and noble qualities, combined with extraordinary powers of body and mind," emerged as a nearly larger-than-life figure in Thompson's epic tales.[110] He was by no means alone. Readers gained fresh insight into other heroes whose names had become tarnished over the years. Remember Baker, who was recalled, if at all, as an irresponsible rabble-rouser, proved to be "one of the most shrewd, sagacious, and coolly calculating" of all the Green Mountain Boys.[111] Matthew Lyon, long the bane of every conservative gentleman, now exhibited a "clear, ardent, and fearless countenance" in which "might be read the promise of what he was to become — the stern democrat, and the well-known champion of the whole right and the largest liberty."[112] Even Ira Allen, driven from Vermont in poverty and ignominy by his Federalist opponents, turned out to be a "Green Mountain Metternich."[113] No reader caught up in Judge Thompson's stories could doubt that when Ira Allen's real story was finally told, it would "show him to have been, either secretly or openly, the originator, or successful prosecutor, of more important political measures, affecting the interests and independence of the state, and the issue of the war in the Northern Department, than any other individual in Vermont." Indeed, the state of Vermont might never have come into being "but for the bold and characteristic project of Ira Allen."[114]

Thomas Chittenden and his Council of Safety, reviled and ridiculed for so long by Isaac Tichenor, Nathaniel Chipman, and their Federalist cohorts, also materialized as simple but true heroes in Thompson's stories. Chittenden, a man of "good sense, great discretion, firmness, honesty of purpose, benevolence, and unvarying equanimity of temper," left "behind him an honest, enduring fame — a memorial of good deeds and useful every-day examples, to be remembered and quoted . . . when the far superior brilliancy of many a contemporary had passed away and been forgotten."[115] Members of the council had displayed not only remarkable wisdom and good judgment but also incredible restraint. They had held positions of extraordinary power, and yet "this power, absolute and dictatorial as it was, they never abused or exercised but for the public good."[116] After reading Thompson's volumes, it must have been a rare individual indeed who did not believe that egalitarians such as those portrayed in these grand stories made up Vermont's great heritage.

Following the appearance of Thompson's *Green Mountain Boys*, the impulse to canonize the state's democratic forebears became irresistible. Daniel Chipman, brother of Nathaniel Chipman and a conservative member of the legal profession himself, published highly laudatory biographies of Seth Warner and Thomas Chittenden. He even appended Jared Sparks's biography of Ethan Allen to his own volume on Warner.[117] B. H. Kinney, a young woodcarver from Bennington County, made Ethan Allen the subject of his first creation. Raised on stories of the exploits of the Green Mountain Boys, Kinney felt the image of the "fearless and true-hearted Hero of Ticonderoga" become stronger as he grew to manhood and "witnessed the neglect of duty to their country, in the pursuit of selfish ends, so characteristic of a considerable portion of the prominent men of this age."[118] The result was an enormous wooden statue of Ethan Allen standing in full military regalia with a look of indomitable determination fixed on his noble brow. Even though Kinney was born long after Allen's death and no portrait had ever been drawn of Allen, thousands of Vermonters came away from the statue convinced that it was an exact likeness of the Green Mountain hero.[119] When the historian Henry De Puy used an engraving of the statue as the frontispiece to a book about Allen and the Green Mountain Boys, such an impression became all the more believable. This was especially true since De Puy's title page included a picture of Allen, drawn with the statue as a model, over a reproduction of Ethan's actual signature. The historian's blending of art and life, imagination and reality, was now complete.

For most Vermonters, De Puy's *Ethan Allen and the Green-Mountain Heroes of '76* (1853) and *The Mountain Hero and His Associates* (1855) bestowed the stamp of historical authenticity on Kinney's likeness and the novels of Daniel Thompson.[120] Indeed, it was often difficult to distinguish between De Puy's history and Thompson's fiction. In fact, De Puy quoted liberally from the judge's novels. Like the figures in those books, in De Puy's portrayal of the Revolutionary period the common people of Vermont endured innumerable hardships and great privation. Nonetheless, between the time they declared themselves an independent republic and the moment they entered the Union as the fourteenth state, "they existed as a thorough democracy; all laws and regulations, as well as the time and manner of their enforcement in particular instances, being decided upon in general meetings of the people."[121] Members of the old Council of Safety, those "Seven Farmers of Vermont," also emerged as staunch patriots. Basing his findings on papers "never before published," De Puy declared that when the full history of the Haldimand negotiations was "properly written," it would reveal beyond the shadow of a doubt that "the odium cast upon the names of these men [the Council of Safety] is grossly unjust." Not only were these individuals "inspired by the purest devotion to the cause of liberty" but their actions "actually kept at bay a large hostile army, which otherwise would have been able to march throughout the northern portion of the union . . . and to crush the hopes of freedom." De Puy left no doubt that Ethan and Ira Allen, Thomas Chittenden, and their associates deserved "the lasting admiration and gratitude of those who enjoy the blessings of the freedom which their services so greatly aided in establishing."[122]

With the publication of De Puy's volumes, the heroic images of Ethan Allen, the Green Mountain Boys, and the common settlers on the Grants achieved legitimacy in the minds of contemporary Vermonters. Caught up in the anxieties and uncertainties of a rapidly changing time, these people gained great comfort from a vicarious association with noble men of a more selfless, communal era. To identify with Ethan Allen and the Green Mountain Boys encouraged them to view themselves and their own society in democratic terms; believing that they still lived in a fluid environment that offered every citizen the same opportunity for social advancement and economic independence gave them a reassuring sense of self-satisfaction and personal accomplishment.

Paradoxically, the Green Mountain Boys, who had overcome an eighteenth-century aristocratic elite, now helped ease the minds of individuals busily engaged in creating a nineteenth-century liberal elite, an elite based more broadly on talent and merit, but an elite nonetheless. It was, however, an elite whose members remained equally blind to their own advantages and the disadvantages of many of those around them. Believing that a nearly perfect opportunity for social mobility already existed in Bennington, and that it existed for everyone, they never questioned their own political, social, or economic beliefs. Men like David Robinson Jr., Hiland Hall, and John S. Robinson quite innocently viewed themselves as the same sort of resolute democrats as those who had fended off New York aristocrats, defeated the British, and forged an independent republic. And they viewed their community as being in every way as true a democracy as the one created by the Green Mountain Boys. Thus, after his election as governor in 1858, Hiland Hall proudly announced to the General Assembly, without the slightest trace of disingenuousness, that Vermont's state government was "emphatically a people's government, being more purely democratic in its character than any other in America, and probably in the world."[123] Like so many others, Hall fervently espoused the principles and ethics of democracy. To substantiate his allegiance to these values, he identified wholeheartedly with Ethan Allen and the Green Mountain Boys. Abstracted from their eighteenth-century egalitarian world, these men became symbols of Vermont's nineteenth-century liberal democracy. The gods of the valleys were now the gods of the hills as well.

Epilogue: A Monument to Democracy

Dawn emerged clear and beautiful in Bennington, Vermont, the morning of August 19, 1891. To the thousands of soldiers and civilians gathering on the grounds of the Soldier's Home and along the streets of the town the pleasant weather was an auspicious beginning to a special day. This day would mark not only the anniversary celebration of Vermont's hundredth year of statehood but also the dedication of a recently completed monument commemorating the American victory at the battle of Bennington on August 16, 1777.[1]

Promptly at 10:00 A.M. a procession of military units, civic organizations, bands, drum corps, and more than one hundred carriages began a grand march through town. The nearly five thousand participants in the parade included the president of the United States, the governors of Vermont, Massachusetts, and New Hampshire, and a great many other prominent military and civilian dignitaries. More than eight thousand people crowded the streets and housetops of Bennington to catch sight of these luminaries and to cheer the bands as they performed martial music along the parade route. When the procession turned onto Main Street it passed beneath the "Triumphal Arch," a temporary structure created for the occasion out of timber and canvas painted to resemble a great stone fortress. One hundred seventy-five young girls from the town's public schools dressed entirely in white sang patriotic songs while perched along the structure's uppermost battlement. A solitary young lady occupied a turret at the very top of the fortress. Dressed as the Goddess of Liberty, she sat on a golden throne holding the American flag. As Benjamin Harrison's carriage approached the arch the president stood and took off his hat. The Goddess of Liberty rose from her throne and returned the salute. Then, as his carriage passed beneath them, the young ladies in white began to sing "America" and showered the president with rose petals.[2]

After passing through the arch the parade began its ascent of a steep hill at the western edge of town. Near the crest it passed old First Church. At this point the procession followed the road as it curved to the right and began to climb yet another incline toward the massive stone monument looming in the distance. Between the church and the monument the parade passed a few scattered homes — all that remained of the original village of Bennington — on its way to State Arms Hill, where the great stone obelisk stood. State Arms Hill, named for the tavern located there, had once proudly been known as Courthouse Hill. The county courthouse, however, had long since been relocated down the hill in the town now bearing the name Bennington. Indeed, even the old State Arms Tavern, constructed before the end of the Revolutionary War and the site of many democratic rallies, would soon be razed in order to make room for a park to enhance the grandeur of the new monument.

Throughout the dedication ceremony and the subsequent banquet celebrating Vermont's centennial anniversary various dignitaries delivered speeches in honor of the occasion. In one manner or another each of them attempted to articulate the larger meaning of the day. All, however, echoed the chaplain's fervent declaration not only that "this is Thy chosen land, and we are Thy people" but that God's word, "the inspiration of personal freedom," had taught Vermont's founding fathers "to sigh for individual liberty." Heeding his entreaty to sanctify the "patriotic lessons" of the day, the speakers eulogized the development of personal freedom within Vermont and took satisfaction in the fact that it had been securely enshrined not only in the democratic institutions of that state but throughout the entire nation.[3]

Each speaker told his version of Vermont's past; together, their stories portrayed a heroic tableau beginning on the New Hampshire Grants in the 1760s. There, in a howling wilderness claimed by both New York and New Hampshire, a small band of "plain, unassuming, upright, resolute, God-fearing men" struggled "not for place or distinction or wealth or power, but to achieve self-government, to establish homes, to create civil institutions that should be truly free, salutary, and enduring." Manfully resisting the aristocratic government of New York, these "yoemen [sic] in that dreadful time showed themselves worthy of the men who had fought under the banner of William the Silent." After declaring themselves an independent republic, Vermonters created their own constitution. "Framed by a rural people, in hardship and poverty . . . its authors neither statesmen nor lawyers," these people toiled "under every discouragement, with such slender acquirements as they had, toward the foundation of a government that might command the respect of mankind." And they succeeded. Vermont was the first state to prohibit slavery and to establish universal male suffrage, and its constitution stood as a bulwark of democracy. Indeed, many of its provisions would become part of the fundamental law of the whole nation.

Nor did the speakers' saga end there. No sooner had the constitution been written than it and the republic it symbolized had to be defended against a British invasion. On August 16, 1777, John Stark, Seth Warner, and the Green Mountain Boys — men lacking bayonets, training, and "everything but hardihood and indomitable resolution" — met the British regulars at Bennington. There, "upon all known rules and experience of warfare, the successful storming, by a hastily organized militia, of an entrenched position at the top of a hill, held by an adequate regular force, would have been declared impossible." But on that fateful day the impossible actually occurred. In one of the great battles of all time, a courageous group of New England militiamen routed a veteran force of disciplined troops and saved not only Vermont but the entire nation.

Vermont's unique struggle as a separate republic came to an end in 1791, when it joined the Union as the fourteenth state. In the opinion of the orators a hundred years later, "absolute freedom and equality were the *Alpha* and *Omega*" of the politics, religion, and social habits of Vermont at that time. "Courageous, honest, persistent, patriotic, God-fearing men," Vermonters had laid the foundations of their state "broad and deep . . . in public and private virtue. The town meeting, the school house, the college, and the church, were its cornerstones." In addition, "there was an universal recognition of duty, obligation and self-sacrifice which made of unlettered men and women, unconscious heroes." Indeed, "true heroism" found "its most congenial soil and noblest growth among the common people." Thus, at the time when Vermont entered the Union "no remnants of colonial magnificence adorned her approach. No traditions of old world aristocracy gave distinction to her presence, or grace to her society. No potency in National politics attracted the parasites of the hour. The luxuries of wealth were unknown to her."

Upon uttering these last sentiments, Edward Phelps, the keynote speaker at the dedication of the monument, asked his listeners: "What shall be the future?" Without giving it a second's thought, he predicted that the new monument would "behold a society, where the great principles of civil and religious liberty shall be slowly but certainly working themselves out, to their final maturity." In this society prosperity would be "more and more widely diffused among common men."[4]

Other speakers developed the same theme. For them, Vermont exemplified the democratic institutions characteristic of late-nineteenth-century American society. President Harrison attributed the existence of such values to the homes, the churches, and the public schools of Vermont. He was absolutely certain that the "devotion to local self-government which originated and for so long maintained the town meeting, establishing and perpetuating a true democracy, an equal, full participation and responsibility in all public affairs on the part of every citizen," remained intact at the very moment when he spoke.[5] For his part, Maj. Gen. Oliver O. Howard, a veteran of Antietam and Gettysburg, fully concurred. In his judgment the home, the church, and the "common school" formed the "fundamental institutions of the land." These were "American Institutions," and he thanked God that they had become universal throughout the United States as a result of the Union victory in the Civil War.[6] Col. Albert Clark of Boston not only agreed with Howard's observations about the solidity of American institutions but believed that the town of Bennington epitomized the values and ideals for which the Revolution and the Civil War had been fought. "The people and the village presented evidence of the great and general beneficence of our political, industrial and social system." In fact, that very morning he had personally visited a factory that, even though idle for the holiday, "showed, with others in the village, an opportunity for popular thrift which dates back and bears relation to the struggle of our fathers, and to their wisdom in securing both the political and industrial independence of this country." Any man, no matter how humble his birth, could make something of himself in an environment where such universal freedom and opportunity prevailed. If the battle monument symbolized American democracy to Clark, the town of Bennington represented the reality of that democracy in everyday life. Here every inhabitant had an equal chance to advance within a social structure devoid of special privilege. Here all citizens participated equally within an atmosphere of individual freedom and economic opportunity.[7]

Regardless of how these speakers revivified the past or how fatuous their presentation of history, they were all certain that the democratic freedom being celebrated that day could be traced directly to the pioneer inhabitants of Bennington. No matter what their conclusions, then, their stories always began along the Walloomsac River more than 130 years earlier. The roots of democracy in Vermont, they unquestioningly believed, had been firmly established in unaltered form by the first settlers on the New Hampshire Grants. Like the yeoman persuasion of a half-century earlier, the cloak of democratic liberalism now enveloped the village within its comforting folds. Historical memory in Bennington blended indistinguishably with that of the nation at large.

Notes

Introduction

1. For a discussion of works dealing with the origins of liberal America see the Essay on Sources.

2. Gordon S. Wood, "Equality and Social Conflict in the American Revolution," *William and Mary Quarterly*, 3rd ser., 51 (1994), 703–16, quotation on 703.

Chapter 1. Separate Paths to the Grants

1. Massachusetts Ecclesiastical Archives, Massachusetts State Archives, Boston, Massachusetts, 13:518–19.

2. Quoted in Lucius R. Paige, *History of Hardwick, Massachusetts* (Boston, 1883), 227.

3. George Whitefield, quoted in C. C. Goen, *Revivalism and Separatism in New England, 1740–1800: Strict Congregationalism and Separate Baptists in the Great Awakening* (New Haven: Yale University Press, 1962), 49.

4. Ibid.

5. Gilbert Tennent, quoted in ibid., 49–50.

6. William G. McLoughlin, *New England Dissent, 1630–1833: The Baptists and the Separation of Church and State*, 2 vols. (Cambridge: Harvard University Press, 1971), 1:340–59.

7. Isaac Backus, *A Fish Caught in His Own Net* (Boston, 1768), 114.

8. Paige, *Hardwick*, 467.

9. Ibid., 34–35.

10. Town Records of Hardwick, Clerk's Office, Hardwick, Massachusetts, 1:x.

11. Ibid., xii–cx.

12. Paige, *Hardwick*, 40–41.

13. John L. Brooke, *The Heart of the Commonwealth: Society and Political Culture in Worcester County, Massachusetts, 1713–1861* (New York: Cambridge University Press, 1989), 124–25.

14. Ibid., 125.

15. Brooke analyzes the Land Bank in ibid., 55–65. He describes Land Bankers themselves as "ambitious men on the make, straining to advance their position against the monetary constraints of the imperial relation" (60–61).

16. Paige, *Hardwick*, 46.

17. Hardwick Town Records, 1:lv–lvi.

18. Paige, *Hardwick*, 467.

19. Ibid., 173–80.

20. Quoted in ibid., 183–84.

21. Ibid.

22. George Whitefield, *George Whitefield's Journals (1737–1741)*, ed. William V. Davis (Gainesville, Fla.: Scholars' Facsimiles & Reprints, 1969), 477.

23. Paige, *Hardwick*, 537.

24. White allied himself with the powerful Williams family of Hampshire County, Massachusetts, who were largely responsible for driving Jonathan Edwards from his pulpit in Northampton (Gregory Nobles, *Divisions throughout the Whole: Politics and Society in Hampshire County, Massachusetts, 1740–1775* [New York: Cambridge University Press, 1983], 36–73).

25. Samuel Robinson, quoted in Paige, *Hardwick*, 184–85.

26. Paige, *Hardwick*, 183–84.

27. Quoted in ibid., 225–26.

28. Quoted in ibid., 182.

29. McLoughlin, *New England Dissent*, 1:391–94.

30. Ibid., 360–85.

31. Paige, *Hardwick*, 315.

32. Ibid., 263–69; Fred Anderson, *A People's Army: Massachusetts Soldiers and Society in the Seven Years' War* (Chapel Hill: University of North Carolina Press, 1984), 3–25.

33. Anderson provides an excellent analysis of the relationship between provincials and professionals in military service during the Seven Years' War (see ibid., esp. 111–41 and 167–95).

34. Rockingham County, New Hampshire, Land Books, County Courthouse, Exeter, New Hampshire, 63:428–29.

35. Paige, *Hardwick*, 467.

36. Livingston-Redmond Manuscripts, Franklin Delano Roosevelt Library, Hyde Park, New York, Box 34.

37. My analysis of land disputes along the Hudson River relies upon Oscar Handlin, "The Eastern Frontier of New York," *New York History*, 18 (1937), 50–75; Irving Mark, *Agrarian Conflicts in Colonial New York, 1711–1775* (New York: Columbia University Press, 1940), 107–63; Patricia Bonomi, *A Factious People: Politics and Society in Colonial New York* (New York: Columbia University Press, 1971), 179–228; and Sung Bok Kim, *Landlord and Tenant in Colonial New York: Manorial Society, 1664–1775* (Chapel Hill: University of North Carolina Press, 1978), 281–415.

38. The Oblong, or Equivalent Lands, was a thin strip of land running along the Connecticut–New York border. It came into being as a result of an agreement confirmed between New York and Connecticut in 1731 fixing a precise

boundary between the two colonies. Previous to this time many individuals had settled in the region under the impression that it lay within Connecticut. As a result, the area became the center of bitter tensions between New England settlers and New York landlords. For the clearest analysis of problems on the Oblong, see Kim, *Landlord and Tenant*, 367–71.

39. Ibid., 395–96.

40. Staughton Lynd, *Anti-Federalism in Dutchess County, New York: A Study of Democracy and Class Conflict in the Revolutionary Era* (Chicago: Loyola University Press, 1962), 38–39.

41. Quoted in ibid., 37.

42. Bonomi, *A Factious People*, 207–8.

43. Quoted in Kim, *Landlord and Tenant*, 282.

44. Land Records, Dutchess County Hall of Records, Poughkeepsie, New York, bk. 5, 166.

45. Anne Grant, *Memoirs of an American Lady, with Sketches of Manners and Scenery in America*, 2nd ed., 2 vols. (London, 1809), 2:219–20.

46. "Examination by Captain Paul Rycant taken at Poughkeepsie, October 7, 1761," in *The Documentary History of the State of New York*, ed. E. B. O'Callaghan, 4 vols. (Albany, N.Y., 1849–51), 3:984–87.

47. Abby Maria Hemenway, ed., *The Vermont Historical Gazetteer*, vol. 3 (Claremont, N.H., 1877), 576–83.

48. Lynd, *Anti-Federalism in Dutchess County*, 47.

49. Testimony of Moss Kent, in Irving Mark and Oscar Handlin, "Land Cases in Colonial New York, 1765–1767: The King v. William Prendergast," *New York University Law Quarterly Review*, 19 (1941), 165–84, quotations on 175.

50. Quoted in Kim, *Landlord and Tenant*, 387.

51. Testimony of Samuel Peters, in Mark and Handlin, "Land Cases in Colonial New York," 183–84.

52. Quoted in Mark, *Agrarian Conflicts in Colonial New York*, 147.

53. Records of the First Congregational Church, Newent, Connecticut, Connecticut State Library, Hartford, Connecticut, 1:29.

54. Ibid., 29–30.

55. Ibid., 31.

56. Frances M. Caulkins, *History of Norwich, Connecticut* (Hartford, Conn., 1874), 256–57.

57. Harry Parker Ward, *The Follett-Dewey Fassett-Safford Ancestry* (Columbus, Ohio, 1896), 160–73.

58. Norwich Town Records, Clerk's Office, Norwich, Connecticut, 2:26.

59. Ibid., 38.

60. Ibid., 29, 32, 38, 54, 71, 77.

61. Newent Church Records, 1:3, 10.

62. Caulkins, *History of Norwich*, 440.

63. Records of the Newent Congregational Society, 1734–1787, Connecticut State Library, Hartford, Connecticut, 2:4–6, 10.

64. Records of the First Congregational Church of Norwich, Connecticut State Library, Hartford, Connecticut, 1:67.

65. Newent Church Records, 1:31.

66. Ibid., 32–33.

67. Caulkins, *History of Norwich*, 320–22.

68. Records of the Separate Society of Newent, Bennington Museum, Bennington, Vermont, 18.

69. Ibid., 21.

70. McLoughlin, *New England Dissent*, 1:363.

71. Ibid., 363–64.

72. Frederic Denison, *Notes of the Baptists and Their Principles in Norwich, Connecticut* (Norwich, Conn., 1857), 19–20.

73. McLoughlin, *New England Dissent*, 1:362–63.

74. Denison, *Notes of the Baptists*, 28–29.

75. Ellen D. Larned, *History of Windham County, Connecticut*, 2 vols. (Worcester, Mass., 1874), 1:469.

76. Ebenezer Frothingham, *Articles of Faith and Practice with the Covenant* (Newport, R.I., 1750), 47.

77. Newent Separate Society, 8–10.

78. Ibid., 10.

79. The Newent Separate Church's covenant appears in ibid., 5–7.

80. Ibid., 17–21.

81. Ibid., 22.

82. For the remarkable array of contacts that Separates formed throughout the New England states, see Isaac Backus Papers, Franklin Trask Library, Special Collections, Andover-Newton Theological School, Newton, Massachusetts.

83. Ward, *Follett-Dewey Fassett-Safford Ancestry*, 164.

84. Paige, *Hardwick*, 264–69.

85. Salisbury Justice Court Records, Town Clerk's Office, Salisbury, Connecticut, vol. 1, September 3, 1765.

86. Ibid.

87. Ibid., October 11 and 27, 1765.

88. Ibid., August 25, 1764.

89. Ibid., September 8, 1764.

90. Charles A. Jellison, *Ethan Allen: Frontier Rebel* (Syracuse: Syracuse University Press, 1969), 11.

91. John Pell, *Ethan Allen* (Boston: Houghton Mifflin, 1929), 20.

92. Michael A. Bellesiles, "Life, Liberty, and Land: Ethan Allen and the Frontier Experience in Revolutionary New England" (Ph.D. diss., University of California, Irvine, 1986), 18–19.

93. Ibid., 20–23.

94. Cornwall Town Records, Clerk's Office, Cornwall, Connecticut, 1:1.

95. Ibid., 4, 6–7.

96. Bellesiles, "Life, Liberty, and Land," 34–38.

97. Ibid., 39–41; Pell, *Ethan Allen*, 6–7; Jellison, *Ethan Allen*, 4–6.

98. Probate Records, District of Litchfield, Town Hall, Litchfield, Connecticut, 1:162.

99. Bellesiles, "Life, Liberty, and Land," 41–43.

100. Salisbury Land Records, Town Clerk's Office, Salisbury, Connecticut, 3:681.

101. Ibid., 763.

102. Ibid., 764.

103. Litchfield Probate Records, 2:82–83.

104. The Salisbury Grand Lists of 1763–65 show Ethan Allen at £42, £125:4:0, and £96:18:0. In 1765 he is rated with his brother Heman (Town Clerk's Office, Salisbury, Connecticut).

105. Salisbury Land Records, 4:203.

106. Henry H. Edes, "Memoir of Dr. Thomas Young, 1731–1777," *Publications of the Colonial Society of Massachusetts* (Boston: By the Society, 1910), 11:2–54; David F. Hawke, "Dr. Thomas Young—'Eternal Fisher in Troubled Waters,'" *New York Historical Society Quarterly*, 54 (1970), 6–29; Pauline Maier, "Reason and Revolution: The Radicalism of Dr. Thomas Young," *American Quarterly*, 28 (1976), 229–49.

107. Henry N. MacCraken, *Old Dutchess Forever! The Story of an American County* (New York: Hastings House, 1956), 321–22.

108. Edes, "Memoir of Dr. Thomas Young," 10.

109. Ibid., 12.

110. Ibid.

111. Quoted in Maier, "Reason and Revolution," 245.

112. Quoted in ibid.

113. Ethan Allen, Preface to *Reason the Only Oracle of Man* (Bennington, 1784); John Pell, "Ethan Allen's Literary Career," *New England Quarterly*, 2 (1929), 585–602, esp. 586.

114. Matt Bushnell Jones, *Vermont in the Making, 1750–1777* (Cambridge: Harvard University Press, 1939), 142–46.

115. Thomas Young, *Some Reflections on the Dispute Between New York, New Hampshire and Col. John Henry Lydius of Albany* (New Haven, 1764), 15.

116. Ibid., 21.

117. Northampton Justice Records, Northampton, Massachusetts, vol. 1, July 15, 1767.

118. Bellesiles, "Life, Liberty, and Land," 53–54.

119. Salisbury Land Records, 4:257; 5:98; 6:76, 90, 131.

120. Rockingham County Land Books, 80:459, 460.

121. Hampden County Deeds, Hall of Records, Springfield, Massachusetts, 10:194.

122. Journal of the Reverend John Ballantine, 1737–1774, Westfield Athenaeum, Westfield, Massachusetts, 20.

123. Ibid., 28.

124. Ibid., 60.

125. John H. Lockwood, *Westfield and Its Historic Influences, 1669–1919* (Westfield, Mass.: By the author, 1922), 59–62, 83–87.

126. Thomas M. Davis and Virginia L. Davis, eds., *Edward Taylor's "Church Records" and Related Sermons: Volume One of the Unpublished Writings of Edward Taylor* (Boston: Twayne, 1981), 461.

127. Lockwood, *Westfield*, 99.

128. Davis and Davis, *Edward Taylor's "Church Records,"* 461.

129. Lockwood, *Westfield*, 86–101.

130. Ibid., 98.

131. Adelburt M. Dewey, *Life of George Dewey and Dewey Family History* (Westfield, Mass., 1898), 844.

132. Davis and Davis, *Edward Taylor's "Church Records,"* 109–12.

133. Ibid., 169–70.

134. Ibid., 265.

135. Hampshire County Probate Court Records, Hall of Records, Northampton, Massachusetts, Box 45, No. 52.

136. Ibid.

137. Hampden County Land Records, County Courthouse, Springfield, Massachusetts, bk. K, 463, 464, 465, 468; bk. M, 352, 353; bk. P, 261, 374, 375; bk. Q, 129; bk. Z, 311.

138. Nobles, *Divisions throughout the Whole*, 38; Dewey, *Dewey Family History*, 855.

139. Quoted in Lockwood, *Westfield*, 333–34.

140. Quoted in Nobles, *Divisions throughout the Whole*, 38.

141. Records of the Westfield Church of Christ, Westfield Athenaeum, Westfield, Massachusetts, 195.

142. Ibid.

143. Ibid., 196.

144. William Breitenbach, "Unregenerate Doings: Selflessness and Selfishness in New Divinity Theology," *American Quarterly*, 34 (1982), 479–502; Joseph A. Conforti, "Samuel Hopkins and the New Divinity: Theology, Ethics, and Social Reform in Eighteenth-Century New England," *William and Mary Quarterly*, 3rd ser., 34 (1977), 572–89; and idem, *Samuel Hopkins and the New Divinity Movement: Calvinism, the Congregational Ministry, and Reform in New England between the Great Awakenings* (Grand Rapids, Mich.: Christian University Press, 1981), provide excellent insights into the principles of this school of thought.

145. Clifford K. Shipton, *Sibley's Harvard Graduates*, vol. 9 (Boston: Massachusetts Historical Society, 1956), 466, 468–72.

146. Lockwood, *Westfield*, 379–80.

147. Journal of John Ballantine, 16.

148. Nobles, *Divisions throughout the Whole*, 57, 216.

149. Quoted in ibid., 57.

150. Breitenbach, "Unregenerate Doings"; Conforti, "Samuel Hopkins and the New Divinity"; idem, *Samuel Hopkins*.

151. Conforti, *Samuel Hopkins*, 65–67, 77–78.

152. Israel Dewey, "Israel Dewey's Letters to the Reverend Mr. Samuel Hopkins" (n.p., [1759?]), quotations on 7–8, 10–11.

153. Quoted in Charles J. Taylor, *History of Great Barrington, Massachusetts* (Great Barrington, Mass., 1882), 194–95.

154. Record of the Conference Held At Stonington, Connecticut, May 29, 1754, Isaac Backus Papers; McLoughlin, *New England Dissent*, 1:433–35.

155. Lockwood, *Westfield*, 470.

156. Hampden County Land Records, 3:228; Dutchess County Land Records, bk. 4, 104.

157. Quoted in Newton Reed, *Early History of Amenia* (Amenia, N.Y., 1875), 30–31.

158. Journal of John Ballantine, 92.

159. Dewey, *Dewey Family History*, 859.

160. Records of the Bennington Church of Christ, Bennington Museum, Bennington, Vermont, 1:2, hereafter Bennington Church Records.

161. Ibid., 2.

162. Ibid., 3.

163. Ira Allen Autobiography, printed in James B. Wilbur, *Ira Allen: Founder of Vermont, 1751–1814*, 2 vols. (Boston: Houghton Mifflin, 1928), 1:1–59; see 36–37.

164. Ibid., 37.

165. Ibid., 37–38.

166. Ibid., 41–42.

167. Cornwall Land Records, Clerk's Office, Cornwall, Connecticut, 2:370, 477.

168. Ira Allen Autobiography, 1–3.

169. Ibid., 5.

170. Ibid., 5–6.

171. Ibid., 6–7.

172. Ibid.

173. Ibid., 8.

174. Ibid., 8–9.

175. Ibid., 9–12.

176. Ibid., 12.

177. Cornwall Land Records, 3:54, 71.

178. Ira Allen Autobiography, 14–15.

179. Ibid., 27–28.

180. Bellesiles, "Life, Liberty, and Land," 55.

181. Ira Allen Autobiography, 15.

182. Ibid., 19–21.

183. Ibid., 38; J. Kevin Graffagnino, " 'The Country My Soul Delighted In': The Onion River Land Company and the Vermont Frontier," *New England Quarterly*, 65 (1992), 24–60.

Chapter 2. The Grants in Jeopardy

1. Isaac Jennings, *Memorials of a Century: Embracing a Record of Individuals and Events Chiefly in the Early History of Bennington, Vt. and its First Church* (Boston, 1869), 213; Lewis Cass Aldrich, *History of Bennington County, Vermont* (Syracuse, 1889), 244.

2. Aldrich, *Bennington County*, 244–45; Abby Maria Hemenway, ed., *The Vermont Historical Gazetteer*, vol. 1 (Burlington, 1867), 145–46.

3. Jennings, *Memorials of a Century*, 210.

4. Bennington Town Records, Town Clerk's Office, Bennington, Vermont, bk. A, February 11, 1762. Pagination is erratic in this volume; therefore, meetings are noted by their date rather than by the page on which the record appears.

5. Ibid., March 31, 1762.

6. Ibid., February 11, 26, 1762; May 9, 1763; August 20, 1766.

7. Ibid., December 18, 1769, and March 28, 1770.

8. See ibid. for the years 1762–70. Nathan Clark is an exceptional case. While never a proprietor, he became a powerful figure within Bennington's town government.

9. Ibid., March 31, 1762.

10. Ibid., April 20, 1763.

11. Bennington Church Records, 1:1 (see chap. 1, n. 160).

12. Ibid., December 29, 1762, 2.

13. Ibid., May 24, 1763, and July 18, 1763, 2.

14. Bennington Town Records, bk. A, November 1, 1763.

15. Bennington Church Records, 1:3.

16. Bennington Town Records, bk. A, October 5, 1763.

17. Ibid., November 1, 1763.

18. Bennington Church Records, 1:12. The vote was taken on May 20, 1764, but was not recorded until June 13, 1768.

19. Ibid., 12.

20. Ibid., 11.

21. John E. Goodrich, ed., *The State of Vermont: Rolls of the Soldiers in the Revolutionary War, 1775 to 1783* (Rutland, Vt.: Tuttle, 1904), 632.

22. Journal of Major Walter Rutherford, July 2, 1765, extract printed in Jones, *Vermont in the Making*, 412–19, quotations on 412–13 (see chap. 1, n. 114).

23. Bennington Church Records, June 19, 1766, 1:7.

24. Ibid., 12.

25. See ibid., 7–21.

26. Jennings, *Memorials of a Century*, 342.

27. O'Callaghan, *Documentary History of New York*, 4:558–60 (see chap. 1, n. 46).

28. Ibid., 570–72.

29. For details of the Hoosic Patent of 1688, see Hiland Hall, *The History of Vermont from its Discovery to its Admission into the Union in 1791* (Albany, N.Y., 1868), 487–88.

30. Jones, *Vermont in the Making*, 106; Harmanus Schuyler to Cadwallader Colden, August 17, 1764, in O'Callaghan, *Documentary History of New York*, 4:575–76.

31. Minutes, Council of New York, September 4, 1764, in O'Callaghan, *Documentary History of New York*, 4:576–77.

32. *New York Gazette*, April 15, 1765; *New Hampshire Gazette*, April 26, 1765.

33. Lords of Trade to Cadwallader Colden, July 13, 1764, in *Documents Relative to the Colonial History of the State of New York*, ed. E. B. O'Callaghan, 10 vols. (Albany, N.Y., 1856–58), 7:642–43.

34. O'Callaghan, *Documentary History of New York*, 4:574–75.

35. Colden to Lords of Trade and Plantations, September 26, 1763, Colden Letter Books, 2 vols., 1760–75, *Collections of the New York Historical Society for the Year 1876–1877*, vols. 9 and 10 (New York, 1877–78), 9:232–37.

36. O'Callaghan, *Documentary History of New York*, 4:37–38.

37. "New York Land Grants in Vermont, 1765–1776," in *Collections of the Vermont Historical Society*, 2 vols. (Montpelier, Vt., 1870–71), 1:147–59; R. C. Benton, *The Vermont Settlers and the New York Land Speculators* (Minneapolis, 1894), 35–36.

38. Jones, *Vermont in the Making*, 110–22.

39. Journals of Major Walter Rutherford and James Duane, made during their trip to Princetown in June and July 1765, printed in ibid., 412–24.

40. Massachusetts State Archives, July 10, 1765, 26:143 (see chap. 1, n. 1). Robinson was a proprietor in a total of seven townships on the Grants (Albert S. Batchellor, ed., *The New Hampshire Grants*, vol. 26 of the *New Hampshire State Papers* [Concord, N.H., 1895]).

41. Grant, *Memoirs of an American Lady*, 2:213 (see chap. 1, n. 45).

42. Quoted in Mark, *Agrarian Conflicts in Colonial New York*, 135 (see chap. 1, n. 37).

43. Grant, *Memories of an American Lady*, 232, 219–20.

44. O'Callaghan, *Documentary History of New York*, 4:584–86.

45. Moore discussed this meeting in a letter to the earl of Shelburne dated June 9, 1767, in O'Callaghan, *Documents Relative to the Colonial History of New York*, 7:930–38.

46. O'Callaghan, *Documentary History of New York*, 4:587. This order appeared in the *Connecticut Courant* (Hartford), July 14, 1766; the *New Hampshire Gazette*, July 18, 25, 1766; the *Boston Gazette*, July 14, 1766, supplement; and the *Boston Evening Post*, August 4, 1766.

47. Jones, *Vermont in the Making*, 123–27; Hemenway incorporates notes from one of these proprietors' meetings in *Vermont Historical Gazetteer*, 1:1026.

48. For an excellent analysis of the activities of Robinson and Johnson throughout the time they worked together, see Jones, *Vermont in the Making*, 132–66.

49. Jones prints this petition in ibid., 404–7. For a copy of Robinson's original petition, see "Petitions to the King, 1766," *Collections of the Vermont Historical Society*, 1:271–88.

50. Jones, *Vermont in the Making*, 406–7.

51. Shelburne to Moore, April 11, 1767, in O'Callaghan, *Documentary History of New York*, 4:589–90.

52. Moore to Shelburne, June 9, 1967, in O'Callaghan, *Documents Relative to the Colonial History of New York*, 7:930–40, quotations on 935, 936, and 938.

53. O'Callaghan, *Documentary History of New York*, 4:609–11.

54. Jones offers a detailed account of these accusations in *Vermont in the Making*, 152–59.

55. Johnson, quoted in Hall, *History of Vermont*, 96.

56. Robinson, quoted in ibid., 96.

57. Diary of William Samuel Johnson, quoted in ibid., 161.

Chapter 3. The Emergence of the Green Mountain Boys

1. Bennington Town Records, bk. A, July 4, 1768 (see chap. 2, n. 4); O'Callaghan, *Documentary History of New York*, 4:617 (see chap. 1, n. 46). As members of the Committee of Bennington, John Fassett, Samuel Safford, and Ebenezer

Wood signed a call for a special meeting of townspeople (Bennington Town Records, bk. A, October 22, 1768).

2. Except where specifically noted, future references to Samuel Robinson indicate Samuel Robinson Jr.

3. The New Hampshire Grants included all of present-day Vermont; however, the conflict with New York concerning overlapping land grants concentrated on the region west of the Green Mountains. For this reason, references to the Grants in this chapter refer exclusively to the area west of the Green Mountains. For events taking place east of the mountains during this same period, see Benjamin H. Hall, *History of Eastern Vermont, From its Earliest Settlement to the Close of the Eighteenth Century* (New York, 1858); and Donald A. Smith, "Legacy of Dissent: Religion and Politics in Revolutionary Vermont" (Ph.D. diss., Clark University, 1981).

4. Colden to the Lords of Trade, February 8, 1764, *Collections of the New York Historical Society*, 9:232–37 (see chap. 2, n. 35).

5. Purchase of New Hampshire grants after the king's order in council was not limited to buyers of small plots. For example, Samuel Robinson purchased one full right in Rupert as well as two hundred acres in Arlington and Shaftsbury on November 16, 1769 (Rockingham County Land Books, 80:363–64 [see chap. 1, n. 34]). And Stephen Fay purchased five rights of Land in Pawlet, one right in Rupert, and one right in Shaftsbury on November 10, 1779 (ibid., 90:201–2).

6. For a discussion of the Walloomsac Patent, which followed the course of that river well into Bennington Township, see Jones, *Vermont in the Making*, 172–73 (see chap. 1, n. 114).

7. Affidavit of Breakenridge and Robinson, February 14, 1770, in O'Callaghan, *Documentary History of New York*, 4:617–19.

8. These petitions, dated October 18 and October 24, 1769, are in the Papers of the Continental Congress, 1774–1789, in the National Archives, Washington, D.C. (microfilmed as M247, r47, i40, vi, pp. 38–47; and M247, r47, i40, vi, pp. 29–31).

9. O'Callaghan, *Documentary History of New York*, 4:615–16.

10. The petition, dated February 22, 1770, is in the Papers of the Continental Congress (M247, r47, i40, vi, pp. 51–54).

11. Edward P. Alexander, *A Revolutionary Conservative: James Duane of New York* (New York: Columbia University Press, 1938), 52–92; Catherine Snell Crary, "The American Dream: John Tabor Kempe's Rise from Poverty to Riches," *William and Mary Quarterly*, 3rd ser., 14 (1957), 176–95.

12. For descriptions of these meetings, see *Connecticut Courant* (Hartford), February 19, March 19, and June 4, 1770.

13. Jellison, *Ethan Allen*, 31–33 (see chap. 1, n. 90); Pell, *Ethan Allen*, 30–31 (see chap. 1, n. 91).

14. Paul Hamlin and Charles Baker offer a graphic description of courtroom etiquette in *Supreme Court of Judicature of the Province of New York, 1691–1704*, 2 vols. (New York: New York Historical Society, 1959), 1:356–78.

15. Quoted in ibid., 358.

16. Quoted in ibid., 2:385–86.

17. Several years after the experience, Ethan Allen noted the "briliant Ap-

pearance" of the plaintiffs and the court. For their part, the defendants, "appearing in but ordinary Fashion . . . made a very disproportionable Figure at Court; and, in fine, Interest, Connection, and Grandeur, easily turned the Case against the forlorn Defendants" (Ethan Allen, *A Brief Narrative of the Proceedings of the Government of New York . . .* [Hartford, Conn., 1774], 7).

18. Hall, *History of Vermont*, 119; Alexander, *Revolutionary Conservative*, 76. It should be noted that Allen did, nonetheless, accept expense money from Duane for his trip from Albany to Bennington (Journal of James Duane, July 4, 1770, quoted in ibid., 76 n. 34).

19. Mark, *Agrarian Conflicts in Colonial New York*, 171–72; Jones, *Vermont in the Making*, 225–27.

20. Hall, *History of Vermont*, 122; Aldrich, *Bennington County*, 254–55 (see chap. 2, n. 1).

21. This petition, dated October 3, 1770, is in the Papers of the Continental Congress, 1774–1789 (M247, r47, i40, pp. 69–70).

22. O'Callaghan, *Documentary History of New York*, 4:661–63.

23. Hemenway, *Vermont Historical Gazetteer*, 1:151 (see chap. 2, n. 2).

24. O'Callaghan, *Documentary History of New York*, 4:687–88. Robinson was indicted at the January 1771 term of the Albany Court and kept in custody until October, when he was freed on bail (Aldrich, *Bennington County*, 50).

25. O'Callaghan, *Documentary History of New York*, 4:686–87.

26. Ibid., 689–90.

27. Ibid., 710–12.

28. Robert Yates provides the fullest account of this expedition in a letter of July 20, 1771, to Duane and Kempe, in the James Duane Papers, New York Historical Society, New York. I have relied on this letter as well as on the affidavits of other participants printed in O'Callaghan, *Documentary History of New York*, 4:732–43; see also Hall, *History of Vermont*, 123–26.

29. Hall, *History of Vermont*, 127–28; Jones, *Vermont in the Making*, 288–89.

30. Bennington Town Records, bk. A, June 26, 1776.

31. The town meeting elected Warner to serve three terms as a highway surveyor (ibid., March 28, 1766, March 29, 1769, March 28, 1770). The proprietors also selected Warner to serve on the committee that assigned town lots in the village proper (Proprietor's records, ibid., March 28, 1770).

32. O'Callaghan, *Documentary History of New York*, 4:730, 762.

33. Ibid., 745.

34. Ibid., 724–29.

35. Hall, *History of Vermont*, 130.

36. O'Callaghan, *Documentary History of New York*, 4:745–47.

37. O'Callaghan, *Documents Relative to the Colonial History of New York*, 8:293 (see chap. 2, n. 33).

38. Ibid., 374–75.

39. O'Callaghan, *Documentary History of New York*, 4:749–55.

40. Ibid., 762; Hall, *History of Vermont*, 128–29.

41. O'Callaghan, *Documentary History of New York*, 4:763–64.

42. Hall prints this proclamation in his *History of Vermont*, 134.

43. Ibid., 135–36.

44. Walter Harriman, "Seth Warner," *Granite Monthly*, 3 (1879), 114–19.

45. Quoted in Hall, *History of Vermont*, 137.

46. Ethan Allen, "Lover of Truth and Reason," *Connecticut Courant*, March 31, 1772.

47. Young, *Some Reflections* (see chap. 1, n. 115). There are striking similarities in both the tone and the language employed by Young and Allen.

48. Allen, "Lover of Truth and Reason."

49. Ethan Allen, "Friend to Liberty and Property," *Connecticut Courant*, April 28, 1772.

50. Having heard of Tryon's boast that he would drive all rioters into the Green Mountains, Ethan Allen and his captains adopted this name in order to mock the governor (Hemenway, *Vermont Historical Gazetteer*, 1:153). Allen first employed the term Green Mountain Boys in print in a letter published in the *Connecticut Courant* on September 22, 1772. New York authorities, however, continued to refer to all rioters as members of the "Bennington Mob."

51. Ira Allen, *The Natural and Political History of the State of Vermont* (London, 1798), 32–33.

52. Breakenridge's petition is dated at Portsmouth, May 19, 1772 (*New Hampshire State Papers*, vol. 28 [Manchester, N.H., 1890], 61–71).

53. O'Callaghan, *Documentary History of New York*, 4:778.

54. Ibid., 777.

55. Ibid., 778–79.

56. William Slade, *Vermont State Papers* (Middlebury, Vt., 1823), 23–24.

57. Allen had his letter, along with those of Tryon and Dewey, published in the *Connecticut Courant* on July 14, 1772.

58. For excellent insight into the influence of the idea of the protection-allegiance compact in the American colonies, see Richard Bushman, *King and People in Provincial Massachusetts* (Chapel Hill: University of North Carolina Press, 1985).

59. Slade, *Vermont State Papers*, 24–29.

60. *Connecticut Courant*, June 9, 1772.

61. O'Callaghan, *Documentary History of New York*, 4:786–92.

62. Ibid., 792–93.

63. Jones, *Vermont in the Making*, 303–12.

64. O'Callaghan, *Documentary History of New York*, 4:793–94.

65. *Connecticut Courant*, November 3, 1772.

66. O'Callaghan, *Documentary History of New York*, 4:799–800.

67. Ibid., 800; Jones, *Vermont in the Making*, 180–85.

68. O'Callaghan, *Documentary History of New York*, 4:846–54.

69. Graffagnino, "The Country My Soul Delighted In" (see chap. 1, n. 183).

70. *Connecticut Courant*, June 1, 1773.

71. O'Callaghan, *Documentary History of New York*, 4:859–60.

72. Ibid., 862–64.

73. Ibid., 856–59. Two years earlier Jonathan Wheat had signed an affidavit naming the principal leaders of the Bennington riots. In addition to the individuals listed by Hough, he had included John Fassett and Moses and Samuel Robinson (ibid., 780–81).

74. Ibid., 871–73.

75. Slade, *Vermont State Papers*, 37–42. The resolutions appeared in the *New Hampshire Gazette* (Portsmouth), April 29, 1774.

76. Slade, *Vermont State Papers*, 49–54. The document appeared in the *New Hampshire Gazette*, May 6, 1774.

77. Allen, *Brief Narrative*.

78. For an analysis of the manner in which gentlemen rationalized their belief that speculation should be carefully restricted to the genteel, see Alan Taylor, *Liberty Men and Great Proprietors: The Revolutionary Settlement on the Maine Frontier, 1760–1820* (Chapel Hill: University of North Carolina Press, 1990), 31–59.

79. Allen, *Brief Narrative*, 5.

80. Ibid., 6–7.

81. Ibid., 7–8.

82. Ibid., 9–10.

83. Ibid., 127.

84. Hall, *History of Vermont*, 187; Slade, *Vermont State Papers*, 36.

85. O'Callaghan, *Documentary History of New York*, 4:893–99.

86. Ibid., 902–3.

87. O'Callaghan, *Documents Relative to the Colonial History of New York*, 8:566–67.

Chapter 4. Newcomers to the Grants

1. David Avery, *A Narrative of the Rise and Progress of the Difficulties which have issued in a Separation between the Minister and the People of Bennington, 1783* (Bennington, 1783), 9.

2. David Avery, notebook entitled "The Case of the Pastor & Church of Wrentham," in *The Papers of David Avery, 1746–1818*, ed. John M. Mulder (Princeton: Princeton Theological Seminary, 1979), microfilm, hereafter cited as *Avery Papers*.

3. Franklin B. Dexter, *Biographical Sketches of Graduates of Yale College, with Annals of the College History*, 6 vols. (New York: Henry Holt, 1885–1912), 3:305–10.

4. For Wheelock's Indian School, see Leon Burr Richardson, *History of Dartmouth College*, 2 vols. (Hanover, N.H.: Dartmouth College, 1932); Baxter Perry Smith, *The History of Dartmouth College* (Boston, 1878); and Frederick Chase, *A History of Dartmouth College and the Town of Hanover, New Hampshire*, 2 vols. (Cambridge, Mass., 1891).

5. Eleazar Wheelock, quoted in Smith, *History of Dartmouth College*, 61.

6. Brooks Mather Kelley, *Yale: A History* (New Haven: Yale University Press, 1974), 75–77.

7. David Avery to Dr. Eleazar Wheelock, December 17, 1767, quoted in Dexter, *Biographical Sketches*, 3:263–64.

8. Quoted in Kelley, *Yale*, 77–78.

9. Jacob W. Johnson and Avery to Sir William Johnson, October 17, 1768, printed in O'Callaghan, *Documentary History of New York*, 4:390–91 (see chap. 1, n. 46).

10. Dexter, *Biographical Sketches*, 3:305–10.

11. David Avery Diary, *Avery Papers*, 17, 9.

12. Ibid., February 7, 1771, 17, 8, 6. The Avery Diary is not consistently paginated; at times reference must be made to the date of the entry rather than to the page number.

13. Ibid., 8.

14. Dexter, *Biographical Sketches*, 3:305–10.

15. Eleazar Wheelock, "A Continuation of the Narrative of the Indian Charity School Begun in Lebanon, in Connecticut; Now Incorporated with Dartmouth-College, in Hanover, in the province of New-Hampshire" ([Portsmouth], N.H., 1773), 14.

16. Avery to Wheelock, November 1, 1776, April 4, 1777, and Wheelock to Avery, August 30, 1773, *Avery Papers*.

17. Avery to Samuel Kirkland, December 25, 1772, ibid.

18. This struggle may be followed in Avery's diary throughout the years 1773–75.

19. Avery to Aaron Putnam, July 18, 1774, *Avery Papers*.

20. Ibid.

21. Ibid.

22. For discussions of New Divinity theology, see Conforti, *Samuel Hopkins* (see chap. 1, n. 144); and Breitenbach, "Unregenerate Doings" (see again chap. 1, n. 144).

23. Avery to Putnam, July 18, 1774, *Avery Papers*.

24. Ibid.

25. Quoted in Jennings, *Memorials of a Century*, 89 (see chap. 2, n. 1).

26. Francis B. Heitman, *Historical Register of Officers of the Continental Army during the War of the Revolution* (Washington, D.C.: Rare Book Shop, 1914), 78.

27. See Avery Diary, April 1777, for details of his dismissal.

28. "The Lord is to Be Praised," undated sermon on Isaiah 30.18, *Avery Papers*, quotations on 12 and 45–46.

29. Sermon on Acts 1.25, delivered April 7, 1776, ibid.

30. Sermon on Ezekiel 18.31, delivered July 9, 1775, ibid.

31. Avery to Hannah Chaplin, January 15, 1776, ibid.

32. Avery to Wheelock, February 13, 1776, ibid.

33. Sermon on Isaiah 6.5, delivered January 19, 1777, ibid.

34. Avery kept a detailed summary of these negotiations in his diary throughout the month of January 1779.

35. Quoted in Samuel Warner, "Wrentham," in *History of Norfolk County, Massachusetts, with biographical sketches of many of its pioneers and prominent men*, ed. Duane Hamilton Hurd (Philadelphia, 1884), 655.

36. These negotiations may be followed in Avery's diary for January and February 1780. See also Bennington Church Records, 1:27–28 (see chap. 1, n. 160).

37. Bennington Church Records, 1:31–34.

38. Ibid.

39. *Haswell's Massachusetts Spy Or American Oracle of Liberty*, August 14, 1777.

40. Patricia L. Parker, *Susanna Rowson* (Boston: Twayne, 1986), 1.

41. John Spargo, *Anthony Haswell, Printer-Patriot-Ballader* (Rutland, Vt.: Tuttle, 1925), 6–7.

42. Ibid., 8–9.
43. Ibid., 7–8.
44. *Bennington Green Mountain Farmer,* March 15, 1814.
45. Spargo, *Anthony Haswell,* 13–14.
46. Ibid., 16–17.
47. Anthony Haswell, quoted in ibid., 17.
48. Ibid., 17–18.
49. Brooke, *Heart of the Commonwealth,* 152–54 (see chap. 1, n. 13).
50. Spargo, *Anthony Haswell,* 126–29.
51. Quoted in Douglas Southall Freeman, *George Washington: A Biography,* 7 vols. (New York: Charles Scribner's Sons, 1948–57), 4:237.
52. Quoted in ibid., 365–66.
53. Quoted in Spargo, *Anthony Haswell,* 131.
54. *Haswell's Massachusetts Spy Or American Oracle of Liberty,* August 14, 1777.
55. Ibid., October 9, 1777.
56. Ibid., November 13, 1777.
57. Ibid., February 12, 1778.
58. Ibid., January 1, 1778.
59. Ibid., December 25, 1777.
60. Ibid., February 12, 1778.
61. Ibid.
62. Ibid., March 26, 1778.
63. *Thomas's Massachusetts Spy Or Oracle of American Liberty,* June 25, 1778.
64. Spargo, *Anthony Haswell,* 25–27.
65. Nathan Baldwin, quoted in ibid., 27–28.
66. E. P. Watson, ed., *Records of the Governor and Council of the State of Vermont,* 8 vols. (Montpelier, 1873–80), 2:12–13, 26, 151, 3:27; J. Kevin Graffagnino, "'We Have Long Been Wishing for a Good Printer in This Vicinity': The State of Vermont, the First East Union, and the Dresden Press, 1778–1779," *Vermont History,* 47 (1979), 33–35.
67. Spargo, *Anthony Haswell,* 35.
68. Nathaniel Chipman to Ebenezer Fitch, October 3, 1778, printed in Daniel Chipman, *The Life of Hon. Nathaniel Chipman, LL.D.* (Boston, 1846), 28–29.
69. Chipman to George Washington, October 10, 1778, printed in ibid., 32–33.
70. Ibid., 9.
71. Ibid., 7.
72. Salisbury Town Records, Town Clerk's Office, Salisbury, Connecticut, 1:160.
73. Ibid., 297.
74. Ibid., 35–36.
75. Ibid., 2:77.
76. Ibid., 1:23–24.
77. Ibid., 29; 2:2, 4, 5, 7, 8, 9; 4:2, 5, 6, 7, 8, 9, 10, 12, 13.
78. Ibid., 1:19.
79. Ibid., 21, 23.
80. Church Records, 1744–1817, Congregational Church of Salisbury, Con-

necticut, stored in the vault of the Salisbury Bank and Trust Company, Lakeville, Connecticut.

81. Ibid.

82. Salisbury Town Records, 2:3.

83. Julia Pettee, *The Rev. Jonathan Lee and His Eighteenth Century Salisbury Parish: The Early History of the Town of Salisbury, Connecticut* (Salisbury, Conn.: Salisbury Association, 1957), 98.

84. Ibid., 102–3.

85. Salisbury Town Records, 2:40.

86. Ibid., 10–11, 12–14, 14–16, 16–18, 77.

87. Ibid., 1:23–24; 4:3, 39, 43, 45, 47, 49, 52, 60.

88. Ibid., 2: 10–11, 12–14, 14–16, 16–18, 212–14; 4:3, 10, 16, 20, 30, 39, 49, 50, 53, 56, 57.

89. Ibid., 2:20, 21, 87, 93, 138, 197, 198.

90. Chipman, *Nathaniel Chipman*, 7.

91. Ibid., 8–9.

92. Ibid., 9–10.

93. Dexter, *Biographical Sketches*, 1:716–17.

94. *The Laws of Yale College in New-Haven in Connecticut, Enacted by the President and Fellows* (New Haven, 1774), 3.

95. For insight into Yale College during the years that Chipman attended, see Edmund S. Morgan, *The Gentle Puritan: A Life of Ezra Stiles, 1727–1795* (New Haven: Yale University Press, 1962), 361–403; Kelley, *Yale*; Leon Howard, *The Connecticut Wits* (Chicago: University of Chicago Press, 1943), 3–33; and Alexander Cowie, *John Trumbull: Connecticut Wit* (Chapel Hill: University of North Carolina Press, 1936), 25–93.

96. *Laws of Yale College*, 6.

97. "Regulations of Yale College," broadside in the collections of Yale University Library, New Haven, Connecticut.

98. Henry F. May provides an excellent analysis of the manner in which Congregational divines employed Locke's *Essay*. See *The Enlightenment in America* (New York: Oxford University Press, 1976), 9–12.

99. William Wollaston, quoted in Howard, *The Connecticut Wits*, 11–13.

100. Wollaston, quoted in ibid., 13.

101. William L. Kingsley, ed., *Yale College: A Sketch of Its History*, 2 vols. (New York, 1879), 1:310, 317.

102. Kelley, *Yale*, 83.

103. Quoted in ibid., 84.

104. Quoted in Anson Phelps Stokes, *Memorials of Eminent Yale Men*, 2 vols. (New Haven: Yale University Press, 1914), 1:313.

105. Daniel Chipman prints the poem in its entirety in *Nathaniel Chipman*, 12–14.

106. Dexter, *Biographical Sketches*, 3:660.

107. Ibid.

108. Anthony Wayne, quoted in Freeman, *George Washington*, 4:571.

109. Quoted in ibid., 579.

110. John C. Miller, *Triumph of Freedom, 1775–1783* (Boston: Little, Brown, 1948), 222.

111. Chipman to Elisha Lee, April 1778, printed in Chipman, *Nathaniel Chipman*, 26–27.

112. Chipman to Washington, October 10, 1778, printed in ibid., 32–33.

113. For the attitudes of officers in the Continental Army, see Charles Royster, *A Revolutionary People at War: The Continental Army and the American Character, 1775–1783* (Chapel Hill: University of North Carolina Press, 1979); Don Higginbotham, "Military Leadership in the American Revolution," *Leadership in the American Revolution* (Washington, D.C.: Library of Congress, 1974), 91–111; Gerhard Kollmann, "Reflections on the Army of the American Revolution," in *New Wine in Old Skins: A Comparative View of Socio-Political Structure and Values Affecting the American Revolution*, ed. Erich Angermann (Stuttgart, Germany: Klett, 1976), 153–76; and James Martin and Mark Lender, *A Respectable Army: The Military Origins of the Republic, 1763–1789* (Arlington Heights, Ill.: Harlan Davidson, 1982).

114. George Washington, quoted in Kollmann, "Reflections on the Army of the American Revolution," 156.

115. Quoted in Royster, *Revolutionary People at War*, 87.

116. Pettee, *The Rev. Jonathan Lee*, 92.

117. Chipman to Fitch, March 20, 1779, printed in Chipman, *Nathaniel Chipman*, 31–32.

118. Uriah Tracey, quoted in David H. Fischer, *The Revolution of American Conservatism: The Federalist Party in the Era of Jeffersonian Democracy* (New York: Harper & Row, 1965), 23.

119. Chipman to Fitch, January 1, 1779, printed in Chipman, *Nathaniel Chipman*, 30.

120. Chipman to Fitch, March 20, 1779, printed in ibid., 31–32.

121. Hemenway, *Vermont Historical Gazetteer*, 3:1143 (see chap. 1, n. 47).

122. Nathan Perkins, *A Narrative of a Tour through the State of Vermont from April 27 to June 12, 1789* (Woodstock, Vt.: Elm Tree Press, 1930), 23.

123. Hemenway, *Vermont Historical Gazetteer*, 1:906 (see chap. 2, n. 2).

124. Daniel Chipman, *A Memoir of Thomas Chittenden, the first governor of Vermont; with a history of the constitution during his administration* (Middleton, Vt., 1849), 9.

125. Ibid., 10.

126. Salisbury Town Records, 1:370.

127. Hemenway, *Vermont Historical Gazetteer*, 1:906.

128. "Births, Deaths, Marriages, Town Meetings, 1740–1780," Salisbury Town Records, 15.

129. Salisbury Town Records, 3:123.

130. Ibid., 3:307; 4:103.

131. Ibid., 3:356, 357, 360.

132. "Births, Deaths, Marriages, Town Meetings, 1740–1780," 97.

133. Salisbury Town Records, 3:634, 676, 678, 733; 4:53, 103, 112, 113, 157, 205, 230, 541.

134. Ibid., 2:10–11.

135. Ibid., 214–17.

136. For an example of the land sales of a proprietor, see the transactions of Thomas Newcomb during the years 1741–42 in ibid., 1:29, 51, 53, 58, 64, 71, 81, 85, 103, 134, 135, 156, 165, 176, 177, 255, 347.

137. "Births, Deaths, Marriages, Town Meetings, 1740–1780," 20.

138. Ibid., 45, 47, 49, 50, 53, 56, 60, 62, 66, 67.

139. Connecticut Archives — Militia Records, 2nd ser., doc. 699, Connecticut State Library, Hartford, Connecticut.

140. Fred Anderson provides wonderful insight into the relationship between provincial troops and British regulars in *A People's Army* (see chap. 1, n. 32).

141. "Births, Deaths, Marriages, Town Meetings, 1740–1780," 71.

142. Charles J. Hoadley, ed., *The Public Records of the Colony of Connecticut*, 15 vols. (Hartford, Conn., 1850–90), 12:295.

143. Oscar Zeichner, *Connecticut's Years of Controversy, 1750–1776* (Chapel Hill: University of North Carolina Press, 1949), 44–77.

144. Hoadley, *Public Records of Connecticut*, 12:651–71.

145. Ibid., 653.

146. Richard Bushman provides a perceptive analysis of the manner in which American colonists interpreted the protection-allegiance covenant in *King and People in Provincial Massachusetts* (see chap. 3, n. 58).

147. Zeichner, *Connecticut's Years of Controversy*, 44–77. Edmund S. Morgan prints these resolutions in his *Prologue to Revolution: Sources and Documents on the Stamp Act Crisis, 1764–1766* (Chapel Hill: University of North Carolina Press, 1959), 62–63.

148. Hoadley, *Public Records of Connecticut*, 12:424.

149. Zeichner, *Connecticut's Years of Controversy*, 57–58.

150. Pettee, *The Rev. Jonathan Lee*, 162–63.

151. Jonathan Lee, *A Sermon delivered before the General Assembly of the Colony of Connecticut, at Hartford, on the day of the Anniversary Election, May 8, 1766* (New London, 1766), 15, 27.

152. *Connecticut Courant* (Hartford), February 10, 24, March 31, 1766, quotation in the March 31 issue.

153. "Births, Deaths, Marriages, Town Meetings, 1740–1780," 56.

154. Ibid., 90; "Salisbury Births, Deaths, Marriages, 1767–1784," Salisbury Town Records, 48, 52; Hoadley, *Public Records of Connecticut*, 12:452, 494, 541, 547, 607, 13:3, 93, 124, 169, 235, 512, 572.

155. Hoadley, *Public Records of Connecticut*, 12:609.

156. Ibid., 13:284.

157. Ibid., 13:578; 14:78.

158. *Connecticut Courant*, December 3, 1764.

159. See esp. Zeichner, *Connecticut's Years of Controversy*, 262 n. 25.

160. *Connecticut Courant*, March 11, 1765.

161. Ibid., May 20, 1765.

162. Quoted in Zeichner, *Connecticut's Years of Controversy*, 59.

163. Hoadley, *Public Records of Connecticut*, 13:382.

164. James B. Wilbur prints excerpts from these documents in *Ira Allen*, 1:44 n. 2 (see chap. 1, n. 163).

165. Hemenway, *Vermont Historical Gazetteer*, 1:907.

166. *State Papers of Vermont*, 17 vols. (Montpelier, Vt.: Secretary of State, 1918–69), 13:52–53.

167. Isaac Tichenor to Jacob Cuyler, November 8, 1782, Papers of the Continental Congress, 1774–1789 (microfilm, M247, r93, i78, v6, pp. 159–61) (see chap. 3, n. 8).

168. Ibid. (M247, r26, i19, vi, p. 627).

169. *A History of Newark, New Jersey* (New York: Lewis, 1913), 384.

170. "Abstract of Wills, 1730–1750," vol. 2, printed in *New Jersey Archives*, 1st ser., 30:566.

171. "Records of the Town of Newark, in New Jersey, from its settlement in 1666, to its incorporation as a city in 1836," printed in *Collections of the New Jersey Historical Society*, 23 vols. (Newark, N.J., 1846–1989), 6:24, 36, 37, 49, 70.

172. Ibid., 51.

173. David L. Pierson, *Narratives of Newark* (Newark, N.J.: Pierson, 1917), 44.

174. "Records of Newark," 107.

175. Ibid., 139.

176. "Abstract of Wills, 1771–1780," vol. 5, in *New Jersey Archives*, 1st ser., 34:526–27.

177. For conditions in New Jersey during this period, see Donald J. Mrozek, "Problems of Social History and Patterns of Inheritance in Pre-Revolutionary New Jersey, 1751–1770," *Journal of the Rutgers University Library*, 36 (1972), 1–19; Dennis P. Ryan, "Landholding, Opportunity, and Mobility in Revolutionary New Jersey," *William and Mary Quarterly*, 3rd ser., 36 (1979), 571–92; and Thomas L. Purvis, "Origins and Patterns of Agrarian Unrest in New Jersey, 1735–1754," ibid., 39 (1982), 600–627.

178. Larry R. Gerlach, *Prologue to Independence: New Jersey in the Coming of the American Revolution* (New Brunswick, N.J.: Rutgers University Press, 1976), 186–89.

179. Rules adopted May 4, 1769, printed in *Pennsylvania Journal*, July 13, 1769.

180. "Abstract of Wills, 1771–1780," vol. 5, *New Jersey Archives*, 1st ser., 34:526–27.

181. For insight into Princeton under Witherspoon, see Thomas J. Wertenbaker, *Princeton, 1746–1896* (Princeton: Princeton University Press, 1946); Francis L. Broderick, "Pulpit, Physics, and Politics: The Curriculum of the College of New Jersey, 1746–1794," *William and Mary Quarterly*, 3rd ser., 6 (1949), 42–68; Ralph Ketcham, "James Madison at Princeton," *Princeton University Library Chronicle*, 28 (1966), 24–54; Sheldon S. Cohen and Larry R. Gerlach, "Princeton in the Coming of the American Revolution," *New Jersey History*, 92 (1974), 69–92; and Mark A. Noll, *Princeton and the Republic, 1768–1822* (Princeton: Princeton University Press, 1989).

182. Samuel Blair, *An Account of the College of New Jersey* (Woodbridge, N.J., 1764), 23.

183. Membership List for the Cliosophic Society, Princeton University Archives, Princeton University Library, Princeton, New Jersey.

184. Gerlach, *Prologue to Independence*, 251.

185. Cohen and Gerlach, "Princeton in the Coming of the American Revolution," 80–81.

186. Gerlach, *Prologue to Independence*, 274–78.

187. *Official Register of the Officers and Men of New Jersey in the Revolutionary War* (Trenton, N.J., 1872), 433, 472, 785.

188. James McLachlan, *Princetonians, 1748–1768: A Biographical Dictionary* (Princeton: Princeton University Press, 1976), 464–66.

189. *Minutes of the Albany Committee of Correspondence, 1775–1778*, vol. 2, ed. Alexander C. Flick (Albany: University of the State of New York, 1925), 1057.

190. For the activities of this group as well as excellent analyses of economic conditions during the Revolution, see Edward Alexander, *Revolutionary Conservative* (see chap. 3, n. 11); Robert A. East, *Business Enterprise in the American Revolutionary Era* (New York: Columbia University Press, 1938); Victor Leroy Johnson, *The Administration of the American Commissariat during the Revolutionary War* (Philadelphia: By the author, 1941); Bernard Mason, "Entrepreneurial Activity in New York during the American Revolution," *Business History Review*, 40 (1966), 190–212; Jonathan Gregory Rossie, *The Politics of Command in the American Revolution* (Syracuse: Syracuse University Press, 1975); E. Wayne Carp, *To Starve the Army at Pleasure: Continental Army Administration and American Political Culture, 1775–1783* (Chapel Hill: University of North Carolina Press, 1984); and Don Gerlach, *Proud Patriot: Philip Schuyler and the War of Independence, 1775–1783* (Syracuse: Syracuse University Press, 1987).

191. Mason, "Entrepreneurial Activity in New York," 203.

192. Quoted in Carp, *To Starve the Army at Pleasure*, 111.

193. Roger Sherman, quoted in Edmund Cody Burnett, *The Continental Congress* (New York: Macmillan, 1941), 396.

194. Joseph Trumbull, quoted in Rossie, *Politics of Command*, 109.

195. Cuyler to Tichenor, September 17, 1777, "Notes and Documents—I: Court Martial of Isaac Tichenor," *Proceedings of the Vermont Historical Society*, 11 (1943), 189–90.

196. Royal Flint to Tichenor, September 10, 1778, ibid., 194.

197. Samuel Herrick and Samuel Robinson to Tichenor, May 4, 1780, ibid., 187–88.

198. Tichenor to Maj. Jonathan Child, January 4, 1779, ibid., 199.

199. George Washington, "General Orders, October 16, 1780," in *The Writings of George Washington*, ed. John C. Fitzpatrick, 39 vols. (Washington, D.C.: Government Printing Office, 1931–44), 20:199–201.

200. Tichenor to ———, October 30, 1780, in "Court Martial of Isaac Tichenor," 207–8.

201. "General Orders, October 16, 1780."

202. *State Papers of Vermont*, 5:124–25, 283–84.

203. Bennington Town Records, bk. A, March 20, 1781 (see chap. 2, n. 4).

204. Goodrich, *Vermont Soldiers in the Revolutionary War*, 424.

205. Ibid., 417; Bennington Town Records, bk. A, September 4, 1781.

206. Archibald Hamilton Rowan, *Autobiography* (Dublin, 1840), 318.

207. Aleine Austin, *Matthew Lyon: "New Man" of the Democratic Revolution, 1749–1822* (University Park: Pennsylvania State University Press, 1981), 7–8; J. Fairfax McLaughlin, *Matthew Lyon, The Hampden of Congress: A Biography* (New York: Wynkoop Hallenback Crawford, 1900), 33–43.

208. Rowan, *Autobiography*, 318.

209. McLaughlin, *Lyon*, 32. Austin gives Lyon's birth as July 14, 1749 (Austin, *Lyon*, 7).

210. Austin, *Lyon*, 8; McLaughlin, *Lyon*, 6–7.

211. The following analysis of the White Boy insurgency relies upon Francis Plowden, *An Historical Review of the State of Ireland*, 2 vols. (London, 1803); William E. H. Lecky, *A History of Ireland in the Eighteenth Century*, 5 vols. (London, 1892); T. Desmond Williams, ed., *Secret Societies in Ireland* (New York: Barnes & Noble, 1973); George C. Lewis, *On Local Disturbances in Ireland; and on the Irish Church Question* (London, 1837); and Michael Beames, *Peasants and Power: The Whiteboy Movement and Their Control in Pre-Famine Ireland* (New York: St. Martin's Press, 1983).

212. Plowden, *Historical Review*, 1:337.

213. Quoted in Lecky, *History of Ireland*, 2:35.

214. Quoted in Beames, *Peasants and Power*, 27.

215. Lewis Collins, *History of Kentucky*, 2 vols. (Covington, Ky., 1882), 2:491; McLaughlin, *Lyon*, 7–8.

216. Austin, *Lyon*, 7; McLaughlin, *Lyon*, 7–8, 14–16.

217. McLaughlin, *Lyon*, 23–27.

218. Richard R. Madden, *The History of Irish Periodical Literature*, 2 vols. (London, 1867), 1:43, 2:373–89; Leslie Stephen and Sidney Lee, eds., *The Dictionary of National Biography* (London: Oxford University Press, 1921–22), 12:231–34 ("Charles Lucas"); Arthur P. I. Samuels, *The Early Life Correspondence and Writings of The Rt. Hon. Edmund Burke* (Cambridge: Cambridge University Press, 1933), 118–19, 180–202.

219. Quoted in Madden, *Irish Periodical Literature*, 2:380.

220. McLaughlin, *Lyon*, 23–27.

221. Austin, *Lyon*, 8–9.

222. *Annals of Congress*, 5th Cong., 1st sess., June 3, 1797, 235.

223. Quoted in Collins, *Kentucky*, 492.

224. Austin, *Lyon*, 9; McLaughlin, *Lyon*, 44–45.

225. McLaughlin, *Lyon*, 65–66.

226. Ibid., 44–47, 59–60, 67; Austin, *Lyon*, 10.

227. Austin, *Lyon*, 10–11.

228. McLaughlin, *Lyon*, 70; Bellesiles, "Life, Liberty, and Land," 44–45 (see chap. 1, n. 92).

229. Edward C. Starr, *A History of Cornwall, Connecticut: A Typical New England Town* (New Haven: Tuttle, Morehouse & Taylor, 1926), 329.

230. Hemenway, *Vermont Historical Gazetteer*, 3:1161–62.

231. Starr, *History of Cornwall*, 329.

232. Austin, *Lyon*, 11–12.

233. Ibid., 13.

Chapter 5. Independence

1. Matthew Lyon, quoted in Austin, *Lyon*, 15 (see chap. 4, n. 207).

2. *Grand committee* is the term employed by Peleg Sunderland in reference to a select committee chosen to serve as civil officers upon the adjournment of the convention (*State Papers of Vermont*, 8:341–42 [see chap. 4, n. 166]).

3. The compact is printed in *Records of the Governor and Council of Vermont*, 2:491–97, quotations on 494 and 496 (see chap. 4, n. 66).

4. The General Association subscribed to by the Albany Committee of Correspondence is printed in *Minutes of the Albany Committee of Correspondence, 1775–1778*, vol. 1, ed. James Sullivan (Albany: University of the State of New York, 1923), 3. The copy of this document in the Vermont Historical Society is referred to as the "Bennington Declaration For Freedom."

5. *Minutes of the Albany Committee of Correspondence*, 1:27, 30, 227–28, 230, 232, 249, 433, 468, 589, 605; Papers of the Continental Congress, 1774–1789 (microfilm, M247, r47, i40, pp. 425, 426, 427, 437) (see chap. 3, n. 8).

6. Ethan Allen, *A Vindication of the Opposition of the Inhabitants of Vermont to the Government of New-York, and of their Right to form an Independent State* (Dresden, N.H., 1779), 10–11.

7. Hall, *History of Vermont*, 199–201 (see chap. 2, n. 29). Col. Benedict Arnold arrived several days later and claimed that his commission from the Massachusetts committee of safety gave him the right to lead the expedition. He was allowed to accompany the force as a volunteer without a command.

8. Ibid., 202–9.

9. Ibid., 209–10.

10. Peter Force, ed., *American Archives*, 4th ser., 6 vols. (Washington, D.C., 1837–46), 2:1339.

11. This list is printed in ibid., 1570.

12. Allen to Jonathan Trumbull, August 3, 1775, printed in ibid., 17–18.

13. For excellent insight into the democratic nature of New Light political thought, see Nathan O. Hatch, "The Christian Movement and the Demand for a Theology of the People," *Journal of American History*, 67 (1980), 545–67; and Stephen A. Marini, *Radical Sects of Revolutionary New England* (Cambridge: Harvard University Press, 1982), esp. 40–59.

14. Bennington Town Records, bk. A, March 29, 1769; March 28, 1770 (see chap. 2, n. 4).

15. Bennington Church Records, "Roll of Members admitted from settlement of Rev. Jedediah Dewey, August 14, 1763 to his death, December, 1778" (see chap. 1, n. 160); Bennington Town Records, bk. A, March 28, 1764–March 26, 1776.

16. Force, *American Archives*, 2:1702–3, 1760–62; 3:243, 469.

17. Gerlach, *Proud Patriot*, 15–34 (see chap. 4, n. 190); Hall, *History of Vermont*, 213–14.

18. Gerlach, *Proud Patriot*, 98.

19. For the rosters of Warner's regiment, see Goodrich, *Vermont Soldiers in the Revolutionary War*, 107–12 (see chap. 2, n. 21).

20. *Records of the Governor and Council of Vermont*, 1:11–13.

21. The petition appears in ibid., 16–19.

22. *Journals of the Continental Congress, 1774–1789*, ed. Worthington Chauncey Ford, 34 vols. (Washington, D.C.: Government Printing Office, 1904–37), 4:405.

23. For insight into the Provincial Congress of New York, as well as James Duane's role in New York politics during this time, see Carl L. Becker, *The History of Political Parties in the Province of New York, 1760–1776* (Madison: University of Wisconsin Press, 1968), 193–276; and Alexander, *Revolutionary Conservative*, 93–157 (see chap. 3, n. 11).

24. *Journals of the Continental Congress*, 4:416.

25. *Records of the Governor and Council of Vermont*, 1:20.

26. Ibid., 21–26.

27. The roll of delegates appears in ibid., 26–27.

28. For activity east of the Green Mountains throughout the Revolutionary years, see Hall, *History of Eastern Vermont* (see chap. 3, n. 3).

29. The "Proceedings of the 'Congress' and 'Committees of Safety' for Cumberland County," printed in *Records of the Governor and Council of Vermont*, 1:313–75, reveal the gradual triumph east of the mountains of radical whigs who were unsympathetic to New York authorities. For an analysis of the close correlation that existed between New Light religious attitudes and opposition to New York authority, see Smith, "Legacy of Dissent" (see chap. 3, n. 3). Smith also provides insight into the formation of a "New Light Brotherhood" on the Grants.

30. *Records of the Governor and Council of Vermont*, 1:28.

31. Ibid., 29–30.

32. Bennington played a disproportionate role in such activities because of a report adopted at Dorset on January 16, 1776, that allotted Bennington the greatest number of delegates (7) of any town represented in the convention (see ibid., 12).

33. Ibid., 36–38.

34. The manifesto appears in ibid., 390–93.

35. Ibid., 40.

36. Ibid., 51.

37. Ibid., 48–51.

38. Ira Allen, *Some Miscellaneous Remarks and Short Arguments, on a Small Pamphlet, dated in the Convention of the Representatives of the State of New York, October 2, 1776, and sent from said Convention to the County of Cumberland, and some Reasons given, why the District of the New Hampshire Grants had best be a State* (Hartford, Conn., 1777), printed in ibid., 376–89.

39. *Records of the Governor and Council of Vermont*, 379.

40. Ibid., 381.

41. *The People the Best Governors: or a Plan of Government Founded on the Just Principles of Natural Freedom* (n.p., 1776), reprinted in Chase, *History of Dartmouth College*, 1:654–63 (see chap. 4, n. 4).

42. Randolph A. Roth, *The Democratic Dilemma: Religion, Reform, and the Social Order in the Connecticut River Valley of Vermont, 1791–1850* (New York: Cambridge University Press, 1987), 34. The pamphlet is generally associated with the New Light coterie at Dartmouth and may have been written by either Eleazar Wheelock or Bezaleel Woodward.

43. *The People the Best Governors*, 654.

44. Ibid., 658, 660.

45. Ibid., 661.

46. *Records of the Governor and Council of Vermont*, 1:52–61.

47. Ibid., 58 n. 2. The composition of this committee is not recorded in the journal of the convention. The research of E. P. Walton, editor of the *Records*, led him to name these four men. Years later, when asked who drafted the Vermont constitution, Jonas Fay responded that he did (Harwood Diary, February 13, 1812, Bennington Museum, Bennington, Vermont).

48. Aaron Hutchinson, *A well tempered Self-Love a Rule of Conduct towards others: A Sermon preached at Windsor, July 2, 1777, before the Representatives of the Towns in the Counties of Charlotte, Cumberland and Glouchester, for the forming the State of Vermont* (Dresden, N.H., 1777), quotations on 11, 27, 19–20, and 40.

49. Since leaving the Oblong, Young had been an ardent member of the Sons of Liberty in Boston and a central figure in the Albany Committee of Correspondence, and as an associate of the Whig Society in Philadelphia he had helped write the Pennsylvania Constitution.

50. Thomas Young, *To the Inhabitants of Vermont, a Free and Independent State, bounding on the River Connecticut and Lake Champlain*, printed in *Records of the Governor and Council of Vermont*, 1:394–96, quotation on 395.

51. For a discussion of these similarities and differences, see John N. Shaeffer, "A Comparison of the First Constitutions of Vermont and Pennsylvania," *Vermont History*, 43 (1975), 33–43; and Gary J. Aichele, "Making the Vermont Constitution: 1777–1824," ibid., 56 (1988), 166–90. Peter S. Onuf places the constitutional history of Vermont within a much broader national framework in "State-Making in Revolutionary Crisis: Independent Vermont as a Case Study," *Journal of American History* 67 (1981), 797–815.

52. John Shaeffer and H. N. Muller argue that the strength accorded the executive branch made the Vermont constitution far less democratic than that of Pennsylvania (see Shaeffer, "First Constitutions of Vermont and Pennsylvania"; and Muller, "Early Vermont State Government, 1778–1815: Oligarchy or Democracy?" *Growth and Development of Government in Vermont*, Vermont Academy of Arts and Sciences Occasional Paper, no. 5 [Waitsfield, 1970], 5–10).

53. *The People the Best Governors*, 656.

54. Ibid., 656–57.

55. *Records of the Governor and Council of Vermont*, 1:62–75.

56. "Proceedings of the Council of Safety, July 8 to August 15, 1777," in ibid., 130–39.

57. For the rosters of these companies, see Goodrich, *Vermont Soldiers in the Revolutionary War*, 26–27.

58. Hall, *History of Vermont*, 261–63; Jennings, *Memorials of a Century*, 146–203 (see chap. 2, n. 1).

59. These resolutions had been passed on June 30, 1777 (*Journals of the Continental Congress*, 8:508–13).

60. Ira Allen, *Miscellaneous Remarks on the Proceedings of the State of New York against the State of Vermont, etc.* (Hartford, 1777), quotations on 9 and 13.

61. *Records of the Governor and Council of Vermont*, 1:76–79.

62. Ira Allen, *Natural and Political History of Vermont* (see chap. 3, n. 51), printed in *Collections of the Vermont Historical Society*, 1:393 (see chap. 2, n. 37).

63. John M. Comstock, *A List of the Principal Civil Officers of Vermont from 1777 to 1918* (St. Albans, Vt.: St. Albans Messenger, 1918), 82.

64. Nathaniel Hendricks, "A New Look at the Ratification of the Vermont Constitution of 1777," *Vermont History*, 34 (1966), 136–40.

65. Until 1808, when Montpelier became the state capital, meetings of the legislature alternated between towns on the east and west sides of the Green Mountains.

66. Hall, *History of Vermont*, 278.

67. Hemenway, *Vermont Historical Gazetteer*, 1:161–62.

68. *State Papers of Vermont*, 12:13.

69. For a discussion of Allen's activities subsequent to his return to the state, see Michael A. Bellesiles, *Revolutionary Outlaws: Ethan Allen and the Struggle for Independence on the Early American Frontier* (Charlottesville: University Press of Virginia, 1993), 148–216.

70. Ethan Allen, *An Animadversory Address to the Inhabitants of the State of Vermont* (Hartford, Conn., 1778), 16.

71. Ibid., 23.

72. Allen, *A Vindication*, 51.

73. Ibid., 36.

74. Ibid., 47–48.

75. The *Narrative* appeared first in serial form in the *Pennsylvania Packet*, November 9, 11, 13, 16, 20, 25, 27, 1779. Subsequently published in book form, it went through a great many editions. All references are to Brooke Hindle, ed., *The Narrative of Colonel Ethan Allen* (New York: Corinth Books, 1961).

76. My discussion of the *Narrative* draws upon Daniel E. Williams, "Zealous in the Cause of Liberty: Self-Creation and Redemption in the Narrative of Ethan Allen," *Studies in Eighteenth-Century Culture*, 19 (1989), 325–47. For a provocative analysis that emphasizes Allen's own self-dramatization in the *Narrative*, see Bellesiles, *Revolutionary Outlaws*, 148–55.

77. Allen, *Narrative*, 78.

78. Ibid., 107.

79. Ibid., 43.

80. Ibid., 62.

81. Ibid., 98.

82. Ibid., 79, 110, 119.

83. Within the first two years the *Narrative* went through eight editions, printed in Boston, Philadelphia, Norwich, Connecticut, and Newbury and Danvers, Massachusetts.

84. Smith, "Legacy of Dissent," 362–63; Roth, *Democratic Dilemma*, 26–28.

85. Samuel Williams, *The Natural and Civil History of Vermont* (Walpole, N.H., 1794), 219.

86. Between 1771 and 1791 Vermont's population rose from 7,644 to 85,425 (see Jay Mack Holbrook, *Vermont 1771 Census* [Oxford, Mass.: Holbrook Research Institute, 1982], xii; I have relied on this work for all census estimates in Vermont prior to 1791).

87. Ibid.

88. Smith, "Legacy of Dissent," 880; Roth, *Democratic Dilemma*, 38–79.

89. For insightful discussions of this phenomenon in various towns, see Charles H. Hubbard and Justus Dartt, *History of the Town of Springfield* (Boston, 1895); Mary R. Cabot, *Annals of Brattleboro, 1681–1895*, 2 vols. (Brattleboro, Vt.: E. L. Hildreth, 1921–22); and Henry S. Wardner, *The Birthplace of Vermont: A History of Windsor to 1781* (New York: Charles Scribner's Sons, 1927). Wardner even includes a chapter entitled "Windsor Gains Some 'Nice People.'" In addition, David Fischer provides highly informative sketches of many of these gentlemen in *Revolution of American Conservatism*, 239–45 (see chap. 4, n. 118).

90. Membership rolls, 1762–80, Bennington Church Records.

91. Bennington Church Records, 1:27.

92. Ibid.

93. Ibid.

94. Ibid., 28.

95. Avery, *A Narrative*, 6 (see chap. 4, n. 1).

96. For the struggle between Strict Congregationalists, who followed the Cambridge Platform, and members of the standing order, who supported the Saybrook Platform, see McLoughlin, *New England Dissent*, 1:340–59; and Goen, *Revivalism and Separatism in New England*, 36–40 (see chap. 1, n. 3).

97. Avery, *A Narrative*, 7–8.

98. Bennington Church Records, 1:35–38; David Avery, "A summary view of the doing of the church of Bennington, 7th March, 1783," *Avery Papers* (see chap. 4, n. 2).

99. Avery Diary, September 25, 1780; David Avery to Benjamin Chaplin, April 5, 1783, Avery Papers.

100. There is a detailed accounting of Mrs. Avery's expenses in the Avery Papers.

101. John M. Mulder, ed., *The Papers of David Avery, 1746–1818* (Princeton: Princeton Theological Seminary, 1979), an introduction accompanying the *Avery Papers*, xxxiii–xxxiv.

102. Avery Diary, August 30, 1783.

103. Abby Maria Hemenway, ed., *Vermont Historical Gazetteer*, vol. 5 (Brandon, Vt., 1891), 29–31.

104. The rate lists for 1780, 1781, and 1782 are in the *Avery Papers*. The rate for 1780 is on the members of the church and the society; those for 1781 and 1782 are for "Voluntary Subscribers."

105. Avery's diary for the years 1780–83 is replete with references to social intercourse with these people. For the clearest example of Avery's penchant for expensive material goods, as well as his pride in associating with men like Tichenor, see Philander [Avery] to Narcissa [Hannah Chapin], May 21, 1782, *Avery Papers*.

106. Avery to Chaplin, April 5, 1783, ibid.

107. Avery to Timothy Dwight, August 25, 1780, ibid.

108. Avery Diary, October 22, 1781.

109. Avery, *A Narrative*, 24–25.

110. Ibid., 26–29.

111. "The congregation in Bennington to the Rev. David Avery," ibid., 35–37. As clerk of the congregation, Tichenor signed this letter.

112. Avery, *A Narrative*, 53–54.

113. For a provocative discussion of the gentleman's perception of disinterestedness, see Gordon S. Wood, "Interests and Disinterestedness in the Making of the Constitution," in *Beyond the Confederation: Origins of the Constitution and American National Identity*, ed. Richard Beeman et al. (Chapel Hill: University of North Carolina Press, 1987), 69–109.

114. Sarah V. Kalinoski, "Sequestration, Confiscation, and the 'Tory' in the Vermont Revolution," *Vermont History*, 45 (1977), 236–46.

115. Austin, *Lyon*, 23–24. For the fullest record of the activities of the Court of Confiscation, see *State Papers of Vermont*, vol. 6.

116. Ibid., 6:24–25 and vol. 2. Thomas Chittenden's name appeared on forty charters, while Ira Allen became a proprietor in thirty-three different townships.

117. Graffagnino reveals how Allen mixed personal and official business in "The Country My Soul Delighted In" (see chap. 1, n. 183).

118. Isaac Miller to Ira Allen, January 30, 1781, Ira Allen Papers, Stevens Collection, Vermont State Archives, Montpelier, Vermont.

119. The Haldimand Negotiations were a complex and tangled affair. For opposing views of the Allens' motives, see Chilton Williamson, *Vermont in Quandary: 1763–1825* (Montpelier: Vermont Historical Society, 1949), 90–126; and Wilbur, *Ira Allen*, 1:292–443 (see chap. 1, n. 163). Bellesiles presents the most balanced and reasonable account of these negotiations in *Revolutionary Outlaws*, 197–211.

120. *Records of the Governor and Council of Vermont*, 3:340.

121. Ibid., 341–42. The quotation appears in an act printed in Slade, *Vermont State Papers*, 392 (see chap. 3, n. 56).

122. For a discussion of lay judges in Vermont in this period, see Samuel B. Hand, "Lay Judges and the Vermont Judiciary to 1825," *Vermont History*, 46 (1978), 205–20.

123. Chipman later reported this incident in the *Annals of Congress*, 5th Cong., 1st sess., 999–1000.

124. Slade, *Vermont State Papers*, 394.

125. *Records of the Governor and Council of Vermont*, 3:343.

126. *State Papers of Vermont*, 3, pt. 2: 37. The bill itself is printed in Slade, *Vermont State Papers*, 442–43, quotation on 443.

127. Ibid., 442.

128. Chipman, *Nathaniel Chipman*, 64 (see chap. 4, n. 68).

129. *Records of the Governor and Council of Vermont*, 3:46–49.

130. *State Papers of Vermont*, 3, pt. 3: 86–87.

131. Ibid., 125–26; *Records of the Governor and Council of Vermont*, 3:349.

132. *State Papers of Vermont*, 3, pt. 3: 154.

133. Ibid., pt. 1, 171. See also *Records of the Governor and Council of Vermont*, 2:89–92.

134. *Vermont Gazette*, September 19, 1785.

135. For discussions of this book, see Arnold Smithson, *Natural Religion in American Literature* (New Haven: College & University Press, 1966), 23–39; and

Bellesiles, *Revolutionary Outlaws*, 217–44. For a sensible interpretation of the controversy over the authorship of the book, see Michael A. Bellesiles, "Works of Historical Faith: Or, Who Wrote *Reason The Only Oracle of Man?*" *Vermont History*, 57 (1989), 69–83.

136. Timothy Dwight, "To the friends of humanity," *American Museum*, October 1787, 410.

137. A great many of these petitions are printed in *State Papers of Vermont*, vol. 8.

138. Ibid., 189–92.

139. Ibid., 216–18.

140. Chittenden's proclamation appeared in the *Vermont Gazette*, August 28, 1786.

141. Chipman, *Nathaniel Chipman*, 18.

142. Chipman published this poem under the pen name "Honestus" in the February 28 and March 6, 1874, issues of the *Vermont Gazette*.

143. Chipman, *Nathaniel Chipman*, 67–69.

144. For details of this disturbance, see Hall, *History of Eastern Vermont*, 548–51.

145. For details of this insurrection, see A. M. Caverly, *History of the Town of Pittsford, Vermont* (Rutland, Vt., 1872), 248–61. Testimony of many of the leaders of the Regulation is printed in the *Vermont Gazette*, February 5, 1787.

146. *Vermont Gazette*, November 27, 1786.

147. Royall Tyler quotes Chittenden to this effect in his report on the Shaysites who fled to Vermont in February 1787 (Royall Tyler Papers, Vermont Historical Society, Montpelier, Vermont).

148. *Vermont Gazette*, January 1, 1787.

149. The results for each town appear in *State Papers of Vermont*, 3, pt. 3: 284–85. The citizens of Bennington, for example, rejected a bank for the issuance of paper money by a vote of 108 to 0.

150. For fresh insight into this rebellion, see Robert A. Gross, ed., *In Debt to Shays: The Bicentennial of an Agrarian Rebellion* (Charlottesville: University Press of Virginia, 1993).

151. *Records of the Governor and Council of Vermont*, 3:119; *State Papers of Vermont*, 3, pt. 3: 270–71.

152. Tyler's report on the Shays men who fled into Vermont (see n. 147 above).

153. *State Papers of Vermont*, 3, pt. 3: 291–92.

154. Ibid., 292–93. The vote was 36 to 24.

155. Ibid., 299–300.

156. Ibid., 309.

157. Slade, *Vermont State Papers*, 543.

158. *Vermont Gazette*, July 24, 31, 1786.

159. Ibid., August 7, 1786.

160. *Vermont Journal* (Windsor), August 28, 1786.

161. *Records of the Governor and Council of Vermont*, 3:95–96; *State Papers of Vermont*, 3, pt. 3: 211–12.

162. *Vermont Journal*, April 25, 1786.

163. *Vermont Gazette,* June 19, 1786.

164. Ibid., August 31, 1786.

165. For details of the Woodbridge transaction, see Williamson, *Vermont in Quandary,* 178–79; and Wilbur, *Ira Allen,* 1:529–30.

166. Slade prints the entire proceedings of the first Council of Censors in his *Vermont State Papers,* 511–44, quotation on 533.

167. Chipman prints this correspondence in his *Nathaniel Chipman,* 70–82. For an excellent analysis of the negotiations between New York and Vermont essential to the latter's admission into the union, see Peter S. Onuf, *The Origins of the Federal Republic: Jurisdictional Controversies in the United States, 1775–1787* (Philadelphia: University of Pennsylvania Press, 1983), 103–45.

168. *Records of the Governor and Council of Vermont,* 3:464–82; Wilbur, *Ira Allen,* 2:1–2; *Vermont Gazette,* January 10, 1791.

169. Smith, "Legacy of Dissent," 880–82.

Chapter 6. Divisions throughout the Town

1. For an analysis of Bennington as a "central place" and a "regional center," see Martyn J. Bowden, Bruce L. LaRose, and Brian Mishara, "The Development of Competition between Central Places on the Frontier: Vermont, 1790–1830," *Proceedings of the Association of American Geographers,* 3 (1971), 32–38; and Bruce L. LaRose, "The Emergence of the Vermont Settlement Pattern, 1609–1830" (M.A. thesis, Clark University, 1967), 95–154.

2. For an itinerary of this trip, see Thomas Jefferson, *The Papers of Thomas Jefferson,* ed. Julian P. Boyd, 25 vols. to date (Princeton: Princeton University Press, 1950–), 20:471–73.

3. The population of Vermont showed a gain of 80 percent between 1791 and 1800, but Bennington's population remained steady.

4. Bennington Town Records, Deeds, vol. A1, 1741–1809.

5. See, e.g., Bennington Superior Court Docket Books, vols. A, 1782–1794, 2–3, 6, and B, 1794–1800, 287–92, Bennington County Courthouse, Bennington, Vermont.

6. Provisioning migrants was a major source of income for many early settlers in western Vermont. For a discussion of this traffic in the Cornwall area, see P. Jeffrey Potash, *Vermont's Burned-Over District: Patterns of Community Development and Religious Activity, 1761–1850* (Brooklyn: Carlson, 1991), 51–52.

7. An analysis of the probate records for Bennington throughout the years 1778–1846 as well as the Bennington County Records, Deeds, vols. A, 1782–1794, B, 1794–1800, and C, 1800–1807; and the Bennington Deed Records, Index, vol, 1, 1762–1892, clearly discloses this growing disparity in wealth. In addition, Bennington's rate list for 1785 reveals that the top 20 percent of Bennington inhabitants held over 75 percent of the wealth of the township. John Page discerned this disparity as early as 1776 ("The Economic Structure of Society in Revolutionary Bennington," *Vermont History,* 49 [1981], 69–84).

8. Bennington was not unique in this regard. Indeed, an analysis of Bennington land records for the period 1762–1800 reveals a striking similarity between landholding patterns there and in Cornwall, where the mean holding of those who settled prior to 1776 was twice that of individuals who settled between

1783 and 1785, triple that of men who came between 1786 and 1790, and four times that of families who settled between 1790 and 1792 (Potash, *Vermont's Burned-Over District*, 52).

9. Bennington Town Records, bks. A and B (see chap. 2, n. 4). See particularly the records of the annual town meetings between 1780 and 1800.

10. List of members admitted between May 27, 1783, and May 31, 1786 (Bennington Church Records [see chap. 1, n. 160]).

11. In his sketch of Job Swift, Franklin B. Dexter notes that Vermont was "very destitute of ministers" (Dexter, *Biographical Sketches*, 2:153 [see chap. 4, n. 3]).

12. Ibid., 151–53; Jennings, *Memorials of a Century*, 92–99 (see chap. 2, n. 1).

13. "Roll of Members admitted from Settlement of Rev. Job Swift, May 31, 1786 to his dismissal June 7, 1801," Bennington Church Records.

14. Jennings, *Memorials of a Century*, 96–98.

15. Bennington Church Records, 1, January 16, July 13, September 11, 1789.

16. *Vermont Gazette*, May 10, June 21, July 26, August 23, September 27, 1793; January 24, 1794.

17. Ibid., August 30, 1793, supplement.

18. Hemenway, *Vermont Historical Gazetteer*, 1:177 (see chap. 2, n. 2).

19. The *Vermont Gazette*, October 18, 1793, printed the election results by county.

20. Chittenden's margins of victory in Bennington in 1794, 1795, and 1796 were four to one, seven to one, and six to one, respectively. In the election of 1797 Moses Robinson carried the town by a nearly six-to-one margin (Bennington Town Records, bk. B, September 2, 1794; September 1, 6, 1796; September 5, 1797).

21. *Vermont Gazette*, August 14, 1786.

22. Ibid., October 9, 1786.

23. Ibid., August 29, 1791.

24. Ibid., August 17, 1792.

25. *Rutland Herald of Vermont*, June 25, 1792.

26. Ibid., September 3, 1792.

27. *Vermont Journal* (Windsor), July 5, 1791.

28. Vermont was initially divided into two congressional districts — eastern and western — with the Green Mountains as the dividing line.

29. Throughout the 1790s Ira Allen struggled to avoid imprisonment for debts resulting from his overzealous land speculations of the previous decade. For the best account of Allen's economic problems, see Graffagnino, "The Country My Soul Delighted In" (see chap. 1, n. 183); and idem, "'Twenty Thousand Muskets!!!': Ira Allen and the *Olive Branch* Affair, 1796–1800," *William and Mary Quarterly*, 3rd ser., 48 (1991), 409–31.

30. By the time he was elected to Congress, Lyon owned saw and gristmills, a tavern, a paper mill, a blast furnace, a forge, and a slitting mill for making nails. For all intents and purposes, he completely controlled the town of Fairhaven. For an excellent analysis of Lyon's entrepreneurial activities, see Austin, *Lyon*, 30–44 (see chap. 4, n. 207).

31. *Rutland Farmer's Library*, April 1, 1793.

32. Paine published part 1 of the *Rights of Man* in 1791; the far more radical part 2 appeared in 1792.

33. For a discussion of the impact of Paine's ideas in America, see Eric Foner, *Tom Paine and Revolutionary America* (New York: Oxford University Press, 1976).

34. *Rutland Farmer's Library*, June 10, 1793.

35. Ibid., February 17, 1794.

36. Quoted in Philip S. Foner, ed., *The Democratic-Republican Societies, 1790–1800: A Documentary Sourcebook of Constitutions, Declarations, Addresses, Resolutions, and Toasts* (Westport, Conn.: Greenwood Press, 1976), 7.

37. *Rutland Farmer's Library*, February 17, 1794.

38. Ibid., February 24, 1794.

39. Foner prints the constitutions and resolutions of these clubs in *Democratic-Republican Societies*, 273–318, quotations on 274. See Eugene P. Link, *The Democratic-Republican Societies, 1790–1800* (New York: Columbia University Press, 1942), for a discussion of these clubs throughout the country.

40. Chipman's letter first appeared in the *New York Herald*, July 14, 1794. Foner reprints it in *Democratic-Republican Societies*, 290–93, quotations on 290–92.

41. For an insightful discussion of the political tensions surrounding Jay's Treaty, see Stanley Elkins and Eric McKitrick, *The Age of Federalism: The Early American Republic, 1788–1800* (New York: Oxford University Press, 1993), 375–449.

42. *Vermont Gazette*, September 4, 1795.

43. Joseph Fay to Thomas Jefferson, September 20, 1791, in *Papers of Thomas Jefferson*, 22:150–51.

44. *Vermont Gazette*, August 7, 1795.

45. *Rutland Farmer's Library*, September 9, 1793.

46. *Vermont Gazette*, January 17, 1794.

47. *Rutland Herald*, August 7, 1797.

48. *Vermont Journal*, April 4, 1798.

49. *Peacham Green Mountain Patriot*, August 24, 1798. For Federalists there was no worse term of opprobrium than *democrat*. For this reason they dubbed individuals supporting the principles of Thomas Jefferson democrats and their political organization the Democratic party.

50. *Vermont Journal*, August 28, 1798.

51. Moses Robinson carried Bennington over Isaac Tichenor by margins of 172 to 29 in 1797 and 232 to 63 in 1798 (Bennington Town Records, bk. B, 104–9).

52. *Vermont Gazette*, July 5, 1798.

53. For insight into Federalist beliefs, see David H. Fischer, *Revolution of American Conservatism* (see chap. 4, n. 118); and James M. Banner Jr., *To the Hartford Convention: The Federalists and the Origins of Party Politics in Massachusetts, 1789–1815* (New York: Alfred A. Knopf, 1970).

54. For their part, followers of Thomas Jefferson referred to themselves as Jeffersonian Republicans, Democratic-Republicans, or simply Republicans. Hereinafter these terms will be used interchangeably.

55. Lyon carried Bennington in the election of 1798 by a margin of 230 to 60 (Bennington Town Records, bk. B, 108–9).

56. For an analysis of the passage of the law as well as the ensuing Federalist purge of Republican opponents, see James Morton Smith, *Freedom's Fetters: The Alien and Sedition Laws and American Civil Liberties* (Ithaca: Cornell University Press, 1956). Austin provides a full treatment of Lyon's career in Congress as well as his trial for sedition in *Lyon*, 90–118.

57. The formal title of the magazine edited by James Lyon was *A Republican Magazine; or Repository of Political Truths*. The title that appeared on each magazine, however, was *The Scourge of Aristocracy*.

58. *Vermont Gazette*, September 29, 1798.

59. Ibid., October 5, 1798.

60. Spargo prints the text of "Patriotic Exultation on Lyon's Release from the Federal Bastille in Vergennes" in *Anthony Haswell*, 233–34 (see chap. 4, n. 41).

61. *Vermont Gazette*, February 14, 1799.

62. Ibid., August 15, 1799.

63. Anthony Haswell, *An Oration delivered at Bennington, Vermont, August 16, 1799. In Commemoration of the Battle of Bennington* (Bennington, 1799), 7.

64. Ibid., 14.

65. Ibid., 8.

66. Ibid., 7.

67. For details of Haswell's arrest, indictment, and trial, see Spargo, *Anthony Haswell*, 58–78; and Smith, *Freedom's Fetters*, 359–73.

68. Spargo, *Anthony Haswell*, 86–87.

69. For an analysis of Freemasonry in this period, see Steven C. Bullock, "A Pure and Sublime System: The Appeal of Post-Revolutionary Freemasonry," *Journal of the Early Republic*, 9 (1989), 359–73.

70. Freemasonry in Vermont included a wide variety of individuals, such as Thomas Chittenden, Ira Allen, Seth Warner, Jonas Fay, Roswell Hopkins, Matthew Lyon, and Nathaniel Chipman (*Records of the Grand Lodge of Free and Accepted Masons of the State of Vermont, From 1794 to 1846 Inclusive* [Burlington, 1879], 9–11, 22–25, 44–48).

71. Ibid., 38–43.

72. Ibid., 74–77.

73. Ibid., 82–85, 127–32.

74. Job Swift, quoted in Fischer, *Revolution of American Conservatism*, 3–5.

75. Job Swift, *Discourses on Religious Subjects* (Middlebury, Vt., 1805), discourse 18, 157–64, quotations on 157–58.

76. Jennings, *Memorials of a Century*, 94–95.

77. *Vermont Gazette*, October 5, 12, 1798.

78. Bennington Church Records, June 7, 1801, 1:61–64.

79. Jennings, *Memorials of a Century*, 356–57.

80. *Vermont Gazette*, November 8, 1802. For the composition of the grand and petit juries in Bennington, see Bennington Town Records, bk. B, 132.

81. *Vermont Gazette*, August 16, 1802, quoted in Jennings, *Memorials of a Century*, 75.

82. Jennings, *Memorials of a Century*, 74.

83. *Journal of Rev. Francis Asbury*, 3 vols. (New York, 1852), 2:274.

84. Quoted in Eleanor Reed, *The Religious Experience of Mrs. Emerson, Late*

Miss Eleanor Reed: Formerly Preceptress of a School in Bennington (Bennington, 1809), 9.

85. Ibid., quotations on 2, 6, and 13.

86. Ibid., 75.

87. *Historical Collections of the Essex Institute* 3 (1861), 272–79.

88. For examples of Joshua Spalding's sermons and hymns, see the following: *Sentiments Concerning the Coming and Kingdom of Christ*, 2nd ed. (Boston, 1841); *The Divine Theory; A System of Divinity, Founded Wholly Upon Christ; which, By one Principle, offers an Explanation of all the Works of God*, 2 vols. (Elizabethtown, N.J.,1808–12); and *The Lord's Songs: A Collection of Composures in Metre, such as have been most used in the late glorious revivals; Dr. Watt's Psalms and Hymns excepted* (Salem, Mass., 1805).

89. Spalding, *Sentiments Concerning the Coming and Kingdom of Christ*, 84.

90. Reed, *Religious Experience of Mrs. Emerson*, 18–20.

91. Ibid., 22.

92. Ibid., 29–30.

93. Ninety-three individuals joined the church during this time ("Members admitted during the revival of 1802–03," Bennington Church Records).

94. Bennington Town Records, bk. B, December 13, 1803, 144–45.

95. Hemenway, *Vermont Historical Gazetteer*, 1:163.

96. Bennington Town Records, bk. B, March 31, 1790.

97. *Vermont Gazette*, July 12, 1790.

98. Bennington Town Records, bk. B, March 28, 1792; March 27, 1793; March 29, 1797; May 29, 1798; December 12, 13, 1803.

99. The act of 1783 exempted individuals from being taxed to support an established religious society if they could prove membership in another church. In 1801 the legislature modified the original law by exempting any person who simply signed a statement claiming that he or she was in disagreement with the majority society. Once residents of Bennington formed a Congregational Society in order to pass a tax to construct a new meetinghouse, 142 individuals signed statements exempting them from such a tax (ibid., November 21, December 31, 1803).

100. Ibid., December 12, 13, 1803.

101. The builders of Bennington's new meetinghouse followed a design found in plate 27 of Benjamin Asher's *Country Builder's Assistant* (Greenfield, Mass., 1797). This was not at all unusual. In fact, Asher's book served as a guide for the majority of Congregational churches constructed throughout New England in the late eighteenth and early nineteenth centuries.

102. Hemenway, *Vermont Historical Gazetteer*, 1:163.

103. The Bennington Church Records include a floor plan of the sanctuary that numbers the pews in order of prestige, lists the original proprietor or proprietors of each pew, identifies church members, and provides the dollar amount paid for each pew.

104. Bennington Town Records, bk. B, March 27, 1805.

105. Daniel Marsh, *A Discourse Delivered at the Dedication of the New Congregational Meetinghouse at Bennington, January 1, 1806* (Bennington, 1806).

106. Bennington Town Records, bk. B, March 31, May 12, 1806. The vote

to settle Marsh was 60 to 19 (Harwood Diary, March 31, 1806 [see chap. 5, n. 47]).

107. Jennings, *Memorials of a Century*, 99.

108. Ebenezer Bradford, *Mr. Thomas Paine's Trial* (Boston, 1795), 12.

109. Richard Harrison, *Princetonians, 1769–1775: A Biographical Dictionary* (Princeton: Princeton University Press, 1980), 275.

110. One young Free-Will Baptist, John Colby, recalled Marsh's kind treatment, as well as his own trepidation at preaching in the new meetinghouse in Bennington in December 1809, in *The Life, Experience, and Travels of John Colby, Preacher of the Gospel. Written by Himself* (Lowell, Mass., 1838), 38–39. The Harwood Diary notes many such visitors; see, e.g., April 27, May 11, June 15, July 6, 20, 27, August 10, 31, October 5, and November 2 for the year 1806 alone.

111. Daniel Marsh, "A Sermon delivered on the 16th of August, 1809, in commemoration of Bennington Battle" (Bennington, 1809), 12.

112. Harwood Diary, May 30, 1808.

113. Ibid., March 29, 1809, March 28, 1810.

114. Ibid., August 25, 1807.

115. *Vermont Gazette*, July 8, 1805, July 7, 1806, July 6, 1807, July 18, 1808; *Bennington Green Mountain Farmer*, July 10, 1809.

116. *Vermont Gazette*, August 18, 1806, August 17, 1807, August 22, 1808; *Bennington Green Mountain Farmer*, August 21, 1809.

117. *Vermont Gazette*, July 10, 1804.

118. Ibid., July 8, 1805.

119. *Bennington Green Mountain Farmer*, August 21, 1809.

120. Ibid.

121. *Vermont Gazette*, May 19, 1806.

122. Ibid., August 17, 1807.

123. Ibid., August 31, 1807.

124. Ibid., August 22, 1808.

125. *Bennington Green Mountain Farmer*, June 3, 1811.

126. *Vermont Gazette*, August 22, 1808.

127. See, e.g., *Bennington Green Mountain Farmer*, December 25, 1809; October 29, November 19, December 2, 1810; August 31, 1812.

128. Ibid., August 31, 1812.

129. *Vermont Gazette*, March 17, 1806.

130. *Bennington Green Mountain Farmer*, January 14, 1811.

131. Harwood Diary, June 7, 1814.

132. Ibid., February 17, 1816.

133. Ibid., August 16, 1809.

134. Harwood was just one of many local Republicans who regularly borrowed copies of David Fay's *Aurora*, the *Intelligencer*, and other prominent Republican papers (see, e.g., Harwood Diary, April 24, June 22, July 15, 1807).

135. For Jeffersonian Republican thought, see John Zvesper, *Political Philosophy and Rhetoric: A Study of the Origins of American Party Politics* (New York: Cambridge University Press, 1977); Lance Banning, *The Jeffersonian Persuasion: Evolution of Party Ideology* (Ithaca: Cornel University Press, 1978); Drew McCoy,

The Elusive Republic: Political Economy in Jeffersonian America (Chapel Hill: University of North Carolina Press, 1980); and Joyce Appleby, *Capitalism and a New Social Order* (New York: New York University Press, 1984).

136. Joyce Appleby, "What Is Still American in the Political Philosophy of Thomas Jefferson?" *William and Mary Quarterly*, 3rd ser., 43 (1986), 287–309.

137. Bennington's population figures for the years 1790–1820 were as follows: 2,350 in 1790; 2,243 in 1800; 2,534 in 1810; and 2,485 in 1820.

138. The persistence rates for heads of households during the years 1790–1820 were 39 percent in 1790; 46 percent in 1800; 37 percent in 1810; and 48 percent in 1820.

139. These conditions were by no means unique to Bennington. Potash discusses strikingly similar circumstances in Middlebury throughout this same period in *Vermont's Burned-Over District*, 61–122.

Chapter 7. The Next Generation

1. Absalom Peters, *Sermon, Preached at Bennington, Vt. on The Lord's Day, Sept. 29, 1822* (Bennington, 1822), 16–18.

2. Absalom Peters, *Life and Time. A Birth-Day Memorial of Seventy Years. With Memories and Reflections for the Aged and the Young* (New York, 1866), 61.

3. Peters, *Sermon*, 17.

4. Peters, *Life and Time*, 56.

5. Ibid., 55–57. Moor's School was the grammar school attached to Dartmouth College. For a discussion of its relationship to the college, see Richardson, *History of Dartmouth College*, vol. 1 (see chap. 4, n. 4).

6. David F. Allmendinger Jr. provides an excellent discussion of the composition of the student body at Dartmouth, as well as other colleges founded in New England during the late eighteenth and early nineteenth centuries, in *Paupers and Scholars: The Transformation of Student Life in Nineteenth-Century New England* (New York: St. Martin's Press, 1975).

7. Ibid., 81–94; Richardson, *History of Dartmouth College*, 1:239–85.

8. Peters, *Life and Time*, 58–60.

9. Only one member of the class of 1799 claimed to be a Christian. A professor noted in 1804 that faith among the students was "never colder since my acquaintance." No religious revival took place on the Dartmouth campus until 1815 (Richardson, *History of Dartmouth College*, 1:275–76).

10. Peters, *Life and Time*, 58.

11. My discussion of the Princeton Theological Seminary draws upon Noll, *Princeton and the Republic*, esp. 272–91 (see chap. 4, n. 181).

12. Bruce Kuklick incorporates an excellent discussion of the emergence of divinity schools during this time in *Churchmen and Philosophers from Jonathan Edwards to John Dewey* (New Haven: Yale University Press, 1985), esp. 66–111.

13. These quotations appear in Noll, *Princeton and the Republic*, 250–51.

14. Elias Boudinot, quoted in ibid., 255.

15. Clifford S. Griffin presents a detailed treatment of these reform societies in *Their Brothers' Keepers: Moral Stewardship in the United States, 1800–1865* (New Brunswick, N.J.: Rutgers University Press, 1960). For an insightful analysis of the larger cultural context within which these societies existed, see Daniel Walker

Howe, "The Evangelical Movement and Political Culture in the North during the Second Party System," *Journal of American History*, 77 (1991), 1216–39.

16. Noll, *Princeton and the Republic*, 258–66, 272–99.

17. Peters, *Life and Time*, 60–62, 65–66.

18. Harwood Diary, September 1, 1835 (see chap. 5, n. 47).

19. Comstock, *Principal Civil Officers of Vermont*, 82–83 (see chap. 5, n. 63).

20. Harwood Diary, March 30, 1808.

21. For descriptions of early Williams College, see Calvin Durfee, *History of William College* (Boston, 1860); Leverett Wilson Spring, *A History of Williams College* (Boston: Houghton Mifflin, 1917); and Allmendinger, *Paupers and Scholars*. The quotation appears in *Williams College: Centennial Anniversary* (Cambridge, Mass., 1894), 229–30.

22. Nathaniel Hawthore, quoted in Allmendinger, *Paupers and Scholars*, 1, 2.

23. Edward A. Kendall, *Travels Through the Northern Parts of the United States in the Years 1807 and 1808*, 3 vols. (New York, 1809), 3:252–56, quotation on 252.

24. See, e.g., Bennington Superior Court Docket Books, C, 1800–1804 (see chap. 6, n. 5).

25. Aldrich, *Bennington County*, 198–99 (see chap. 2, n. 1).

26. *Vermont Gazette*, August 21, 1827.

27. Ibid., July 6, 1830. Jackson's supporters in Bennington variously referred to themselves as Republicans, Democratic-Republicans, or Democrats.

28. Ibid., July 27, 1830.

29. Ibid.

30. Ibid.

31. Ibid., August 17, 1830.

32. Ibid., October 20, 1834.

33. Ibid., November 8, 1834.

34. Ibid., August 9, 1831; May 8, 29, June 18, July 24, December 18, 1832; June 25, 1833; June 24, July 15, August 21, December 30, 1834; January 20, 1835; February 24, April 26, 1836; August 20, 1839.

35. Ibid., August 30, 1836.

36. Ibid., August 20, 1839.

37. George Shepard, *The Complete Works of Rev. Daniel A. Clark, With a Biographical Sketch, and an Estimate of His Powers as a Preacher*, 2 vols. (New York, 1848), 1:xxiii–xxiv.

38. Ibid., xxv.

39. Jennings, *Memorials of a Century*, 107–11 (see chap. 2, n. 1).

40. Shepard prints Clark's sermon, "Mirror of Nature," delivered in Bennington in 1827, in *Works of Clark*, 1:92–103, quotations on 93, 101, and 102.

41. Ibid., xxv.

42. Ibid., x–xii.

43. Ibid., xiii–xiv.

44. Ibid., ix.

45. My discussion of Samuel Stanhope Smith draws upon Noll, *Princeton and the Republic*, 185–213, quotations on 201–3.

46. Ibid., 228–29.

47. Clark's name does not appear on the original petition, and he was not among the 126 students suspended by the faculty ("Resolves and Minutes of the Faculty," March 31, 1807, Princeton University Archives).

48. Noll, *Princeton and the Republic*, 237.

49. Clark, quoted in Shepard, *Works of Clark*, 1:xv.

50. Noll, *Princeton and the Republic*, 240–71.

51. Henry K. Rowe, *History of Andover Theological Seminary* (Newton, Mass.: Thomas Todd, 1933), and Leonard Woods, *History of the Andover Theological Seminary* (Boston, 1885), provide descriptions of the seminary as well as of its faculty and students.

52. Lois Banner includes an analysis of these activities in "Religion and Reform in the Early Republic: The Role of Youth," *American Quarterly*, 23 (1971), 677–95, esp. 684–87.

53. Quoted in Shepard, *Works of Clark*, 1:xix.

54. Ibid., xviii.

55. Shepard prints a letter that Clark wrote to his in-laws for the ostensible purpose of congratulating them on their conversion from Socinianism to orthodoxy. The letter actually constitutes a lecture displaying Clark's intolerance for any who do not accept his beliefs (see ibid., xviii–xx).

56. *The History of the Town of Amherst, Massachusetts* (Amherst, 1896), 199–200. No reason is given for Clark's dismissal. Shepard says only that "charges were brought against him affecting his character; and some of them, if sustained must have destroyed his standing and influence" (Shepard, *Works of Clark*, 1:xxi).

57. Bennington Church Records, 2:205–6 (see chap. 1, n. 160).

58. Ibid., 206–8.

59. Herbert Stebbins Walbridge, *The History and Development of North Bennington Vermont* (Rutland, Vt., 1837), 54–56.

60. Bennington Town Records, bk. C, 150–51 (see chap. 2, n. 4).

61. Zadock Thompson, *History of Vermont, Natural, Civil and Statistical* (Burlington, 1842), pt. 3, 18–20.

62. Ibid., 18–19, quotation on 18.

63. Aldrich, *Bennington County*, 295.

64. Family Genealogical Files, Bennington Museum, Bennington, Vermont; John Spargo, *The Potters and Potteries of Bennington* (Boston: Houghton Mifflin, 1926); Hamilton Child, *Gazetteer and Business Directory of Bennington County, Vt.* (Syracuse, 1880), 84–114; Aldrich, *Bennington County*, 295–303. The census of 1850 lists P. L. Robinson as the wealthiest man in Bennington Township.

65. Herbert Cornelius Andrews, *Hinsdale Genealogy: Descendants of Robert Hinsdale of Dedham, Medfield, Hadley and Deerfield* (Lombard, Ill.: Alfred Hinsdale Andrews, 1906), 98–99.

66. Goodrich, *Vermont Soldiers in the Revolutionary War*, 786 (see chap. 2, n. 21).

67. Walbridge, *North Bennington*, 54–55; Marcus A. McCorison, "Vermont Papermaking, 1784–1820," *Vermont History*, 31 (1963), 213; *Vermont Gazette*, March 14, 1785, April 4, 1791, November 9, 1792, May 8, 1795.

68. McCorison, "Vermont Papermaking," 213; Walbridge, *North Bennington*, 554–55; Will of Joseph Hinsdill, Probate Records, Bennington, Vermont, 3: 34–45.

69. *Bennington World,* September 5, 1808.

70. *Bennington Green Mountain Farmer,* July 17, 1809.

71. Ibid., May 28, 1810.

72. Ibid., December 14, 1813.

73. *Vermont Gazette,* June 18, August 20, September 17, 1816; July 29, December 2, 1817; April 7, 14, 1818; March 27, April 3, 1821; February 5, 1822.

74. Bennington tax list for 1820 (reconstructed from individual tax slips found in the Hiland Hall Papers, Park-McCullough House, North Bennington, Vermont, bk. C, sec. 12, folders 23 and 25).

75. Stephen lost all three of his elder brothers—Joseph, Daniel, and Norman—within a two-year period, 1820–22 (Andrews, *Hinsdale Genealogy,* 139–45).

76. Walbridge, *North Bennington,* 54–55.

77. Bennington Church Records, 2:42–43.

78. Bennington Town Records, bks. A–D.

79. Ibid., bk. C, March 28, 1821, March 22, 1822, March 26, 1823, March 31, 1824, March 21, 1827.

80. Ibid., March 27, 1816, continued under June 24, 1816.

81. *Vermont Gazette,* July 14, 1818.

82. Hinsdill's advertisement, "Families Wanted," *Bennington Journal of the Times,* March 27, 1829.

83. Hinsdillville bears a striking resemblance to the mill hamlets described by Anthony F. C. Wallace in *Rockdale: The Growth of an American Village in the Early Industrial Revolution* (New York: Alfred A. Knopf, 1978). In this work Wallace provides a wonderfully complete analysis of all aspects of life in and around the cotton mills in these isolated villages.

84. Harwood Diary, November 17, 1835.

85. *Seventh Report of the Vermont Bible Society, October 20, 1819,* pamphlet in the Vermont Historical Society.

86. *Vermont Gazette,* September 17, 1822, September 16, 1823, September 18, 1827, September 15, 1829, January 18, 1831; *Journal of the Times,* October 24, 1828.

87. Peters, *Life and Times,* 62–63.

88. *Vermont Gazette,* September 2, 1823.

89. Shepard, *Works of Clark,* 1:xxii–xxv.

90. Bennington Seminary, catalogs for April 1829, October 1834, and October 1835, Vermont Historical Society.

91. *Fourth Report of the Directors of the Northwestern Branch of the American Education Society, January 24, 1824,* pamphlet in the Vermont Historical Society. Allmendinger incorporates a discussion of the Society in *Paupers and Scholars,* 64–78.

92. Wendell Phillips Garrison and Francis Jackson Garrison, *William Lloyd Garrison, 1805–1879: The Story of His Life Told by His Children,* 4 vols. (New York, 1885), 1:116–17.

93. *Vermont Gazette,* July 7, 1829.

94. John Myers, "The Beginning of Antislavery Agencies in Vermont, 1832–1836," *Vermont History,* 36 (1968), 126–41; Aldrich, *Bennington County,* 279–80;

Vermont Gazette, November 5, December 24, 31, 1833; *Boston Liberator*, January 11, 1834.

95. *Second Annual Report of the Vermont Anti-Slavery Society*, February 16, 17, 1836, pamphlet in the Vermont Historical Society.

96. *Vermont Gazette*, February 13, 1821.

97. Ibid., February 3, 1824.

98. Ibid., January 9, 1827.

99. Harwood Diary, February 28, 1828; *Journal of the Times*, February 20, 1829.

100. Rush Welter, *Bennington, Vermont: An Industrial History* (New York: Columbia University Library Services, 1959), 13–14.

101. *Christian capitalism* is the term Wallace uses to describe the socioeconomic attitudes of the manufacturers of Rockdale. My discussion of Hinsdill's attitudes benefits from Wallace's analysis.

102. *Vermont Gazette*, February 26, 1828.

103. Jennings, *Memorials of a Century*, 317–18; Sarah Robinson, *Genealogical History of the Families of Robinsons, Saffords, Harwoods, and Clarks* (Bennington, 1837), 32.

104. See, e.g., *Vermont Gazette*, December 27, 1803.

105. Jennings, *Memorials of a Century*, 317–18, 323.

106. See, e.g., James Merrill, *The Happiness of America: An Oration delivered at Shaftsbury, on the Fourth of July, 1804* (Bennington, 1804); and idem, *An Oration delivered at the Meeting-House in Bennington on the 4th of July, 1806* (Bennington, 1806).

107. *An Oration delivered in Bennington*, 24–25.

108. Hemenway, *Vermont Historical Gazetteer*, 1:171–72 (see chap. 2, n. 2).

109. Jennings, *Memorials of a Century*, 245.

110. Aldrich lists the names of twenty-eight lawyers admitted to the bar in Bennington in the two decades before Merrill began to practice (*Bennington County*, 200). Merrill appeared in the docket book of the Bennington Superior Court only once for the year 1806 and on rare occasions throughout 1807 (Bennington Superior Court Docket Books, C).

111. Hemenway, *Vermont Gazetteer*, 1:171–72; Jennings, *Memorials of a Century*, 817–18.

112. For details of the contested election, see *Annals of Congress*, 16th Cong., 1st sess., January 1820, 860–66.

113. *Bennington Green Mountain Farmer*, February 24, 1812, March 29, July 12, 1814, August 21, 1815; *Vermont Gazette*, August 20, 1816; July 8, 1817; August 25, 1818; July 27, 1819.

114. *Vermont Gazette*, February 15, 1820, February 13, 1821, January 13, 1824.

115. Jennings, *Memorials of a Century*, 318; Comstock, *Principal Civil Officers of Vermont*, 27–28, 83, 306.

116. Harwood Diary, August 30, 1815.

117. Ibid., September 2, 1817. In this election Bennington gave majorities to Isaac Tichenor for governor, to Aaron Robinson for state representative, and to all the Federalist candidates for the state council.

118. An analysis of voting returns for the town of Bennington during the years 1794–1860 reveals that Republicans totally dominated elections for the Vermont General Assembly during the period 1794–1811. From 1812 to 1860, however, Republicans (Democrats) won this position only three times. Previous to 1813 the town never gave a majority to a Federalist gubernatorial candidate; indeed, Isaac Tichenor often lost his own town by lopsided margins of four and five to one. Between 1813 and 1820, when the party no longer offered a slate of candidates for state positions, Federalist candidates won the town three times. In 1817 Isaac Tichenor even carried the town in an election that saw his opponent emerge victorious in the state by nearly a two-to-one margin. In addition, the citizens of Bennington chose a Federalist as moderator of their annual town meeting every year during the period 1813–29 (Bennington Town Records, bks. B, C, and D).

119. Vermont's population rose from 30,000 in 1781 to 85,000 in 1791, 154,000 in 1800, and 217,00 in 1810. These increases represent gains of 150 percent, 80 percent, and 40 percent, respectively. There was only an 8 percent increase between 1810 and 1820 (Lewis D. Stillwell, *Migrations from Vermont* [Montpelier, Vt., 1948], 95).

120. Ibid., 124–96.

121. William Rossiter, "Vermont: An Historical and Statistical Study of the Progress of the State," *American Statistical Association*, n.s., 98 (March 1911), 387–454. Rossiter identifies ten towns — Burlington, Rutland, Barre, Montpelier, St. Albans, St. Johnsbury, Bennington, Brattleboro, Bellows Falls, and Colchester — that outstripped all others in the state. Bennington's population, for example, increased by 75 percent between 1820 and 1860, while that of the entire state grew by only 16 percent. During the decade 1850–60 the state's population decreased by 1.8 percent, while Bennington's increased by 12 percent. Paul Goodman presents a helpful analysis of the uneven spread of wealth that resulted from this process in his *Towards a Christian Republic: Antimasonry and the Great Transition in New England, 1826–1836* (New York: Oxford University Press, 1988); see esp. 120–46.

122. Goodman, *Towards a Christian Republic*, 125–28.

123. Bennington's social and economic structure closely resembles that of what Edward M. Cook considers a "major county town" in *The Fathers of the Towns: Leadership and Community Structure in Eighteenth-Century New England* (Baltimore: Johns Hopkins University Press, 1976), 174–77. It is also quite similar to the structure Robert Doherty analyzes as a market and administrative center throughout his *Society and Power: Five New England Towns, 1800–1860* (Amherst: University of Massachusetts Press, 1977).

124. *Vermont Gazette*, June 20, 1820.

125. Ibid., June 27, 1820.

126. Ibid., February 19, 1822.

127. Bennington Church Records, 2:55–63, 110, 107–8.

128. Harwood Diary, December 29, 1827.

129. Merrill served as editor of the *Gazette* from June 19, 1827, until January 17, 1832.

130. *Vermont Gazette*, July 8, 1828. The need to celebrate national holidays in

the traditional manner became a litany for Merrill (see, e.g., ibid., August 19, 1828, January 7, 1829, and August 23, 1831).

131. Ibid., April 7, 28, July 14, 1829. Hiram Harwood refers specifically to the "Pioneer" party in Bennington (Harwood Diary, March 7, 1837). The name comes from the Pioneer Line, a Sabbath-keeping stage and boat line formed in New York in 1828.

132. *Vermont Gazette*, January 20, 1829.

133. Ibid., July 27, 1830.

134. Jackson constantly referred to the "real people" as constituting "the bone and sinew of the county." Marvin Meyers offers a perceptive analysis of the meaning Jackson gave to these terms in his *Jacksonian Persuasion: Politics and Belief* (Palo Alto: Stanford University Press, 1957); see esp. 16–32.

135. See esp. *Vermont Gazette*, August 17 and September 7, 1830.

136. Ibid., August 30, 1836.

137. Hiland Hall, address to the Stratton Mountain Convention, Hall Papers.

138. *Niles' National Register* (Baltimore), August 1, 1840, 340.

139. Sage's City assumed the name North Bennington in 1828.

140. Walbridge, *North Bennington*, 13.

141. Hiland Hall, brief memoir of his father, Hall Papers.

142. Hemenway, *Vermont Historical Gazetteer*, 5:84 (see chap. 5, n. 103).

143. Aldrich, *Bennington County*, 506.

144. Hiland Hall, notes on his childhood, Hall Papers.

145. Ibid.

146. Ibid.

147. Record Book, Sons of Liberty, Bennington, Vermont Historical Society, 1–9.

148. Ibid., 7, 11, 15, 22, 23.

149. Harwood Diary, December 15, 1813.

150. Record Book, Sons of Liberty, 10, 17, 25, 34–36.

151. Ibid., 64–68.

152. Hiland Hall, notes on his life through the year 1830, Hall Papers.

153. Ibid.

154. Ibid.

155. Henry D. Hall, *Memoir of Hon. Hiland Hall, LLD* (Boston, 1887); Aldrich, *Bennington County*, 506; Hemenway, *Vermont Historical Gazetteer*, 5:85.

156. Aldrich, *Bennington County*, 506; Hemenway, *Vermont Historical Gazetteer*, 5:85.

157. James D. Richardson, ed., *A Compilation of the Messages and Papers of the Presidents, 1789–1897*, 10 vols. (Washington, D.C., 1896–99), 2:316.

158. Daniel Walker Howe provides an excellent discussion of the ideological underpinnings of the American System in *The Political Culture of the American Whigs* (Chicago: University of Chicago Press, 1979); see esp. 137–40.

159. Hiland Hall to Dolly Hall, October 21, 1827, Hall Papers.

160. Hiland Hall to Henry Hall, May 19, 1839, ibid.

161. The quotations are from Hall's speech to the Bennington Probate District Colonization Society, delivered at a celebration on July 4, 1829 (*Vermont Gazette*, July 14, 1829).

162. Hiland Hall, "Notes on Education," Hall Papers, box C, sec. 11, folder 23.

163. Hiland Hall to Dolly Hall, December 15, 1839, Hall Papers.

164. Dolly Hall to Hiland Hall, January 4, 1840, ibid.

165. Hiland Hall to Henry Hall, October 20, November 6, 1839, ibid.

166. For the documents relating to this controversy, see *Vermont Gazette*, January 20, 1829.

167. Bennington Academy, catalog for the summer and fall terms ending November 23, 1831, Vermont Historical Society.

168. "Roll of members admitted from the settlement of Rev. Daniel A. Clark June 13, 1826 to his dismissal October 2, 1830," Bennington Church Records.

169. Harwood Diary, August 28, 1830.

170. Ibid., October 14, 1830.

171. Ibid., December 29, 1827; Dolly Hall to Hiland Hall, February 18, 1837.

172. Harwood Diary, February 10, 1837.

173. Minutes of the June 9, 1832, meeting, Hall Papers. Isaac Tichenor noted on this copy that Hall wrote the resolution regarding wool and cotton manufactories.

174. Hiland Hall, "How I became a member of Congress," Hall Papers.

175. Hiland Hall, "Bennington County Convention," ibid.

176. Hiland Hall to David Robinson, jr., March 8, 1834, ibid.

177. *Register of Debates in Congress*, 23rd Cong., 1st sess., 1834,10, pt. 3, 3944.

178. Ibid., 3944–45.

179. Ibid., 3945–46.

180. Hiland Hall to David Robinson Jr., April 2, 1838, Hall Papers.

181. Walter Hill Crockett, *Vermont: The Green Mountain State*, 3 vols. (New York: Century History, 1921), 3:310–11.

Chapter 8. Tensions Persist

1. For the election results mentioned in this and the subsequent paragraph, I have drawn upon vols. 2 and 3 of Crockett's *Vermont* (see chap. 7, n. 181).

2. For an excellent analysis of this phenomenon, see Roth, *Democratic Dilemma*, 80–116 (see chap. 5, n. 42).

3. Bennington Town Records, bk. B, September 3, 1812 (see chap. 2, n. 4).

4. Ibid., March 31, 1813.

5. *Bennington News-Letter*, April 14, 1813.

6. Bennington Town Records, bk. B, September 7, 1813.

7. See esp. *Vermont Gazette*, April 21, 1806.

8. For the election results discussed in the following paragraph, see the minutes of the annual March and September meetings for the years 1813–19 (Bennington Town Records, bks. B and C).

9. Tensions ran so high during the freemen's meeting in 1819 that participants were unable to elect a representative even after five ballots (ibid., bk. C, 23–24).

10. For insight on how the war served the Federalist cause in Vermont, see Williamson, *Vermont in Quandary*, 258–76 (see chap. 5, n. 119); John Duffy, "Broadside Illustrations of the Jeffersonian-Federalist Conflict in Vermont,

1809–1816," *Vermont History*, 49 (1981), 209–22; and Edward Brynn, "Patterns of Dissent: Vermont's Opposition to the War of 1812," ibid., 40 (1972), 10–27.

11. For an analysis of the way local merchants extended their influence over the rural economy, see Christopher Clark, *The Roots of Rural Capitalism: Western Massachusetts, 1780–1860* (Ithaca: Cornell University Press, 1990), 156–91.

12. *Bennington Green Mountain Farmer*, April 16, 1812.

13. Ibid., May 1, 1812.

14. Ibid., September 7, 1813.

15. Ibid., May 10, 1814.

16. Ibid., May 6, 1816.

17. Harwood Diary, May 30, 1808 (see chap. 5, n. 47).

18. Ibid., March 30, 1808.

19. Ibid., March 20, 1818.

20. Ibid., April 23, 1819.

21. Ibid., June 18, 1820.

22. Jennings, *Memorials of a Century*, 300 (see chap. 2, n. 1).

23. Bennington Church Records, 1, January 28, 31, 1820 (see chap. 1, n. 160).

24. Ibid., April 25, 1820.

25. Peters, *Life and Time*, 60–61 (see chap. 7, n. 2).

26. In that year Isaac Tichenor had defeated O. C. Merrill for the position of moderator, Aaron Robinson bested William Haswell for clerk, and Moses Robinson Jr. defeated General David Robinson for first selectman (Harwood Diary, April 8, 1819).

27. Ibid., March 29, 1820.

28. Bennington Church Records, 2, April 4, 1820.

29. Ibid., May 28, 1820.

30. Ibid., May 29, 1820.

31. Harwood Diary, June 20, 1820.

32. Bennington Church Records, 2, July 5, 1820.

33. *Vermont Gazette*, March 6, 31, 1821.

34. Harwood Diary, January 12, 1821.

35. Ibid., March 28, 1821.

36. Ibid., September 4, 1821.

37. *Vermont Gazette*, December 18, 1821.

38. Ibid., February 19, 1822.

39. For examples of these letters, see "ABC Scholars," "ABCX Scholars," and "Senex," in ibid., January 8, 15, and 22, 1822; the quotation is from "Senex," January 8, 1822.

40. Harwood Diary, March 27, 1822.

41. Ibid., April 13, 1822.

42. *Vermont Gazette*, May 7, 1822.

43. Harwood Diary, January 7, 1823.

44. Ibid.

45. *Vermont Gazette*, June 24, 1823.

46. Ibid., April 5, 1825.

47. Ibid., March 26, 1822.

48. Ibid., April 23, May 28, 1822.

49. Harwood Diary, April 19, 1822.

50. Ibid., April 20 and 22, 1822.

51. *Vermont Gazette*, April 30, May 7, 21, 28, 1822, quotation on May 21.

52. Ibid., August 27, 1822.

53. Ibid., September 3, 1822. The exchange between "The Hermit of Mt. Anthony" and "A man in Society" exemplifies the dialogue taking place within Bennington over the role of missionaries in American society (ibid., August 27, September 3, October 1, 8, 1822).

54. Peters, *Sermon*, 20–21 (see chap. 7, n. 1).

55. Harwood Diary, September 30, 1822.

56. *Vermont Gazette*, October 1, 1822.

57. Ibid., November 5, 1822.

58. Harwood Diary, September 2, 1823.

59. *Vermont Gazette*, October 22, 1822. "Friend" cited John Bigland, *The History of England from the earliest period, to the close of the year 1812* (London, 1813).

60. Bennington Church Records, 2:7–14.

61. Ibid., 38–39.

62. Ibid., 41.

63. Ibid., 42.

64. Ibid., 115–17.

65. Ibid., 51–55.

66. Ibid., 55–57.

67. *Records of the Grand Lodge*, 272, 277, 281 (see chap. 6, n. 70).

68. *Vermont Gazette*, January 13, 1824.

69. Ibid., January 27, 1824.

70. Ibid., February 3, 1824.

71. See, e.g., ibid., July 8, 1817, August 26, 1823, and July 13, 1824.

72. Ibid., January 9, 1827.

73. Ibid., March 26, 1822. For other letters by "Z," see ibid., April 16, May 14, July 23, September 24, 1824; June 21, July 26, 1825.

74. Ibid., April 16, 1822.

75. For a discussion of this phenomenon from a national perspective, see Rowland Berthoff, "Independence and Attachment, Virtue and Interest: From Republican Citizen to Free Enterpriser, 1787–1837," in *Uprooted Americans: Essays to Honor Oscar Handlin*, by Richard Bushman et al. (Boston: Little, Brown, 1979), 99–124.

76. *Vermont Gazette*, July 16, 1822.

77. See, e.g., ibid., September 23, 1823.

78. Harwood Diary, May 5, 1824.

79. Ibid., November 19, 1825.

80. Ibid., May 8, 13, 1824.

81. Ibid., November 23, 1825.

82. Bennington Church Records, 2:126–28.

83. Ibid., 129–34.

84. *Vermont Gazette*, December 20, 1825.

85. Bennington Church Records, 2:129–34. The committee included Ste-

phen Hinsdill, Erwin Safford, Aaron Robinson, Noadiah Swift, Uriah Edgerton, and Luman Norton.

86. Ibid., 135–38.

87. *Vermont Gazette*, June 20, 1826.

88. Ibid., June 27, 1826.

89. Ibid., July 11, 1826.

90. Harwood Diary, October 15, 1826.

91. Ibid., December, 17, 1826.

92. Ibid., March 4, 1827.

93. One hundred twenty-six individuals joined the church during the time Clark served as pastor (Bennington Church Records, "Roll of members admitted from settlement of Rev. Daniel A. Clark June 13, 1826 to his dismissal October 12, 1830").

94. Harwood Diary, March 26, 1827.

95. Ibid., March 2, April 17, 1827.

96. Ibid., May 29, 1817.

97. Ibid., April 30, 1827.

98. *Vermont Gazette*, July 10, 1827.

99. Ibid., July 24, 1827.

100. Ibid., August 21, 1827.

101. Harwood Diary, December 19, 1826, January 20, 1827.

102. *Vermont Gazette*, May 23, 1826.

103. Ibid., May 30, 1826.

104. Harwood Diary, September 5, 1826.

105. Ibid., September 11, 1826.

106. Ibid., September 3, 1827.

107. Ibid., August 22, 1827.

108. Ibid., September 3, 1827.

109. *Vermont Gazette*, September 11, 1827.

110. Ibid.

111. Harwood Diary, December 29, 1827.

112. *Vermont Gazette*, December 25, 1827.

113. Harwood Diary, December 29, 1827.

114. Ibid., February 14, 1828.

115. Ibid., March 26, 1828.

116. Clark's address appeared in the *Vermont Chronicle*, August 15, 1828.

117. Darius Clark maintained proprietorship of the paper but turned the editorial duties over to Merrill.

118. *Vermont Gazette*, July 8, 1828.

119. *Bennington Journal of the Times*, October 3, 1828. Henry S. Hull actually founded the *Journal* to promote Adams's presidential campaign paper.

120. Harwood Diary, October 29, 1828.

121. *Journal of the Times*, October 3, 1828.

122. Ibid., October 10, 1828.

123. Ibid., January 16, 1829; *Vermont Gazette*, January 20, 1829.

124. *Journal of the Times*, January 16, 1829.

125. Ibid.

126. *Vermont Gazette*, January 20, 1829.

127. Both academies listed the members of the student body in their annual catalog. These catalogs are in the collections of the Vermont Historical Society.

128. See esp. *Journal of the Times*, January 16 and February 6, 1829.

129. Ibid., February 6, 1829.

130. Ibid., January 16, 1829.

131. *Vermont Gazette*, April 7, 1829.

132. Ibid., March 31, 1829.

133. Bennington Church Records, 2:152–53.

134. Harwood Diary, July 4, 1830.

135. Ibid., July 3, 1830.

136. *Vermont Gazette*, February 17, 1829.

137. Ibid., April 28, 1829.

138. Ibid., May 12, 1828.

139. Harwood Diary, July 26, 1830.

140. *Vermont Gazette*, August 4, 1829.

141. Harwood Diary, July 16, 25, 1830.

142. Ibid., August 28, 1830.

143. Bennington Church Records, 2:160–63.

144. Harwood Diary, October 14, 1830.

Chapter 9. Paeans to the Green Mountain Boys

1. Bennington Church Records, 2:163–64 (see chap. 1, n. 160).

2. Ibid., 164.

3. Ibid., 165–67.

4. Ibid., 168.

5. Gridley's conduits to Finney were Rev. Nathaniel Beman, pastor of the First Presbyterian Church in Troy, and Rev. Horatio Foote, a fiery evangelist active throughout eastern New York, Vermont, and Massachusetts. For a full account of Finney and his coworkers, see Keith J. Hardman, *Charles Grandison Finney, 1792–1875: Revivalist and Reformer* (Syracuse: Syracuse University Press, 1987).

6. For Finney's techniques, see Paul E. Johnson, *A Shopkeeper's Millennium: Society and Revivals in Rochester, New York, 1815–1837* (New York: Hill & Wang, 1978). I have relied on Johnson's analysis in this and the following paragraph.

7. Harwood Diary, June 25, 1831 (see chap. 5, n. 47).

8. Bennington Church Records, 2:172; Peters, *Life and Time*, 64 (see chap. 7, n. 2).

9. Bennington Church Records, Roll of members admitted from October 12, 1830, to February 21, 1832.

10. Harwood Diary, July 4, 1831.

11. Bennington Church Records, 2:175–76.

12. Jennings, *Memorials of a Century*, 112–15 (see chap. 2, n. 1).

13. Harwood Diary, March 13, 1833.

14. The minutes of the Congregational Society include the Articles of the Society as well as a list of all members. These minutes are in the Bennington Church Records.

15. For a detailed description of the techniques employed by Hooker and Foote, see Hooker's account of the revival in the *Vermont Chronicle* (Bellows Falls), December 27, 1833.

16. Harwood Diary, December 11, 1833.

17. For the clearest analysis of this process, see Hiland Hall to Henry Hall, May 19, 1839, Hall Papers (see chap. 7, n. 74).

18. Aldrich, *Bennington County*, 280 (see chap. 2, n. 1).

19. For a description of Murray's activities, see Myers, "Antislavery Agencies in Vermont," 126–41 (see chap. 7, n. 94).

20. *Vermont Gazette*, December 24, 31, 1833, quotation on December 31. Murray incorporated a detailed account of the arguments employed against him in a letter published in the *Boston Liberator*, January 11, 1834.

21. *Boston Liberator*, January 11, 1834.

22. Harwood Diary, December 15, 1834.

23. Haswell, a younger son of old Anthony Haswell, took over as editor of the *Gazette* on January 17, 1832.

24. *Vermont Gazette*, September 29, October 6, 1835, quotations in the October 6 issue.

25. Isaac Jennings, *The One Hundred Year Old Meetinghouse of Christ in Bennington, Vermont* (Cambridge, Mass.: Riverside Press, 1907), 36.

26. *Vermont Gazette*, August 21, 1827.

27. Ibid., August 26, 1828.

28. Ibid., June 24, 1823.

29. Ibid., April 5, 1825.

30. For the rosters of these schools, see the catalogs of the Bennington Academy, the Bennington Seminary, and the Union Academy in the East Village in the Vermont Historical Society.

31. The Harwood Diary contains excellent discussions of these votes; see, e.g., April 1, 1831, March 6, 1834, and March 29, 1837.

32. *Vermont Gazette*, September 23, 1823.

33. Ibid., August 18, 1829.

34. Harwood Diary, March 31, 1833.

35. For examples of these discussions, see ibid., March 25, 1835, and March 29, 1837.

36. *Bennington Green Mountain Farmer*, February 19, 1816; *Vermont Gazette*, June 18, 1816.

37. Harwood Diary, February 10, 1837.

38. *Vermont Gazette*, February 14, 1826.

39. Ibid., May 25, 1824, January 31, 1826.

40. For a wonderful example of this rhetoric, see the *Vermont Gazette*, September 11, 1827.

41. "Rules for Christian Mechanics, Merchants, etc." *Vermont Chronicle*, November 26, 1835.

42. For Anti-Masonry in Vermont, see Goodman, *Towards a Christian Republic* (see chap. 7, n. 121). My discussion of the movement draws upon Goodman's insights.

43. *Manchester Horn of the Green Mountains*, March 22, 1830. For an outstand-

ing discussion of the way Anti-Masonry divided churches, social organizations, and the town elite in Rochester, see Johnson, *A Shopkeeper's Millennium.*

44. Quoted in Goodman, *Towards a Christian Republic,* 128.

45. *Vermont Luminary* (East Randolph), August 5, 1829.

46. Quoted in Goodman, *Towards a Christian Republic,* 125.

47. *Woodstock Liberal Extracts,* July 1829.

48. Goodman, *Towards a Christian Republic,* 122–29.

49. *Rutland Herald,* quoted in the *Danville North Star,* October 4, 1831.

50. David Palmer, *An Address Delivered before St. John's Lodge, No. 41, Thetford, Vermont . . . 1829* (Hanover, N.H., 1829).

51. Quoted in the *Boston Masonic Mirror,* August 3, 1833.

52. *Vermont Gazette,* March 3, 1829.

53. Anti-Masonry shattered most denominations in Vermont. However, divisions within the Congregational clergy were the most bitter. As a result, a great many Congregational ministers took the lead in attacking Masons within their churches and throughout their communities (Goodman, *Toward a Christian Republic,* 130–34).

54. *Vermont Gazette,* September 8, 1829.

55. Ibid., June 11, 1833.

56. Ibid., April 16, 1833.

57. Goodman, *Towards a Christian Republic,* 139–40, 286 n. 76.

58. *Vermont Gazette,* July 9, 1833.

59. In this election Henry Clay received 805 votes; Andrew Jackson, 692; and William Wirt, 333 (ibid., November 19, 1832).

60. Bennington Town Records, bk. C, 145 (see chap. 2, n. 4).

61. Ibid., bk. D, 22–23; *Vermont Gazette,* September 9, 1834.

62. These statistics are drawn from the records of the annual March meetings for the years 1820–40 in Bennington Town Records, bks. C and D.

63. The Anti-Masonic party experienced only minimal success in the state's ten most successful commercial towns (Burlington, Rutland, Barre, Montpelier, St. Albans, St. Johnsbury, Bennington, Brattleboro, Bellows Falls, and Colchester) (Goodman, *Towards a Christian Republic,* 128–29, 282 n. 28).

64. Harwood Diary, February 10, 1837; Dolly Hall to Hiland Hall, February 18, 1837, Hall Papers.

65. Dolly Hall to Hiland Hall, February 18, 1837, Hall Papers.

66. The two families settled in Grand Rapids, Michigan, where Hinsdill started a woolen factory and Ballard became pastor of the First Congregational Church and principal of the local academy (Andrews, *Hinsdale Genealogy,* 141–45 [see chap. 7, n. 65]; *History of Kent County, Michigan* [Chicago, 1881], 849, 872–77).

67. Harwood Diary, March 2, 1837.

68. *Vermont Gazette,* August 30, 1836.

69. Ibid., August 13, 1839.

70. Ibid., August 25, 1840.

71. For examples of this rhetoric, see the reports of Democratic conventions in ibid., August 12, 1834, January 20, 1835, January 10, 1836, September 3, 1839, and June 2, 1840.

72. Ibid., August 28, 1832.

73. For editorials in favor of these principles, see ibid., January 17, 24, November 7, December 26, 1826; January 9, October 16, 1827; April 8, May 27, 1828.

74. "Things Which Every National Republican Must Believe," ibid., August 28, 1832.

75. *Vermont Gazette*, September 3, 1839.

76. Harwood Diary, September 11, 1830.

77. *Vermonter*, July 21, 1835. A single issue of this paper is in the Hall Papers.

78. *Vermont Gazette*, August 21, 1840.

79. Crockett, *Vermont*, 3:313 (see chap. 7, n. 181).

80. The Whig majority in the state senate was 28 to 2; in the house the majority was 178 to 59 (ibid., 311).

81. Whig presidential electors won by a vote of 392 to 290, Hall's margin was 413 to 325, and Isaac Weeks defeated Alvah Rice for the General Assembly by a vote of 408 to 328 (Bennington Town Records, bk. D, 96, 98).

82. Hiland Hall, draft of a speech, Hall Papers.

83. *Register of Debates in Congress*, 23rd Cong., 1st sess., 1834, 10, pt. 3, 3948–49.

84. Ibid., 3945.

85. Hiland Hall, address to the Stratton Mountain Convention, Hall Papers.

86. Hiland Hall, "Notes for speeches on the Battle of Bennington," ibid. This toast honors Chittenden and the members of his Council of Safety for their participation in the Haldimand negotiations of 1781–82.

87. *Register of Debates in Congress*, 3944, 3947.

88. *Vermont Gazette*, March 25, 1834.

89. Ibid,. August 12, 1834.

90. Ibid., August 20, 1839.

91. Ibid., July 31, 1840.

92. Ibid., August 20, 1839.

93. By 1820 the top 10 percent of the population in Bennington owned well over a third of its wealth. This income distribution grew increasingly more skewed with the passage of time (Bennington rate lists, 1785, 1820; manuscript census lists for 1850 and 1860, Vermont Historical Society, microfilm). Of the wills probated during the 1840s, those of the richest 10 percent accounted for over 40 percent of the town's wealth (Bennington Probate Records, vols. 18–22 [see chap. 7, n. 68]).

94. Persistence rates for heads of household in Bennington from 1790 to 1850 were 39 percent, 46 percent, 37 percent, 48 percent, 40 percent, 34 percent, and 33 percent, respectively. In 1850 — the first year in which all inhabitants, rather than just heads of household, were listed — the persistence rate for those who were not heads of household was 23 percent.

95. The following discussion of competition between Bennington and the East Village relies upon Hemenway, *Vermont Historical Gazetteer*, 5:33–37 (see chap. 5, n. 103).

96. After the courthouse burned to the ground on March 26, 1869, the county located the new courthouse in the East Village, which by this time had assumed the name Bennington.

97. Hemenway, *Vermont Historical Gazetteer*, 1:141 (see chap. 2, n. 2).

98. Ibid., 5:35–36; census of 1850.

99. Census of 1850.

100. Stillwell, *Migration from Vermont*, 196–97 (see chap. 7, n. 119). As early as 1816 the local press carried notices in which agents advertised their ability to deliver "laborers, mechanics or any other class of emigrants" (*Vermont Gazette*, September 17, 1816).

101. Harwood Diary, January 8, 1829.

102. Zadock Thompson, *History of the State of Vermont from its Earliest Settlement to the Close of the Year 1832* (Burlington, 1833), 63.

103. Ibid., 157.

104. Jared Sparks, *Library of American Biography*, 25 vols. (Boston, 1834–48), 1:243–44, 331–32.

105. Ibid, 354–55.

106. Daniel P. Thompson, *The Green Mountain Boys: A Historical Tale of the Early Settlement of Vermont* (New York, 1839), 186–87; idem, *The Rangers or The Tory's Daughter: A Tale Illustrative of the Revolutionary History of Vermont and the Northern Campaign of 1777*, 10th ed. (Boston, 1890), 4.

107. Thompson, *Rangers*, 4.

108. Ibid., 155.

109. Thompson, *Green Mountain Boys*, 323.

110. Ibid., 45, 123.

111. Ibid., 167.

112. Thompson, *Rangers*, 9.

113. Thompson, *Green Mountain Boys*, 65.

114. Thompson, *Rangers*, 20, 11.

115. Ibid, 9.

116. Ibid., 6.

117. Daniel Chipman, *Memoir of Colonel Seth Warner* (Middlebury, Vt., 1848); idem, *Thomas Chittenden*.

118. B. H. Kinney, letter quoted in Henry De Puy, *Ethan Allen and the Green Mountain Heroes of '76* (Buffalo, N.Y., 1853), xvii.

119. Ibid., xvi.

120. Ibid.; Henry De Puy, *The Mountain Hero and His Associates* (Boston, 1855).

121. De Puy, *Mountain Hero*, 176–77.

122. De Puy, *Ethan Allen*, 411.

123. *The Journal of the Senate of the State of Vermont*, October sess., 1858 (Ludlow, Vt., 1858), 18.

Epilogue: A Monument to Democracy

1. Full descriptions of the events, as well as complete transcripts of the speeches delivered on this day, appear in *The Dedication of the Bennington Battle Monument, and Celebration of the Hundredth Anniversary of the Admission of Vermont as a State, At Bennington, August 19, A.D., 1891* (Bennington: Banner Book and Job Printing House, 1892).

2. Ibid., 68–76.

3. The composite picture of Vermont history that follows draws upon speeches printed in ibid., 77–96.

4. Ibid., 96.

5. Ibid., 106.

6. Ibid., 117–18.

7. Ibid., 126.

Essay on Sources

This book relies predominantly upon sources found in a wide variety of locations scattered throughout New England. These include the offices of town and county clerks, village athenaeums, local museums, and the research institutions of metropolitan Boston. In addition, numerous county and town histories and genealogical studies yielded invaluable insights into the lives of the individuals and groups under investigation. Citations to all these appear in the notes, but some merit special mention. Without the rare books and manuscripts found in the Boston Public Library, the Massachusetts Historical Society, the Congregational Library of Boston, the Massachusetts Historical and Genealogical Society, Widener Library of Harvard University, the Andover Divinity School Library of Harvard University, Houghton Library of Harvard University, the Vermont Historical Society, the Vermont State Library, and the Bennington Museum this book simply could not have been written. In addition, the archives at the Park-McCullough House in North Bennington, Vermont, yielded a treasure trove of material.

The town, probate, court, and land records of Bennington, found in the town clerk's office and the county courthouse in Bennington, were absolutely indispensable, as were the records of the First Church of Christ, Bennington, located in the Bennington Museum. I also found myself returning again and again to four nineteenth-century works dealing with Bennington: Isaac Jennings, *Memorials of a Century: Embracing a Record of Individuals and Events Chiefly in the Early History of Bennington, Vt. and its First Church* (Boston: Gould & Lincoln, 1869); Lewis Cass Aldrich, *History of Bennington County, Vermont* (Syracuse: D.

Mason, 1889); Hamilton Child, *Gazetteer and Business Directory of Bennington County, Vt.* (Syracuse: Journal Office, 1880); and Abby Maria Hemenway, ed., *The Vermont Historical Gazetteer,* 5 vols. (1867–91). No understanding of the revolt on the New Hampshire Grants and the revolutionary government of Vermont would be possible without constant reference to E. B. O'Callaghan, ed., *The Documentary History of the State of New York,* 4 vols. (Albany, N.Y.: Weed, Parsons, 1849–51); and to E. P. Watson, ed., *Records of the Governor and Council of the State of Vermont,* 8 vols. (Montpelier: J. & J. M. Poland, 1873–80). Finally, the *Vermont Gazette,* published in Bennington under various titles from 1783 to 1850, was absolutely indispensable to my research. The Vermont State Library has a complete set of this paper in bound volumes. It also has the *Gazette* and many other early Vermont newspapers on microfilm.

A sizable amount of scholarship focusing on the early history of Vermont has appeared over the years. Recent work that was extremely helpful to me includes Aleine Austin, *Matthew Lyon: "New Man" of the Democratic Revolution, 1749–1822* (University Park: Pennsylvania State University Press, 1981); Randolph A. Roth, *The Democratic Dilemma: Religion, Reform, and the Social Order in the Connecticut River Valley of Vermont, 1791–1850* (New York: Cambridge University Press, 1987); William J. Gilmore, *Reading Becomes a Necessity of Life: Material and Cultural Life in Rural New England, 1780–1835* (Knoxville: University of Tennessee Press, 1989); Michael A. Bellesiles, *Revolutionary Outlaws: Ethan Allen and the Struggle for Independence on the Early American Frontier* (Charlottesville: University Press of Virginia, 1993); and P. Jeffrey Potash, *Vermont's Burned-Over District: Patterns of Community Development and Religious Activity, 1761–1850* (Brooklyn: Carlson, 1991). Two essays by J. Kevin Graffagnino provided special insight into the life of Ira Allen and his colleagues: "'The Country My Soul Delighted In': The Onion River Land Company and the Vermont Frontier," *New England Quarterly,* 65 (1992), 24–60, and "'Twenty Thousand Muskets!!!': Ira Allen and the *Olive Branch* Affair, 1796–1800," *William and Mary Quarterly,* 3rd ser., 48 (1991), 409–31. Donald A. Smith's dissertation, "Legacy of Dissent: Religion and Politics in Revolutionary Vermont" (Clark University, 1981), proved to be an important source of information regarding the religious affiliations of early settlers in Vermont.

A number of older works also offer valuable perspectives on life in early Vermont. *Vermont in the Making, 1750–1777* (Cambridge: Harvard University Press, 1939), by Matt Bushnell Jones, is essential to understanding the struggle between New York and New Hampshire for control of the Grants. Charles A. Jellison's *Ethan Allen: Frontier Rebel* (Syracuse: Syracuse University Press, 1969) and John Pell's *Ethan Allen* (Boston: Houghton Mifflin, 1929) provide solid accounts of the life and times of the leader of the Green Mountain Boys. James B. Wilbur's *Ira Allen: Founder of Vermont, 1751–1814*, 2 vols. (Boston: Houghton Mifflin, 1928), although reverential, is a wonderful source of information regarding political life in early Vermont. Chilton Williamson offers a far more critical perspective on the Allens in his *Vermont in Quandary: 1763–1825* (Montpelier: Vermont Historical Society, 1949). In addition, Walter Hill Crockett's three-volume *Vermont: The Green Mountain State* (New York: Century History, 1921) proved to be a steady source of essential information on the early history of the state.

A great deal of the current historical literature dealing with various of the other states and the nation has influenced my thinking over the years. Foremost among this scholarship is the debate among scholars today over the origins of liberal America. The essays published in "*The Creation of the American Republic, 1776–1787*: A Symposium of Views and Reviews," *William and Mary Quarterly*, 3rd ser., 44 (1987), 549–640, offer the best introduction to this subject. For the clearest juxtaposition of conflicting views regarding the identification of the groups most responsible for the emergence of liberalism in Revolutionary America as well as the significance of this phenomenon within our society, see Barbara Clark Smith, "The Adequate Revolution," Michael Zuckerman, "Rhetoric, Reality, and the Revolution: The Genteel Radicalism of Gordon Wood," and Gordon A. Wood, "Equality and Social Conflict in the American Revolution," in *William and Mary Quarterly*, 3rd ser., 51 (1994), 684–716. For the later period Charles Sellers, *The Market Revolution: Jacksonian America, 1815–1846* (New York: Oxford University Press, 1991), and William E. Gienapp, "The Myth of Class in Jacksonian America," *Journal of Policy History*, 6 (1994), 232–59, represent opposite sides of the historical dialogue over whether class tensions developed in America as a result of the emergence of liberalism.

Works dealing with American political culture in the late eighteenth and early nineteenth centuries are legion. Principal among those that have influenced my analysis of the late colonial and Revolutionary era are Richard Bushman, *King and People in Provincial Massachusetts* (Chapel Hill: University of North Carolina Press, 1985); Fred Anderson, *A People's Army: Massachusetts Soldiers and Society in the Seven Years' War*

(Chapel Hill: University of North Carolina Press, 1984); Bernard Bailyn, *The Ideological Origins of the American Revolution* (Cambridge: Harvard University Press, 1967); Gordon A. Wood, *The Creation of the American Republic, 1776–1787* (Chapel Hill: University of North Carolina Press, 1969); Gregory Nobles, *Divisions throughout the Whole: Politics and Society in Hampshire County, Massachusetts, 1740–1775* (New York: Cambridge University Press, 1983); and Eric Foner, *Tom Paine and Revolutionary America* (New York: Oxford University Press, 1976). Two insightful books that go well beyond this era are John L. Brooke, *The Heart of the Commonwealth: Society and Political Culture in Worcester County, Massachusetts, 1713–1861* (New York: Cambridge University Press, 1989); and Alan Taylor, *Liberty Men and Great Proprietors: The Revolutionary Settlement on the Maine Frontier, 1760–1820* (Chapel Hill: University of North Carolina Press, 1990).

For the early national period and beyond, I have drawn most heavily on Gordon A. Wood, *The Radicalism of the American Revolution* (New York: Alfred A. Knopf, 1992); Ronald P. Formisano, *The Transformation of Political Culture: Massachusetts Parties, 1790s–1840s* (New York: Oxford University Press, 1983); David H. Fischer, *The Revolution of American Conservatism: The Federalist Party in the Era of Jeffersonian Democracy* (New York: Harper & Row, 1965); James M. Banner Jr., *To the Hartford Convention: The Federalists and the Origins of Party Politics in Massachusetts, 1798–1815* (New York: Alfred A. Knopf, 1970); John Zvesper, *Political Philosophy and Rhetoric: A Study of the Origins of American Party Politics* (New York: Cambridge University Press, 1977); Drew McCoy, *The Elusive Republic: Political Economy in Jeffersonian America* (Chapel Hill: University of North Carolina Press, 1980); Joyce Appleby, *Capitalism and a New Social Order* (New York: New York University Press, 1984); Charles Sellers, *The Market Revolution: Jacksonian America, 1815–1846* (New York: Oxford University Press, 1991); Daniel W. Howe, *The Political Culture of the American Whigs* (Chicago: University of Chicago Press, 1979); Marvin Meyers, *The Jacksonian Persuasion: Politics and Belief* (Palo Alto: Stanford University Press, 1957); and Paul Goodman, *Towards a Christian Republic: Antimasonry and the Great Transition in New England, 1826–1836* (New York: Oxford University Press, 1988).

Religious thought and behavior are central to my analysis of Bennington, and a number of important studies have influenced my view of the subject. Most prominent among these are Alan Heimert, *Religion and the American Mind from the Great Awakening to the Revolution* (Cambridge: Harvard University Press, 1966); Philip Greven, *The Protestant Temperament: Patterns of Child-Rearing, Religious Experience, and the Self in Early America* (New York: Alfred A. Knopf, 1977); Bruce Kuklick, *Churchmen and Philosophers from Jonathan Edwards to John Dewey* (New Haven: Yale University Press, 1985); C. C. Goen, *Revivalism and Separatism in New England, 1740–1800: Strict Congregationalism and Separate Baptists in the Great Awakening* (New Haven: Yale University Press, 1962); William G. McLoughlin, *New England Dissent, 1630–1833: The Baptists and the Separation of Church and State*, 2 vols. (Cambridge: Harvard University Press, 1971); Stephen A. Marini, *Radical Sects of Revolutionary New England* (Cambridge: Harvard University Press, 1982); Nathan Hatch, *The Democratization of American Christianity* (New Haven: Yale University Press, 1989); Paul E. Johnson, *A Shopkeeper's Millennium: Society and Revivals in Rochester, New York, 1815–1837* (New York: Hill & Wang, 1978); William Breitenbach, "Unregenerate Doings: Selflessness and Selfishness in New Divinity Theology," *American Quarterly*, 34 (1982), 479–502; and Joseph A. Conforti, "Samuel Hopkins and the New Divinity: Theology, Ethics, and Social Reform in Eighteenth-Century New England," *William and Mary Quarterly*, 3rd ser., 34 (1977), 572–89.

A knowledge of rural economic change is also essential to an understanding of the transformation of society and culture in Bennington from the late eighteenth through the early nineteenth century. Much recent research dealing with this phenomenon has centered on a dialogue between "market" and "social" scholars. The former view market forces as the key determinants of economic and social change; the latter emphasize the power of social forces not only to shape society but to influence the form that market forces assume within any particular culture. For the former, see especially Winifred B. Rothenberg, *From Market-Places to a Market Economy: The Transformation of Rural Massachusetts, 1750–1850* (Chicago: University of Chicago Press, 1992). James Henretta, "Families and Farms: *Mentalité* in Pre-Industrial America," *William and Mary Quarterly*, 3rd ser., 35 (1978), 3–32, and Christopher Clark, "Household Economy, Market Exchange, and the Rise of Capitalism in the Connecticut Valley, 1800–1860," *Journal of Social History*, 13 (1979), 169–89, are particularly good examples of the latter. Throughout this book, which attempts to synthesize the two approaches, I draw most heavily upon Christopher Clark, *The Roots of Rural Capitalism: Western Massachusetts, 1780–1860* (Ithaca: Cornell University Press, 1990); Allan Kulikoff, *The Agrarian Origins of Ameri-*

can Capitalism (Charlottesville: University Press of Virginia, 1992); and the essays in Steven Hahn and Jonathan Prude, eds., *The Countryside in the Age of Capitalist Transformation* (Chapel Hill: University of North Carolina Press, 1985). Over the last several decades a great many scholars have published excellent studies dealing with the emergence of factory towns in the Northeast. Of these, Anthony F. C. Wallace's *Rockdale: The Growth of an American Village in the Early Industrial Revolution* (New York: Alfred A. Knopf, 1978), Jonathan Prude's *The Coming of the Industrial Order: Town and Factory in Rural Massachusetts, 1810–1860* (New York: Cambridge University Press, 1983), and Judith McGaw's *Most Wonderful Machine: Mechanization and Social Change in Berkshire Paper Making, 1801–1860* (Princeton: Princeton University Press, 1981) proved to be the most helpful to my analysis of factory development in Bennington.

Index

Library of Congress Cataloging-in-Publication Data

Shalhope, Robert E., 1941–
    Bennington and the Green Mountain boys : the emergence of liberal
democracy in Vermont, 1760–1850 / Robert E. Shalhope.
        p.   cm — (Reconfiguring American political history)
    Includes bibliographical references and index.
    ISBN 0-8018-5335-4 (alk. paper)
        1. Bennington (Vt.) — Politics and government.   2. Vermont — Politics
and government — To 1791.   3. Vermont — Politics and government —
1775–1865.   4. Democracy — Vermont — History.   I. Title.   II. Series.
F59.B4S53   1996
974.3′8 — dc20   96-791